Spatial Justice After Apartheid

This book considers the question of spatial justice after apartheid from several disciplinary perspectives – jurisprudence, law, literature, architecture, photography and psychoanalysis are just some of the disciplines engaged here. However, the main theoretical device on which the authors comment is the legacy of what in Carl Schmitt's terms is *nomos* as the spatialised normativity of sociality. Each author considers within the practical and theoretical constraints of their topic, the question of what *nomos* in its modern configuration may or may not contribute to a thinking of spatial justice after apartheid.

On the whole, the collection forces a confrontation between law's spatiality in a "postcolonial" era, on the one hand, and the traumatic legacy of what Paul Gilroy has called the "colonial *nomos*", on the other hand. In the course of this confrontation, critical questions of continuation, extension, disruption and rewriting are raised and confronted in novel and innovative ways that both challenge Schmitt's account of *nomos* and affirm the centrality of the constitutive relation between law and space. The book promises to resituate the trajectory of *nomos*, while considering critical instances through which the spatial legacy of apartheid might at last be overcome.

This interdisciplinary book will appeal to scholars of critical legal theory, political philosophy, aesthetics and architecture.

Jaco Barnard-Naudé is Professor of Jurisprudence and Co-Director of the Centre for Rhetoric Studies (CRhS) at the University of Cape Town's (UCT) Law Faculty, South Africa. From 2020 to 2021, he was a Research Professor in the Free State Centre for Human Rights at the University of the Free State, South Africa. He is a past recipient of the UCT Fellows' Award and was the British Academy's Newton Advanced Fellow in the Westminster Law and Theory Lab at the University of Westminster Law School, UK, from 2017 to 2020. Jaco holds a B2-rating from the South African National Research Foundation (NRF) and is also a past Honorary Research Fellow of the Birkbeck Institute for the Humanities, Birkbeck College, University of London, UK. He publishes widely in the fields of Jurisprudence, Law and Literature, Spatial Justice, Queer Legal Theory, Contractual Justice after Apartheid and Transitional Post-Apartheid Justice.

Julia Chryssostalis is Principal Lecturer and Co-Director of the Westminster Law and Theory Lab at the University of Westminster Law School, UK. She became an academic after practising law as a lawyer in Athens, Greece, while chairing the Human Rights Education Committee of the Greek Section of Amnesty International. She has held Visiting Fellowships at the European University Institute in Florence, Italy, Princeton University, USA and University of Cape Town, South Africa. Her current work is in the interface of critical legal theory and law and humanities exploring the different names and figures of *nomos*.

Part of The
Law and The Postcolonial
series

series editors
Denise Ferreira da Silva, Queen Mary University of London, UK
Mark A. Harris, La Trobe University, Australia

for information about the series and details of previous and forthcoming titles, see

https://www.routledge.com/Law-and-the-Postcolonial/book-series/LAWPOSTCON

a GlassHouse book

Spatial Justice After Apartheid

Nomos in the Postcolony

Edited by Jaco Barnard-Naudé and
Julia Chryssostalis

Routledge
Taylor & Francis Group
a GlassHouse Book

First published 2022
by Routledge
4 Park Square, Milton Park, Abingdon, Oxon OX14 4RN

and by Routledge
605 Third Avenue, New York, NY 10158

a GlassHouse book

Routledge is an imprint of the Taylor & Francis Group, an informa business

British Library Cataloguing-in-Publication Data
A catalogue record for this book is available from the British Library

Library of Congress Cataloging-in-Publication Data
A catalog record has been requested for this book

ISBN: 978-1-138-55937-0 (hbk)
ISBN: 978-1-032-28810-9 (pbk)
ISBN: 978-0-203-71277-1 (ebk)

DOI: 10.4324/9780203712771

Typeset in Bembo
by Deanta Global Publishing Services, Chennai, India

Contents

Contributors

Barbara Boswell is a feminist literary scholar and creative writer with research and teaching interests in Black diasporic women's writing, Black South African women's literature and queer theory. Currently she is an Associate Professor and Head of Department of English Literary Studies at the University of Cape Town. She is the author of *And Wrote My Story Anyway: Black South African Women's Novels as Feminism* (Wits University Press, 2020) and *Grace: A Novel* (Modjaji Books, 2017), winner of the University of Johannesburg Debut Creative Writing Prize.

Victoria J. Collis-Buthelezi is Associate Professor in English at the University of Johannesburg (UJ) and Director of UJ's Centre for the Study of Race, Gender and Class. She is a senior research fellow at the Johannesburg Institute of Advanced Studies (JIAS) and a research associate at the Institute for Research in African American Studies (IRAAS) at Columbia University, USA. Her research is on Black intellectual and literary histories and has appeared in *Small Axe*, *Callaloo*, *boundary2* and the *UK Journal of Arts and the Humanities*. Her current book project explores global frames for understanding Blackness in early twentieth-century Cape Town. Collis-Buthelezi is on the editorial committee for *Small Axe* and an editor of the Polity *Critical South* book series as well as Peter Lang's *Race and Resistance in the Long Twentieth Century*.

Sean Christie lives in Cape Town, South Africa and has been contributing his writing to books, newspapers and magazines since 2007, including *The Guardian*, City Press, *Business Day*, African Cities Reader, Cityscapes, Chimurenga, Neue Rundschau, Kwani? and New Contrast. In 2016, Christie's first non-fiction book, *Under Nelson Mandela Boulevard – Life Among the Stowaways*, was published by Jonathan Ball Publishers. In 2015, Christie was awarded a Taco Kuiper prize for his journalism on the Tanzanian stowaways and in 2014 he won the business and economics category at the CNN/Multichoice African Journalist of the Year Awards. In 2011, he was awarded the Open Society Initiative of Southern Africa's Fellowship in Foreign Policy, and in 2012 he was awarded a Climate Change Media Partnership fellowship. Christie was born in Zimbabwe.

Isolde de Villiers is a lecturer in the Department of Mercantile Law at the University of the Free State, South Africa. Her research focuses on spatial justice from a feminist perspective and the ways in which aspects of law, business and commerce intersect with the spatiality of the overlooked city of Bloemfontein/Mangaung and surroundings.

Loretta Feris was the Deputy Vice-Chancellor for Transformation and Student Affairs at UCT from 2017 to March 2021. She is also a Professor of Law in the Institute of Marine and Environmental Law at the University of Cape Town (UCT), South Africa where she taught natural resources law, pollution law and international environmental law until 2017 when she took up executive office. She holds the degrees BA (law), LLB and LLD from the University of Stellenbosch, South Africa and LLM from Georgetown University, USA.

Derrick Higginbotham is an Associate Professor in the Department of English at the University of Hawai'i at Mānoa, whose primary teaching and research interests are late medieval and early modern English literary cultures, especially drama, queer theory/gender studies, ecocriticism and economic criticism/Marxisms. He is also a Research Associate in the Department of English at the University of Johannesburg. He is finishing his book, *Winners and Wasters: Queer Desire, Economics, and the Theater in Premodern England*, and he has published articles in *Exemplaria*, *Shakespeare in Southern Africa* and *Early Modern Black Diaspora Studies*. He co-directs *Oecologies*, a research cluster on premodern ecocriticism, and co-edits the Routledge book series *Critical Junctures in Global Early Modernities* with Nicolas R. Jones.

Antjie Krog is a poet, writer, journalist and professor emeritus at the University of the Western Cape, South Africa. Her books include *Country of My Skull* (1998), *A Change of Tongue* (2004) and *Begging To Be Black* (2009). Her latest collection of poetry was published in Afrikaans as *Mede-wete* and in English as *Synapse*. She has won the Stockholm Award from the Hiroshima Foundation for Peace and Culture, the Open Society Prize from the Central European University and the Hertzog Prize.

Iain Low is an architect and professor emeritus at the University of Cape Town, South Africa where his research in space and transformation focusses on the rewriting of type within contexts of radical contestation. Post-graduation he practised and lived in Lesotho for ten years prior to taking up a Fulbright scholarship at Penn. He was a Pew Fellow at the American Academy in Rome, Italy and is editor of the Digest of South African Architecture and, most recently, academic adviser to the new African Futures Institute [AFI] in Accra, Ghana.

Joel M. Modiri is Associate Professor and Head of the Department of Jurisprudence, University of Pretoria, South Africa. His research and teaching interests lie broadly in the area of legal and political philosophy, critical race theory, Black political thought and African jurisprudence. He is currently working on a number of projects elaborating on Black Consciousness and Pan-Africanism as a critique of post-apartheid political rationality/ies.

Johnny Miller is a photographer and multimedia storyteller based in South Africa and the USA. He is interested in exploring inequality, architecture, displacement and climate justice from the ground and from the air. He is currently a Senior Fellow at Code For Africa, a Senior Atlantic Fellow for Social and Economic Equity at the London School of Economics and the co-founder of africanDRONE.

David Southwood's photos can be viewed at the South African National Gallery, where his work made up part of three shows in 2010, two of which were broad surveys of South African art, the Finnish Museum of Photography, the Christoph Merian Stiftung, the collection of the Constitutional Court of South Africa, the Goethe Institut, the Spier Art Collection and private collections in South Africa and abroad. He has been awarded multiple residencies. He has contributed to and been featured in publications like Adbusters, COLORS, ID, *The New York Times* magazine, New York Magazine and Wallpaper. He has also edited photo editions of magazines, taught at universities and written for the art press. He has had invitations to talk at Yale University, USA (The MacMillan Center Council on African Studies and School of Architecture), the International Centre of Photography, Ohio State University, USA, the University of South Dakota, USA, the Universities of Cape Town and Stellenbosch, South Africa and many other tertiary institutions.

Karin van Marle joined the Department of Public Law, University of the Free State (UFS), South Africa in February 2019. Before joining the UFS she worked as Professor in the Department of Jurisprudence, University of Pretoria, South Africa where she taught jurisprudence at undergraduate and postgraduate levels for many years. Several doctoral and research master's students completed their studies under her supervision and she currently supervises a number of postgraduate students working in the field of critical jurisprudence, law and transformation and feminist theory. Her research falls within the broad field of law and the humanities and involves critical theory, legal philosophy and jurisprudence. Her work on post-1994 jurisprudence engages with the crisis of modernity and a rethinking of law and legal theory along the lines of fragility, finitude and a "giving up of certitudes". She is an ethical feminist and her research and writing are inspired by and embedded in feminist theory. She has published widely in national and international journals and books. She serves on the international editorial boards of *Law and Critique*, *Feminist Legal Studies* and the international advisory board of *Legalities Journal*. She is an adjunct professor at Southern Cross University, Australia and is a Fellow at the Stellenbosch Institute for Advanced Study (STIAS), South Africa.

Chapter 1

Apartheid remains

Nomos, law and spatiality in post-apartheid South Africa

Jaco Barnard-Naudé and Julia Chryssostalis

"we ought to stop circumscribing the *nomos*; we ought to invite new worlds"
(Cover 1983, 68)

The province of post-apartheid jurisprudence

It is widely acknowledged that the enactment of the so-called "post-apartheid" Constitutions marked a historical break with the apartheid regime and buried the entire legal edifice associated with it – both in terms of its organising principles as well as its administrative instruments. The 1996 "final"[1] Constitution mandates the transition to post-apartheid law and, in the famous words of South Africa's former Chief Justice, Pius Langa, makes transformation a

> permanent ideal, a way of looking at the world that *creates a space* in which dialogue and contestation are truly possible, in which new ways of being are constantly explored and created, accepted and rejected and in which change is unpredictable but the idea of change is constant.
> (Langa 2006, 354, emphasis added)

The universal appeal of the 1996 Constitution lies undoubtedly in its rejection of what it calls in its preamble the "divisions of the past" and its promise of overcoming these divisions in the process of the becoming of a post-apartheid being-in-common. Many scholars have studied the juridico-political meanings and conditions of possibility of such a being-in-common. They have done so, however, predominantly from the point of view of what we would call an institutional transition – a transition, in other words, from what the literature routinely refers to as a profoundly racist, authoritarian parliamentary oligarchy (Mureinik 1994, 32; Salazar 2002, xvi) to a constitutional democracy which protects the rule of law, the supremacy of the Constitution and a set of fundamental rights and freedoms. In the course of these explorations of what post-apartheid might and must entail juridically, much attention has also been devoted to the Constitution's protection of a set of "postliberal" socioeconomic rights (Klare 1998, 151–156; Baxi 2013, 32).

DOI: 10.4324/9780203712771-1

At the mainstream, liberal-conservative end, these discussions represent the South African transition as the replacement of an authoritarian government and a system of racialised capitalism with a liberal democratic government (Ackermann 2004; Du Toit and Kotzé 2011; Woolman and Swanepoel 2012) and a racially "neutral", but now aspirationally neoliberal (Bond 2014; Terreblanche 2002), political economy. From this aspect, South Africa's transformation is seen as institutionally no different from those that have taken place in a number of other countries that have seen the end of undemocratic government since the end of the 1980s. These range from formerly communist European countries to South America and, most recently, the rise and fall of the Arab Spring. These discussions tend to view the work of transformation in the face of the legacy of apartheid as the undoing of the legal apparatus of oppression through the institutionalisation of democracy, fundamental human rights, a substantive rule of law and juridicised processes of an ill-defined "reconciliation" (Sibanda 2011, 494).

At the other, "critical" end, the notion of "transformative constitutionalism", famously defined by Karl Klare (1998, 150) as "an enterprise of inducing large-scale social change through nonviolent political processes grounded in law", has focused on constitutional rights application, adjudication (especially of the common law), judicial outcomes and legal culture as the primary sites of intervention and transformation, albeit that discussions at this end readily accept the "post-liberal" aspects of the 1996 Constitution, notably the notion of "substantive equality", promoted primarily by, on the one hand, the Section 9 prohibition of unfair discrimination and, on the other, the progressive realisation of socioeconomic rights.

Despite former Chief Justice Langa's (2006) warning that the levelling of the socioeconomic playing field would be crucial in promoting a lasting transformative constitutionalism (Langa 2006, 352), this discourse has also found it difficult – save for a few notable exceptions (for example Van Marle 2010, 628–45; Cornell 2012, 324–32; Cornell and Van Marle 2015, 1–8; Coggin 2016, 434–51; Strauss 2019, 135–68) – to move beyond a narrow institutional account and consideration of law, giving rise in recent years to several critiques (Sibanda 2011, 482–500; Modiri 2012, 405–36; Madlingozi 2017, 123–47; Modiri 2018, 300–25) of transformative constitutionalism as elaborated in the leading literature. The gist of these critiques consists in the charge that there is too much constitutionalism and not enough transformation in transformative constitutionalism, as presently conceived. These critiques focus on the limited role that transformative constitutionalism can be expected to play in the alleviation of apartheid-induced poverty and highly disproportionate inequality when it is left exclusively in the hands of an unelected elite of judges and an untransformed legal profession (Sibanda 2011, 492–93). Of late, this critique has broadened to include the Constitution itself, leading Tshepo Madlingozi (2017, 123) in a widely discussed recent article, to coin the term "neo-apartheid constitutionalism" (see also Ramose 1998).

Apartheid remains

The current project takes a different approach. It reads liberal and transformative constitutionalism's preoccupation with the inevitable post-apartheid "politics of law" (its strenuous denial at the liberal end and its resolute affirmation at the transformative end) as symptomatic of its neglect, at least until very recently, by and large to appreciate the centrality of space in apartheid's abhorrently racist "law and order". If as Iain Low (2003, 34) puts it, "space is the construct that most effectively maintained apartheid's grand plan and continues to ensure the endurance of its legacy", what, in our view, these different ways of examining the post-apartheid legal order miss, is precisely the spatial inscription of apartheid's racist normativity. For us, it is therein that apartheid's concrete specificity lies, in that apartheid was not simply a brutally oppressive regime amongst other brutally oppressive regimes around the world, but at its very core a juridicised system of racialised *spatial* ordering, which took the primary form of segregation, implemented and entrenched by means of a plethora of legal enactments and planning and housing policies, meticulously administered through its various enforcement mechanisms. Moreover, once this racist spatial ordering was instituted and maintained, apartheid did everything in its power to raise that order and ordering to the power of a "natural" ontology, or what Derrida (1985, 292) in his famous essay on apartheid, called a "quasi-ontological segregation".

While it is certainly true that the Interim Constitution, when describing itself, resorted to a spatial metaphor which has stuck, namely, that of the bridge between the apartheid past and the post-apartheid future,[2] our contention is that the spatiality of the bridge, and the modernist spatial aesthetics used in the "architectural framing of post-apartheid constitutionalism" (Le Roux 2007, 60) more generally, is exhausted in its metaphoricity. By understanding transformation in terms of a linear, ineluctably forward movement from one side of the constitutional bridge to the other that has already taken place by the adoption of the Constitution itself, the metaphor has meant that the Constitution has, ironically, been largely unable to function – in concrete terms – as the very bridge to the post-apartheid radically "brave new world", that it envisaged itself to be. As Andreas Philippopoulos-Mihalopoulos (2011, 189–190) writes: "metaphors can become too comfortable. They start working against the objective of confluence, facilitating instead a distance between, in this case, law and space". This is precisely, in our view, what has happened to the metaphor of the bridge in the South African Constitution: instead of producing the confluence of space and law, the fixation on the metaphor of the bridge has instead produced and sustained a divergence, or mismatch, between, on the one hand, the promise of a new post-apartheid normative landscape of inclusion and justice and, on the other, the continued normality of spatial segregation and injustice. In this way, the fixation on metaphoricity becomes a symptomatic indication of the problem, rather than a marker pointing in the direction of a solution (Antaki 2013, 48). To put it simply: the post-apartheid legal order, with the Constitution positioned at its foundation, has been unable to address adequately the racialised spatial injustice that lies at apartheid's core and that the transition to the "post"-apartheid has, by necessity, to redress.

Within both mainstream and critical jurisprudence, then, the nexus between apartheid and spatiality has remained underexplored, at best. Drucilla Cornell and Karin van Marle's (2015) reflections on *ubuntu* and space is a notable exception. Philippe-Joseph Salazar's (2004, 132–156) reflections on space and rhetoric in the context of the post-apartheid legal order, is another. The recent work of Isolde de Villiers has also formed a critical counter-balance to the dearth of spatiality in critical jurisprudence (see, for example, De Villiers 2016; Van Marle and De Villiers 2013). In other disciplines, notably urban studies, architecture, geography and literature, there has been work in which apartheid is considered for the inherently spatial order that it is (see, for example, Judin and Vadislavich 1999; Bremner 2010; Robinson 1997, 365–86; Coetzer 2013; Home 2014, 75–85; Parnell 1997, 891–906). However, even in these disciplines the relationship between apartheid spatiality and the role of law in achieving and maintaining the racialised ordering that it represented, is only incidentally examined. By and large, the closest that scholars in these disciplines have come to a consideration of the role of law in the spatial arrangements of apartheid is in terms of a fairly narrow Foucaultian institutional governmentality (see Robinson 1997, 366).

The failure to examine the *legal* character of the apartheid (and concomitantly the post-apartheid) spatial order, has resulted in the failure to take, as the point of departure for the "large-scale social change" envisioned for South Africa, both the way in which and the extent to which apartheid's regime was literally "built" by law – in other words, that a defining feature of apartheid was that its law did not restrict itself to normative or institutional confines, but had at its very centre the obsessive preoccupation with concrete spaces and with spatiality. From the outset, apartheid set upon the earth and morphed into the physical spaces of the "setting-apart" policy: first and foremost, apartheid envisioned its legal order as a visible, spatialised order. The "Whites Only" sign – apartheid's most paradigmatic public sign – both marked out the specific space as segregated and, at the same time, condensed the general norm of segregation that animated the apartheid order.

Through law, apartheid's juridical apparatus created highly regulated concrete spaces of racial segregation, dispossession, exclusion, exploitation, displacement, forced relocation and migration, as well as constant surveillance – the notorious pass laws and the policies of forced removal and relocation on which it was premised, are exemplars in this regard. Apartheid's desire was fundamentally a desire for the perfect coincidence of the "legal" enunciation with the "legal" enunciated, of the normative with the concrete. It was in this sense that apartheid indeed set itself up as racism's "last word" (Derrida 1985, 290). Stated differently, if what is at stake in apartheid is the perfect coincidence between the fact and norm of its racialised spatial order and ordering, then apartheid, at its most basic level, involves the profoundly reductive inscription of the fact within the norm and of the norm within the fact, such that within its order it is imperative that the racist norm is inhabited factually *and* the racialised fact is inhabited normatively.

Viewed in this way, apartheid completely eschews the modes of traditional jurisprudential enquiry, situated as the latter is along the persistent divide between positivism and natural law. The positivist approach to apartheid characteristically denies the normativity of its facts, while the natural law approach denies the legal facticity of its norms. In these discussions, apartheid is regarded as just another oppressive regime amongst others, with both approaches typically positing the "solution" at the level of the law. In other words, both positivism and natural law imagine the solution as a law that is more just, fair, democratic, etc. In the case of apartheid South Africa, this imagination famously congealed around the notion of human rights for all. As for the so-called "third path" theorists, Ronald Dworkin (2004, 16) himself rejected the application of law as integrity to the apartheid legal order, on the basis that "legality can no longer serve" under such an order. And rightly so, for the truth of the matter is that legality was *made* to serve apartheid to the point that legality itself was illegalised (Sitze 2013, 7–9).

As for post-apartheid legality, the break that Dworkin and the rest of the liberal tradition imagine, although clear at the constitutional level, is hardly apparent at the level of the everyday spaces that people inhabit. What marks the post-apartheid condition is this highly prominent spatial remainder from its apartheid past. Because apartheid worked simultaneously, intently and intensely at the level of both the fact *and* the norm, it has shaped South African reality in a highly particular way. Unless there is a simultaneously intent and intensive intervention at the level of concrete juridicity as well – that is, at the level of what Njabulo Ndebele (1991) calls "the ordinary", at the level of everyday injustice, inequality and segregation – merely transforming the norm will neither produce a post-apartheid legal spatiality, nor a truly post-apartheid polity. This is not to contest the significance of the interventions that have taken place at the level of concrete juridicity, but rather to locate a profound deficit at this level.

The wager of both liberal and transformative constitutionalism has been that replacing the master-norm of apartheid would not only transform the subordinated norms but would also quickly transform the facts on the ground through a distinct "politics of law", broadly aligned with transformation, *ubuntu*, non-racialism and reconciliation. This, at least, would explain the focus in the early literature on the judiciary and the legal profession as the primary vehicles through which this conception of transformation of the legal order would take place. Notwithstanding the pronounced intellectual battle between liberal and transformative constitutionalism (however radically conceived) over the extent to which the South African legal order as a whole must be transformed, neither has as yet connected its legal sensibilities sufficiently with the extent to which apartheid normed and formed, as well as formed and normed, the ordinary, everyday life of the polity. There, apartheid remains. It does not follow that a new, horizontally effective Constitution, the simultaneous institutional dismantling of apartheid and the unfolding of a new language of law in most legislative and judicial pronouncements, translates as a *fundamental* shift in the experience of injustice in the spaces that people inhabit: where they habitually live, are allowed to live, can work, are able to move (to), build a house, take a train, go to the toilet, hospital, school, take a drink of water, have a meal, shop, play, relax, be/become educated, have sex, love each other. These spaces continue to be dominated by a spatial common sense that has normalised if not naturalised the everyday experience of spatial injustice of the apartheid "racial *nomos*" (Gilroy 2014, 68).

This is also not to devalue the crucial work that transformative constitutionalism has done in terms of a reconsideration of property rights and other legal devices that apartheid used in its attempt to normalise dispossession, exploitation and vast inequality. Indeed, the South African Constitution, while protecting private property, continues to legitimise the government's land reform strategy and, as indicated, goes on to entrench an array of socioeconomic rights to address the legacy of dispossession and displacement. A number of scholars have devoted their attention to this facet of post-apartheid property law (see, for example Van der Walt 2009) and the progressive adjudication of socioeconomic rights (Liebenberg 2010; Brand 2005, 1–56). Other interventions aimed at the eradication of dispossession and exploitation include progressive labour legislation, consumer protection law, broad-based Black economic empowerment and a governmental strategy of improved service delivery, which is deplorably riddled with widely reported incompetence, corruption and indeed "state capture".

These efforts have failed to bring about a fundamental shift in the structural injustices that continue to persist and have even been exacerbated, according to some statistics, more than 25 years after the institutional dismantling of apartheid. As Shane Graham (2009, 2) observes, although many of the "policies of spatial regimentation" have collapsed in post-apartheid South Africa, "the racial legacy of apartheid is perpetuated by the remains of its built environment and by conservative elements in the society that struggle to limit wealth and privilege to those (white and black, now) who already possess it" (2). These failures are, of course, not unrelated to what Sampie Terreblanche (2002, 96) has pinpointed as the elite compromise reached between the corporate sector and a leadership core of the African National Congress before 1994, one which ensured not only a democratic but also a "neoliberal transition" for South Africa.

Thus, while the neoliberal hegemony that has been in place since the late nineties has been subjected to significant critique in other disciplines and whilst these critiques have had a distinct materialist focus, the dominant jurisprudential approaches in post-apartheid South Africa up to now have been unable to advance a progressive critique that reaches beyond law's institutional normativity. In treating apartheid as predominantly a set of juridico-institutional norms and administrative regulations (not significantly dissimilar from other authoritarian and oppressive regimes), these approaches have not adequately addressed the concrete order of apartheid's legality and thus the *singularity* of apartheid's injustice. For that which made of apartheid a singularly unjust and oppressive regime and that which allows the injustice, that lies in its core and animates it, to be perpetuated in the "new", post-apartheid South Africa, consists in the way in which apartheid translated the normativity of its order into a concrete reality of divided, grossly unequal, racial ordering that is spatially entrenched.

Nomos

Nómos (plural, *nómoi*), the Greek word for law, refers in modern Greek to the concept of law and to laws in general (as in "the laws of the state"), as well as to specific legislative instruments (as in "Law xyz"). *Nómos* in ancient Greek is usually translated into English as "custom" or "law", even though it is only roughly in the fifth century BC that *nómos* begins to be used to describe written "laws" or "norms", and the sense of *nomos*-"law" begins to become commonplace. Until then, a number of other words were used to signify law (whatever law meant for the Greeks during this time), while *nómos* was characterised by a remarkable plurality, polyvalence and expansiveness (Laroche 1949; Ostwald 1969; Zartaloudis 2018).

In fact, *nomos* enters the Greek lexicon as two words, the oxytone *nomós* (νομός) and the paroxytone *nómos* (νόμος)[3]. As Emmanuel Laroche (whose extensive study of the linguistic root *nem-* across different periods and dialects of ancient Greek has been of pivotal importance for our understanding of the semantic history of *nomos*) has convincingly argued, the oxytone *nomós*, which signifies pasture for animals in undivided land, and a habitat without limits for human beings (Laroche 1949, 119, n.18), is Homeric and "primary", while the paroxytone *nómos* is post-Homeric and "secondary". Its appearance is situated at some point after the composition of the Homeric poems and before the end of the eighth century BC (166) and it is first met with in Hesiod.[4] Until roughly the fifth century BC, *nómos* has an extraordinary variety of meanings. These range from a "normal order of things", "a way of living or acting" for humans or animals, and a "normal or proper way in which something is done" (e.g. when carrying out a ritual sacrifice, farming or administering a remedy), to a "commonly held belief", a "linguistic usage", a "customary practice", a "ritual process" and "the mores of a particular group of people" (Ostwald 1969, 20–54).

In addition, at some point in the seventh century BC, Terpander, one of the most famous musicians of the time, is said to have invented a particular style of song, the *citharoedic nomos*, which he used in order to sing the Homeric epic: with the aid of *cithara* (lyre), he would wrap melodies around the verses. The invention of *citharoedic nomos* inaugurated what, according to Thomas Mathiesen, is "the most intriguing" of all the musico-poetic forms of ancient Greek music (Mathiesen 1999, 58), a style of song "of great complexity, and one that came to be associated with virtuoso performers" (58). Despite a number of other styles being added to the *citharoedic nomos* in subsequent years, as a musical genre, *nómos* was conventionally formed and fixed, so much so that both the composer and the performer were bound by its "rules", and yet it remained open to local variation. By the fifth century BC, alongside this technical musical sense, *nomos* also came to mean "melody", "tune", "song", "hymn" and "air", and specifically "any melody with a definite identity or character: the songs of different birds, a mourner's song, the songs in a particular musician's repertory, and so forth" (West 1992, 212).

It remains unclear exactly how *nómos* came to signify "law". As Laroche notes in the opening lines of his chapter on *nomos*, "[n]o truly satisfactory etymology has been proposed for [it]" (Laroche 1949, 163). True, *nomos* belongs to the family of words of the pre-Homeric verb *némein* (νέμειν), which means "to assign", "allot" or "distribute". In its most ancient and prevalent sense, *némein* refers to a concrete act of "distributing", or "dealing out" (Laroche 1949), an act of "ritual" distribution of food to guests at a feast (Zartaloudis 2018). Alongside this sense of *nemein*, there are also numerous so-called "pastoral" uses of the word, in both the active voice *nemō* (νέμω), "to graze", and the middle voice *nemomai* (νέμομαι), "grazing" for domestic animals. In Homeric times, these pastoral senses (of the middle voice especially) stabilise to signify "to enjoy, devour, exploit, and possess", mainly an allotted piece of land, and from this "to inhabit" (Laroche 1949, 10). Yet, as Zartaloudis has observed, following Laroche, these acts of distribution or allotting do not carry the sense of "formal appropriation or a 'juridical' or other, sense of uniform or equal 'division'" (Zartaloudis 2018, xxviii). According to Laroche, there is no connection between *nomos* and *nemein* apart from the common linguistic root, **nem-* (νεμ-), and he is critical of both the view that traces directly *nomos*-law to *nemō*-distribute (Laroche 1949, 177),[5] and the view that traces it to the pastoral sense of *nemō*-graze (206, n. 2).

In other words, contrary to the popular account that identifies the origin of *nómos*-law, to *nemō*-distribute, and hence to an "original" distribution, a *distributio primaeva*, Laroche insists that *nómos*-law in both of its early senses as "a way of life", or "a way of doing" and as "melody", derives from a subsequent, post-homeric, sense of *nemō* (νέμω), "arrange", "divide into parts", "place in order" and "govern", and maintains that the etymological connection between *nómos*-law and *nemō*-distribute, was created much later, in the work of fifth century philosophers. Similarly, according to Laroche, *nomós*-pasture/habitat, along with other pastoral words such as *noméfs*-shepherd and *nomás*-nomad, derive from the pastoral senses of *nemō* and not from any distribution of pastureland between the beasts or the shepherds. *Nemō* here refers to the spreading out of the animals across an unlimited space, a mountainside perhaps, a forest, or the flat expanse around a city (Deleuze [1968] 1994, 309, n.6), For Laroche, therefore *nomós*-pasture belongs to an entirely different semantic line than *nómos*-law, so much so in fact that he does not exclude the possibility of the existence of a separate, different *-nom* (-νομ) group, to which *nomós* belongs. Finally, Laroche is also sceptical about the possibility that *nómos*-law derives from *nómos*-song,[6] despite the well-known ancient Greek practice of singing the laws, and argues that *nómos*-law and *nómos*-song develop in parallel more or less during the same period, from the sense of *nemō* as "arrange", "govern" and "order", which is central to these uses of *nomos*. It is telling in this respect that *nomos* comes to replace *cosmos* in designating "order" in post-homeric Greek. Indeed, the idea of "order of some kind", of an arrangement according to some sort of norm that is appropriate or valid in a given situation, is according to Ostwald the underlying "root idea" of *nómos* from the start (Ostwald 1969, 20) – provided of course that by "norm" here we do not refer to a formal normativity (of law) but an "ethological ordering" (Zartaloudis 2018, xxxv), an established way of doing something in a given setting.

In recent times, the term *nomos* has been used to refer to a "meaningful order" of socio-normative enworlding and has been taken up by Peter L. Berger (1967) and Peter L. Berger and Thomas Luckmann (1966), and of course Robert Cover (1983, 4–68). For Cover, in particular, *nomos* is a normative universe that we inhabit. "We constantly create and maintain a world of right and wrong, of lawful and unlawful, of valid and void" (4), he writes. In other words, we are constantly engaged in the juridical enworlding of reality. This universe, however, is not entirely made up of "the rules and principles of justice, the formal institutions of the law, and the conventions of a social order" (4). For Cover, no rules and principles, no formal institutions of the law exist outside a variety of narratives that locate them and provide them with meaning. Law in this sense is not merely a system of rules that we simply observe but a world that we inhabit (5). Law and narrative are inextricably linked, for it is the stories that we tell about the rules that give rules their meaning, and this meaning is "our" meaning, precisely because these are "our" stories. It is in this way that law is grounded in narrative. Undoubtedly, notwithstanding the affinities between the way in which Cover and we use *nomos*, there are also significant differences. Although in his account Cover uses extensively the language of spatiality in order to explain the many ways in which a normative world is both inhabited and emplaced, his concept of *nomos*, developed as it is in terms of narrativity, lacks a concrete spatial situatedness – unless we start thinking of narrativity in a broader sense, one that is not limited to language and text but comes to include other surfaces of inscription, such as the city or our physical/material environment. Cover for one, nonetheless, seems to maintain a distinction between the normative world and the physical/material world, with narratives being the "trajectories plotted upon the material reality by our imagination" (5).

For us, the value of deploying the concept of *nomos* lies, on the contrary, in the way in which a different "tradition" of very disparate thinkers that range from Gianbattista Vico (2020), Carl Schmitt (2003) and Hannah Arendt (1990, 1998, 2006, 2007), to Gilles Deleuze (1994), Giorgio Agamben (1998), Paul Gilroy (2014), Pierre Legendre (1992; 2001), Peter Goodrich (2006) and Jacques Rancière (2001), find in *nomos* "the ways that law's earthly ensigns render spatially visible the normed forms of our sociality" (Chryssostalis 2022). To begin with, and long before the so-called "spatial turn" in the critical Humanities, Carl Schmitt's *The Nomos of the Earth in the International Law of the Jus Publicum Europaeum* ([1950] 2003), considered that the Greek word *nomos* is a word that names law's "terrestrial fundament", the unity of space and law, of order and orientation/localisation (Schmitt 2003, 47; Agamben 1998, 19). Tracing it to *nemein* – "to divide" and "to pasture" – *nomos*, according to Schmitt, originally signifies "the initial measure and division of pastureland, that is, the land appropriation as well as the concrete order contained in it and following from it" (Schmitt 2003, 70). For Schmitt, *nomos* is the Law of the law, "both more than law and expressive of law" (Goodrich 2006, 28), the root and *ratio* that "nourishes" all individual laws and renders visible the norms of sociality and the forms of power and domination. Its ground is land appropriation, an act that knows no law, a historical fact before any law, a lawless fact that makes law, in other words, a norm making fact, "the full immediacy of a legal power unmediated by laws" (Schmitt 2003, 73). At the beginning of every *nomos*, argues Schmitt, we thus find the "public sign" (42) of a concrete order grounded in the land, the marks through which "the orders of human social life become apparent" (42), the inscriptions through which "the forms of ownership and human proximity, [...] of power and domination, become visible" (42): the fence, the wall, the enclosure, the line in the soil, the furrow in the field. *Nomos*, in this sense, thus names the site of the visibility of the normative, in Rancière's terms (Rancière 2001), the measure that renders the normative sensible, in other words, the form of a normative order as it appears, and is experienced, in its concrete, spatial instantiation etched on the ground and grounded in the soil, precisely "the immediate form in which the political and social order of a people becomes spatially visible" (Schmitt 2003, 70).

It needs to be noted that for Schmitt, *nomos* is not just any word and any concept, but an *Urwort*, a word that takes us back to the beginning, to the "primal scene" of all law and order, namely the scene of the original *Landnahme*, or land seizure, through which a given order becomes "rooted" to its physical location. Land appropriation is key to Schmitt's notion of *nomos*. Not only is it the original sense of *nomos*, according to Schmitt, it is also "the archetype of a constitutive legal process" (47) the primeval law-founding event (*Ereignis*) that creates the "most radical title" from which all other titles and, most significantly, the original entitlement to name, derive. At the same time, *nomos* establishes the "inner measure" (69) of all "subsequent regulations" (78) as well as the outer marks through which a given order becomes visible, concrete. *Nomos* thus names the originary and primordial relation of law to the earth and to the soil, law's spatiality and concreteness, the unity of order and emplacement, which law, in both its normativist and its positivist variants, has long lost and forgotten. In positing *nomos*, as a primeval and "constitutive act of spatial ordering" (71) established by land appropriation, against law's oblivion of its own earthly rootedness, Schmitt sets out to retrieve and restore law's "original, spatial character" (75) and develop a theory of law as "concrete order" (234), i.e. a theory of law as a unity of order (*Ordnung*) and its localisation or emplacement (*Ortung*) that is rooted to the soil. As such, *nomos* in its Schmittian iteration complicates the simplistic understanding of law as the legality of "the functional mode of a state bureaucracy" (71) which concerns itself merely with "enactments of acts emanating from the central command-post responsible for this bureaucracy" (71). Its insight is that it allows us to start appreciating the different ways in which the normativity of our relations with others (and the physical world) are materially inscribed.

Despite their hugely divergent interpretations of *nomos*, both Schmitt (2003, 71; 78) and Arendt (1998, 63–64) refer to *nomos* as quite literally the walls of the polis, that is, the spatial demarcation of the normative political community, the concrete manifestation of the boundary by way of which the inside and the outside is constituted. Richard Ek (2006, 365) points out that for Schmitt the *nomos* of the earth was the spatial ordering "conceptualized on the basis of an 'us inside–them outside' divide". Quoting Trier, Schmitt (2003, 74) notes that nomos is a fence-word: "'In the beginning was the fence. Fence, enclosure, and border are deeply interwoven in the world formed by men, determining its concepts.'" Schmitt went on to consider this meaning of *nomos* as the coincidence of space and law in the context of the imperialist and colonialist projects. On this he wrote the following:

> The history of colonialism in its entirety is as well a history of spatially determined processes of settlement in which order and orientation are combined. At this origin of land appropriation, law and order are one; where order and orientation coincide, they cannot be separated.
>
> (Schmitt 2003, 81)

Almost 70 years after Schmitt wrote these words, Achille Mbembe would echo them in a way that magnifies Schmitt's claim: "colonial war [...] is ultimately, if not the matrix of the *nomos* of the Earth in the last instance, then at least a privileged means of its institutionalization" (Mbembe 2019, 4).

The colonial *nomos* at the Cape

Eight years after the arrival, in 1652, of the Dutch at the Cape of Good Hope, Jan van Riebeeck planted a hedge of bitter almonds at the trading post that he was tasked to establish and maintain on behalf of the Dutch East India Company (VOC) (the latter has, of course, in recent years, become widely recognised as the world's first multinational corporation). Van Riebeeck's hedge was planted with the explicit purpose of keeping out "the KhoiKhoi cattle herders who inhabited this southernmost tip of the African continent, with the mountain barrier behind" (Sparks 1990, xiii). In the words of the late Alistair Sparks, the hedge effectively "cut off Van Riebeeck's little white community from the great African continent stretching away to the north, creating their own little enclave of Europe – six thousand miles from home".[7]

As such, the hedge marked the first European land appropriation in Southern Africa as "a constitutive act of spatial ordering" (Schmitt 2003, 71). Through this land appropriation, the first colonial unity of order and emplacement was constituted, which grounded colonial law – as Roman-Dutch law – both internally, between the early settlers amongst themselves, and externally, vis-à-vis those to whom Sparks refers as the "KhoiKhoi cattle herders", that is to say, South Africa's indigenous peoples. As such, the hedge instituted the first colonial *nomos* at the Cape of Good Hope and marked the boarders of the first geographical jurisdiction of colonial law in South Africa.

Viewed in this way, Van Riebeeck's hedge constituted the first colonial polity in South Africa through the self-closure of a community as "an inside over against an outside" (Lindahl 2006, 882). Van Riebeeck's hedge did not, however, simply function to keep the KhoiKhoi out, for it also demarcated the line beyond which no law – except for the Darwinian law of nature – applied. From the point of view of both the VOC, the state authority in the Netherlands and Van Riebeeck as their representative, the legal status of the territory beyond the hedge remained as it had been found upon European arrival at the Cape. In other words, it remained as *a-nomos* or, to put it in today's terms, it remained as lawless. Given that this territory was populated by the KhoiKhoi, the hedge did not merely indicate *where* colonial law did not apply, but also – and this is critical – to *whom* it did not apply. What we have in Van Riebeeck's hedge, then, is also the first instantiation of colonial sovereignty, constituted on the basis of an included exclusion (Agamben 1998, 11). From the outset, the colonial *nomos* constitutes itself by way of an exclusion which is included in its unity of order and emplacement. This is the exclusion – the alienation, in fact – of the indigenous people of South Africa from the title of the land and any entitlement to the colonial polity.

This brings us to the relationship between the colonial *nomos* and racism. Paul Gilroy (2014, 29) describes the former as "a place so bleak and bloody that the archive of cruelty incubated there can strip the narrative of European progress of its halo". Gilroy (32) also argues that the distinguishing feature of the colonial *nomos* was "the enduring double standard to which it gave rise", a double standard, he writes, which both enframed and defined the unfolding of European empire. The double standard was precisely this: that "[p]eace and law would dwell inside its borders while the chaos and conflict that Marx would later name 'wild justice' reigned, catastrophically, outside" (32). At the Cape, the whole point of Van Riebeeck's hedge was this "double standard", for the effect of the demarcating line of the hedge beyond which no law applied, was precisely that "peace and law would dwell inside its borders", while "wild justice" would catastrophically reign outside. As Richard Marback (2004, 255) writes: "The boundary line of the hedge gave physical expression to colonial categories. Ordered European spaces of economic power enabled and naturalized the extraction of resources and the exploitation of labor in the unordered natural spaces of Africa".

In the form of the included exclusion to which Van Riebeeck's hedge gave rise, we can already see the rudiments of what Michel Foucault (2003, 62) would, centuries later, name as "state racism" and what Gilroy (2014, 33) calls the "racializing power" of the colonial *nomos*. However, at the Cape the included exclusion and the racialising power of the colonial *nomos* soon took on a different, if intricately connected, form. It is highly pertinent for the purposes of this discussion that, in his Tanner Lectures, when Gilroy first mentions the colonial *nomos*, he describes it as a *nomos* "of [...] slavery warranted by race" (21).[8] Here it is necessary to mention another critical effect of the land appropriation marked by Van Riebeeck's hedge, namely that it cut off the KhoiKhoi from their traditional grazing lands. As one historical source notes, "within fifty years of the establishment of the Dutch settlement, the indigenous communities near Table Bay, despite heroic struggles on their part, had been dispossessed of their lands and their independent means of existence had come to an end" (South African History Online 2011).

At the same time as Van Riebeeck was dispossessing the KhoiKhoi from their land, it became increasingly clear that the incipient colonial economy at the Cape "could not function without the use of slave labour" (South African History Online 2011). While it is true that slaves were first imported to the Cape from the Gulf of Guinea, Madagascar, India, Indonesia and Mozambique, it is also true that, as South African historian Russel Viljoen (2001, 30) puts it, "[a]s a result of blatant dispossession and displacement, with subjugation to follow, the Khoikhoi were left little choice but to become servants", specifically, "landless laborers eking out a living on white farms".

It is thus hardly an overstatement to write, as former South African State President, Thabo Mbeki (1999, 96) did in 1999 in an article about race and reconciliation, that "it became impossible to continue the civilizing mission except through the enslavement of the people to the law, the whip, and the gallows". As Arendt pointedly remarks in *The Origins of Totalitarianism* (1958), the European settlers "lived on their slaves exactly the way natives had lived on an unprepared and unchanged nature" (194). This means, that "the Cape became not just a society in which some people were slaves, but a fully-fledged slave society" (South African History Online 2011) and that the most important social feature of a slave society is the high degree of stratification and polarisation between those who are slaves and those who are not. While the

VOC "did not institute a codified form of racial classification, the fact is that slaves were black and slave owners were white" (South African History Online 2011).

Gilroy (2014, 54) accordingly has every reason to name the colonial *nomos* as a "racial *nomos*" of which he writes that it declined to accommodate either the agency or the suffering of the dominated. In this, he is echoing Foucault, who, in his famous *Society Must Be Defended* lecture of 1976 wrote that "[r]acism first develops with colonisation" (257). It is, accordingly, as if the unitary combination of order and emplacement that constituted the colonial, racial *nomos* was, from the outset, accompanied by a much darker, ostensibly subterranean, no less unitary and no less constitutive combination of dispossession (a *dis-order*, after all) and enslavement (a *dis-placement*, after all) – an appropriation – that indeed strips the narrative of European progress of any halo.

It is in this unitary combination of dispossession and enslavement that the excluded inclusion finds the basic form which it would follow for three centuries in South Africa, a form according to which Black people were excluded from the polity only to have their labour included as an economic "resource". As such, slavery represents the point at which what Agamben (1998, 10) calls "bare life" is inscribed in the unity of order and emplacement that the colonial *nomos* founds by way of its racialising power. In this way, slavery is a classical biopolitics as Foucault described it in his lectures on the subject at the Collège de France. It is what Gilroy (2004, 44) calls the "biopolitical force" of the colonial order or *nomos*.

What slavery means from the point of view of Schmitt's *nomos* is thus that the appropriation is no longer confined to land – from this point on, it is also bare life that is *appropriated* by the colonial *nomos*: here, we need only to remind ourselves that according to the Roman-Dutch law that the VOC brought to the Cape, slaves were *property*. The slave, as a labourer in their relation with a master owner, is, in the colonial setting at least, an embodiment of that appropriation by way of which they are included as property and excluded as human. Gilroy's argument, moreover, allows us to understand that this inscription of bare life in the colonial *nomos* has always been racial – it was Black life that was inscribed as bare life in the unity of order and emplacement of the colonial, racial *nomos* and it was Black life that was included in the colonial polity only by way of its exclusion. To resort, finally, to the contemporary idiom: it was Black life that did not matter to the colonial *nomos*, or mattered only to the extent that it merely represented the *animal laborans*.

Racism, then, was critical to the very instantiation of this *nomos* of the colonial polity, because it was what made the included exclusion on which it depended, possible. To put it in Foucault's (2003, 255) terminology, the racism of the colonial *nomos* created the "caesura" in the population by way of which colonial sovereignty came into its own. Indeed, as Anthony King wrote in 1985 in his seminal work on the colonial city,

> the idea of race [...] is essentially an urban product, and very much a colonial urban product. Though race has a biological basis and geographical location, it is also socially produced [...] it was in the colonial city where races were in permanent contact and, in contact, were defined in contradistinction to each other.
>
> (King 1985, 21)

The *nomos* of apartheid

For King (1976, 14),

> the major explanatory variable [of the colonial city] is dominance [...] which partially accounts for the fact that [...] the component sectors of the colonial city were kept separate, deliberately preventing the development of those characteristics of diffusion and interaction which are invariably assumed in any definition of the city.

It is in the colonial urban settlement that the indigenous people of the country are excluded and segregated from the sector inhabited by representatives of the colonising society. In rooting "to the soil the first manmade barrier marking the line that would come to divide the highly stratified white and native communities of South Africa for so many centuries" (Hogan 2012, 29), Van Riebeeck's hedge furnished the blueprint for the system of dispossession and racist exploitation that would carry on for three centuries in South Africa.

The remains of Van Riebeeck's hedge are today still visible in the Kirstenbosch National Botanical Gardens, located on the slopes of Table Mountain. But the remains of the hedge are represented by much more than those few wild almond plants that survive at Kirstenbosch today. In 1958, Rycroft (1958, 23) called Van Riebeeck's hedge the "oldest living monument of European settlement" (Rycroft 1958, 23) at the Cape. Many years later, in his 1990 book, *The mind of South Africa*, Alistair Sparks (1990, xiii–xiv) demonstrates how a direct and concrete link can be traced from Van Riebeeck's first inscription of colonial exclusion, to apartheid's "geography of exclusion", demonstrating Schmitt's point that all subsequent divisions (distributions and productions) follow from the original division that marks the first land appropriation:

> Stand there beside the strip of hedge in the Kirstenbosch Garden and look north – in the middle distance are the twin cooling towers of Athlone Power station [...] to the left and west of that line lie the white suburbs of Claremont, Kenilworth, Rondebosch, Newlands, Mowbray, Wynberg and Pinelands. On the sandy flats to the right and east of it lie the 'coloured' townships – Athlone, Hazendal, Bonteheuvel, Heideveld, Bellville, Elsies River, Lavender Hill and Mitchells Plain – and beyond them, in a descending order of social status, the black townships and squatter camps

> of Langa, Nyanga, Gugulethu, Crossroads and Khayelitsha. There before you lies apartheid in all its obscenity (xiii–xiv).

This is apartheid, then, as apart-ness, the "spectacle of empire as separation" (Hogan 2012, 29), "a spatial ordering of society through segregation and sub-urbanization: dividing and distancing being central to the politics and culture of apartheid" (Hall 2012, 1); and its law as a rigid spatial ordering that originates in land appropriation. Mbeki (1999, 96) concludes his reflections on the hedge stating that "[t]oday, where Jan van Riebeeck's hedge once stood, railroad tracks separate the black and white quarters of Cape Town". He is talking about post-1994 South Africa. As it stands, the remains of Van Riebeeck's hedge continue to serve as a poignant spatial marker from which apartheid's spatial legacy can be traced to this day.

In a 2004 budget speech, the Western Cape Minister of Environment Planning, Tasneem Essop, noted that "almost 300 years later, the architects of apartheid continued Van Riebeeck's act of separation by legislating the 'hedge' into existence through the Group Areas Act" (Essop 2004, as quoted in Barnard-Naudé 2009, 186). The Group Areas Act 41 of 1950 was perhaps the most notorious legal device by way of which the apartheid government furthered its politics of racial oppression. It created separate residential areas in accordance with racial classification (all developed urban areas were designated "white only" while under- or undeveloped areas were assigned to Black people). This Act also led to the notorious forced removals by the apartheid government of people who lived in the "wrong" areas, notably the forced removal of the original residents of Cape Town's District Six.

But the Group Areas Act was a fairly late arrival on the scene in the systematic dispossession and subjugation of South Africa's Black population. The Natives Land Act 27 of 1913, which was the first major piece of segregation legislation passed by the newly formed Union Parliament of 1910, is commonly regarded as the point at which the land appropriations that preceded it was formally legalised, on the one hand, and as providing the legalised spatial structure for the system of apartheid that would "officially" follow later in the twentieth century, on the other hand.[9] As Jacques Derrida (1987, 13) noted in his essay on Nelson Mandela, the failure of the apartheid system to cover up the basic founding violence of its colonial origin, meant that it could only keep itself alive by way of the "pathological proliferation of juridical prostheses (laws, acts, amendments)" that were "destined to legalize to the slightest detail the effects of fundamental racism, of a state racism, the unique and the last in the world" (18). It is the same Derrida who, in his essay on apartheid would describe it as follows:

> APARTHEID: by itself the word occupies the terrain *like a concentration camp*. System of partition, barbed wire, crowds of mapped out solitudes. [...] The word concentrates separation, raises it to another power and sets

> separation itself apart [...] By isolating being apart in some sort of essence [...] the word corrupts it into a quasi-ontological segregation.
>
> (Derrida 1985, 292 (emphasis added))

The link that Derrida makes between apartheid and the concentration camp is, of course, anything but coincidental. It is a commonly known fact that the concentration camp was invented in South Africa by the British during the Anglo-Boer War. It is significant that the great theorist of the camp as "the *nomos* of the modern", Giorgio Agamben, mentions at the beginning of the chapter on the spatiality of the camp in *Homo Sacer* (1998, 166), these very same "'concentration camps' into which the English herded the Boers toward the start of the century". It is also worth recalling that Hannah Arendt's *The Origins of Totalitarianism* notes that concentration camps emerged for the first time during the Boer War and that, from the beginning, they were used to contain what she refers to as "undesirable elements" (Arendt 1968, 440). For Agamben the paradigm of the camp is, of course, defined by the fact that it represents that combination of order and "localization" where the exception is normalised, where norm and exception collapses into what he calls a "real zone of indistinction".

Adam Sitze (2013) has definitively revealed the juridical/normative correspondent of the spatiality of the camp in the way in which the English jurisprudence of sovereignty functioned in the colonial and apartheid setting. In his genealogy of the South African Truth and Reconciliation Commission, Sitze argues that the two principles of sovereignty in *salus populi suprema lex esto* in the form of political sovereignty and the rule of law as legal sovereignty, *constitutionally* lodge the exception in the heart of the norm. Sitze then goes on to show how, in the case of South Africa, the exception and the norm collapsed into a real zone of indistinction as a result of the way in which the indemnity convention was operationalised during colonial-apartheid.

To understand how this worked, one has to note, first that, from the outset, apartheid, in order to maintain itself, could not but have recourse to violent, repressive state action. In order to legitimise this violence juridically, it could not but have recourse to a routine invocation of the indemnity convention, originally theorised by Dicey as an *exceptional* device of political sovereignty that would work in the service of legal sovereignty (Sitze 2013, 4). The effect of invoking the indemnity convention was, of course, the exoneration of state officials from criminal responsibility for their conduct during uprisings, revolts, riots and general civil disobedience.

The reliance on indemnity, however, was so frequent during colonial-apartheid that it became a "norm of South African governance" (Sitze 2013, 73). With reference to the Sharpeville massacre, for instance, Sitze writes that by 1961 "indemnity had become so predictable and normal a part of South African law" that "one South African [member of parliament] would even argue that the truly unprecedented event would have been for Parliament not to pass an indemnity act following the Sharpeville massacre" (72–3). What is crucial for our argument is that this use of indemnity does not start with grand apartheid. Sitze shows how, at least since the 1912 Police Act, indemnity was integrated into "normal" South African legislation to the extent that such integration "dissolved the intricate balance that Dicey attempted to achieve between law and convention" (74). As a result, Sitze argues that the whole period of colonial and apartheid rule could be characterised as a state of exception in which legality and illegality themselves collapsed into a zone of indistinction.

This does not mean that, spatially speaking, the whole of South Africa amounted to a camp. Rather, the *nomos* of colonialism and apartheid created very specific places where the state of exception prevailed nomically, that is to say, as concrete order. To state it differently, the state of exception was *emplaced* and where it was so emplaced, the place was spatially normativised as a camp. The state of exception did not prevail in Cape Town's white suburbs or in the business centres of South Africa's cities – it prevailed in those spaces to which Black people were confined and, more often than not, in the places and spaces where they laboured, most notably, of course on the mines where the notorious lack of occupational health and safety repeatedly translated into those infamous mining disasters of the apartheid era. As for the spaces to which Black people were residentially and socially confined, they had many names under apartheid – "homelands", "trusts", locations, townships. They were defined by the fact that they were reserved for Black people, that Black people were confined there in mostly sub-human, grossly unequal social conditions and finally by the fact that the police force and the army were a law unto themselves in those spaces. It was in relation to these spaces that the apartheid legal order invoked the indemnity convention on a routine basis and it was in relation to events that occurred in these spaces that the apartheid legal order set up its biopolitical Commissions of Inquiry to whitewash its own wrongdoing.

As a result, it would be mistaken to think of South Africa's colonial-apartheid laws of dispossession, such as the Native Land Act, "merely" as legislation by way of which 7% of the land was allocated to so-called Native Reserves outside of which Black people could not buy land. For, in addition to this gross dispossession and internal displacement, the purpose of this law was normatively to spatialise the state of exception in relation to South Africa's Black population. To put it differently, the ultimate purpose of legislation such as the Native Land Act and the Natives (Urban Areas) Act, as well as of the "pathological" "proliferation of juridical prostheses (laws, acts, amendments)" that followed[10] from it, was to restrict definitively the Black population of South Africa to those spaces where the state of exception prevailed or could easily be made to prevail. In this way, the spatial planning of colonial-apartheid amounted to the instantiation of the spatiality of the camp.

In post-apartheid South Africa, it is also these spaces that remain largely untransformed and that are spaces today where, what Sitze (2013, 193), relying on the work of Richard Rive, calls the "normal emergency", prevails. These are the spaces in which the law and rights of the Constitution are applicable, meaning that they apply, for most part, in a theoretical sense alone. In effect, the neoliberalisation of the South African state has brought with it an abandonment of the very people who the Constitution's bridge was meant to include. These are also the very people who are most in need of basic services and indeed of the law. The state's biopolitical entitlement to "make live and let die" (Foucault 2003, 241), originally established by the *nomos* of colonial-apartheid, thus continues. Specific parts of the population remain abandoned to the exception that the apartheid state created for them. While elements of this apparatus have been displaced through transformative constitutionalism, the post-apartheid spatial order continues starkly, too starkly, to resemble that of apartheid. Nowhere is this clearer than in the untransformed spatial configuration of the post-apartheid city – fundamentally, its business centre-suburb-township model of apartheid spatial planning persists and has not yet been successfully reimagined.

The ubiquitous spatial injustice of continuing conditions of *de facto* segregation and exploitation (the "normal emergency") suggests that the question of post-apartheid spatial justice must become central to facing the challenges of transformation in contemporary South Africa. The post-apartheid government acknowledged the glaring hiatus of spatial justice in its transformation strategies when it included in the 2011 version of the National Development Plan (2011, 246) a vague definition of spatial justice as the requirement that "[t]he historic policy of confining particular groups to limited space (ghettoisation and segregation) and the unfair allocation of public resources between areas [must] be reversed".[11] Subsequently, Minister Lindiwe Sisulu (2014) stated in her address at the 6th Planning Conference of the South African Planning Institute in October 2014 that

> [o]ur most immediate need after 1994 was the urgent need for shelter, a roof over our people's heads and the restoration of their dignity. Ten years down the line we realized that even as we were building houses, we were doing no more than recreating Apartheid in a democracy. This is a sad indictment of our planning.

The recent enactment of the Spatial Planning and Land Use Management Act 16 of 2013, which came into force in April 2015, represents a concrete intervention aimed at the transformation of the spatial legacy of injustice left by apartheid. It introduces a "uniform, effective and comprehensive system of spatial planning" and requires that spatial planning and land use management must promote "social and economic inclusion". These developments indicate that the time has come for critical jurisprudence in the postcolony to focus its attention explicitly on the spatial dimension of law as *nomos*, reminding itself not only of law's impossibly necessary and necessarily impossible responsibility to do justice, but also of Andreas Philippopoulos-Mihalopoulos's (2015, 181) adage that "there can be no justice which is not spatial".

The chapters

Each of the chapters in this collection speaks directly to different aspects of the troubling legacy of the *nomos* of apartheid, to the racism at its core, and, especially, to its continuation in a time attenuated as "post-". In this way, the chapters address the continuation of the kind of spatial injustice that lies at the core of apartheid's *nomos*, reminding us that, as Karin van Marle (2010, 635) puts it, apartheid may be "post-" but it is by no means "past".

Joel Modiri's essay opens the collection by deftly taking stock of the condition of "post"-apartheid spatiality, situating it firmly within the historically neglected problematic of the co-constitutive relationship between law, race and space in South Africa. Modiri warns that without centrally positioning race and racism within the enquiry into the conditions of possibility of spatial justice after apartheid, we risk understating the proportions of the problem. Arguing that it is "a *ruse* to refer to South Africa as substantively 'post-apartheid' since the spatial design of that which the term 'post-apartheid' claims to have overcome (colonial-apartheid), remains firmly etched on the ground and soil of South Africa", Modiri echoes the concern of this introductory chapter that it is not simply land appropriation which is at stake in the "making of a colonial *nomos*", but indeed also the appropriation of "bodies and minds".

Drawing on seminal literature in critical race theory, Modiri goes on to consider what he calls the "racial ontology of space", which converts indigenous people into strangers in their own country. With reference to our earlier invocation of Derrida's point that apartheid isolates being apart into a "quasi-ontological" segregation, Modiri would disagree: if the "ontology of space" in the racist context is racial alienation, then apartheid raises being apart to the level of ontology proper. In other words, as a spatial project, apartheid is not merely "quasi-ontological", it is ontological through and through.

Modiri considers this alienating conversion through which the racial *ontology* of space proceeds, as fundamental to the way in which the "racial *nomos*", in turn, unfolds. Indeed, spatial inequality "emanates from the racist inscription of the Otherness-of-the-Black onto the surface of the material world". In a similar vein, Denise Ferreira da Silva (2009) has argued that raciality produces both the "subject of ethical life" and what she calls the "subjects of *necessitas*": "the racial subaltern subjects whose bodies and territories, the global present, have become places where the state deploys its forces of self-preservation" (da Silva 2009, 224). Interestingly, Ferreira Da Silva retrieves from Schmitt's rendering of *nomos* the possibility of comprehending instances of racial violence as "moments of political/symbolic 'land-reappropriation'". For these instances of racial violence merge disciplinary and juridical power by imposing an "order and orientation" that legitimises itself in advance.

While Modiri's reading of Schmitt, on the other hand, is at pains to emphasise the ways in which *The Nomos of the Earth* reads "as an apologia for colonialism", his exposition (relying on the work of Nuttall and Mbembe) that "there is no metropolis without a necropolis" comes close to Ferreira Da Silva's. Indeed, Modiri's argument that necropower creates "death-worlds" and that "[n]ecropolitics and necropower are thus fundamentally spatial and racialised at the same time", seem to echo Ferreira Da Silva's point. What remains, then, central in both Modiri and Ferreira Da Silva's reading of *nomos* is the problematic of appropriation beyond the initial land appropriation. Modiri's answer to the land appropriation and the "political/symbolic" land re-appropriations of which both he and Ferreira Da Silva write in resonating terms, is given in the form of Razack's notion of "unmapping", which Modiri argues could supplement or indeed supplant the notion of spatial justice. "To unmap", Modiri writes, is to "denaturalise the spatial order, to ask how spaces came to be composed as they are and to undermine the racialist worldviews that such spaces rest upon". Modiri associates unmapping explicitly with Mogobe Ramose's call for a "*post-conquest* – and not merely post-apartheid" South Africa and, in so doing, he calls for "recovering the lost sovereignty and title to territory of the indigenous African peoples". In the context of ongoing debates about land, land ownership and decolonisation in South Africa, Modiri's argument could not be more pressing.

Julia Chryssostalis's contribution follows immediately and is in dialogue with Modiri's reading of Schmitt's account of modernity and colonialism, while focusing on the question of what comes – what *could* come – after the colonial moment and its *nomos*, thus setting the scene, so to speak, for one of the themes of this collection, namely that of thinking *nomos* "otherwise" (Chryssostalis 2013), after the end of apartheid and colonialism. Reading closely Herman Melville's novella *Benito Cereno* (Melville 1856), a piece of literature that Schmitt read intensely and used extensively, so much so that he came to identify with the central character, Chryssostalis breaks with Schmitt's interpretation, according to which *Benito Cereno*, as the "myth of unresolved situations" and impossible choices, provides a way for him to justify his involvement with the Nazi regime, and proposes, against Schmitt, a very different reading of Melville's novella. Taking us back to the opening scene of the story, when the American captain boards the Spanish slave ship, oblivious to the fact that this had been taken over by its human cargo, Chryssostalis argues that this moment offers a rare staging of the "tarrying with the negative" that characterises every post-revolutionary situation, and of the "relative opacity", as Fanon puts it, in which "each generation must discover its mission, fulfil it or betray it" (Fanon 1963, 206). This condition, she argues, is the situation in which the symbolic link breaks, and this break opens up a number of different possibilities of how to reconstitute it. Taking her cue from Melville, Schmitt and Fanon respectively, Chryssostalis goes on to sketch three different configurations of postcolonial becoming.

The first one envisages the restoration of the racial *nomos* and the racialised logics of modern coloniality and as such is characterised by the "the loop of the modern colonial death drive" that reinstates the "abyssal line" (De Sousa Santos 2007) of the colonial *nomos*, which reduces the rest of the world to "zones of nonbeing", disposability and exploitation, and their lands to *terrae nullius*, or "lands of nobody", that is, "nobody-that-counts", "nobody-like-us". The second one oscillates between on the one hand, a new *nomos* of "no Nomos", in which both the law, through its empty universalisation, becomes rootless, ungrounded, separated from its terrestrial fundament, and its object is radically transformed, given that it can no longer be based on the appropriation of land; and on the other hand, a new *nomos* of new "amity lines", that heralds a new pluriversal global order of the world. Finally, the third configuration does not provide us with an already made image of postcolonial becoming but instead sketches its conditions of possibility, namely the disordering of the previous colonial nomos and the undoing of the racialised "amity lines" that organise it, "ex-scribing" them from the soil, in order to inscribe new lines of sociality and "disenclosure" (Mbembe 2017), and thus decolonised postcolonial worlds.

Karin van Marle's chapter engages especially the last two trajectories of *nomos* as explained by Chryssostalis, by focusing on the contemporary debate about ownership and belonging in South Africa. Arguing that the notion of "unlearning" is "pivotal" in the understanding of possibilities of response to the legacy of apartheid's *nomos*, Van Marle is principally concerned with the relationship between land appropriation as a law-founding/law-preserving violence, on the one hand, and with epistemic violence and the imposition of language, on the other. Relying on the work of Walter Mignolo, Van Marle considers "spatiality as a relation" to be inextricably bounded up with epistemology and language. In the colonial context, being alive to this entanglement of space and language entails an understanding that, to use Mignolo's words, "language is the companion of the empire". *Nomos* does not instantiate and consolidate itself all by itself – it does so in and through the violent imposition of a colonial symbolic order.

Nowhere is the inextricability between *nomos* and language more apparently the case than in the gesture of naming. Van Marle reviews Schmitt's position on the relationship between *nomos, nahme* (taking) and naming, before discussing recent instances of naming/renaming in post-apartheid South Africa. Arguing that the controversies about the renaming of streets and the abolition of Afrikaans as a medium of instruction at the University of Pretoria (as elsewhere), fundamentally affect spatial relations that bear on cohabitance, inhabitance and belonging, Van Marle insists that the loss of the name as well as the loss of the language is intimately related to the loss of territorial power.

These instances of what one could call the transformation of the name, then, demand an unlearning that is central to the becoming of decolonial spatiality – of "living differently and ethically in the postcolony". For Van Marle, the "continued assertion of space through naming and language", on the part of those who are losing the power to name, stands in direct contrast to the ethical notion of reconfiliation in the work of Magobe Ramose. By way of a discussion of the work of JM Coetzee on the failure of love, and Antjie Krog on being "land-owned as opposed to being landowner", Van Marle illustrates what the unlearning that she is concerned with might entail.

Following Van Marle's chapter, we republish here with the permission of the author, a poem by Antjie Krog in the original Afrikaans and as translated into English, from her collection *Mede-wete/Synpase* (2014). The poem is entitled "inventory of my poetic bankruptcy" and its repetition of the word "spaces" suggest that the "poetic bankruptcy" of the poet and, by extension, of poetic justice, is intimately bounded up with spatiality. For the "spaces" that Krog renders in poetry are inexorably spaces of injustice, spaces, one could say, as the poet does, where it is not possible for life to be lived (justly).

Like Van Marle, Barbara Boswell also involves literature in exploring the past and present of spatial exclusion in South Africa, but whereas Van Marle focuses on the critique of the *nomos* from within what JM Coetzee (1988) once called "white writing", Boswell turns to the much neglected authorship of Black South African women, bringing her piece to turn on the trope of "black feminist geography" as articulated by Katherine McKittrick. Boswell argues that the work of these writers explores resistant spatial practices by Black South African women which function to counter the "taken-for-granted instantiation of South African spatial order" in the colonial-apartheid *nomos*. Boswell refers to such resistant spatial practices as "place-making" and she illustrates how such places are made in the novels of Miriam Tlali and Lauretta Ngcobo, describing these novelists as the "first writers to produce a critical black feminist geography through their fiction".

Boswell then turns to two poems (one by Koleka Putuma and the other by Diana Ferrus) which she describes as products of the "political moment" of the RhodesMustFall and FeesMustFall protest movements at South African universities. These movements themselves contested the continued spatial exclusion of students from university campuses due to the legacy of colonialism, imperialism and apartheid. For Boswell, Ferrus's poem provides a literary opportunity both to take stock of the way in which the racial *nomos* appropriated people as well as space by way of the institution of slavery and forced labour more generally. In Putuma's poem, "Mountain", Boswell sees a reflection of the continuation of that *nomos* in the arrangements of private property after apartheid – arrangements through which private property have come detrimentally to encroach on the notion of public ownership: "For the white woman guarding her parcel of land from black trespasses, the dogs, the fences and the very mountain structures her experience of dominion over territory, producing a taken-for-granted ownership of this domain". Yet, Boswell deftly argues that the very presence of the Black body in this space produces a "critical black geography" that contests the foundations of this *nomos*. In both poems, the target remains the appropriative logic of *nomos* in the service of what Boswell calls "white supremacist domination". Yet, in conclusion, Boswell insists that the work of authors like Ferrus and Putuma dare to produce a "post-apartheid, oppositional *nomos*", a counter-*nomos*, then, that points to the limits of democratic law in securing spatial justice after apartheid.

Victoria Collis-Buthelezi's essay is in critical conversation with Boswell. Collis-Buthelezi takes Lauretta Ngcobo's *And They Didn't Die* as her point of departure to explore the ways in which "the *nomos* (or the spatialized normativity) of the white (suburban) South African home operates as a site of production of black female subjectivity". Collis-Buthelezi argues that Ngcobo offers "a feminist recounting of systemic productions of South African black female subjectivity(ies) under the *nomos* of apartheid". This essay is concerned with continuation and remainder – how the *nomos* of apartheid "'remains' emplaced onto black women's bodies", how it continues to endure in "post"-apartheid South Africa. "If the *nomos* of the white SA *oikos* appropriated (and incorporated) black female subjects by completely de-personalising them, the post-apartheid economic order, or *oikonomia*, continues to deny black female subjectivity full personhood", Collis-Buthelezi writes. Here, then, we have a similar concern as the one voiced by Modiri and Ferreira Da Silva – the extension of colonial-apartheid land appropriation to the appropriation of the Black body, specifically the Black female body. Collis Buthelezi recalls how, under colonial-apartheid Black women's movement "and thus their *emplacement*" was "state regulated" and she continues to focus on how the production of the South African home as a space, simultaneously produced the Black female body as a servant/maid/"meid". This historical production and reproduction of the Black female body has not gone away post-apartheid, Collis-Buthelezi insists, while arguing that it "reorganizes" the production of Black female subjectivity "in general".

Furthermore, Collis-Buthelezi vividly illustrates the intertwinement, the constitutive intertwinement, of the material spatial ordering with the ordering of the Black female body in the home, drawing attention to the way in which the home is a nomic order, a concrete order in which *nomos* and *oikos* are combined to produce a spatial arrangement that corresponds to the "normative architecture" of colonial-apartheid, a normative architecture of separation that has not been superseded by the dawn of the "famed rainbow nation". Yet Collis-Buthelezi is at pains to illustrate how Ngcobo's writing and Black South African female writing in general provide examples of how Black women refuse, resist and subvert this production of themselves as servants in the *nomos* of the *oikos*. Tracing the line of correspondence of Ngcobo's novel from Olive Schreiner's *The Story of an African Farm*, to Sol Plaatje's *Mhudi*, Collis-Buthelezi comes to a consideration of the impossibility of inter-racial friendship in the South African home. "What", she asks, "is a declaration of friendship and love for a black woman when expressed through violence and coercion and when the very conditions of black female subjectivity are oppressive?" The "*meid*'s rooms" that remain in post-apartheid South Africa "as a fact of the built domesticity" of the White South African home, Collis-Buthelezi concludes, begs us to break down the "structures of affect that continue to perpetuate white supremacy and patriarchy in the continued commodification of black female subjectivity".

Remaining within the ambit of literature, Jaco Barnard-Naudé turns to the work of JM Coetzee to consider what he calls an "*un*colonial spatial justice" after apartheid. Barnard-Naudé reads Coetzee's *Waiting for the Barbarians* (1980) as representing, in allegorical form, the pervasive spatial normativity and the normativised space of apartheid's *nomos*. He goes on to argue that this *nomos* is fundamentally disrupted in the novel's ministration scenes in which the main character, a magistrate in a frontier town, takes into his care a "barbarian" girl who has been tortured, maimed and blinded by the brutal operation of the *nomos* of Empire. Barnard-Naudé reads the ministration scenes as a series of liminal encounters within which a discursive (and thus spatial) transformation begins to take place in the magistrate who, as he argues earlier in the essay, becomes in the course of the novel a "coloniser who refuses". Relying on the psychoanalysis of Jacques Lacan, Barnard-Naudé shows how the embodied encounters between the magistrate and the girl unleash an analytical experience for the magistrate – an experience which unmoors him from the master-signifier of Empire and which comes to represent the beginnings of an *un*colonial, but not decolonial, spatial justice after apartheid.

Like Collis-Buthelezi, Barnard-Naudé's chapter is critically concerned with the "post"-apartheid condition in which white colonisers continue to live with the colonised in the same country, albeit in radically stratified spaces that mark the continuation of the legacy of apartheid spatiality. Like Van Marle, Barnard-Naudé relies on the notion of unlearning – specifically, on the idea of unlearning Empire – to consider the responsibility of the coloniser who refuses. To be sure, the white population of present-day South Africa consists to a great extent of colonisers who (still) accept, but Barnard-Naudé's concern is with those colonisers who refuse, have begun to refuse, would like to refuse the implicitly racist tautologies that mark their discourse and thus their socio-spatial bonds. In characterising the ministration scenes in *Waiting for the Barbarians* as instances of a rudimentary *un*colonial spatial justice, Barnard-Naudé is implying that the coloniser who refuses must be considered at a certain distance from the signifier of "decolonisation", unentitled to claim it. In this, Barnard-Naudé is arguing that the spatial project of the coloniser who refuses entails a radically different nomic responsibility than that of the colonised and that such a responsibility begins with the unlearning of Empire and could be characterised as the quest for an *un*colonial spatiality.

In Derrick Higginbotham's essay, literature creates the space to reflect on the continuation of a different, yet related, dimension of the legacy of the *nomos* of apartheid. This is the continuation, after formal decolonisation, of a heteropatriarchal *nomos* in the (Zimbabwean) postcolony. Higginbotham's focus is Tendai Huchu's 2010 novel, *The Hairdresser of Harare*, which is set during the time of the Mugabe government's notorious Operation Murambatsvina during which thousands of informal structures in the country were declared illegal and arbitrarily demolished. Higginbotham reads such a postcolonial operation of governmentality as echoing the actions of colonial governments and indeed of the abhorrent spatial practices of apartheid's forced removal policies. For Higginbotham, Huchu situates the novel at the time of Operation Murambatsvina as if to underscore the state's power to "re-organise a country's *nomos*".

Yet, Higginbotham is interested in the ways in which these governmental operations are symptomatic of the postcolonial state's creation of included exclusions at the level of citizenship. Huchu's novel focuses specifically on how a heteropatriarchal *nomos* displaces women and sexual minorities. Higginbotham's focus is on the gay character, Dumisani, who is outed in the course of the novel and who is, as a result, not simply rendered out-of-place, or as occupying a non-place, but who indeed ultimately becomes placeless (*a-topos*). Higginbotham approaches such placelessness as a queer state "betwixt and between nations" – a queerness from which it may be possible to contemplate that which lies beyond the heteropatriarchal displacements of the *nomos* of the closet. Like Collis-Buthelezi's chapter in this collection, Higginbotham is at pains to underscore the profound sense in which an oppressive *nomos* renders other spatialities, other subjectivities and indeed other relationalities, impossible – the *nomos* produces space at the same time as it produces preferred categories of people, preferred relationships and prohibited affinities.

Isolde de Villiers shifts the focus back to "post"-apartheid South Africa where she attributes the continuation of the *nomos* of apartheid to the proclivity, in a "post"-apartheid era, for the production of abstract space. Arguing along similar lines to Rachel Langford (2003) that the colonial conception of space coincides, in its most important aspects, with Henri Lefebvre's conceptualisation of the space of capitalism as "abstract space", De Villiers underscores a point that has been made by Langford (2003, 117), namely that:

> one of the spatial discourses characteristic of the high colonial period was a utilitarian representation of space: the physical elements making up the space of the colonies are seen only as objects for consumption, in the form of portions of knowledge or resources for commercial exploitation.

As regards the historical position, De Villiers relates the production of apartheid's racist spaces as the production of abstract space through the notorious sanitation syndrome's language of infestation, sanitation and separation. In terms of the contemporary, De Villiers focuses on South Africa's administrative capital, Pretoria/Tshwane, to elaborate an argument that the sanitation syndrome plays a key role in understanding the continuation of apartheid's *nomos*. Here, De Villiers turns to the 2011 evictions at Schubart Park in the Tshwane inner city, in order to show how the (colonial) language of the sanitation syndrome continued to be enlisted, in order to style the evictions ("forced removals", as she, rightly, calls them) as evacuations and to justify them as necessary.

At the same time, De Villiers is interested in how the relationship between race and space is harnessed in resistant spatial practices. In this regard, she relies on the work of South African performance artist, Steven Cohen, to show how Cohen's site-specific performance emplaces whiteness at the site of a post-apartheid forced removal. By doing so, Cohen's work, *Chandelier*, enlists whiteness to disrupt whiteness and provides important directions for an itinerary of resistance to the continuation of apartheid's *nomos*.

All of the chapters in this collection are at pains to illustrate the many different ways in which the *nomos* of apartheid remains, endures, continues. Following De Villiers's chapter is a photo essay by the celebrated photographer, Johnny Miller, which serves as a visual illustration of the continuation of apartheid's *nomos*. In the text accompanying these photographs, Miller writes that "[s]ome informal settlements in these photographs did not exist during apartheid, they are fully modern creations, of a poisonous environment of fear and exclusion which continues to entrap our cities". Miller's larger project is entitled "unequal scenes" and his introduction of the trope of "inequality" through these visual elaborations stands in stark contrast with the South African Constitution's commitment to the "achievement of equality", illustrating as it does the profound mismatch between the abstract constitutional re-imagination of *nomos* and the spatial, concrete and material continuation of the *nomos* of apartheid.

Loretta Feris and Jaco Barnard-Naudé circle back to Collis-Buthelezi's "structures of affect" to argue in their chapter on "sense of place" for the importance of virtual displacement in detecting the ways in which the neoliberal orientation of the post-apartheid dispensation extends the, or a, *nomos* of apartheid. Virtual displacement refers to situations where, as a result of development projects, local communities experience displacement even though they remain in the same physical location. In other words, they experience displacement not because they are forced to relocate physically but instead because their "sense of place" is radically altered as their natural environment is profoundly impacted by various development projects. In situations like these, people become placeless (*a-topos*) in two ways: they occupy a non-place, a place that is no longer "there" as far as they are concerned, and are out-of-place, disemplaced, in their own locality because they feel no connection to the place in its "new" form.

The law treats differently physical and virtual displacement. Whereas physical displacement is recognised for its negative human rights impact, virtual displacement is not. The loss involved in the latter thus remains unmarked and unaccounted for. As a consequence, and insofar as the post-apartheid Constitution promises a normative space that has a place for everyone, the unaccounted character of the loss involved in virtual displacement means that the injury of the placeless becomes also a normatively placeless injury, an injury that can find no place in the new normative space of post-apartheid South Africa. As such, this is an injury that is *a-topos*, and hence *a-nomos*, outside the domain of the law, a normatively unintelligible injury, without possibility of redress; a profound injustice.

Ferris and Barnard-Naudé argue therefore that the distinction between physical and virtual displacement cannot be maintained. Traditional notions of displacement should be revised to include "virtual" displacement, especially since displacement in the postcolony "has not failed to take place along racialized lines that continue to be as pronounced as they were during apartheid". This in turn will allow the loss of sense of place to be indexed within the post-apartheid normative dispensation in a two-fold manner. First, by conceptualising it in the context of an existing right such as the right to the environment in the Constitution, while, at the same time, re-imagining the legal process in ways that could "capture the multiplicity of [people's] connections to place and space" and spatialise the constitutional right to the environment. Protecting a sense of place, thus, disrupts the appropriative, extractivist and racialised logics of the *nomos* of the postcolony and becomes significant in re-configuring our relationship to the earth and with each other in a post-apartheid, ("actively") postcolonial *nomos*.

Schmitt famously argued that originally the sea has no *nomos*, although he does go on to write about "sea-appropriations" in the *Nomos of the Earth* (Schmitt 2003, 37). "On the open sea", Schmitt writes, "there were no limits, no boundaries, no consecrated sites, no sacred orientations, no law, and no property" (43). David Southwood's photo essay on the Tanzanian stowaway community of Cape Town, provides a visual complement to Schmitt's thinking in this regard. The members of this community travel thousands of miles across the sea not only in an effort to escape the *nomos* of their country of origin, in which they have no place, but also along the very routes that were originally appropriated by the sea powers both for the purpose of colonising overseas territory and for the transport of goods and people between the colonies amongst themselves and between the colonies and the metropole. In this way, the movement of these people not only trace, but also draw attention to the fact that the appropriation of the sea precedes the appropriation of land on the African continent. No wonder that Schmitt writes of the sea-appropriations as "world-historical events of revolutionary significance" (44).

Engaging Southwood's essay upon having read Ferris and Barnard-Naudé's chapter on sense of place, one is also invariably given to think the sense of place of this most marginal of marginal communities, paradoxically occupying precarious spaces within the very heart of central Cape Town (they thus also draw attention to how the periphery can exist in the very heart of the centre). As Southwood's essay shows, the members of these communities literally live under the bridges of Cape Town, amongst the brute concrete structures and remnants that offer almost no solace. Whereas many of these people come to Cape Town under the most dangerous of circumstances in the hope of finding a new *nomos* and a place in it, their situation is no more itinerant on land than it is at sea. Their lives are plagued by placelessness, rightlessness and precarity, by devastation and abandonment, by a constant sense of having to be in motion, by having no sense of a place where one can rest one's head, no home. As illegal immigrants who have no hope of coming within the purview of the post-apartheid *nomos*, their lives remain both *a-topos* and *a-nomos*. Southwood's essay powerfully suggests that the lives of those who literally exist in a non-place between land and sea, constitutes an important remainder of the colonial *nomos* and it evocatively shows these "invisible" people as the remains of colonisation understood as the quintessentially modernist project spread across the oceans. We have placed this essay between a chapter on sense of place and Iain Low's chapter on writing the city otherwise, precisely to draw attention to those who can so easily, if unwittingly, be left behind by both sense of place and the idea of overwriting the postcolonial city.

Finally, then, Iain Low's contribution moves in a similar direction to that of Ferris and Barnard-Naudé in seeking ways to "over-write" colonial-apartheid *nomos* yet does so from a different perspective. Low's starting point in his chapter is that "the single most enduring legacy of colonial apartheid – the 'master' legacy of the 'master's' legacy – is the spatial one". If, as we argue here, apartheid was in its core a repugnant juridicised system of racialised and racist *spatial* ordering, then for Low the task of architecture and planning in a postcolonial, post-apartheid context is that of spatial transformation, of rewriting the city otherwise, that is to say, of rewriting the city in ways that actively undo the racialised and racist logics that continue to form and norm its space. Carrying out this task, moreover, "depends to a great extent on how we do and do not *practise* architecture", and Low goes on to demonstrate that the immense task of rewriting the South African *nomos* beyond that of apartheid and colonialism has begun through

> a consistent, although liminal, intentional practice [of rewriting architectural type] in those post-apartheid architectures that can be characterised as having brought into being the signs of a city otherwise, or of an otherwise city, that is, a city critically 'conscious' of the Other which it has denied for so long.

Through a fascinating *excursus* in, and reflection on, a number of different projects, which in the last 25 years have attempted to contest the norm(alis)ed form of apartheid spatiality in post-apartheid South Africa and rewrite the city in ways critically distinct from those that colonial-apartheid used to inscribe its forms of urban life and sociality, Low argues that these diverse projects share a number of features: they "have produced 'new spaces' and building types", have challenged "the hegemony of the architectural profession and related professions [...] by co-productive modes of engagement through design and implementation" and have paid "close attention to the production of localities" by being "more cognisant of the relational and contextual underpinnings that give rise to particular specificities". As such, these "new spaces" simultaneously make space, unmake space and engage in new practices of spacing, emplacement and localisation. And in doing so, for Low, they provide us with a glimpse of what an emergent *nomos* of the postcolony might look like.

Conclusion

Schmitt (in)famously stated in 1962, as the wave of decolonisation was breaking over the Anglo-European world, that "anti-colonialism does not have the capacity to forge the beginning of a new spatial order in a positive way" (Schmitt in Ulmen 2003, 31). This statement was foreshadowed by the exasperated statement in his *Glossarium* of 1948, that the "new Nomos of the Earth" was "no more Nomos" (Schmitt in Pottage 2019, 170). It is true that the context of both these statements is Schmitt's lament for what he saw as the collapse of the Eurocentric spatial order of international law after the Second World War. However, given that the theory of *nomos* as international order is inseparable in *The Nomos of the Earth* from the theory of *nomos* as the spatialised normativity of all law, these statements exhibit a profound scepticism as regards the capacity of the concept of *nomos* itself to be transformed beyond the Eurocentricity in which it was founded and grounded.

The chapters in this collection each invite us to imagine, against Schmitt, the possibility of a new spatial ordering, conceived in a positive way – a *nomos* that temporally comes after apartheid and colonialism, but that is also *after* the eradication of apartheid and colonialism, in other words a *nomos* that (also) has a teleological orientation. As such, the collection asks after the conditions of possibility of a decolonial nomos – a *nomos* that would be *for* the postcolony and of the postcolony – and thus beckons the possibility of a *nomos* "otherwise" (Chryssostalis 2013), that is, thought, formed and normed from the position of the Other, from the position of those who are beyond the pale of Schmitt's *Nomos of the Earth*, namely Fanon's *Wretched of the Earth*.

In order to begin this task of thinking, forming and norming *nomos* otherwise, the collection insists that we cast our critical gaze both into the past and onto the "post"-apartheid present in order not only to diagnose what exactly was/is at stake in a *nomos* of colonial-apartheid, but also to attend to the myriad ways in which that *nomos* is duplicated, reduplicated and continued in a time after the formal dismantling of the apartheid legal order, mired as it is in the vicissitudes of the neoliberal capitalist hegemony. In this it responds to the project, proposed by André van der Walt in 2009, to imagine property "from the margins". As Brenna Bhandar (2018, 184) has recently reminded us, there is in fact "a rich and vibrant history of the marginalized creating counterlegalities and subverting modern laws of private property as a form of resistance to colonial capitalist modes of governance". In addition, Bhandar (185) recalls Van der Walt's insistence that "what constitutes a view from the margins is not just about the experience and perspective of the disenfranchised; it is also about positioning oneself as a legal theorist on the margins of settled law".

This collection unapologetically situates itself "on the margins of settled law", repeatedly asking not only after the exact nature of what went before, but, most importantly, also asking after what is still to come, what can still be. In this way, it invites us to think *nomos* beyond the "abyssal line" (De Sousa Santos 2007, 45), beyond the priority of appropriation and beyond, indeed, settled law as the "proper" of property. Work on this collection was concluded before the landmark judgment in the *Adonisi*[12] case which has been widely celebrated as a rare juridical "win" for those on the margins of post-apartheid spatial planning and spatial development. While the judgment signals a willingness on the part of legal authority to engage with the coincidence of space and law (and its legacy in South Africa), it is our hope that in future research the impact of the *Adonisi* judgment will be evaluated as a new nomic beginning for the postcolony and as an instance of, or milestone on the road to, spatial justice after apartheid. At the same time, the collection was finished in the midst of a third wave of the Covid-19 pandemic in South Africa – a pandemic the "management" of which has been marked by governmental practices of spatial exclusion and forced removal. As such, it has exacerbated the plight of the marginalised in South Africa and has relegated thousands of people to spaces on the margins of our cities, towns and farms, exposing them once again to existing and new forms of profound spatial injustice in the postcolony. In the space between the hope that the *Adonisi* judgment signals and the despair that the pandemic has brought, we hope that this collection will provide further opportunities for engagement, contestation and reflection – the kind of thinking, in other words, that enables us, urgently so, to "invite new worlds"; indeed, not only to "invite" these new worlds, but also to work together, through scholarly legal activism, to bring them concretely into being. Such work from the margins and on the margins is, in our view, critical for the work of "disenclosure" that is, according to Achille Mbembe (2021, 63) involved in any project of decolonisation:

> by disenclosure we understand the taking apart and disassembling of fences, barriers and enclosures. But, for the disenclosure of the word to happen, it is necessary to detach oneself from oneself, precisely in order to confront what is coming and what, in coming, causes other resources of life to spring up.

Whether such a radical "disenclosure" would still warrant the name of *nomos*, whether *nomos*, thought "otherwise", can disclose such a world; these are the critical questions that the present collection invites us to ponder.

Acknowledgments

The writing of this piece and the editorial work on this collection was made possible through a British Academy Newton Advanced Fellowship held by Jaco Barnard-Naudé in the Westminster Law and Theory Lab in the School of Law at the University of Westminster, between 2017 and 2020 (award reference no. AF160177). Julia Chryssostalis was the Co-Investigator on the project. We wish to thank the British Academy for the research funding received in terms of this grant, as well as the University of Westminster and the University of Cape Town for additional research funding and grant administration support. The editors are indebted to the participants of the Cape Town Spatial Justice Colloquium, that was convened in April 2016 in Cape Town (where this project began) and funded by the South African National Research Foundation and the Faculty of Law, University of Cape Town; as well as to the various speakers and participants who contributed to the project's seminar series, held in London and Cape Town between 2017 and 2020, specifically Brenna Bhandar, Philip Briel, Carrol Clarkson, Peter Fitzpatrick, Sarah Keenan, Leopold Lambert, Renisa Mawani, Shaun McVeigh, Stewart Motha, Andreas Philippopoulos-Mihalopoulos, Alain Pottage, Jacqueline Rose, Rory Rowan, Mandisa Shandu, Karin van Marle and Thanos Zartaloudis.

Finally, we are grateful to Maria Drakopoulou and Connal Parsley for inviting us to present earlier versions of this piece at the Kent Law School Staff Seminar at the University of Kent, and at the 2019 Kent Summer School in Critical Theory in Paris, and to the participants in these events. We would also like to thank the participants of the Cape Town Spatial Justice Laboratory held in 2019 in part at the District Six Museum, where this introduction was delivered as the opening masterclass. We are especially indebted in this regard to Mandy Sanger who created the space within the museum for engagement and community participation, and to Iain Low who has not only been a constant intellectual companion in the project, but who also played a critical role in the organisation and delivery of the laboratory. Above all, we would like to thank our contributors for their engagement with this project, their sustained support, understanding and commitment, and for trusting us with their thought, indeed thinking with us through the *nomos* of the postcolony and the conditions of possibility of spatial justice in the postcolony.

Notes

1 As Drucilla Cornell (2008, 18) writes, "there can be no final Constitution because it will be up to the people of South Africa continually to transform this country as guided by the great ideas of dignity, equality and justice".

2 For an example of its use by the courts, see *Azapo v The President of the Republic of South Africa* 1996 (4) SA 671 (CC). For early criticisms of the bridge metaphor, see De Vos 2001 and Van Der Walt 2001.

3 For this brief account of early *nomos*, and *nemein*, we draw on Chryssostalis (2022, forthcoming).

4 *Works and Days* 276–80; and 388–9; *Theogony* 66; and 416–7; and fr. 20 (Porphyrius, *De abstinentia* ii.18). On this, see Laroche,1949, 164-6, and 171-2; Ostwald, 1969, 21; and more extensively Zartaloudis, 2018, 171–81.

5 For Laroche, the account that traces *nomos*, "law" to *nemō*-distribute, is superficial, does not take into account the semantic diversity of *nomos* found in the older ancient texts and neglects its historical development and chronology (163). Whereas *nomos*, "order", "melody", is post-homeric, the active verb *nemō* (νέμω), "distribute", and its pastoral sense, "take to pasture", the middle verb *némomai* (νέμομαι), "graze", and the noun *nomós* (νομός), "pasture", are all pre-Homeric (7–12 and 176). On the origin of *nomos*, see further Laroche (1949, 163–4, 177 and 187). Also Ostwald 1969, 9–10, and references therein (10, n. 2) and extensively Zartaloudis (2018).

6 Although this seems as a plausible possibility as Zartaloudis has convincingly argued (2018, 339–96).

7 The hedge of bitter almonds was regarded as the second-best option to a canal that was originally planned (see Samuelson 2014, 806). The original intention was thus to cut off the peninsula from the rest of the continent and turn it into an island – an extraordinary plan, driven by a will to geographical insularity which would go as far as re-forming, in the sense of redrawing the form of, the very earth on which the settlers found themselves.

8 Gilroy's reference is to "plantation slavery" and from this it is clear that he has America in mind, but our contention is that the argument applies with equal force to colonisation in Africa and South Africa.

9 Further examples of segregationist legislation passed after 1910 include the following: The Natives (Urban Areas) Act 21 of 1923, the The Native Administration (Black Administration) Act 38 of 1927, The Slums Act 53 of 1934, The Development Trust and Land Act (Native Trust Act) 18 of 1936, The Native (Urban Areas) Consolidation Act 25 of 1945, The Asiatic Land Tenure and Indian Representation Act (Ghetto Act) 28 of 1946, Prevention of Illegal Squatting Act 52 of 1951, the Reservation of Separate Amenities Act 49 of 1953, the Natives Resettlement Act 19 of 1954, The Promotion of Bantu Self-Government Act 46 of 1959, the Bantu Homelands Citizenship Act (National States Citizenship Act) 26 of 1970, the Bantu Homelands Constitution Act (National States Constitutional Act) 21 of 1971, the Black Affairs Administration Act 45 of 1971 and the Black Communities Development Act 4 of 1984.

10 See Note 5 above.

11 The Draft National Spatial Development Framework of September 2018, defines "spatial justice" as follows: A need to:

- Ensure redress in terms of access to the economic opportunities and locational benefits that the country and its cities, towns and rural areas offer, including well-located, productive land;
- Include inclusion of previously excluded areas in the national space economy; and
- Pursue intergenerational justice in (1) the location and pattern of settlement development, and (2) the use of natural resources. See Department of Rural Development & Land Reform and Department of Planning, Monitoring & Evaluation. 2018.

12 *Adonisi and Others v Minister for Transport and Public Works Western Cape and Others; Minister of Human Settlements and Others v Premier of the Western Cape Province and Others* [2020] ZAWCHC 87.

References

Ackermann, Lourens W.H. 2004. "The Legal Nature of the South African Constitutional Revolution." *New Zealand Law Review* 4: 633–679.

Agamben, Giorgio. 1998. *Homo Sacer. Sovereign Power and Bare Life*. Translated by Daniel Heller Roazen. Stanford, CA: Stanford University Press.

Antaki, Mark. 2013. "From the Bridge to the Book: An Examination of South Africa's Transformative Constitutionalism's Neglected Metaphor." In *Genres of Critique: Law, Aesthetics and Liminality*, edited by Karin van Marle and Stewart Motha, 49–74. Stellenbosch: SUN Press and STIAS.

Arendt, Hannah. 1968. *The Origins of Totalitarianism*. San Diego: Harcourt Inc.

Arendt, Hannah. 1990. *On Revolution*. London: Penguin Books.

Arendt, Hannah. 1998. *The Human Condition*. 2nd ed. Introduction by Margaret Canovan. Chicago, IL and London: The University of Chicago Press.

Arendt, Hannah. 2006. *Che cos'è la politica? [What Is Politics?]*. Edited by U. Ludz and translated by M. Bistolfi. Turin: Giulio Einaudi.

Arendt, Hannah. 2007. "The Great Tradition I. Law and Power." *Social Research* 74 (3): 713–726.

Barnard-Naudé, Jaco. 2009. "At the Walls of Athens: What Remains?" *Law and Critique* 20: 177–192.

Baxi, Upendra. 2013. "Postcolonial Legality." In *A Companion to Postcolonial Studies*, edited by Henry Schwarz and Sangeeta Ray, 540–555. Malden, MA: Blackwell Publishing.

Berger, Peter L. 1967. *The Sacred Canopy: Elements of a Sociology of Religion*. New York: Anchor Books.

Berger, Peter L. and Luckmann, Thomas. 1966. *The Social Construction of Reality. A Treatise in the Sociology of Knowledge*. New York and London: Penguin Books.

Bhandar, Brenna. 2018. *Colonial Lives of Property: Law, Land, and Regimes of Ownership*. Durham, NC: Duke University Press.

Bond, Patrick. 2014. *Elite Transition: From Apartheid to Neoliberalism in South Africa*. 2nd ed. London: Pluto Press.

Brand, Danie. 2005. "Introduction to Socio-Economic Rights in the South African Constitution." In *Socio-Economic Rights in South Africa*, edited by Danie Brand and Christof Heyns, 1–56. Pretoria: PULP (Pretoria University Law Press).

Bremner, Lindsay. 2010. *Writing the City into Being: Essays on Johannesburg, 1998–2008*. Johannesburg: Fourthwall Books.

Chryssostalis, Julia. 2013. "Reading Arendt 'Reading' Schmitt: Reading *Nomos* Otherwise?" In *Feminist Encounters with Legal Philosophy*, edited by Maria Drakapoulou, 158–184. Abingdon: Routledge.

Chryssostalis, Julia. 2022. "Nomos is an Air: Hearing as a Juridical Faculty." In *Hearing*, edited by Danilo Mandic et al., forthcoming. London: Westminster University Press.

Coetzee, J.M. 1988. *White Writing: On the Culture of Letters in South Africa*. Sandton: Century Hutchinson (Radix).

Coetzer, Nicholas. 2013. *Building Apartheid: On Architecture and Order in Imperial Cape Town*. Abingdon: Routledge.

Coggin, Thomas. 2016. "Redressing Spatial Apartheid: The Law of Nuisance and the Transformative Role of Social Utility and the Right to the City." *South African Law Journal* 133 (2): 434–451.

Cornell, Drucilla. 2008. "Bridging the Span toward Justice: Laurie Ackermann and the Ongoing Architectonic of Dignity Jurisprudence". In *Dignity, Freedom and the Post-Apartheid Legal Order*, edited by AJ Barnard-Naudé, Drucilla Cornell and François du Bois, 18–46. Cape Town: Juta.

Cornell, Drucilla. 2012. "A Call for a Nuanced Constitutional Jurisprudence: Ubuntu, Dignity, and Reconciliation." In *Ubuntu and the Law: African Ideals and Post-Apartheid Jurisprudence*, edited by Drucilla Cornell and Nyoko Muvangua, 324–332. New York: Fordham University Press.

Cornell, Drucilla, and Karin van Marle. 2015. "Ubuntu Feminism: Tentative Reflections." *Verbum et Ecclesia* 36 (2): 1–8. https://doi.org/10.4102/ve.v36i2.1444.

Cover, Robert M. 1983. "Foreword: Nomos and Narrative." *Harvard Law Review* 97 (1): 1–68.

Da Silva, Denise Ferreira. 2009. "No-bodies: Law, Raciality and Violence." *Griffith Law Review* 18 (2): 212–236.

Deleuze, Gilles. 1994. *Difference and Repetition*. Translated by Paul Patton. New York: Columbia University Press.

Department of Rural Development & Land Reform and Department of Planning, Monitoring & Evaluation. 2018. *National Spatial Development Framework Draft*. https://www.dpme.gov.za/keyfocusareas/gwmeSite/The%20PME%20Forum%202018/FINAL-DRAFT-NSDF-September-2018-B-1.pdf.

Derrida, Jacques. 1985. "Racism's Last Word." Translated by Peggy Kamuf. *Critical Inquiry* 12 (1): 290–299.

Derrida, Jacques. 1987. "The Laws of Reflection: Nelson Mandela, in Admiration." In *For Nelson Mandela*, edited by Jacques Derrida and Mustapha Tlili, 13–42. New York: Seaver Books.

De Sousa Santos, Boaventura. 2007. "Beyond Abyssal Thinking: From Global Lines to Ecologies of Knowledges." *Review* 30 (1): 45–89.

De Villiers, Isolde. 2016. "Leibniz, Lefebvre and the Spatial Turn in Law." *HTS Theological Studies* 72 (1): 1–6.

De Vos, Pierre. 2001. "A Bridge Too Far? History as Context in the Interpretation of the South African Constitution." *South African Journal on Human Rights* 17: 1–33.

Du Toit, Pierre, and Hennie Kotzé. 2011. *Liberal Democracy and Peace in South Africa: The Pursuit of Freedom as Dignity*. New York: Palgrave Macmillan.

Dworkin, Ronald. 2004. "Keynote Address." *Acta Juridica*: 1–17.

Ek, Richard. 2006. "Giorgio Agamben and the Spatialities of the Camp: An Introduction." *Geografiska Annaler* 88 (4): 363–368.

Essop, Tasneem. 2004. "Budget speech 2004/2005: Department of environmental affairs and development planning". *Polity Archive. http://www.polity.org.za/article.php?a_id=135428.*

Fanon, Frantz. 1963. *The Wretched of the Earth*. Translated by Constance Farrington and a preface by Jean-Paul Sartre. New York: Grove Press.

Foucault, Michel. 2003. *"Society Must Be Defended": Lectures at the Collège de France, 1975–76*. Translated by David Macey and edited by Arnold I. Davidson. New York: Picador.

Gilroy, Paul. 2004. *After Empire: Melancholia or Convivial Culture?* Abingdon: Routledge.

Gilroy, Paul. 2014. "The Tanner Lectures on Human Values: Lecture I: Suffering and Infrahumanity; Lecture II: Humanities and a New Humanism." February 21. https://tannerlectures.utah.edu/Gilroy%20manuscript%20PDF.pdf.

Goodrich, Peter. 2006. "A Theory of the Nomogram." In *Law, Text, Terror*, edited by Peter Goodrich, Lior Barshack and Anton Schütz. London: Glasshouse Press/Routledge-Cavendish.

Graham, Shane. 2009. *South African Literature After the Truth Commission: Mapping Loss*. New York: Palgrave Macmillan.

Hall, Suzanne M. 2012. "Book Reviews: *Writing the City into Being: Essays on Johannesburg, 1998–2008* by Lindsay Bremner; *City of Extremes: The Spatial Politics of Johannesburg* by Martin J. Murray." *Antipode* 44 (4): 1–3.

Hesiod. 2006. *Theogony, Works and Days, Testimonia.* Translated by G. W. Most. Loeb Classical Library 57. Cambridge Mass. and London: Harvard University Press.

Hogan, Sarah. 2012. "Of Islands and Bridges: Figures of Uneven Development in Bacon's New Atlantis." *Journal for Early Modern Cultural Studies* 12 (3): 28–59.

Home, Robert. 2014. "Legal histories of planning and colonialism." In *Routledge Handbook on Cities of the Global South*, edited by Susan Parnell and Sophie Oldfield, 75–85. Abingdon: Routledge.

Judin, Hilton, and Ivan Vladislavic, eds. 1999. *Blank: Architecture, Apartheid and After.* Rotterdam: Nai.

King, Anthony D. 1976. *Colonial Urban Development: Culture, Social Power and Environment.* London: Routledge.

King, Anthony D. 1985. "Colonial Cities: Global Pivots of Change." In *Colonial Cities*, edited by Robert J. Ross and Gerard J. Telkamp, 7–32. Dordrecht: Martinus Nijhoff Publishers.

Klare, Karl. 1998. "Legal Culture and Transformative Constitutionalism." *South African Journal on Human Rights* 14: 146–188.

Langa, Pius. 2006. "Transformative Constitutionalism." *Stellenbosch Law Review* 17 (3): 351–360.

Langford, Rachael. 2003. "Challenging the Colonization of Space: Exteriors and Interiors in the Films of Ousmane Sembène and Souleymane Cissé." In *Francophone Post-Colonial Cultures: Critical Essays*, edited by Kamal Salhi, 114–125. Oxford: Lexington Books.

Laroche, Emmanuel. 1949. *Histoire de la racine nem- en grec ancien (νέμω, νέμεσις, νόμος, νομίζω).* Paris: Librairie C. Klincksieck.

Legendre, Pierre. 1992. *Les Enfants du texte. Étude sur la fonction parentale des États.* Paris: Fayard.

Legendre, Pierre. 2001. *De la societé comme texte. Linéaments d'une anthropologie dogmatique.* Paris: Fayard.

Le Roux, Wessel. 2007. "Bridges, Clearings and Labyrinths: The Architectural Framing of Post-Apartheid Constitutionalism." In *Post-Apartheid Fragments. Law, Politics and Critique*, edited by Wessel Le Roux and Karin Van Marle. Pretoria and Leiden: University of South Africa Press/Brill.

Liebenberg, Sandra. 2010. *Socio-Economic Rights: Adjudication Under a Transformative Constitution.* Claremont, IL: Juta.

Lindahl, Hans. 2006. "Give and Take: Arendt and the *Nomos* of Political Community." *Philosophy & Social Criticism* 32 (7): 881–901.

Low, Iain. 2003. "Space and Transformation: Architecture and Identity." *Digest of South African Architecture*, 7: 34–38.

Madlingozi, Tshepo. 2017. "Social Justice in a Time of Neo-Apartheid Constitutionalism: Critiquing the Anti-Black Economy of Recognition, Incorporation and Distribution." *Stellenbosch Law Review* 28 (1): 123–147.

Marback, Richard. 2004. "A Tale of Two Plaques: Rhetoric in Cape Town." *Rhetoric Review* 23 (3): 253–268.

Mathiesen, Thomas. 1999. *Apollo's Lyre: Greek Music and Music Theory in Antiquity and the Middle Ages.* Lincoln, NE: University of Nebraska Press.

Mbeki, Thabo. 1999. "Haunted by History: Race and National Reconciliation in South Africa." *Harvard International Review* 21 (3): 96, 95.

Mbembe, Achille. 2017. *Critique of Black Reason*. Translated by Laurent Dubois. Durham, NC and London: Duke University Press.
Mbembe, Achille. 2019. *Necropolitics*. Translated by Steven Corcoran. Durham, NC: Duke University Press.
Mbembe, Achille. 2021. *Out of the Dark Night: Essays on Decolonization*. Johannesburg: Wits University Press.
Melville, Herman. 1856. "Benito Cereno." In *The Piazza Tales*, 109–271. New York: Dix and Edwards and London: Sampson Low, Son & Co.
Modiri, Joel M. 2012. "The Colour of Law, Power and Knowledge: Introducing Critical Race Theory in (Post-)Apartheid South Africa." *South African Journal on Human Rights* 28 (3): 405–436.
Modiri, Joel M. 2018. "Conquest and Constitutionalism: First Thoughts on an Alternative Jurisprudence." *South African Journal on Human Rights* 34 (3): 300–325.
Mureinik, Etienne. 1994. "A Bridge to Where? Introducing the Interim Bill of Rights." *South African Journal on Human Rights* 10 (1): 31–48.
National Planning Commission. 2011. *National Development Plan: Vision for 2030*. November 11. https://cisp.cachefly.net/assets/articles/attachments/36224_npc_national_development_plan_vision_2030_-lo-res.pdf.
Ndebele, Njabulo. 1991. *South African Literature and Culture: Rediscovery of the Ordinary*. Introduction by Graham Pechey. Manchester: Manchester University Press.
Ostwald, Martin. 1969. *Nomos and the Beginnings of Athenian Democracy*. Oxford: Clarendon Press.
Parnell, Susan. 1997. "South African Cities: Perspectives from the Ivory Tower of Urban Studies." *Urban Studies* 34 (5/6): 891–906.
Philippopoulos-Mihalopoulos, Andreas. 2011. "Law's Spatial Turn: Geography, Justice and a Certain Fear of Space." *Law, Culture and the Humanities* 7 (2): 187–202.
Philippopoulos-Mihalopoulos, Andreas. 2015. *Spatial Justice: Body, Lawscape, Atmosphere*. Abingdon: Routledge.
Pottage, Alain. 2019. "Holocene Jurisprudence." *Journal of Human Rights and the Environment* 10 (2): 153–175.
Ramose, Mogobe. 1998. "Justice and Restitution in African Political Thought." In *The African Philosophy Reader*, edited by P.H. Coetzee and A.P.J. Roux, 541–570. London: Routledge.
Rancière, Jacques. 2001. "Ten Theses on Politics." Translated by Rachel Bowlby with Davide Panagia. *Theory & Event* 5 (3): https://doi.org/10.1353/tae.2001.0028.
Robinson, Jennifer. 1997. "The Geopolitics of South African Cities." *Political Geography* 16 (5): 365–386.
Rycroft, H.B. 1958. "The Van Riebeeck Hedge at Kirstenbosch: Past, Present and Future." *Journal of the South African Forestry Association* 31 (1): 21–23.
Salazar, Philippe-Joseph. 2002. *An African Athens: Rhetoric and the Shaping of Democracy in South Africa*. Mahwah, NJ: Lawrence Erlbaum Associates, Publishers.
Salazar, Philippe-Joseph. 2004. "The Joint Sitting of Parliament, 15 April 2003: A Rhetorical View of the Reparation Debate." In *To Repair the Irreparable: Reparation and Reconstruction in South Africa*, edited by Erik Doxtader and Charles Villa-Vicencio, 44–65. Cape Town: David Philip.
Samuelson, Meg. 2014. "(Un)Lawful Subjects of Company: Reading Cape Town from Tavern of the Seas to Corporate City." *Interventions* 16 (6): 795–817.

Schmitt, Carl. 2003. *The Nomos of the Earth in the International Law of the Jus Publicum Europaeum*. Translated and annotated by G. L. Ulmen. New York: Telos Press Publishing.
Sibanda, Sanele. 2011. "Not Purpose-Made! Transformative Constitutionalism, Post-Independence Constitutionalism and the Struggle to Eradicate Poverty." *Stellenbosch Law Review* 22 (3): 482–500.
Sisulu, Lindiwe. 2014. "6th Planning Africa Conference of the South African Planning Institute." October 21. https://www.gov.za/address-l-n-sisulu-mp-minister-human-settlements-6th-planning-africa-conference-south-african.
Sitze, Adam. 2013. *The Impossible Machine: A Genealogy of South Africa's Truth and Reconciliation Commission*. Ann Arbor, MI: The University of Michigan Press.
South African History Online. 2011. "History of Slavery and Early Colonisation in South Africa." South African History Online, June 2. https://www.sahistory.org.za/article/history-slavery-and-early-colonisation-south-africa.
Sparks, Allister. 1990. *The Mind of South Africa: The Story of the Rise and Fall of Apartheid*. Cape Town: Jonathan Ball Publishers.
Strauss, Margot. 2019. "A Historical Exposition of Spatial Injustice and Segregated Urban Settlement in South Africa." *Fundamina* 25 (2): 135–168.
Terreblanche, Sampie. 2002. *A History of Inequality in South Africa, 1652–2002*. Pietermaritzburg: University of Natal Press.
Ulmen, Gary L. 2003, "Translator's Introduction." In *The Nomos of the Earth in the International Law of the Jus Publicum Europaeum*. Translated and annotated by G. L. Ulmen. New York: Telos Press Publishing.
Van der Walt, André J. 2001. "Dancing with Codes: Protecting, Developing and Deconstructing Property Rights in a Constitutional State." *The South African Law Journal* 118: 258–311.
Van der Walt, André J. 2009. *Property in the Margins*. Oxford: Hart Publishing.
Van Marle, Karin. 2010. "Jurisprudence, Friendship and the University as Heterogeneous Public Space." *The South African Law Journal* 127 (4): 628–645.
Van Marle, Karin, and Isolde de Villiers. 2013. "Law and Resistance in the City of Pretoria: Space, History and the Everyday." *Australian Feminist Law Journal* 38 (1): 129–145.
Vico, Giambattista. 2020. *The New Science*. Translated and edited by Jason Taylor and Robert Miner. New Haven, CT and London: Yale University Press.
Viljoen, Russel. 2001. "Aboriginal Khoikhoi Servants and Their Masters in Colonial Swellendam, South Africa, 1745–1795." *Agricultural History* 75 (1): 28–51.
West, Martin L. 1992. *Ancient Greek Music*. Oxford: Clarendon Press.
Woolman, Stu, and Jonathan Swanepoel. 2012. "Constitutional History." In *Constitutional Law of South Africa*. 2nd ed., edited by Stuart Woolman, Michael Bishop and Jason Brickhill, 2-1–2-49. Cape Town: Juta.
Zartaloudis, Thanos. 2018. *The Birth of Nomos*. Edinburgh: Edinburgh University Press.

Chapter 2

Un/mapping Black life

On estranged spatialities, colonial *nomos* and the ruses of "post"-apartheid

Joel M. Modiri

> Law creates the space, the subjects, the choreography, the words, the incentives, and the pleasures of the everyday practices of domination and submission.
>
> (Farley 2002, 150)

> The category of space is discursively produced and ordered. Just as spatial distinctions like West and East are racialised in their conception and application, so racial categories have been variously spatialised more or less since their inception into continental divides, national localities, and geographic regions. Racisms become institutionally normalized in and through spatial configuration just as social space is made to seem natural, a given, by being defined in racial terms.
>
> (Goldberg 1993, 185)

First thoughts

In this paper, I offer provisional notes on the relation between race, spatiality and coloniality in the context of the putatively "new South Africa" with the aim of calling that proclaimed newness into question. I want to offer a distinctly political rendering of space as a crucial instrument in the making of the colonial world and in the distribution of human value according to the hierarchies of racial difference fabricated within the European colonial imaginary. That is to say that I wish to highlight the relentlessly spatial nature of the colonial project: colonisation and coloniality are first and foremost impositions on space. The global hegemony of the idea of Europe consists largely in its deep imprint on the landscape. Through the spatial and aesthetic fiction of *terra nullius* (or the "empty land" myth[1] in the South African context), colonisation clears away the indigenous inhabitants of the land and violently inaugurates a global racial hierarchy. Colonisation "links space with race and race with personhood" (Mills 1997, 50) by constructing the European subject (whiteness) as the embodiment of civilisation and humanity while imbuing indigenous and racialised communities with the value of absence, sub-personhood and ontological negation.

The making of a colonial *nomos* in South Africa and the colonised world at large has its origins not only with what Carl Schmitt identified as the

DOI: 10.4324/9780203712771-2

world-historical act of "land-appropriation that founds an order" (Schmitt 2003, 80) but also with the appropriation of bodies and the thoroughgoing (but never total) decimation of African cultural, epistemological and spiritual systems. At the level of the symbolic order, these appropriations of lands, bodies and minds set in motion a structure of colonial subjection that reduces its victims to things so that they become *beings-for* their captors and conquerors (Spillers 1987, 67): "That order, with its sequence written in blood, represents for its African and indigenous peoples a scene of *actual* mutilation, dismemberment and exile" (Spillers 1987, 67).

From the perspective of the place we call "South Africa", the question of law and *nomos* cannot be separated from the problem of conquest and antiblackness. Insofar as *nomos* invokes that which is constitutive or foundational to a legal and political order, I will argue that any theoretical investigation into the *nomos* of (this part of) the Earth must take European colonial domination and white supremacy to be the source of South Africa's present contradictions and divisions (Magubane 2007, 15). Following this cue, these reflections on space, *nomos* and the postcolony will take off from a critical race lens which provides us with a "revisionary theoretical cartography" and "redrawing of the map of the political" (Mills 1998, 121) that will analytically recentre the frequently evaded problematics of race, colonial racism and white supremacy in any given scene of analysis. This will also highlight the violence, dispossession and dehumanisation that accompanied the ascendance of Western modernity and the formation of the present geopolitical order (see Mignolo 2011).

The racialised character of South African space is an outcome of the colonial *nomos* that was installed through the violent onslaught of European conquest, set in motion in 1652 with the arrival of the first European settler-colonialists on these shores (see Delport and Lephakga 2016). Through land dispossession, labour exploitation, unequal spatial distribution, economic deprivation, state violence, epistemicide and psycho-social alienation, a now almost four-century long system of white supremacy has been entrenched in both the physical world (as socio-spatial structure) and the psychic world (as ideology and consciousness). As such, the problem of colonial *nomos* cannot be easily relegated to the past, since landlessness continues to define the Black condition.[2]

South African spaces – in which the majority of Black people remain confined to under-resourced rural areas and underdeveloped townships, and whites mostly live on large arable farms and in upmarket suburbs – continue to adhere to the logics and demarcations of colonial-apartheid. Distance, aversion, contempt, control, stratification and the fear of contamination and extinction are central components of the spatial imaginary of colonial-apartheid, hence the historical segregation of racial groups and the concomitant socioeconomic inequalities between them. Twenty eight years after the *formal* demise of white minority rule, the persistence of this spatial imaginary is symptomatic of the limits of the post-1994 project of national reconstruction and transitional justice, which centred largely on human rights and constitutionalism as drivers of social transformation (Mutua 1997).

As I have argued elsewhere, the lack of attention to the *spatial* dimension of South Africa's long history of racial oppression and injustice has left the structure and ideology of colonial-apartheid very much intact in the public and private life of South Africa (see Modiri 2012; Modiri 2015). It is thus a *ruse* to refer to South Africa as substantively "post-apartheid" since the spatial design of that which the term "post-apartheid" claims to have overcome (colonial-apartheid), remains firmly etched on the ground and soil of South Africa.[3] The spatial vision of colonial-apartheid was accompanied by a political ontology in terms of which blackness was constructed in opposition to humanity proper and relegated to a wasted social existence. From this reading then, the politics of spatial justice must address itself to the undoing of the colonial *nomos* that could also annul the world of the conqueror embodied in the structural foundations of South Africa.

I shall develop this argument first by drawing on Saidiya Hartman's (2007) recollection of the historical construction of Black subjectivity through loss and displacement. As I will read her, the production of the Black subject as a *stranger* – to the self, the land and to humanity itself – constitutes the primary spatial violence of colonisation and enslavement of African peoples. I shall thereafter extend Hartman's insights through an engagement with the relationship between space and race, and specifically the racialised character of space, as theorised in critical race theory and settler-colonial studies. This will then be related to the South African context with reliance on the thinking of Frantz Fanon and his description of the Manichean character of colonial racism. This turn towards Fanon is also a turn away from Schmitt, as a way of registering objection to the powerful traces of the colonial in Schmitt's own spatial geography. Finally, the notion of "unmapping" is proposed as a concrete project of spatial justice and decolonisation that could unsettle and undo the settler-colonial *nomos* of "South Africa".

This chapter represents only an initial blush of an argument that aims to recall the settler-colonial foundations of "South African" law as the *central* problematic for post-1994 critical jurisprudence. Drawing on critical race theory, African philosophy and settler-colonial studies, the aim is to question the certainties of white settler hegemony in South Africa and to unsettle the authority of laws and epistemologies imposed on indigenous African people through colonial violence. A persistent feature of South African legal discourse has been the erasure or "unknowing" (Vimalassery, Hu Pegues and Goldsten 2016) of the historical fact of settler-colonialism and its connection to the dominance of whiteness and Eurocentrism in the *present context*. The negotiated political settlement that has given rise to the new constitutional dispensation together with scholarly work in law, the humanities and social sciences which is ideologically aligned to this dispensation operate on this view as "epistemologies of ignorance" (see generally Sullivan and Tuana 2007) that work to preclude the problem of settler-colonialism and conquest from critical inquiry and from the demand for justice and reparation (see Ramose 2003, 575; Cavanagh 2017, 304). It will turn out that even critical traditions of legal scholarship in South Africa are implicated in this current of anti-decolonisation insofar as they presume white settler entitlement to indigenous lands to be a given, affirm the dominance of European and Euro-American paradigms of law and politics and evade the problem of conquest (see Madlingozi 2017; Modiri 2018, 4–5). This is the background against which the present investigation into space takes place.

Estrangement as/and the racial ontology of space

> The dispersal of humans out of the motherland to other parts of the world introduced estrangement and alienation among human beings. This manifested itself in the denial by some human beings that Africa is their motherland. They used their pink colour, often mistaken as "white", to claim separation and difference from Africans.
>
> (Ramose 2016, 547)

From the perspective of Black critique, the bloody beginnings of the relation between race and space are rooted in the 15th-, 16th- and 17th-century European colonial expansions and encounters in Africa and the Americas which resulted in the dispossession and exploitation of Africans on indigenous lands as well as the forced transportation and enslavement of African bodies in the New World.[4] The encounter of Africans with Western civilisation historically represents a moment of profound *displacement* in which Africans on the continent and in the diaspora would come to inhabit a world that is not of their choosing or making; a world that compels their negation, defined by the cultural and epistemic terms of their white European antagonists. In short, "they [were] recast as objects in a world of subjects", ontologically produced as the non-human against which (white) humanity would define and reproduce itself (Wilderson 2010, 96).

The African-American historian Saidiya Hartman famously described the colonial occupation of African lands and the genocidal dispossession and enslavement of Africans as a *loss of the mother.* This "loss of the mother" for her signals a primordial expulsion from the World of Beings, an *estrangement* (Hartman 2007). She recounts her own experience in Ghana as she was retracing the genealogy of African-American peoples and upon arrival she was referred to as *Obruni* – "a stranger. A foreigner from across the sea" (Hartman 2007, 3). This, Hartman recalls, "forced [her] to acknowledge that she didn't belong anyplace" (Hartman 2007, 4). "The domain of the stranger is always an elusive elsewhere" she continued. (Hartman 2007, 4). Having been born in another country as a descendant of enslaved Africans whose progeny would continue to experience brutal subjugation, discrimination and disenfranchisement,

Hartman also felt like an alien in the United States. This led her to consider the historical homologies between Black subjectivity and the experience of being a stranger.

Hartman writes that "the most universal definition of the slave [and in the context of South Africa, we could add colonized native] is a stranger" (Hartman 2007, 5). Torn from the bonds of family, community, nation, polity and world, deprived of the integrity of kinship, subjected to unspeakable dishonour and violation, the slave or colonised native comes to define the paradigmatic position of the outsider. And racial blackness comes to stand in as the paradigmatic expression of the slave condition, expressing not simply inferiority but as Fanon would conjecture, "nonexistence" (Fanon 2008, 106).

The estrangement described here applies not only to the diasporic Black experience, but also to white settler societies such as South Africa. The anomaly of settler-colonialism inheres precisely in its conversion of the indigenous peoples into strangers and "foreigners in the country of their birth" (Badat 2009, 125–26). Hartman's reflections serve as a prelude to the argument that spatial inequality, rather than being a simple problem of physical environment and location, emanates from the racist inscription of the Otherness-of-the-Black onto the surface of the material world. It is through this inscription that successive colonial-apartheid regimes have implemented legal-spatial technologies that limit or prohibit Black land ownership, enforce segregation, facilitate forced removals, evictions and imprisonment and mandate the expulsion of racial Others to the peripheries of urban space. Colonialism, slavery and racism generate spatial arrangements in which a vertical order of the human permeates everyday relations and requires the colonised to remain constantly within the space and place dictated by the coloniser. This process involves not only a reconfiguration of space, but also a redefinition of the terms of humanity, belonging and subjectivity.

The two great and unceasing historical formations of white supremacy – colonisation/dispossession and slavery/captivity – have functioned to erase for the African the grounds of subjectivity, of being a Subject among other subjects, through the demarcation and reorganisation of living spaces in accordance with the ideological prescripts of what Malcolm X named "white-world supremacy" (Malcolm X, 2011). The European interdiction of African lives and lands that gave rise to the racial-spatial configuration of the modern world as we know it (what Jared Sexton (2015, 166) following Dionne Brand, calls "a tear in the world") serves as a critical starting point for reflecting on spatial justice, power, memory and national reconstruction, particularly in the context of the place currently known as "post-apartheid South Africa". In the section that follows, I reflect on the colonial organisation of South African space and relate this to the ways in which "Black lives are still imperilled and devalued by a racial calculus and political arithmetic that were entrenched centuries ago" (Hartman 2007, 6).

Racialised space

To understand the spatial organisation of South Africa, it is necessary to understand "how social relations take on their full force and meaning when they are enacted physically in actual spaces" (Lipsitz 2011, 5). Posed in the context of cultural geography by George Lipsitz, the problem of "how racism takes place" principally concerns the ways in which the racialisation of space and spatialisation of race reproduces and deepens inequality, perpetuates white supremacy and exacerbates black disadvantage. Lipsitz's project is closely related to Sherene Razack's exploration of how "place becomes race through the law" (Razack 2002, 1). What her account emphasises is the role of law and policy in maintaining racial hierarchies and in constituting racialised space. As Lipsitz writes of racialised space:

> Racialized space shapes nearly every aspect of urban life. The racial imagination that relegates people of different races to different spaces produces grossly unequal access to education, employment, transportation, and shelter. It exposes [black communities] disproportionately to environmental hazards and social nuisances while offering whites privileged access to economic opportunities, social amenities, and valuable personal networks. The lived experience of race takes place in actual spaces, while the lived experience of place draws its determinate logic from overt and covert understandings of race.
>
> (Lipsitz 2011, 6)

Lipsitz (2011, 25–50) argues that a core feature of racialised space is the privileging of a "white spatial imaginary" whereby white racial myths of purity, superiority and entitlement to privilege manifest in the concrete organisation of spaces (i.e. the reservation for whites of large cities, exclusive neighbourhoods and upmarket properties and the simultaneous relegation of Blacks to the peripheries of urban spaces (slums, labour reserves, plantations, prisons, townships, shantytowns, ghettoes)). The spatial ordering engendered by the white spatial imaginary thus follows the logic of racial capitalism which exposes Blacks to labour exploitation and precarious living conditions in order to protect the socioeconomic interests of whites, appreciate their wealth and enhance their standard and quality of living. But more than its economic implications, Lipsitz suggests that this spatial imaginary also

> has cultural as well as social consequences. It structures feelings as well as social institutions. The white spatial imaginary idealizes "pure" and homogeneous spaces, controlled environments, and predictable patterns of design and behavior. It seeks to hide social problems rather than solve them. The white spatial imaginary promotes the quest for individual escape rather than encouraging democratic deliberations about the social

> problems and contradictory social relations that affect us all. The suburb is not only an engine of self-interest, but also a place that has come to be imbued with a particular moral value consistent with deeply rooted historical ideals and illusions.
>
> (Lipsitz 2011, 29)

An important caution relayed by Lipsitz is that the long-term effects of this unequal racialisation of space that produces Black people's "geographically organized vulnerability" (Lipsitz 2011, 55) is a *problem for everybody*. It values white property over Black life, and produces a dangerous overconcentration of poverty, pollution, disease, crime and violence and, while promoting among whites a culture of privatism, fear and anxiety; it ferments racial conflict and resentment (Lipsitz 2011, 20).

Lipsitz poses this white spatial imaginary against what he calls a "Black spatial imaginary" (Lipsitz 2011, 51–70). Imbued with the history and experience of resistance and struggle carried by Black people, a Black spatial imaginary proceeds from a recognition of the importance of public spaces where political memory, cultural activism and spiritual ritual could be enacted (Lipsitz 2011, 52–54). In a Black spatial imaginary, schools, neighbourhoods, churches, taverns and hair salons among others are linked to the struggles of Black communities to make a home, develop a collective and affirming sense of self and centrally to politicise communities to reflect on their reality and condition (Lipsitz 2011, 53). In this regard, Lipsitz argues that a Black spatial imaginary should be considered as a model for democratic citizenship (Lipsitz 2011, 56), and I would add, spatial justice. We could note here, in passing, the resonance between Lipsitz's account of a Black spatial imaginary and the principle of African humanness (*ubuntu/botho*).

The paradoxes of "post"-apartheid space

The nominally "new" South Africa harbours fundamental tensions between reconciliation and justice, democratisation and liberation, between forgiving and forgetting, past and future, freedom and equality, white power and Black freedom, between optimism and rage and between prosperity and wretchedness. To put this in a more spatial register, this tension manifests in the lives, experiences and histories of those who walk and drive over the famous "bridge" from apartheid authoritarianism to "post"-apartheid constitutional democracy and those who live and die beneath it.[5]

The colonial-apartheid "past", its divisions and devastations, is still visible on the surfaces of South Africa's urban and rural spaces, its townships and informal settlements, its taxis and trains – spaces where most of Black life moves and takes place. Not only are many of the untransformed spaces inhabited by Black life deliberate constructions of the colonial-apartheid regime(s), functioning to maintain spatial segregation and inequality between racial groups, they are also marked by severe deprivation, squalor, decay and impaired mobility and access to socioeconomic opportunities and political voice.

As we see in the news, on our way to work and when we drive to the airport, or to visit family, the spatial environments largely inhabited by the majority of Black South Africans are often overcrowded and dingy, lacking the usual comforts of room for recreation and socialising and for forming and sustaining familial, friendship and sexual bonds. They do not facilitate privacy and safety and they are generally not aesthetically pleasing. They also do not provide easy access to socioeconomic opportunities, or any other form of empowerment and mobility: they are not places where significant economic, political and legal decisions are made; they are not the places where middle-class life takes place; they are the dark margins of urban life – the dark side of the new South Africa. These spaces are also environmentally hazardous: they are the spaces we see when we hear of so-called "open toilets",[6] of shack fires, of rodent infestations, high rates of cholera and malaria and other diseases.

The terror, injustice and oppression of colonial-apartheid materialises physically or ergonomically in the organisation, sanitation and appearance of spaces and places where the majority of Black people live. They cannot be denied or erased as easily as the voices and memories of those who refuse co-optation into the dominant rainbow-nation narrative. Accordingly, the unjust conditions of misery and poverty that still characterise those spaces should be read as an index of the continuing exclusion and marginalisation of Blacks from the official narrative of "post"-apartheid transformation. They register the inequalities and disadvantages that Blacks still experience as a result of colonial-apartheid and which are *continuing* due to the lack of reparation and the new constitutional dispensation's failure to actualise new post-conquest ways of being and belonging. But the problems I have adumbrated above go deeper than their precarious material and empirical dimensions. Rather, as instances of structural antiblackness, they function as part of a symbolic geography of death, disaster and dereliction that consigns Blacks to a permanently unliveable existence. The profusion of laws, policies and rights aimed at improving service delivery, rural development, urban renewal and other schemes could not address this geography in full without abolishing the colonial *nomos* by which the functioning and existence of South Africa is governed.

Colonial/anticolonial *nomos*

These reflections take their cue from Frantz Fanon's (2004) meditations on spatiality in the context of colonial racism in which he illustrated his claims tellingly with reference to apartheid South Africa (3). For Fanon, colonial racism produces a bifurcated or Manichean divide between the zone of beings and the zone of nonbeings which materialises physically in the spaces occupied by the colonisers and the colonised (4–7). For Fanon, the world (or sector) of the colonised native is "not complementary to the European sector", the white world (4). As he tells us: "The two confront each other, but not in the service of a higher unity. Governed by a purely Aristotelian logic, they follow the dictates of mutual exclusion: There is no conciliation possible, one of them is superfluous" (4). As Fanon describes it, the white world, what he calls the colonist's sector "is a sector built to last, all stone and steel. It's a sector of lights and paved roads, where the trash cans overflow with strange and wonderful garbage, undreamed-of leftovers" (4). In contrast, the Black world, the colonised's sector

> the native's quarters, the shanty town, the Medina, is a disreputable place [...] You die anywhere, from anything. It's a world with no space, people are piled one on top of the other, the shacks squeezed tightly together. This sector is a famished sector.
>
> (4).

Fanon then goes on to describe a world divided in this way as a compartmentalised world that is first and foremost structured by racial violence and economic exclusion:

> This compartmentalized world, this world is divided in two, is inhabited by different species. The singularity of the colonial context lies in the fact that economic reality, inequality, and enormous disparities in lifestyles never managed to mask the human reality. Looking at the immediacies of the colonial context, it is clear that what divides this world is first and foremost what species, what race one belongs to.
>
> (Fanon 2004, 5)

In this description of the Manichean divide between the world of the coloniser and the colonised, we find in Fanon an account of a '*nomos* of the earth' *and* a *nomos* of the postcolony. Indeed, we find in Fanon an account of *nomos* as rivalling, indeed decolonising, Schmitt's Eurocentric account. By highlighting the inescapably "concrete and spatial" character of *nomos*, Schmitt does assist us in understanding how the constitutive act of land appropriation and dispossession is foundational to the making of the modern world (Antaki 2004, 322–323). Schmitt, in addition, takes the colony to the be the "basic spatial fact of the modern *nomos*" (Kalyvas 2018, 25) and views "modernity and colonialism as co-original and co-constitutive" (Kalyvas 2018, 35). Insofar as he provides an extensive account of the colonial underpinnings of the modern world order and international law, he remains a compelling interlocutor for postcolonial and anticolonial critique.

But this is also the same Schmitt who writes explicitly from within Europe's violent conquest of the rest of the world and who as a result re-naturalises self-made colonial myths concerning the superiority of Western culture and political rationalism as well as racist depictions of the non-Western world as uninhabited, desolate and chaotic (Kalyvas 2018, 36–37). Schmitt, of course, is quite incapable of providing a normative critique of the injustice of conquest, given that his argument in *The Nomos of the Earth* takes conquest as given – affirms it even – as "merely" one of the ways in which land appropriation takes place. Indeed, his *Nomos of the Earth* reads disturbingly as an apologia for colonialism. In his own words, Schmitt appears to suggest that the intellectual and civilisational advancement of the European not only *enables* but *entitles* him to conquer non-European peoples (Lossau 2011, 252). As he writes in relation to the conquest of the Americas:

> Discoveries were made without prior permission of the discovered. Thus, legal title to discoveries lay in higher legitimacy. They could be made only by peoples intellectually and historically advanced enough to apprehend the discovered by superior knowledge and consciousness.
>
> (Schmitt 2003, 132)

Schmitt's troubling celebration of the Eurocentric global order depends crucially upon what Cedric Robinson identified as the ignorance and destruction of the non-European past (Robinson 1983, 81). According to Robinson, it was only through this ignorance and erasure of the pasts of non-European life-worlds that the "architects of European consciousness" could construct the false worldview "that the measure of mankind was indeed the European" (Robinson 1983, 99).

Schmitt's political background as an avowed Nazi (Lossau 2011, 251) does him no favours in the way of redeeming his image as a European supremacist. Reading Schmitt through Fanon's eyes is instructive for discerning the dark side of *nomos*, for seeing how Schmitt's account is also an account of the formation of what Mills calls "global white supremacy" (Mills 1998, 98–99). The amity lines that Schmitt takes as demarcating the fundamental distinction between the European space of order and a non-European space of disorder is more accurately read from the view of the Global South as an "abyssal line" premised on the "radical denial of co-presence" and the extermination of that which lives "on the other side of the line" (Santos 2007, 48; Kalyvas 2018, 37–39). The Eurocentric moral and political cartography of Schmitt's abyssal amity lines conceives of those "beyond the line" as savage, lawless and subhuman, and thereby treats everything which occurs beyond the line – European racism, violence and subjugation – as "outside [of] the legal, moral and political values recognized on this [the European] side of the line" (Minca and Rowan 2016, 223). This ensures that the false universality, rationality and morality of European culture is not compromised by its imperial and colonial excesses. The abyssal nature of the amity lines inheres in the absolute divide between the zone of being and the zone of nonbeing that it constructs through which the visibility and superiority of "this [white European] side of the line" (the zone of being) is secured through the *imagined* vanishing and non-existence[7] of those on "the other (dark, non-European) side of the line" (Santos 2007, 45).

At this point, Fanon can be read in conjunction with Sarah Nuttall and Achille Mbembe's argument that "there is no metropolis without a necropolis" (Nuttall and Mbembe 2008, 21). The white world, the metropolis, is always secured through the exploitation and slow destruction of its Other, the Black(ened) world, the necropolis. The metropolis is, to use Nuttall and Mbembe's phrase, "produced by what lies beneath the surface" (Nuttall and Mbembe 2008, 21). Not only is there a hierarchy between these spaces, but there is also a parasitic relationship between them – the identity, security and privileging of the metropolis is always acquired through the exploitation, degradation and Othering of the necropolis. A crucial element of Mbembe's theorisation of necropower and necropolitics pertains to what he draws out as the political intimacy between race and death (Mbembe 2003, 17). He points to the plantation and the colony (Mbembe 2003, 21–27) as paradigmatic examples of "forms of social existence in which vast populations are subjected to conditions of life conferring upon them the status of the living dead" (Mbembe 2003, 40).

For Mbembe, following Fanon, the colony is a formation of terror "predicated on the racial denial of any common bond between the conqueror and the native", reducing the latter to savage life (Mbembe 2003, 22). Making specific reference to South Africa, Mbembe extended this argument specifically to the township as emblematic of the structural violence of late modern colonial sovereignty (Mbembe 2003, 25). He refers to the *township* as a "peculiar spatial institution scientifically planned for the purposes of control" (Mbembe 2003, 26). This form of control is intimately bound to the workings of necropower, the creation of "death-worlds" and "topographies of cruelty" (Mbembe 2003, 40). The plantation, the colony, the township and the homeland are all presented by Mbembe as instances where space provided "the raw material of sovereignty and the violence it carried with it" (Mbembe 2003, 24). Necropolitics and necropower are thus fundamentally spatial and racialised at the same time.

This is not unrelated in our current context to the mass number of poor Black labourers, domestic workers and gardeners who daily commute in the early hours of the morning to suburbs not to visit or to run their own errands but to work and serve those who inhabit those spaces only to return much later in the afternoon or evening to rest and repeat this tragic cycle of servitude and powerlessness. How else are we to consider for example the stark contrasts between the affluent suburbs and hotspots of Cape Town and the leafy wine estates of Stellenbosch vis-à-vis the Cape Flats, and the townships of Gugulethu and Khayelitsha; or the differences between Sandton's corporate-by-day and party-at-night aesthetic in comparison to Alexandra and the as yet unglamorous parts of Soweto township?

This segregated form of spatial organisation – which continues to persist in "post"-apartheid South Africa – then corresponds to, mirrors and is continuous with the central binary logic of white supremacy. White supremacy is premised on a "perverse ontological designation by race" (Birt 1997, 209), whereby differences in skin colour are essentialised in the construction of a distinction between white and Black, so that whiteness represents humanity and all its Great Virtues (goodness, beauty, morality, intelligence, wealth, art, civilisation etc) and blackness symbolises the negation and or corruption of those virtues. The racialisation of space is thus modelled on precisely these normative valuations about Blacks and whites and so come to correspond to the taxonomy of the human that is promulgated by white supremacy. In a sense, these spaces give material or tactile form to negative and long-held racist beliefs about Blacks; about chronic dysfunction and disintegration in Black families, about the violence and excess of Black sexual and social life, the carelessness of Black youth (owing to drug and alcohol abuse), and to colonial associations of blackness with inferiority, impurity and immorality.

This is a trite point, for we know that most of the spaces and places where Black life takes place and where Black bodies move were historically demarcated for those who do not belong, who do not fit into the ideal mould of any given national imaginary in part because they do not fit into any specific mould of the human. Spatial organisation and in particular segregation is always a part of how power and vulnerability are differentially distributed and it is central as well to the maintenance of social stratification and inequality. It is telling that most legal reforms in "post"-apartheid South Africa such as the delivery of basic services and housing policies takes the existence of these places for granted, treating them as normal, as just the way things are – not considering the system of racial capitalism that produced them and the racial interests of whites that seek to maintain the boundaries between those racial spaces.

Most perversely, townships and informal settlements – because they are tolerated and do not elicit outrage (again because rather than being seen as unjust and undignified they are seen as normal places for Black people to live in) – have become available for romanticisation, commodification and depoliticisation as evidenced in their instrumentalisation as sites for the production of music videos, for political campaigns during elections and even as models for exotic holiday resorts. The normalisation of townships as proper and unproblematic spaces for Black inhabitation attests to what Sexton more generally calls "the obscurity of Black suffering" (Sexton 2007, 120).

Unmapping "South Africa"

I have so far been attempting to theoretically draw out the connection between spatial injustice, white supremacy and settler-colonialism. My argument is that these three formations historically cohere into the idea of "South Africa" as we know it today. Indeed, the very anointing of this territory as "South Africa" is the outcome of the reconciliation between the two European conquering powers (the Boers and the English) that gave rise to the Union of South Africa in 1910. This Union was underwritten by a pact – what Mills (1997) would call a "racial contract" – which prescribed white dominance and rule over Africans and African lands and the legal sanctioning of racial inequality and the political marginalisation of Blacks (Fredrickson 1981, 179–198). Historically, this racial contract in turn produced a racial bond between whites in which they were socialised to view their interests as fundamentally irreconcilable with the advancement of political rights and economic opportunities for Blacks. Put another way, the formation of whiteness and white identity in 20th-century South Africa was inextricably bound to the absolute necessity of Black subordination. Even the name "South Africa" emanates from the Anglo-Boer colonial imagination and is itself the product of the ongoing epistemic and political violence of setter-colonialism.

It is therefore this fact of South Africa as a settler-created polity and not merely the excesses of colonial and apartheid violence that is the fundamental (spatial) injustice of South Africa. Notions of spatial justice centred on inclusion, the right to the city and the right to a home may risk redrawing a white settler mythology if they do not confront conquest, dispossession and the exploitation of African land and labour as the foundational predicaments in the very creation of "South Africa". When settler-colonialism, and the concomitant impositions of white power on the South African landscape, is not treated as a problem of justice, the violence of colonial conquest and the accompanying racist thesis concerning the inhumanity of the Africans is converted into an incontestable and naturalised historical fact, out of reach from the demands of justice.

The notion of spatial justice in South Africa could be supplemented or indeed supplanted by the notion of "unmapping" postulated by Sherene Razack as a way of making visible and contesting settler-colonial spatial configurations. Such unmapping begins by reclaiming the living memory of the indigenous conquered peoples "whose lands were stolen and whose communities remain imperilled" (Razack 2002, 5). To unmap is therefore to denaturalise the spatial order, to ask how spaces came to be composed as they are and to undermine the racialist worldviews that such spaces rest upon (Razack 2002, 5). Razack further describes "unmapping" as a way of countering colonial conceits of mastery and ownership implied in imperial acts of "mapping" (Razack 2002, 12). Razack writes:

> Just as mapping colonized lands enabled Europeans to imagine and legally claim that they had discovered and therefore owned [indigenous lands], unmapping is intended to undermine the idea of white settler innocence (the notion that European settlers merely settled and developed the land) and to uncover the ideologies and practices of conquest and domination.
>
> (Razack 2002, 4)

I associate Razack's call for 'unmapping' with Mogobe Ramose's argument for a *post-conquest* – and not merely post-apartheid – South Africa (Ramose 2001). A post-conquest South Africa, according to Ramose, demands the undoing of the illegitimate "right of conquest" that is the basis of white supremacy in South Africa by attending to and recovering the lost sovereignty and title to territory of the indigenous African peoples which were usurped in the unjust wars of colonisation.

Ramose's contrasting of a post-conquest social order against a post-apartheid order correlates with his distinction between decolonisation and democratisation – with the latter representing the faulty negotiated political settlement of the new South Africa, and the former representing the unrealised liberation of South Africa from the bondage of colonisation. For Ramose, the new constitutional dispensation of South Africa represents an impediment to decolonisation (Ramose 2001). This is most clearly expressed in the constitution's perpetuation of spatial injustice through the protection of property rights gained through centuries of land dispossession, displacement, forced removals and systematic economic deprivation.

The notion of unmapping concretely connects the call for spatial justice to the exigency of decolonisation. For Ramose, decolonisation involves the "dissolution of the conqueror's South Africa" (Ramose 2003, 507). It seeks to effect a fundamental alteration in the power relations, and the epistemological and ontological framework, of South African society. Decolonisation aspires not merely to the enfranchisement and inclusion of the "oppressed" into existing frameworks and spaces, but a fundamental reconstitution of new frameworks and spaces. This involves dissolving the very categories of coloniser/colonised, settler/native and Black/white as material social realities and not merely nominal juridical labels. Decolonisation thus abolishes the polity as imagined and instantiated by the European colonialist and as such marks the true end of the white settler State.

The prophet-theoretician of Black Consciousness, Steve Biko, also insists on the inseparability of liberation and decolonisation. Having exposed non-racial integration and liberal humanist inclusion as counter to decolonisation, Biko sets out to explain his conception of a liberated and decolonised South Africa. Repeatedly utilising the metaphor of the "table" to describe "South Africa", Biko makes clear that decolonisation is not a mere inversion in power relations or a simple "turning of tables" (Biko 2012, 108). It also does not amount to acceding to white power and seeking a "place at the white man's table" (Biko 2012, 23). Instead he writes:

> We knew he had no right to be there; we wanted to remove him from our table, strip the table of all trappings put on it by him, decorate it in true African style, settle down and then ask him to join us on our own terms if he liked.
>
> (Biko 2012, 75)

The naming of this land as "South Africa" and the creation of political, legal and cultural systems based on the epistemological paradigm of the conqueror is an artefact of colonial sovereignty which must be redressed if authentic liberation and decolonisation is to be actualised. Such a reversal would anticipate as well the annulment of the spatial imaginary of the conqueror, thereby signalling an end to townships, slums, shantytowns, and homelessness and to gated communities, gentrification and overpriced suburbs. Such a decolonisation is a precondition for what Ramose describes as "reconfiliation" (Ramose 2012), the coming together of brothers and sisters, the restoration of the oneness of humanity and the creation of a new and emancipatory spatial ethics.

The vision of decolonisation proffered by anticolonial African philosophers such as Ramose and Biko was ultimately occluded from the terms of the negotiated political settlement that delivered South Africa's constitutional democracy (Madlingozi 2017, 137). I would argue that this failure to substantively decolonise South African law and society has resulted in an unreconciled society that has not yet reckoned with the injustices of the past and present, a Black majority that continues to experience the constitution's promise of legal equality and freedom as hollow and a polity whose moral and political geography is still conflicted by a centuries-old racial antagonism.

Closing remarks

In this chapter, I sought to trace the connections between race, colonialism and spatial injustice through an engagement with the historical and ongoing experiences of estrangement and suffering that resulted from the European colonisation of African lands and the forced transporting of enslavement of African bodies. The relentlessly Manichean and abyssal colonial *nomos* that underpinned this history also carried with it a racial metaphysics which denied Black people ontological presence and human relationality. It is in this historical moment that the problems of spatial inequality and spatial justice are located.

Writing specifically from within the context of "South Africa", I argued for an apprehension of the history of settler-colonialism, which is the source of the present organisation of power and the present arrangement of space, as *the* fundamental (spatial) injustice of our time. The racialisation of space relegates the Black majority to a reality of social death, first through symbolically recasting them as foreigners or "spatial aliens" to South Africa and then through locking them into sites of inhabitation such as townships and rural areas which reproduce misery, deprivation and powerlessness. Certainly, here in South Africa and other parts of the world, race and space are powerfully linked in shaping human lives, relationships, opportunities and life-chances. The social construction of race and the physical construction and organisation of space have historically been mutually constitutive. This is most evident in how the key terms of colonial racism – dispossession, segregation, exclusion, containment, removal, stratification – invoke a spatial idiom as well.

The argument throughout this chapter has been that the continuation of racialised space into South Africa's constitutional democracy troubles triumphalist and optimistic readings of the "new South Africa" and confronts those readings with the persistence of racism and the cartographical and ontological afterlife of "white South Africa". Indeed, the incomplete abolition of apartheid that can be seen through the racialised spaces of "post"-apartheid South Africa exemplifies precisely the futility of erasure: hegemonic attempts to erase and to officially legislate new narratives and laws will always be subverted by the inerasable and incontestable traces of the unresolved colonial-apartheid "past". In this vein, the notion of "unmapping" linked to decolonisation provides a promising path for enacting a practice and politics of spatial justice that is historically sensitive to the settler-colonial foundations of South African space. By contesting the spatial imaginary of the conquerors who named and mapped this territory, the possibility of "giving this country back to itself" is called into being. I end with the haunting words of Biko:

> It does not mean simply because whites have been living in this country that you cannot give this country back to itself. We believe that we have to reject their economic system, their political system, and values that govern human relationship, in order to establish the kind of society that we as indigenous people want here. And that kind of society is not exclusively for us. It is for everybody who is here – but it has trappings which are obviously indigenous. To get to that stage we have to be properly orientated to being ourselves, into a proper force to know what the alternative is about, to live it within ourselves.
>
> (Biko 1971, 7)

Notes

1 On the differences between the uses of the idea of *terra nullius* and "empty land" in South African colonial history, see Boisen 2017.

2 The 2017 *Land Audit Report* published by the South African Government's Department of Rural Development and Land Reform determined that White South Africans (who make up less than 10% of the population) own 72% of farms and agricultural holdings, followed by "Coloureds" at 15%, Indians at 5% and Africans at an alarming 4%.

3 This is not to posit a seamless continuity between the colonial-apartheid order (1652–1994) and post-1994 constitutional democracy. The argument is rather that the path of institutional and legal changes in the early 1990s that brought about constitutional democracy in South Africa remain incomplete, disjunctive and deeply flawed. These changes have not, in other words, resulted in substantive socioeconomic, spatial, cultural and existential change. For a deeper exploration of this argument, see Modiri 2018, 39–81.

4 The historiography on this point is contested as is the division often drawn between North and sub-Saharan Africa. Davidson (1980, 53) in *The African Slave Trade* tracks the "first recorded skirmish of Europeans and Africans South of the Sahara" to 1441. In the South African context, 1510 is the recorded date of the first colonial encounter with the Portuguese. For other commentators (Wynter 1995 and Magubane 2007, for

example), 1492 marks the beginning of the Age of Empire and the modern founding of white supremacy. I have also chosen to refrain from the designation of "Black Africa". Thus, the colonial encounter has its "bloody beginnings" in the 15th century, even though the time between the 17th and the 19th centuries is the most decisive and comprehensively recorded period of colonial formation, rule and anticolonial resistance.

5 The "bridge metaphor" was first introduced into post-1994 South African constitutional theory by the late Etienne Mureinik (1994) to capture the aspirations of social transformation embedded in the shift from the apartheid legal order to the constitutional democratic dispensation. Since then, it has been a major theme of South African legal theory and criticism.

6 "Open toilets" refer to unsafe, unenclosed toilets and pit latrines where users must defecate or urinate out in the open. Public attention was drawn to the issue of open toilets most prominently in the wake of the death of five-year-old Michael Komape who fell and drowned in a pit toilet at his school in rural Seshego, Limpopo Province. *Komape v Minister of Basic Education* 2018 JDR 0625 (LP).

7 The ontological negation of blackness and the imposition of non-existence on the colonised is always an incomplete process; thoroughgoing but never total; *an imagined and then instituted political ontology from the view of the coloniser that can never exhaust the totality of human reality*. There can never be in reality a total nonbeing, but only a negative/negated being. That negativity is itself a form of subjectivity and is also the source of resistance, struggle and alternative imaginaries.

Bibliography

Antaki, Mark. 2004. "Carl Schmitt's Nomos of the Earth". *Osgoode Hall Law Journal* 42 (2): 317–334.

Badat, Saleem. 2009. *Black Man, You are On Your Own*. Braamfontein: Steve Biko Foundation.

Biko, Steve. 1971. "Steve Biko Interviewed by Greg Lanning". In *Gerhart Archives*, Volume 5. Braamfontein: Steve Biko Foundation.

Biko, Steve. 2012 [1978]. *I Write What I Like*. Johannesburg: Picador Africa.

Birt, Robert. 1997. "Existence, Identity and Liberation". In *Existence in Black: An Anthology of Black Existential Philosophy*, edited by Lewis R. Gordon, 203–214. New York: Routledge.

Boisen, Camilla. 2017. "From Land Dispossession to Land Restitution: European Land Rights in Africa". *Settler Colonial Studies*, 7(3): 1–9.

Cavanagh, Edward. 2017. "Settler Colonialism in South Africa: Land, Labour and Transformation 1880–2015". In *Routledge Handbook of the History of Settler Colonialism*, edited by Edward Cavanagh and Lorenzo Veracini, 291–308. Abingdon: Routledge.

Davidson, Basil. 1980. *The African Slave Trade*. Oxford: James Currey Ltd.

Delport, Terblanche and Lephakga, Tshepo. 2016. "Spaces of Alienation: Dispossession and Justice in South Africa". *HTS Teologiese Studies/Theological Studies* 72(1). http://www.hts.org.za/index.php/HTS/article/viewFile/3567/pdf_1.

Fanon, Frantz. 2004 [1963]. *The Wretched of the Earth*. New York: Grove Press.

Fanon, Frantz. 2008 [1967]. *Black Skin, White Masks*. London: Pluto Press.

Farley, Anthony. 2002."The Poetics of Colorlined Space". In *Crossroads, Directions and a New Critical Race Theory*, edited by Francisco Valdes, Jerome McCristle Culp and Angela P. Harris 97–158. Philadelphia, PA: Temple University Press.

Fredrickson, George. 1981. *White Supremacy: A Comparative Study in American and South African History*. Oxford and London: Oxford University Press.

Goldberg, David Theo. 1993. *Racist Culture. Philosophy and the Politics of Meaning*. Oxford: Blackwell.

Hartman, Saidiya. 2007. *Lose Your Mother: Journeys Along the Atlantic Slave Route*. New York: Farrar, Straus and Giroux.

Kalyvas, Andreas. 2018. "Carl Schmitt's Postcolonial Imagination". *Constellations* 25: 35–53.

Komape v Minister of Basic Education. 2018. JDR 0625 (LP).

Lipsitz, George. 2011. *How Racism Takes Place*. Philadelphia, PA: Temple University Press.

Lossau, Julia. 2011. "Postcolonialism". In *Spatiality, Sovereignty and Carl Schmitt: Geographies of the Nomos*, edited by Stephen Legg, 251–259. London: Routledge.

Madlingozi, Tshepo. 2017. "Social Justice in a Time of Neo-Apartheid Constitutionalism: Critiquing the Anti-black Economy of Recognition, Incorporation and Distribution". *Stellenbosch Law Review* 28: 123–147.

Magubane, Bernard. 2007. *Racism and the Construction of the Dispensable Other*. Pretoria: UNISA Press.

Malcolm, X. 2011. *The End of White World Supremacy*, edited by Imam Benjamin Karim. New York: Arcade Publishing.

Mbembe, Achille. 2003. "Necropolitics". *Public Culture* 15 (1): 11–40.

Mbembe, Achille. 2017. *Critique of Black Reason*, translated and introduced by Laurent Dubois. Durham, NC: Duke University Press.

Mbembe, Achille and Nuttall, Sarah. 2008. "Introduction: Afropolis". In *Johannesburg: The Elusive Metropolis*, edited by Sarah Nuttall and Achille Mbembe, 1–36. London: Duke University Press.

Mignolo, Walter. 2011. *The Darker Side of Western Modernity: Global Futures, Decolonial Options*. Durham, NC: Duke University Press.

Mills, Charles. 1997. *The Racial Contract*. Ithaca, NY: Cornell University Press.

Mills, Charles. 1998. *Blackness Visible: Essays on Philosophy and Race*. Ithaca, NY: Cornell University Press.

Minca, Claudio and Rowan, Rory. 2016. *On Schmitt and Space* [eBook]. Abingdon and Oxon: Routledge.

Modiri, Joel. 2012. "The Colour of Law, Power and Knowledge: Introducing Critical Race Theory in (Post-)Apartheid South Africa". *South African Journal on Human Rights* 28: 405–435.

Modiri, Joel. 2015. "Law's Poverty". *Potchefstroom Electronic Law Journal* 18 (2): 224–273.

Modiri, Joel. 2018. *The Jurisprudence of Steve Biko: A Study in Race, Law and Power in the Afterlife of Colonial-Apartheid*. Unpublished PhD thesis, University of Pretoria.

Mureinik, Etienne. 1994. "A Bridge to Where? Introducing the Interim Bill of Rights". *South African Journal on Human Rights* 10: 31–48.

Mutua, Makau. 1997. "Hope and Despair for a New South Africa: The Limits of Rights Discourse". *Harvard Human Rights Journal* 10: 63–114.

Ramose, Mogobe. 2001. "An African Perspective on Justice and Race". *Polylog: Forum for Intercultural Philosophy* 3. https://them.polylog.org/3/frm-en.htm.

Ramose, Mogobe. 2003. "I Conquer, Therefore I am the Sovereign: Reflections Upon Sovereignty, Constitutionalism and Democracy in Zimbabwe and South Africa". In *The African Philosophy Reader*, edited by P.H. Coetzee and A.P.J. Roux, 543–589. New York: Routledge.

Ramose, Mogobe. 2012. "Reconciliation and Reconfiliation in South Africa". *Journal on African Philosophy* 5: 20–39.
Ramose, Mogobe. 2016. "Teacher and Student with a Critical Pan-Epistemic Orientation: An Ethical Necessity for Africanising the Educational Curriculum in Africa". *South African Journal of Philosophy* 35 (4): 546–555.
Razack, Sherene. 2002. *Race, Space and the Law: Unmapping a White Settler Society*. Toronto: Between the Lines.
Robinson, Cedric. 1983. *Black Marxism: The Making of the Black Radical Tradition*. Chapel Hill, NC: The University of North Carolina Press.
Santos, Boaventura de Sousa. 2007. "Beyond Abyssal Thinking: From Global Lines to Ecologies of Knowledge". *Review* 30 (1): 45–89.
Schmitt, Carl. 2003. *The Nomos of the Earth in the International Law of the Jus Publicum Europaeum*, translated by Gary Ulmen. New York: Telos Press.
Sexton, Jared. 2007. "The Obscurity of Black Suffering". In *What Lies Beneath: Katrina, Race and the State of the Nation*, edited by South End Press Collective, 120–132. Cambridge, MA: South End Press.
Sexton, Jared. 2015. "Unbearable Blackness". *Cultural Critique* 90: 159–178.
Spillers, Hortense J. 1987. "Mama's Baby, Papa's Maybe: An American Grammar Book". *Diacritics* 17 (2): 64–81.
Sullivan, Shannon and Tuana, Nancy, eds. 2007. *Race and Epistemologies of Ignorance*. Albany, NY: State University of New York Press.
Vimalassery, Manu, Hu Pegues, Juliana and Goldstein, Alyosha. 2016. "On Colonial Unknowing". *Theory and Event* 19 (4).
Wilderson, Frank. 2010 *Red, White & Black: Cinema and the Structure of US Antagonisms*. Durham, NC: Duke University Press.
Wynter, Sylvia. 1995. "1492: A New World View". In Race, Discourse and the Origin of the Americas: A New World View, edited by S. Wynter, V. Lawrence Hyatt and R. Nettleford, 5–57. Washington, DC: Smithsonian Institution Press.

Chapter 3

On the *San Dominick*

Thinking *nomos* and postcolonial becoming with Melville, Schmitt and Fanon

Julia Chryssostalis

Schmitt and Melville's *Benito Cereno*

In November 1982, in an interview with Fulco Lanchester, originally published in the Italian review of constitutional law, *Quaderni Costituzionali*, the German jurist Carl Schmitt – one of the most important thinkers of the twentieth century and a controversial figure of repellent political allegiances, who, as crown jurist of the Reich, actively participated in the Nazi regime between 1933 and 1936 – speaking towards the end of the interview about his place in twentieth-century German and European history, suggested it was "apt to invoke the myth of Benito Cereno" at that point. And proceeded to ask: "Do you know Melville's story, the myth of unresolved situations?" (Lanchester 2005, 182–183). Schmitt's polite and innocent-sounding question to his interlocutor, a professor of comparative constitutional law at the University of Rome La Sapienza, who had an in-depth knowledge of his writings, was of course somewhat disingenuous. Anyone familiar with Schmitt's work, would know that Schmitt had been "invoking" the "myth" of Benito Cereno for some time. Indeed, *Benito Cereno* is "probably the work of world literature which Schmitt cite[s] most frequently" (Mohler, as cited in Sollors 2020, 403) – although he never wrote about it, as he did in the case of Shakespeare's *Hamlet* (Schmitt 2009) and Däubler's *Nordlicht* (1916).

Herman Melville's novella *Benito Cereno* tells the "strange history" of a slave mutiny in the Pacific Ocean. It was originally published in serial form, over the course of three months, October, November and December 1855, in the antislavery journal, *Putnam's Monthly Magazine*, and then published in its entirety (with some minor revisions) in *The Piazza Tales* (Melville 1856). The historical context of its writing and publication is significant as it is framed by at least four politically charged and widely reported and discussed legal decisions regarding slavery: the Fugitive Slave Act (1850), which allowed former masters of fugitive slaves to require officials in free states to arrest anyone suspected of being a fugitive only on a claimant's sworn testimony of ownership, and criminalised the obstruction of the arrest and return of an allegedly fugitive slave; the Kansas–Nebraska Act (1854), which opened these newly

DOI: 10.4324/9780203712771-3

acquired territories to the expansion of slavery, by giving settlers a say on whether to permit slavery or not; the Supreme Court decision in the *Amistad* case (1841),[1] which ruled that the "negroes" on board the ship were not "lawful slaves" but were "natives of Africa and kidnapped there, [...] illegally carried to Cuba, and illegally detained and restrained on board of the Amistad" and that therefore, when "they asserted their liberty and took possession of the [ship], and endeavoured to regain their native country, [...] they [could] not be deemed pirates or robbers in the sense of the law of nations"; and finally, the very prominent and hotly contested fugitive slave-rendition case of Anthony Burns (1854) in Boston, in which the court ordered the return of Burns to his Southern master under the Fugitive Slave Act, finding that the Act was constitutional, albeit "wicked and cruel", yet conceding that it was not for the court to decide whether the statute was a "harsh one or not".[2] Melville's novella then first appeared "amidst [a whole range of] intense debates about the domestic remnants of transatlantic slavery" (Tripp 2017, xx) and a few years before the American Civil War. Although it converses with, and comments on, these controversial legal decisions, it was generally regarded as a sea adventure and largely ignored or neglected by critics (Feltenstein 1947, 245) at the time. It was not until well after the "Melville revival" of the 1920s that it was rediscovered and widely viewed as an obscure masterpiece.

The plot of the story is closely based on purported actual events that took place near a small, uninhabited island off the coast of central Chile in 1805 and that one Amasa Delano, an American captain and explorer, distantly related to Franklin Delano Roosevelt, recounts in the eighteenth chapter of his book, *A Narrative of Voyages and Travels in the Northern and Southern Hemisphere* (Delano 1817), under the title, "Particulars of the Capture of the Spanish Ship *Tryal*, at the Island of St. Maria, with the Documents Relating to That Affair". Melville's heavy reliance on Delano's story was not discovered until 70 years or so after the novella's publication, when Harold Scudder located Delano's travelogue (Scudder 1928). Yet as Shari Goldberg astutely observes,

> Delano's "original" already reads as a rewriting insofar as it gathers several accounts and types of writing, and as such it not only contains "tensions and gaps" but occasionally contradictory bits of information. What Scudder proclaimed as critical bedrock was, in effect, that Melville chose as his subject not a series of known events, but a text that already exposed the divergence between "history" as it occurred and the writing that later recorded it.
>
> (Goldberg 2009, 6)

What becomes clear, and interesting, therefore, about Melville's appropriation of Delano's story is precisely that the correlation between the two texts "exponentializes, rather than reduces, this divergence" (*ibid.*). And that curiously it is Melville's fiction that in the end historicises the events recorded by Delano.

In the novella, Melville retains the names of the American and the Spanish captains and of the small uninhabited island, in whose bay most of the action takes place. The story is narrated by an omniscient observer and presented as an uneven "triptych" (9), comprising three separate sets of events focusing in turn on Delano, Cereno and the relationship between the two. The first and longest section recounts Amasa Delano's time on board the Spanish ship from the moment he arrives to offer his assistance to the instant that, in "a flash of revelation illuminating in unanticipated clearness his host's whole mysterious demeanour" (Melville 1856, 298), he realises that the slaves are in control of the ship, and Cereno is their hostage, and enlists his crew to end the mutiny and free the Spanish captain and his remaining crew. The second section consists of excerpts from the notarised deposition of Benito Cereno that was submitted to the Lima tribunal that heard the case against the mutineers. In it, Cereno explains the story from the beginning, when he sailed from the port of Valparaiso with destination that of Callao, with passengers, 36 crew, and 160 "blacks" belonging mostly to his friend, Don Alejandro Aranda. His account, which describes all the events on the ship, once corroborated by the depositions of the surviving sailors, will subsequently constitute the basis for the court's decision and its capital sentences for the mutinous slaves. Finally, the third and last section contains some of the conversations between the two captains discussing the events in St. Maria during the boat passage to Lima, and describes the end of Babo, the leader of the mutiny, and that of Cereno in a monastery on Mount Agonia.

Told in this way, what characterises the narration of the story is that it "proceeds … by seeming to speak and explain but in fact withholding" (Goldberg 2009, 10), leaving something always unexplained and unresolved, deferring the moment of providing "the best account" (Melville 1856, 164) to a future point. Moreover, this "narrative muteness", Goldberg compellingly argues, characterises not only the overall narration of the story but also the narration of each set of events. The first section is dominated by Delano's continuous failed attempts to understand correctly what is happening around him, in other words, to pierce the muteness of the situation he is in. By contrast, Cereno never fulfils the expectation, stemming from his authoritative position, to provide Delano with a full account of what is happening. Every time he sets out to explain, "[h]e falters, he chokes, he whispers, he faints, he cringes" (Goldberg 2009, 10). In short, the overall effect of his speech is not to reveal but to add to his general "mysterious demeanour" (Melville 1856, 298) instead. Further, when Cereno has the opportunity in his deposition to explain how everything did happen, his speech is

> set up with a generalized doubt regarding its production of the truth, uncertainty as to how one might distinguish the ravings [of someone "not

> undisturbed in his mind by recent events" (311)] and the affirmed facts, and the divestment of the very voice expected to offer it.
>
> (Goldberg 2009, 11)

For Cereno's deposition, notarised by Don Jose de Abos and Padilla, is presented as a third-person transcription of his speech. The only "I" in Cereno's testimony that "certif[ies] and declare[s]" (Melville 1856, 312) is that of Don Jose.

At the same time, if Cereno's speech is always blocked, both at sea and on dry land, the slaves' speech is entirely foreclosed. On the ship, when they speak, their speech to Delano is nothing but noise, and when they have an opportunity to speak in front of the two captains, they speak only in character – when Babo speaks, for instance, he does so in accordance with the script of the dutiful and self-effacing slave. Alternatively, they remain silent – either because silence seals off their interaction away from Delano's reading, its unintelligibility adding to the "strangeness" of the ship; or because silence is already scripted as an act of acceptable defiance in conditions of generalised submission, as in the case of Atufal, who is obediently paraded every two hours in chains in order to ask Cereno for forgiveness in a spectacle of mastery and docility. By contrast, in the Lima court, "being defendants in a 'criminal cause'" (312), "their testimony [is nowhere] solicited" (Nelson 1992, 122). Their speech is suppressed. Their voice is ventriloquised in Cereno's testimony and their speech invoked only to indict them. When towards the end of the extract from Cereno's deposition, the notary adds that all "this is known and believed because the negroes have said it" (Melville 1856, 337), it becomes clear that, from the point of view of the settler-colonial legal system, the only meaningful content that their speech can carry, the only way, that is, that their voice can be credited to them as *phonē semantikē*, is in order to confirm their wilful participation in the revolt (Nelson 1992, 122). Melville's text reflects therefore the symbolic and juridical foreclosure of the speech of slaves, ex-slaves and accused fugitives, and as such may be thought "to represent justice's perversion as an archive of silence, empty of the content it is expected to hold" (Goldberg 2009, 7). After all, at the time of Melville writing, following the passing of the Slave Fugitive Act and in the wake of the Anthony Burns case, it was clear that the very institutional structures entrusted and authorised to provide a hearing, were notable, as Brook Thomas notes, not for the speech they guaranteed but for the speech they prohibited (Thomas 1987, 42). *Benito Cereno* is thus a work of fiction that, as Dana Nelson has persuasively argued, "has something important to say about the operations of racism" (Nelson 1992, 109). Moreover, it does so in a remarkable way, by reflexively framing its context on a symbolic level through its "rigorous examination of the 'imaginary' mechanisms of colonialist mentality" (JanMohamed 1985, 66).

With this in mind, it is undoubtedly puzzling that it is this particular work of fiction that Schmitt uses in order to explain his own role in German and

European twentieth-century history, and that he frames *Benito Cereno* as a "myth of unresolved situations" to do so. To be sure, Melville's novella is a suspenseful, dark, richly woven, fin-de-siècle, Gothic tale that affords multiple readings at multiple levels: about black and white, the ontological basis of race and its political construction, good and evil, elites and masses, fate and freedom, contingency and necessity, reality and appearance, awareness and misrecognition, truth and illusion, blindness and vision, muteness and voice, historical event and historical record, fact and fiction, force and consent. Further, Melville himself, as Faye Halpern observes, "does not give us a stable point from which to figure out how to interpret the mutiny and its aftermath". Indeed, even on the central issues of race and slavery, it remains uncertain what position Melville or the novella are taking or proposing (Nelson 1992, 109; Sollors 2020, 410). In addition, as Werner Sollors remarks, Melville's "open mode of narration [leaves] many "blanks", and this makes the text "particularly hospitable to the dynamism of its reception by various readers" (Sollors 2020, 410).

Schmitt's interest in *Benito Cereno* appears to have begun not long after the novella was published in Germany in 1938. By then, Schmitt had been forced to resign from some of his commitments after he came under attack in 1936 in the SS newspaper *Das Schwarze Korps* and was put under the surveillance of the SD (*Sicherheitsdienst*, the intelligence agency of the SS) (Sollors 2020, 401–402). During the early 1940s, he and his friend, Ernst Jünger, read Poe and Melville, and had numerous exchanges about the literary merits of the two authors. Schmitt developed a deep admiration for Melville, an intense fascination with *Benito Cereno* and an extensive identification with the title character. Indeed, from fairly early on, Schmitt read in Cereno's persona, the captive captain forced to remain silent and compliant to the orders of the mutinied slaves in charge of the ship, his own position *vis-à-vis* the Nazi regime controlled by the SS. As Jünger wrote in his diary, after a conversation he had with Schmitt on 16 October 1941, Schmitt

> compared his situation with that of the white captain who was under the rule of the black slaves in Melville's 'Benito Cereno' and in that context he quoted the saying, "*Non possum scribere contra eum, qui potest proscribere*" [I cannot write against someone who has the power to turn me into an outlaw].[3]
>
> (Jünger, in Sollors 2020, 405–406)

From this point on, gradually, Schmitt appears to have appropriated Cereno's persona, and this seems to have provided him with a (convenient) narrative foil to try and explain (and justify) his involvement and complicity with the Nazi regime, and to do so from two perspectives. First from a subjective, personal one: in a long statement Schmitt prepared in Nuremberg, for instance, there is a point where it is as if Schmitt speaks wearing the mask of Cereno, giving an account of his actions on the ship: "I acted against such opponents carefully and avoided polemical responses, according to the wisdom of the ancient saying: *non possum scribere contra eum, qui potest proscribere*" (Schmitt in Sollors 2020, 406, fn 17). Second, from an objective perspective, invoking "Cereno's myth" this time, the "myth" of "unresolved situations". This is the case, when in *Ex Captivitate Salus* (or "Deliverance from Captivity"), authored while in isolation during a period of arrests and internments (culminating in Nuremberg) between August 1945 and April 1947, he writes:

> In Germany Benito Cereno, the hero of Melville's story, has become a symbol of the situation of the intelligentsia in a mass system...Each situation has its secret, and each scientific discipline contains its own *Arcanum*. I am the final conscious representative of the *jus publicum Europaeum*, the last one to have taught and studied it in an existential sense, and I experience its end in the same way that Benito Cereno experienced the journey of the pirate ship. This means that it is the time and the place for silence.
>
> (Schmitt 2017, 60–1; translation slightly modified)

Tierno Galván articulates well the Schmittian reading of the "impossible" choice confronting the European intelligentsia on the Nazi ship-of-state: faced with the Nazi barbarism, fleeing and "emigrating to the friendly ship of Mr Delano" (Galvan in Agamben 2017, 460) might have been preferable than staying and collaborating. Yet how could any member of the European elite, and particularly Schmitt, from his self-proclaimed position as last representative of the *jus publicum Europaeum*, "simply bid adieu to Europe?" (*ibid.*). None of this, of course, can ever provide sufficient justification, and hence any form of exculpation, for Schmitt's reprehensible role and activities during the Nazi regime. As Giorgio Agamben rightly notes, unlike Benito Cereno,

> Schmitt was at no point forcibly made to take part … He willingly collaborated with the government of the pirated ship and repeatedly sought to give juridical form to the new constitution of National Socialist Germany.
>
> (Agamben 2017, 461)

Indeed, even more than that, he appears to have "contributed to the radicalization of [a number of] Nazi positions" (Sollors 2020, 401).[4]

My focus, therefore, in the rest of this essay is not Schmitt's reading of Melville's novella. In fact, I want to move away from Schmitt's interpretation and appropriation of *Benito Cereno* and return to the beginning of Melville's story, and specifically to the scene in which the American captain boards Cereno's ship. For part of the argument pursued here is to propose a markedly different reading from the one focused on good and evil, free action and constraint, elites and masses, friends and foes. Or how, or when,

Delano, like another Oedipus, is going to pierce the opacity of the situation, decipher its secret and grasp its truth, realising finally that the apparent order on the ship hides a hideous disorder. Rather, the reading that I am putting forward here requires us to stay with the doubling that Melville's narration produces, with its staging of Delano's arrival on the Spanish ship, as an encounter with an unknown, opaque space, and observe what he does, how he repeatedly tries (and fails) to read the situation he finds himself in. For the question that Melville raises is not so much how or when Delano will comprehend the truth of the situation he is in – a situation that looks "normal" but in reality is the emerging alternative "other" of the "civilised" space of European modernity: a postrevolutionary, decolonised space, where the former colonial authority is under the rule of its former slaves. Rather, the key question for Melville, I suggest, is this: once captain Delano does realise what the truth is, where is it that *he*, as descendant of the first anticolonial revolution and citizen (and representative) of the New World, will stand with respect to it? To put it differently, the question that Melville poses is the following: once Delano realises that the Eurocentric symbolic order, that he thought he found himself in, is a sham, and that the social link normed by a European colonial and racist modernity is broken, what will *he* do? Will he align himself with the "civilised" nations and help reconstitute the old, colonial, Eurocentric order? Will he deem Europe to be "indefensible"[5] in establishing and perpetuating (by its own standards) such barbarism and hence side with the newly freed "wretched of the earth"? Will he seek to establish a new order? Or refrain from doing so, step back and leave other possibilities to materialise? In the rest of this piece, I sketch, following Melville, Schmitt and Fanon, three possible ways of configuring postcolonial becoming.

On the *San Dominick*

> *Mundus est fabula*
> The world is a stage/The world is a fable

The *San Dominick* is Benito Cereno's ship in Melville's novella. It is a decrepit former Spanish Manila galleon, a popular Asian trading vessel in the Spanish empire until the late eighteenth century, used to transport precious goods from one colonial port to another: from Manila to Acapulco and back. Most of the action in Melville's novella takes place on the *San Dominick*, somewhere in the Pacific Ocean, in the year 1799. Melville's choice of year is not accidental. The year 1799 is the last of the century that saw the beginning of the Age of Revolution against despotism and tyrannical government: first, with the American Revolution and the birth of "the first new nation, the child of the first anti-colonial revolution … and [ironically] the first modern settler state" (Mamdani 2015, 608); then, with the French Revolution and its "civic-bourgeois universalism" (Balibar 2016) that, in *declaring* that "men are born free and with equal rights" to "liberty, property, safety and resistance to oppression", provides the original political matrix of the modern imaginary for the democratic refounding of the social; and finally, with the Haitian Revolution, the "only successful slave revolt in history" (James (1938) 2001, xviii), that, in defeating "in turn the local whites and the soldiers of the French monarchy, a Spanish invasion, a British expedition of some 60,000 men, and a French expedition of similar size under Bonaparte's brother-in-law" (*ibid.*), not only defeated the most powerful European nations of the day, while also precipitating the end of the transatlantic slave trade, but achieved (what was considered unthinkable at the time) the establishment of the first "Negro state" endowed with a constitution that abolished slavery and discrimination on the grounds of race.

Benito Cereno is Melville's most political work. It is a story about colonialism, slavery, racism and white metropolitan fears of slave uprisings on both land and sea and of the proliferation throughout the Americas of "black empires" – which is precisely what Haiti called itself in its first post-independence Constitution of 1805. The main events of the story take place on board the *San Dominick*, "in the harbour of St. Maria, a small, desert, uninhabited island" (Melville 1856, 109) that Melville relocates off "the southern extremity of the long coast of Chile" (*ibid.*), at the very southern end of the world. This move is significant because it inscribes the "finisterrial" liminality of the ship's location both geographically, by placing it "at the tip of the [southern] hemisphere, straddling an imagined critical edge between the (trans)Atlantic and the (trans) Pacific" (Tripp 2017, 9); and existentially, on the "final waters" (Melville cited in Tripp 2017, 6) of an oceanic liminality, not simply "in the radical contingency and vulnerability of thalassic existence" (Gilroy 2014, 54), but in the vast, empty space of the "blank ocean" (Melville 1856, 150), away from social custom, normative codes, entrenched hierarchies and the symbolic moorings that these provide to apprehend reality; in short, in the unworldly "lawlessness and loneliness" (Melville 1856, 141) of a worldly blind spot.

The *San Dominick* is thus also a stage. Not just because it provides the fictional *pegma* on which the dramatic events, that eventually reveal the "truth" of the situation on board this "strange" ship, unfold – namely, that the ship has been taken over by its would-be human cargo and is heading to Senegal, no longer following its prescribed route. But mainly because it stages two conflicting readings of the world and of what takes place therein: one in which things are "black and white", starkly clear and certain, because already coded epistemically through the political ontologies of race and ordered through the entrenched phantasmatic hierarchies of the colonial world and its fabular colourlines; and one in which things are "gray",[6] without any "true colours",[7] and hence "odd", uncoded, uncertain, shifting, yet-to-be-determined, constantly potentially otherwise; and where power, authority and order, once without their racial and racist imperial ground, are reduced to mere spectacle. Being on the *San Dominick*, in other words, does not take us back to a fictional desert island, a pre-political and a-nomic, state of nature. Far from it. What we witness instead is the envisioning of, what must have appeared at the time as, a far more radical, unsettling and unthinkable possibility: namely, not simply that the appearance of order may hide a darker reality, but that the *mise-en-scène* of normal conventions of colonial reality and sociality, that takes place on the ship to distract the American unsuspecting captain, is a masquerade, a masterly, subtle ruse, orchestrated and carried out by the "civilised" world's very shadow, its ontological negative, the invisible, nameless human beings of the colonial world's "zone of non-being" (Fanon (1952) 1986), the "no-bodies" (Ferreira da Silva 2009), the "damned" of the earth (Fanon 1961).

Melville's account of the events on the *San Dominick* provides therefore a glimpse of a broader "unthinkable" possibility: that the ship's black "cargo", the West African slaves that had taken over the ship, could also be the subjects of reason and instrumental rationality, the subjects of freedom and action and heroism, the subjects of history. They could organise, plan and carry out a successful revolt, destroy their oppressor and take control (of the ship and their destiny), deploying violence ferociously to overcome their opponent, threatening it to ensure compliance, and using any means available to them to achieve their objective: make an agreement with the captain of the ship to spare him and his remaining crew so that the latter could take them to Senegal to safety, and use the display of servitude and docility as a ruse so as not to raise suspicion. In other words, what Melville's Gothic record of the events reveals is the "unimaginable" possibility that the objects of the symbolic economy of racial capitalism and colonialism could occupy the position of subject. Indeed, a subject that is so conscious and deeply knowledgeable of the rules that form and norm their being that they are able to replicate them to perfection and use them for their own ends. In this respect then, Melville's account resonates with the thrust of CLR James' history of the Haitian Revolution some 80 years later. As James explains in his foreword to the 1980 edition of *The Black Jacobins*, his aim was to "write a book in which Africans or people of African descent instead of constantly being the object of other peoples' exploitation and ferocity would themselves be taking action … and shaping other people to their own needs" (James (1938) 2001, xv). And it is precisely this aspect of the "events that shook up Saint-Domingue [the site of the Haitian Revolution] from 1791 to 1804" that rendered them ""unthinkable facts" in the framework of Western thought" (Trouillot cited in Tripp 2017, 11). Moreover, if Matt Clavin is right, when, in considering the extensive use of Gothic historical narratives to recount the events in Saint-Domingue, he convincingly argues that "the Gothicization of the Haitian Revolution reinforced its unthinkability" (Clavin 2007, 5), then Melville's use of the stylistic grammar of the Gothic in *Benito Cereno* could be seen as underscoring precisely this ontologically "unimaginable" character of the events on the *San Dominick* – *San Dominick* being of course another name for Saint-Domingue; that is, not only the site of the Haitian Revolution but also where the transatlantic slave trade began.[8]

Yet simply to identify the *San Dominick* with Saint-Domingue would doubtless miss the point. For as Sava Klickovic aptly notes echoing John Locke,[9] "the whole world is the *San Dominick*" (Klickovic, cited in Agamben 2017, 468). Indeed, what Captain Delano first encounters upon climbing the side of this "large and populous ship" (Melville 1856, 150) is an "unusual" scene: a "clamorous throng of whites and blacks" (149) along with "a nondescript crew such as Lascars or Manilla men" (150), that together combine into "a shadowy tableau" of "strange costumes, gestures and faces" (151). What Delano stumbles upon on the *San Dominick*, in other words, is an odd, unworldly, postcolonial world from an emergent future, a "peculiar" cosmopolis without colonial, cultural and racial divisions, the "complex global world" (Tripp 2017, xx) in its multiplicity and plurality, unmarked, uncoded and unordered, without visible hierarchies, or other dividing lines, and hence for Delano, an opaque, alien, unreadable world: "a strange house, with strange inmates, in a strange land" (Melville 1856, 150).

Delano, however, as we know, does not realise until late in the day, literally at the eleventh hour in fact, what it is that he sees on the ship; namely, that the ship's "good order" has been overturned, the captain is captive and the ship is ruled by its former human cargo. Delano realises this, moreover, only because he is forced to do so, when Benito Cereno makes a desperate attempt to warn him of the danger that he and his ship are in, jumps in Delano's boat and Babo tries to kill him. It is only then, in that instant, that a "flash of revelation" sheds light on the whole "strangeness" of the situation and Delano finally understands what he has been unwilling to see all along while on the *San Dominick*. Yet by that point, we also have no longer any doubt, if we ever had any, about which side Delano is going to take. For from the beginning, the narrator of the story has been carefully detailing Delano's "perceptual strategy" (Nelson 1992, 111) in trying to figure out the strangeness (Melville 1856, 140–55 *passim*) of the ship and exposing the "Manichean binarity which undergirds [its] colonialist conceptual structure" (Nelson 1992, 111).

Indeed, even before boarding the *San Dominick*, where the narrator sees "gray" or "no colors", Delano sees the ship as a "whitewashed monastery after a thunderstorm" filled with "dark moving figures [...] as of Black Friars pacing cloisters" (Melville 1856, 145). And then, while on board the ship, he never stops making everything he sees fit into this framework, even though it may not quite fit, forcing the evidence, and explaining away his discomfort and unease or relying blindly on "the ever-watchful Providence" (291). As such, as Dana D. Nelson perceptively observes,

> [t]he conceptual binary of black and white that rules Delano's perception also organises his interpretation of events, which in turn is governed by a body of assumptions about the essential nature of each color. Before

> Delano can even make out figures on the ship his imagination is "coloring" them – transferring a dualistic scheme onto diversely coloured and heretofore *unseen* humans. So when Delano boards the ship, he can take the slaves "genially", relying on his certitude that "whites" are "by nature the shrewder race" and that "blacks" are "too stupid" to worry over. [...] It is impossible for Delano to entertain the notion of "black" power. It is equally impossible for him to envision a fellow "white" without it [...] Delano cannot read through the will to power that constitutes a blind spot in colonial epistemology [...] But Babo clearly has done so – he counts precisely on Delano's complacent reading of "black" and "white" for the success of his plan.
>
> (Nelson 1992, 111)

The aftermath, therefore, to the moment of revelation on the ship is unsurprisingly bleak: Delano overpowers Babo, and with the help of his crew, captures the *San Dominick*, frees Benito Cereno and brings the surviving mutineers to Lima to face justice. Following trial, Babo is sentenced to death, his body is "burnt to ashes" and his severed head is "fixed on a pole in the Plaza", where it meets, "unabashed, the gaze of the whites" (Melville 1856, 353), and from where it looks, across the Plaza and across the Dimac river, St. Bartholomew's church and the monastery on Mount Agonia, the resting places of Don Aranda and Don Benito, respectively.

Melville, Schmitt and Fanon on modern *nomos* and the becoming of postcolonial becoming

For Melville, then, the future of anticolonial revolution, along with the prospect of establishing a new postcolonial order, is grim. In fact, there does not seem to be a future. Past, present and future, Melville says in the novella, all merge, all "seem[] one" (298). In siding with the old colonial powers, the New World (represented here by Delano) proves unable to carry out its historical task of leading the rest of the world to a future new order of freedom and equality for all. Its anticolonialism reveals itself to be out of sync with its ideals. For it is clearly not directed to the structures of colonial domination, violence and oppression, of racial *nomos* and of the racialised logics of appropriation and extractivism that organise the European colonial order, but, if opportune, to those that control them, to those that are in charge – with the view of taking their place, or at least of taking a share of their dominions as the old imperial world wanes away. Melville is scathing and simultaneously prescient in his indictment: ultimately, the New World is caught in the loop of the eternal return of the same old Eurocentric imperial order. Its emancipatory ideals are caught in the necropolitical power game ordered by the colonial *nomos* of the modern. Indeed, the New World will not stop being caught in the loop of the modern colonial death drive as long as it sees itself as part of the world's "civilised" nations and seeks to restore the "fraternal unreserve" (347) between them. Or to put it differently, it will not stop being caught in the cycle of colonial domination as long as it continues to follow the lead of the Old World and accept the "abyssal line" (De Sousa Santos 2007) of the colonial *nomos*, that reduces the rest of the world to "zones of nonbeing", disposability and exploitation, and their lands to *terrae nullius*, 'lands of nobody', that is, "nobody-that-counts", "nobody-like-us".[10] Babo's gesture, whereby Christopher Columbus, one of the figureheads of the age of discovery, is replaced with the skeleton of the slave trader, Don Aranda, as figurehead of the *San Dominick*, and the command "follow your leader" is written below his bones in chalk, should be read not only as Babo's chilling reminder to the Spaniards of who is in charge of the ship but also as a statement of the stark truth about the state of the world: if death in the form of the remains of the slave trader has replaced the explorer as existential figurehead of the "civilised" world, this is precisely because colonial exploitation and slavery have long replaced discovery as its existential journey.

The "final tragedy" of *Benito Cereno* therefore is clearly not that Delano cannot identify with Cereno, as Eric Sundquist, the Melville scholar, thinks (Sundquist 1987, 100). Rather, following Dana Nelson's insightful analysis, it can be argued that the tragedy in Melville's novella is twofold. On the one hand, it is tragic that both Delano and Cereno fail to identify with Babo's humanity, even though they both experience, albeit Delano fleetingly, the horror and dehumanisation of Babo's position, of "being [...] rendered Object/Other under [someone else's] authority" (Nelson 1992, 127). On the other hand, it is also tragic that both Delano and Cereno fail to see the horror, brutality and inhumanity of the systems that they are part of, racial capitalism, colonialism and slavery, and only see the ferocity of the revolt and the threat that it poses to their own status as Subjects of power and authority (*ibid.*). As a result, despite Aranda being avenged, the Spanish ship recaptured, Cereno saved, the mutinied slaves brought to justice and "good order" restored, law, justice, order, authority and the good, are now hollowed out. The gap that the story renders visible in the social link, between what is lawful and what is good, between law and justice, order and authority, remains open, unresolved, without catharsis or closure. It is now clear that there is nothing "good" about the order that is being restored with the recapture of the ship, and nothing just about the justice being done in the Lima court. In the end, it is not slavery that is put on the dock but its victims. It is not its brutal racial and racist *nomos* that are deemed an aberration by the legal authority of the court, but the revolt against slavery that is judged as criminal, and Babo, voiceless, dispossessed once more of his capacity to speak, deprived of humanity and subjectivity once again during the trial, the one that is sentenced to a "silent end". The order of things is such that Cereno is not held accountable for his part in the perpetuation of slavery and colonialism. Indeed, as Schmitt observes revealingly, it would be Kafkaesque to have Cereno on trial on charges of piracy "in front of a special court for the fight against Spanish imperialism" (Schmitt in Sollors 2020, 407).[11] After all, the very purpose of the statements made in Cereno's deposition is precisely "to show the court that from the beginning to the end of the revolt it was impossible for the deponent and his men to act otherwise than they did" (Melville 1856, 342). Babo's impaled head becomes thus the emblem of Cereno's guiltlessness.[12]

Hence ultimately the "final tragedy" of *Benito Cereno* is the impasse and impossibility of postcolonial becoming. For insofar as the forces of anticolonialism remain divided, unable or unwilling to undo the racial *nomos* of the old colonial order, they end up either co-opted or crushed. The novella leaves no space for alternatives, for utopian possibility (Ganser 2018, 228) or "remedial action" (Levine in Ganser, *ibid.*). Instead, we are left at a dead end, in an "aprogressive [narrative] of modernity" (Huang in Ganser, *ibid.*), stuck between a foundering colonialism and an exhausted anticolonialism that never reaches liberation, trapped in "a despairing (even sinister) collapse of history into timeless, repeated and unavoidable oppression" (Nelson 1992, 127); without interruption or transcendence. In the end, the emerging new global order lead by the New World, remains organised by the old racial *nomos*, and as such remains haunted by an ineliminable remainder, the spectral shadow of the "negro" (Melville 1856, xx) – even if it remains persistently oblivious to it.

It is not difficult to appreciate here why *Benito Cereno* speaks so directly to Carl Schmitt, not only at a personal but also at an intellectual level. Even if Schmitt does not share Melville's liberal politics and his antislavery position, he shares his view in *Benito Cereno* that the American self-perception of being exceptional in, and pushing forward, world history is self-complacent (Ganser 2018, 228) and wilfully blind to the darkness at the heart of both its emancipatory politics and its global hegemonic ambitions. Moreover, it is not difficult to imagine that Schmitt would recognise, in the image of the "peculiar" postcolonial cosmopolis that Melville describes when Delano boards the *San Dominick*, precisely the image of the world in the wake of decolonisation and the "foundering" of "the traditional Eurocentric order of international law" (Schmitt 2003, 39). For as Schmitt laments, the recognition of newly independent states in international law, and, after World War II, their admission to the United Nations in growing numbers, created a "new, *imponderable* situation" (Schmitt in Blanco and del Valle 2014, 4; my emphasis). According to Schmitt,

> a disorganised mass of […] heterogeneous states, lacking any special or spiritual consciousness, […] a chaos of reputedly equal and equally sovereign states […] in which a common bracketing of war no longer was feasible, and for which not even the concept of civilization could provide any concrete homogeneity.
>
> (Schmitt 2003, 234)

came to replace the old global order of European empires. This shift was warranted by the increasing "spacelessness of a general universalism" (230) in international law and the growing practical impossibility of bracketing war "beyond the line" that separated Europe from the "free" space of the New World and the colonies – a transformation that began intellectually with the dissolution of "the distinctive territorial status of colonial overseas lands", on which "the whole [modern] spatial structure of the Earth in international law was based" (221), and was completed historically with the introduction of air power in warfare, that is, a new form of warfare in world history that upset any sense of territorial demarcations (Hussain 2011, 245)[13] that organised the modern spatial order of the world.

Schmitt's treatise on *The Nomos of the Earth in the international law of the jus publicum Europaeum* (Schmitt 2003), originally published in 1950 yet largely written between 1942 and 1945 (in other words, during the very time that *Benito Cereno* was on his mind), deals precisely with the advent and unravelling of the global order of European empires and the establishment and subsequent irrevocable waning of the spatial normative structure that organised world order in the modern period, namely the "old *nomos* of the earth" (39), in which the *jus publicum Europaeum* was grounded.

This "old *nomos*", the first "*nomos* of the Earth" proper, according to Schmitt, was made possible with the age of discovery, and was established with the age of conquest, when, through exploration and contest, "the earth was encompassed and measured by the global consciousness of the European peoples" (49), or, more concretely, when the European powers "appropriated, divided and utilized the planet" (352). Before the late fifteenth century and early sixteenth century therefore, that is, before the discovery of the Americas and the circumnavigation of the planet, there could not be any *nomos* "of *the Earth*" as such, since "the great oceans of the world were inaccessible to human power" (352) and a global, all-encompassing concept of the earth was lacking (53 and 55). It was precisely this "unrepeatable historical event", in Schmitt's view, that by unifying the world geographically, created for the first time a sense of the world on a global scale and inaugurated a new epoch of spatial normative ordering of the earth. Moreover, this new global ordering posited Europe as its geopolitical centre and, beside it "a vast, formerly unknown, non-European space [...] as *free space*, as an area open to European occupation and expansion" (87; emphasis in the original). The "European struggle for this new world" (*ibid.*) in turn gave rise to a new "nomic topology" (Otero 2005, 387), or dispensation, of the world, by drawing new "internal divisions [...] within the framework of one and the same spatial order" (Schmitt 2003, 92). These divisions were not merely conceptual but physical (Hussain 2011, 245), concrete, spatial, inscribed geographically and determined cartographically, along global demarcation lines based on the earth's spherical nature, "the first scientific concept of the true form of our planet" (Schmitt 1996, 32).

In Schmitt's account of the emergence of this new *nomic* dispensation, the "following distinctions and divisions were characteristic of the *nomos* of the earth" (Schmitt 2003,183): first, the distinction between firm land and free sea, *terra firma* and *mare liberum*; and second, the division between the territory of European states and that of colonial lands (184). The "first [such] global lines of division and distribution" (*ibid.*) of the world were the *rayas*, the divisional lines established through treaties between the Portuguese and Spanish princes, "both recognising the same spiritual authority and the same international law" (91). Yet the *rayas*, as a historical type of global lines, were essentially premised on a premodern, medieval, schema of the world, predicated on the *respublica Christiana*, and as such they proved inadequate "for the purpose of the exploitative distribution of a global order between two burgeoning mercantilist states" (Miéville 2005, 173–174). At the same time, however, crucially, the *rayas* represented a form of *nomic* thinking, "global linear thinking" Schmitt calls it (Schmitt 2003, 87), that survived in later types of divisional lines of the world, such as the amity, or friendship, lines, which first appeared in secret treaties between the English and the French in the sixteenth century. The amity lines were a world apart from the *rayas* (90). They split the earth into two distinct zones: a European "inside", that is to say, territory inside European interstate, international law, where "treaties, peace and friendship applied" (92); and a colonial "beyond", that is, territory on "free colonial soil outside Europe", meaning both soil "free to be occupied as long as it did not belong to a state in the sense of internal European interstate law" (198), and territory that remained "outside the legal, moral and political values recognised on this side of the line", where "force could be used freely and ruthlessly" (94). Schmitt explains the significance of the amity lines for the modern world order when he writes that at this

> line, Europe ended and the "New World" began. At any rate, European law i.e. "European public law," ended here. Consequently, so, too, did the bracketing of war achieved by traditional European international law, meaning that here the struggle for land-appropriations knew no bounds. Beyond the line was an "overseas" zone in which, for want of any limits to war, only the law of the stronger applied.
>
> (93–4)

The amity lines thus "created an abyss between freedom (the lawlessness of the state of nature) and an orderly 'civil' mode of existence" (95), between colonial territory and European soil, between a conflict zone outside Europe and a sphere of peace and order ruled by European public law (97), between exception and norm (98). In doing so, these lines did not establish only the division of the earth into state territory and colonial territory but importantly, as Andreas Kalyvas observes, they also put into full play the rule of colonial difference (Kalyvas 2018, 40) that was constitutive of the spatial structure of the *jus publicum Europaeum* (Schmitt 2003, 199) and gave rise to the "special *territorial status of the colonies*"[14] (*ibid.*; emphasis in the original). It is therefore a crucial element in Schmitt's unconventional account of how this Eurocentric global order emerged that the *nomos* of the modern era, this *ordo ordinans* of the modern world, that came about with the European colonial expansion, "did not derive essentially from internal European land-appropriation and territorial changes but rather from the European land-appropriation of a non-European new world" (183). In other words, for Schmitt, the history of international law during this period is also the history of colonialism,[15] and in turn colonialism is "co-original and co-constitutive" with modernity (Kalyvas 2018, 36).[16]

When it comes to the decline of this Eurocentric spatial order now, it is true that Schmitt does not provide a coherent or linear account of this in his work (Loughlin 2015, 81; Kalyvas 2018, 40). On the one hand, he sees as the main reason for the decline of the European order the emergence of the United States and its rise into a global power that was able "to upset the spatial order of the European world [by drawing a new global line on the earth, that of the Western hemisphere] and to introduce a new concept of war into world history" (Schmitt 2003, 100)[17] with the entry of air power in warfare. On the other hand, it is also the case that he locates the beginning of the decline of this Eurocentric order of the world, "in terms of intellectual history", in the American War of Independence (*ibid.*), in other words, in the first anticolonial revolution; and locates the end of "traditional, specifically European international law" to the moment when the overseas colonial territory, loses its distinctive territorial status and becomes indistinguishable from, and equivalent to, state territory, in the sense of European soil (199). At that point, "the core concept of the traditional interstate European international law was thrown into disorder" (226). For "the concept of the colonies", Schmitt maintained, "contained an ideological burden that affected, above all, European colonial powers" (199). The constitutive role of the colony for the modern *nomos* of the earth, and its *jus publicum Europaeum*, is evidenced, Kalyvas perceptively observes, both in the making and the unmaking of European international law and its modern global order (Kalyvas 2018, 35). The colony, in Schmitt's history and theory of international law, at once "sustained the Eurocentric order, set off its dissolution and brought the demand for another order" (*ibid.*)

What then of the postcolonial becoming of the modern world in Schmitt's post-war writings? Does he provide an account of the emerging international order after the fading of the Eurocentric *nomos* into a universal, abstract and rootless law? And if so, does he approach this from the perspective of a European continent whose position in the world has been relativised (217), so that it is "no longer the centre of gravity of the world" (Mbembe 2017, 1), no longer "the sacral centre of the earth" (Schmitt 2003, 226)? Does he trace the contours of a new *nomic* dispensation of the world from the point of view "of the vanishing colony" (Kalyvas 2018, 44)? At different points in the post-war period, Schmitt attempts to think the transformation of the global order brought about by the process of decolonisation and the decline of the modern European *nomos*. In 1948, for instance, in an entry in his private notes collected in the *Glossarium* from the 18th of July, reflecting on the growing significance of the economy on the world stage and the waning of the *jus publicum Europaeum*, the picture he paints is grim:

> The most terrible transformation of the world, which is effected by mindless aggrandisement of power, consists in the fact that things that are beyond the measure of our physical senses are now rendered visible, audible, and perceptible: perceptible and therefore capable of being possessed. The new concept of property or rather the domination of functions: *eius regio, eius economia*, henceforth: *eius economia, eius regio*. That is the new *Nomos* of the earth; no more *Nomos*.
>
> (Schmitt in Pottage 2019, 170)

The enormous shift, in other words, that this new epoch brings about, according to Schmitt, is not only that the law becomes rootless, detached from its terrestrial fundament, but its object is also radically transformed. Things no longer have any elemental, tangible substance. They are now visible, audible, perceptible and hence "capable of being possessed" yet "beyond the measure of our physical senses". As a consequence, their appropriation does not follow any longer the earthbound, "elemental paradigm of Nomos" (Pottage 2019, 171). As Alain Pottage insightfully observes, appropriation now "becomes a contingent effect of the articulation of an ecology of discourses, technologies, media and affects", since what renders these artefacts perceptible, and hence capable of being possessed and appropriated is precisely the technical and economic practices and discourses that create them (*ibid*). At the level of world order, where what we have is a free, global economy, that ignores all territorial demarcations and destroys the old amity lines, by simultaneously overstretching and undermining them (Schmitt 2003, 226), the 'sphere' of interstate, international law is increasingly determined by the 'space' of economic power (Pottage 2019, 170), and hence, the spatial structure of the modern world, as defined by the old *nomos* of the earth, is dissolved, spelling a catastrophic transformation, for Schmitt, that is marked by disorientation, confusion and disorder. For *Nomos* having disappeared, the *nomos* of the earth being no more, the world has become a-*Nomos*, lacking any comprehensive spatial order (Schmitt 2003, 186), and any unity of order (*Ordnung*) and orientation (*Ortung*). For this is now a world, which having a "technical-industrial existence", has all its orientations destroyed, and as such it is a world that has become rootless, u-*topos* (178), adrift – like the *San Dominick*.

In the years that follow, however, and especially from the *Nomos of the Earth* onwards, Schmitt appears to abandon this bleak image of the world, without *nomos* and without *topos*, in which the very paradigm of appropriation is altered. In *Nomos of the Earth*, he proclaims that "in such times of disorientation, the essential juridical task becomes that of properly ascertaining the reality of a fading and a rising *nomos* and of disclosing the derivation of each" (182), and dedicates the last part of his book, part four, to the "question" of a new *nomos* of the earth. It is thus clear that now Schmitt no longer seems to think that the end of the modern *nomos* of the earth spells out the end of *nomos* as such. Instead, throughout the book he maintains that, *nomos* being "a fundamental process of apportioning space", encapsulating "the structure-determining convergence of order and orientation in the cohabitation of peoples", it is something that is "essential to every historical epoch" (78). Indeed, as

> [e]very new age and every new epoch in the coexistence of peoples, empires, and countries, of rulers and powerful nations of every sort, is founded on new spatial divisions, new enclosures, and new spatial orders of the earth.
>
> (79)

Now that the first global *nomos* of the earth has ended, the issue is to discern the new global *nomos* that is emerging, as "[h]istorically speaking, new amity lines are on the agenda" (322). The "dilemma" he foresees at this point is between two options, *universum* and *pluriversum*, in short, between the "global monopoly of a single power, or [...] an ordered pluralism of large spaces (*Großräume*) ... themselves ordered and coexisting" (243). In a later essay, "The New *Nomos* of the Earth" (351–55), originally published in 1955, he adds a further possible configuration that the new *nomos* could take. The first one is the familiar one of a "complete unity of the world", a global political union under "a sole sovereign", who "would appropriate the whole earth – land, sea, and air – and would divide and manage it in accord with his plans and ideas" (354); the second is "to retain the balance structure of the previous *nomos*" and bring it up to date, by establishing hegemonic control over both sea and air power (355). Finally, the third one is that of a global order with a new, multipolar equilibrium, made up of several relatively independent blocs or *Großräume*, on condition that these are "differentiated meaningfully and are homogeneous internally" (*ibid.*).[18]

Admittedly, Schmitt's attempts to think the new global reality are tentative and, as Kalyvas notes, "lack the analytical rigour and conceptual sharpness of his previous studies" (Kalyvas 2018, 44). Schmitt never explains for instance how these independent blocs would come about, how they would be distinct from each other and internally unified. He also never explains, how war would be bracketed in such a system, or whether land appropriation would continue to be relevant for the emergence of the new nomos in an era marked by the expansion of technology and the dissolution of elemental, tangible substances as ground of juridical objectivity. In the third possibility that he envisages in the essay on the "New *Nomos*" there is little detail. This is also the case in subsequent essays,[19] although he does flesh out more the contours of this postcolonial, multipolar, polycentric order.[20] In general terms, what is coming after the disintegration of the European spatial order is neither "boundlessness nor a nothingness hostile to *nomos*" (355). And yet, it is difficult to disregard the tension in his post-war writings between on the one hand trying to imagine a post-European, postcolonial, multipolar, world order, grounded along a new set of amity lines, and on the other his dismissal of anticolonial movements and the postcolonial world as able to "generate the beginning of a New spatial order in positive terms" (Schmitt in Blanco and Del Valle 2014, 5); or indeed the idea that appropriation, once it is disconnected from the tangibility of the earth's soil, becomes an a-nomic, boundless, all-devouring, logic that mediates all human relations to the world as such.

Still, if Schmitt leaves us in this "unresolved situation" when imagining the postcolonial becoming of the world, it is Frantz Fanon that provides us guidance in the uncharted and often treacherous waters of postcoloniality, of "new" beginnings and "independent" becomings. Fanon's, *The Wretched of the Earth* (Fanon 1963), his classic, influential (and controversial), revolutionary text, provides an ethics and politics of decolonisation as a process and project of radical unmaking and remaking of the world and humanity. Written at the height of the Algerian War of Independence (in which Fanon was personally involved), during a period shaped by the intensification of the Cold War and the waning of the European empires in Asia, Africa, the Caribbean, the Middle East and the Mediterranean, as national liberation struggles redrew the geopolitical atlas of the world, it combines a gritty realism with a poetic, fervent language of revolutionary anger along with passages of patient contemplation and profound insight that make its "deliberately universalized level of analysis" (Bhabha 2004, xvi) utterly compelling, leading it to become, in Stuart Hall's words, the "Bible of decolonisation" (Hall in Bhabha, *ibid*.).

Famous for its phenomenology of violence as the key "counterontological force" (Ciccariello-Maher 2017) driving the agenda of anticolonial liberation, Fanon is clear that decolonisation is not a process that concerns only the former colonies. "Decolonization", he says, "sets out to change the order of the world" and as such "is obviously, a program of complete disorder" (Fanon 1963, 36) for it puts into question coloniality, "the colonial situation", as such (*ibid*.). In saying this, he is of course surprisingly close to Schmitt and his reading of the effect that decolonisation, and the dissolution of the distinct status of the colony, have on the world. Three themes provide the focus of Fanon's analysis in the *The Wretched of the Earth*: a phenomenology of the structures of the colonial world that need to be overcome in the process of decolonisation; an attentive reading of the psychic and affective life of coloniser and colonised; and an exploration of the complex dynamics of postcoloniality.

For the purposes of this piece, I want to focus on the first theme, namely on Fanon's phenomenology of colonial structures. According to Fanon, "[t]he colonial world is a world divided into compartments" (37). In Rancière's terms, we would say that in Fanon's account, colonial difference organises the order of the normatively sensible (Barnard-Naudé and Chryssostalis 2022, xx). For "[t]he colonial world is a world cut into two … The zone where the natives live is not complementary to the zone inhabited by the settlers" (Fanon 1963, 38). And he goes on:

> The settlers' town is a strongly built town, all made of stone and steel. It is a brightly lit town; the streets are covered with asphalt, and the garbage cans swallow all the [remainders], unseen, unknown and hardly thought about. [...] The settler's town is a well-fed town, an easygoing town; its belly is always full of good things. The settlers' town is a town of white people, of foreigners. [...] The town belonging to the colonized people, or at least the native town, the Negro village, the medina, the reservation, is a place of ill fame, peopled by men of evil repute. They are born there, it matters little where or how; they die there, it matters not where, nor how. It is a world without spaciousness; men live there on top of each other, and their huts are built one on top of the other. The native town is a hungry town, starved of bread, of meat, of shoes, of coal, of light.
>
> (39)

In other words, the colonial world is a "system of compartments" (37), that are ruled by entirely different standards, and it is precisely this compartmentalisation of the normative world of the colony, this "division into [normative] compartments" (52) that marks coloniality, that is emblematic of the normative world of "the colonial situation". Moreover, for Fanon, this compartmentalisation is a division that is spatially inscribed: its ordering is apparent, visible, experienced concretely, through its spatial instantiation of different standards of normativity and sociality. Colonial difference, finally, is instituted in the "geographical layout" of the colony, in the enclosures that institute "the norms, the play of social life" (Goodrich 2006, 30), the normed forms of sociality, "the forms of ownership and human proximity, [...] of power and domination (Schmitt 2003, 42). So "if we examine closely this system of compartments", Fanon continues, "we will at least be able to reveal the lines of force it implies" (Fanon 1963, 37–38). These dividing lines, these 'lines of force", are invariably lines of exploitation and disposability, abyssal lines, dividing the world of the colony into zones of normality and zones of exception, "zones of being" and "zones of non-being", zones of those who "count" and those who "don't". In the colonies, these dividing lines are marked by barracks and police stations; in capitalist societies, they are internalised, dividing lines that run under the skin, in "the structure of moral reflexes handed down from father to son" (38), of what is considered "good and proper", the marks of "civility" and "normality". And it is by revealing these lines of force, that order and organise the colonial world, that it becomes possible, especially in a postcolonial context, to trace their continued presence, unearth their (often) sublimated colonial geography, in order to undo them, and decolonise the world of the colony.

So for Fanon, the undoing of the "colonial situation", of the colonial *nomos* (Gilroy 2014, 29), cannot but go through the undoing of the spatial ordering of coloniality, the topography that organises colonial normativity and its "order of the sensible" (Rancière 2001), "the immediate form in which the [colonial] order … becomes spatially visible" (Schmitt 2003, 70), we could say paraphrasing Schmitt. It is precisely "this approach to the colonial world, its ordering and its geographical layout", Fanon argues, that "will allow us to mark out the lines on which a decolonized society will be reorganized" (Fanon, 1963, 38). And these new lines, for Fanon, that will reorganise "decolonised society", will not be drawn only through regime change, new constitutional dispensations or changes in positive law. They will be drawn only after the divisions and enclosures of the colonial world have been exscribed (Hanafin 2004); in short, only after the world of the colony has been disenclosed (Mbembe 2017).

Acknowledgements

In memoriam, Peter Fitzpatrick. I am deeply grateful to Jaco Barnard-Naudé for inviting me to UCT in September–October 2012 and to him and Pierre de Vos, as well as the Faculty of Law and HUMA for hosting me. The visit marked the beginning of our collaboration on *nomos* in the postcolony; and more generally, our work on the spatial inscription of the norms of sociality, coloniality and spatial (in)justice. I would like to thank him for sharing this journey with me, and for his intellectual companionship, comraderie and friendship. This piece would have never been written without him – let alone completed – especially without our conversations over the years, and his understanding and attentive care under very difficult circumstances. I would also like to thank Patrick Hanafin for reading earlier drafts and for discussing some of the ideas I put forward here, Costas Douzinas for his advice and critical support, and of course the sisterhood that provided respite from other commitments at crucial moments: Maria Chryssostalis, Jane Eames, Jo Alexandre and Karen Mann.

Notes

1 *United States v. Libellants and Claimants of The Schooner Amistad*, 40 U.S. (15 Pet.) 518 (1841).
2 On the significance of Burns and its impact on public opinion, see Cover, 1975, 178 ff.
3 Jünger is also cited in Agamben, 2017, 459, in a slightly different translation. The Latin saying that Schmitt uses comes from Ambrosius Theodosius Macrobius, a fifth century, Neoplatonist Roman scholar, but in Macrobius's version, this maxim has a much weaker formulation, as Macrobius originally writes: *non est enim facile in eum scriberequi potest proscribere* [it is *therefore not easy* to write against someone who has the power to turn me into an outlaw] (Sollors, 2020, 406 fn. 17.)
4 Moreover, following Jean-François Kervégan, it should be noted here that Schmitt's intellectual engagement with Nazism did not end in 1936, when he came under attack by the SS, but lasted until 1942, although after 1936 became less extreme (Kervégan, 1999, 72, n. 10).
5 It should be noted that this is precisely Aimé Césaire's indictment at the beginning of his *Discourse on Colonialism* (Césaire, 2000, 32).

6 "Everything was mute and calm; everything grey", writes Melville at the beginning of *Benito Cereno.*

> The sea, though undulated into long roods of swells, seemed fixed, and was sleeked at the surface like waved lead, that has cooled and set in the smelter's mould. The sky seemed a grey mantle. Flights of troubled grey fowl, kith and kin with flights of grey vapours among which they were mixed, skimmed low and fitfully over the waters.
>
> (Melville, 1856, 140-141)

7 "[T]he stranger, viewed through the glass, showed no colours; though to do so upon entering a haven however uninhabited ... was the custom among peaceful seamen of all nations" (Melville, 1856, 141)
8 On this point, see further James, (1938) 2001, 3.
9 When, in the "Second Treatise of Government", he famously says that "all the World was America" (Locke, (1689) 1988, §49, 301).
10 Cf. here Schmitt, 2003, 198–99.
11 Schmitt writes in the *Glossarium*, in his entry for 30 November 1947:

> I would very much like to [...] write a sequel to B.C. on a different level. B.C. in court. Perhaps the mood should be combined with elements from Franz Kafka's novel *The Trial*. Should B.C. end this way, in a Kafkaesque trial? Horrifying.
>
> BC charged with piracy in a court that does not permit discussions of his "premises". Will he step on that carpet of concepts [*Begriffsteppich*]? Will he be silent? The problem of all political trials? In front of an admiralty court (he has a chance); in front of a special court for the fight against Spanish imperialism (he would not stand a chance) (cited in Sollors, 2020, 407).

12 Cf. here Nelson, 1992, 123, for whom "Babo's punishment becomes an emblem of 'white' guiltlessness" more generally. In her view, the purpose of the trial was not to find the slaves guilty but to absolve the "whites" on the ship of any responsibility towards the community of white male Subjects.
13 On this point, see further Hussain, 2011.
14 This meant that

> [t]he land-appropriating state did not need to respect any rights [whether of public or private property (whether of *imperium* or *dominium*)] to the soil existing within the appropriated land, unless these rights somehow were connected with the private property of a member of a civilised state belonging to the order of interstate, international law.
>
> (Schmitt, 2003, 198–99)

15 Earlier, in *Land and Sea*, Schmitt said something similar, when he located "[t]he meaning, the heart of the law of the Christian European peoples" in "the dividing up of the new territories" (Schmitt 2015b, xx). In *Nomos of the Earth*, there can be no division without appropriation, and so "the heart of European law" is now to be found in the appropriation of the non-European territories in the new world.
16 In recent years, the significance of colonial expansion for the development of international law is widely accepted. See for instance generally, Anghie, 1996; and 2005; Grewe, 2000; Koskenniemi, 2002; and Miéville, 2005. Anghie points out the striking resemblance between the arguments of post-colonial and Third World scholars and Schmitt's account of the origin of the European global order in land appropriation (Anghie 2012, 1074), as well as their fundamental difference: whereas Schmitt laments

the dissolution of this order, Third World scholars denounce its injustice and are critical of its very existence.

17 On this point, see further Kalyvas, 2018, and extensive references therein.

18 In his post-war writings, Schmitt reworks his theory of *Großräum*, of large spaces or regional blocs, which he originally developed in 1939. *Großräum* is the most controversial concept he ever developed due to its association with Nazi expansionist foreign policy (Schmitt, 2011), and one reason for his arrest and detention in Nuremberg from 1945–47 (Schmitt 1987a; Schmitt 1987b, 102).

19 See Schmitt 1995; Schmitt 2015a.

20 On Schmitt's attempt to think and envisage possible post-Eurocentric global alternatives, see Kalyvas, 2018, who significantly underplays the tension between an a-nomic logic of appropriation and a new nomos of the world in his work.

References

Agamben, Giorgio. 1998. *Homo Sacer. Sovereign Power and Bare Life*, translated by Daniel Heller Roazen. Stanford, CA: Stanford University Press.

Agamben, Giorgio. 2005. *Un giurista davanti a se stesso*. Vicenza: Neri Pozza.

Agamben, Giorgio. 2017. "A Jurist Confronting Himself: Carl Schmitt's Jurisprudential Thought." In *The Oxford Handbook of Carl Schmitt*, edited by Jens Meierhenrich and Oliver Simons, 457–69. Oxford: Oxford University Press.

Anghie, Anthony. 1996. "Francisco de Vitoria and the Colonial Origins of International Law." *Social and Legal Studies* 5 (3): 321–36.

Anghie, Anthony. 2005. *Imperialism, Sovereignty and the Making of International Law*. Cambridge: Cambridge University Press.

Anghie, Anthony. 2012. "Identifying regions in the history of international law". In *The Oxford Handbook of the History of International Law*, edited by B. Fassbender and A. Peters, 1058–1078. Oxford: Oxford University Press.

Balibar, Etienne. 2016. "The idea of Revolution: Yesterday, Today and Tomorrow." Originally the Keynote Lecture at the International Society for Intellectual History Conference, "Rethinking Europe in Intellectual History," University of Crete, Rethymnon, 3 May 2016, it appears as revised for a lecture on May 6 at the MEGARON Lecture Hall in Athens, as part of the "Birkbeck in Athens Lectures in Critical and Cultural Theory" in Uprising 1/13 Revolution Seminar, organised by the Columbia Center for Contemporary Critical Theory, Columbia University. http://blogs.law.columbia.edu/uprising1313/etienne-balibar-the-idea-of-revolution-yesterday-today-and-tomorrow/

Barnard-Naudé, Jaco and Julia Chryssostalis. 2022. "Apartheid remains: nomos, law and spatiality in post-apartheid South Africa." In *Spatial Justice After Apartheid:* Nomos *in the Postcolony*, edited by Jaco Bernard- Naudé and Julia Chryssostalis, 1–38. Abingdon: Routledge.

Beebee, Thomas O. 2006. "Carl Schmitt's Myth of Benito Cereno." *Seminar: A Journal of Germanic Studies* 42 (2): 114–34.

Bhabha, Homi. 2004. "Foreword: Framing Fanon." In Frantz Fanon, *The Wretched of the Earth*, translated by Richard Philcox, with commentary by Jean-Paul Sartre and Homi Bhabha, vii–xli. New York: Grove Press.

Blanco, John D. and del Valle, Ivonne. 2014. "Reorienting Schmitt's *Nomos*: Political Theology and Colonial (and Other) Exceptions in the Creation of Modern and Global Worlds." *Política Común* 5: 1–22. https://doi.org/10.3998/pc.12322227.0005.001

Césaire, Aimé. 2000. *Discourse on Colonialism*, translated by Joan Pickham. New York: Monthly Review Press.
Ciccariello-Maher, George. 2017. *Decolonizing Dialectics*. Durham, NC: Duke University Press.
Clavin, Matt. 2007. "Race, Revolution and the Sublime: The Gothicization of the Haitian Revolution in the New Republic and the Atlantic World." *Early American Studies: An Interdisciplinary Journal* 5 (1): 1–29.
Cover, Robert M. 1975. *Justice Accused: Antislavery and the Judicial Process*. New Haven, CT: Yale University Press.
Da Silva, Denise Ferreira. 2009. "No-Bodies. Law, Raciality and Violence". *Griffith Law Review* 18 (2): 212–36.
Delano, Amasa. 1817. *A Narrative of Voyages and Travels in the Northern and Southern Hemisphere: Comprising Three Voyages Around the World; Together with a Voyage of Survey and Discovery, in the Pacific Ocean and Oriental Islands* (Vol. 1). Boston, MA: Printed by E.G. House for the author.
De Sousa Santos, Boaventura. 2007. "Beyond Abyssal Thinking: From Global Lines to Ecologies of Knowledges." *Review* 30 (1): 45–89.
Fanon, Frantz. (1952) 1986. *Black Skin, White Masks*. Translated by Charles Lam Markmann. London: Pluto Press.
Fanon, Frantz. 1961. *Les damnés de la terre*. Paris: François Maspero.
Fanon, Frantz. 1963. *The Wretched of the Earth*, translated by Constance Farrington and a preface by Jean-Paul Sartre. New York: Grove Press.
Feltenstein, Rosalie. 1947. "Melville's "Benito Cereno"." *American Literature* 19 (3): 245–55.
Ganser, Alexandra. 2018. "From the Black Atlantic to the Bleak Pacific: Re-reading Benito Cereno." *Atlantic Studies* 15 (2): 218–37.
Gilroy, Paul. 2014. "The Tanner Lectures on Human Values: Lecture I: Suffering and Infrahumanity; Lecture II: Humanities and a New Humanism." February 21. https://tannerlectures.utah.edu/Gilroy%20manuscript%20PDF.pdf
Goldberg, Shari. 2009. "Benito Cereno's Mute Testimony: On the Politics of Reading Melville's Silences." *Arizona Quarterly: A Journal of American Literature, Culture and Theory* 65 (2): 1–26.
Goodrich, Peter. 2006. "A Theory of the Nomogram." In *Law, Text, Terror*, edited by Peter Goodrich, Lior Barshack and Anton Schütz, 13–33. London: Glasshouse Press/Routledge-Cavendish.
Grewe, William G. 2000. *The Epochs of International Law*, translated by Michael Byers. Berlin: De Gruyter.
Halpern, Faye. 2008. "In Defense of Reading Badly: The Politics of Identification in 'Benito Cereno', Uncle Tom's Cabin, and Our Classrooms." *College English* 70 (6): 551–77.
Hanafin, Patrick. 2004. "The Writer's Refusal and the Law's Malady." *Journal of Law and Society* 31 (1): 3–14.
Hussain, Nasser. 2011. "Air Power." In *Spatiality, Sovereignty and Carl Schmitt: Geographies of the Nomos*, edited by Stephen Legg, 244–50. London and New York: Routledge.
James, C. L. R. (Cyril Lionel Robert). (1938) 2001. *The Black Jacobins: Toussaint L'Ouverture and the San Domingo Revolution*. With an Introduction and Notes by James Walvin. London and New York: Penguin Books.
Kalyvas, Andreas. 2018. "Carl Schmitt's Postcolonial Imagination." *Constellations: An International Journal of Critical and Democratic Theory* 25 (1): 35–53.

Kervégan, Jean François. 1999. "Carl Schmitt and 'World Unity'." In *The Challenge of Carl Schmitt*, edited by Chantal Mouffe, 54–74. London: Verso.

Koskenniemi, Marti. 2002. *The Gentle Civilizer of Nations: The Rise and Fall of International Law 1870–1960*. Cambridge: Cambridge University Press.

Lanchester, Fulco. 2005. "Un giurista davanti a se stesso. Intervista a Carl Schmitt." In *Carl Schmitt, Un giurista davanti a se stesso*, edited by Giorgio Agamben, 151–83. Vicenza: Neri Pozza.

Locke, John. (1689) 1988. *Two Treatises of Government*, edited with an Introduction and notes by Peter Laslett. Cambridge: Cambridge University Press.

Loughlin, Martin. 2015. "Nomos." In *Law, Liberty and the State. Oakshott, Hayek and Schmitt on the Rule of Law*, edited by David Dyzenhaus and Thomas Poole, 65–95. Cambridge: Cambridge University Press.

Mamdani, Mahmood. 2015. "Settler Colonialism: Then and Now." *Critical Inquiry* 41 (3): 596–614.

Mbembe, Achille. 2017. *Critique of Black Reason*. Translated by Laurent Dubois. Durham, NC and London: Duke University Press.

Melville, Herman. 1856. "Benito Cereno." In *The Piazza Tales*, 140–353–. New York: Dix and Edwards and London: Sampson Low, Son & Co.

Miéville, China. 2005. *Between Equal Rights. A Marxist Theory of International Law*. Leiden and Boston, MA: Brill.

Nelson, Dana. 1992. *The World in Black and White: Reading Race in American Literature, 1638–1867*. Oxford: Oxford University Press.

Otero, Carlos A. 2005. "From the *Nomos* to the Meridian." *The South Atlantic Quarterly* 104 (2): 381–88.

Pottage, Alain. 2019. "Holocene Jurisprudence." *Journal of Human Rights and the Environment* 10 (2): 153–75.

Rancière, Jacques. 2001. "Ten Theses on Politics." Translated by Rachel Bowlby with Davide Panagia. *Theory & Event*, 5(3). doi:10.1353/tae.2001.0028.

Schmitt, Carl. 1916. *Theodor Däublers "Nordlicht": Drei Studien über die Elemente, den Geist und die Aktualität des Werkes*. Munich: Georg Müller.

Schmitt, Carl. 1987a. "Interrogation of Carl Schmitt by Robert Kempner." *Telos* 72: 97–107.

Schmitt, Carl. 1987b. "On Grossraum, the Hitler regime, and collaboration. Answers to Allegations." *Telos* 72: 107–29.

Schmitt, Carl. 1995. Die Ordnung der Welt nach dem zweitenWeltkrieg. In *Carl Schmitt, Staat, Grossraum, Nomos: Arbeiten aus den Jahren 1916–1969*, edited by Günter Maschke, 592–618. Berlin: Duncker & Humblot.

Schmitt, Carl. 1996. "The Land Appropriation of a New World." *Telos* 109: 29–80.

Schmitt, Carl. 2003. *The Nomos of the Earth in the International Law of the Jus Publicum Europaeum*, translated and annotated by G. L. Ulmen. New York: Telos Press Publishing.

Schmitt, Carl. 2009. *Hamlet or Hecuba. The Introduction of Time into the Play*, translated by David Pan and Jennifer Rust. New York: Telos Press Publishing.

Schmitt, Carl. 2011. "The *Grossraum* Order of International Law with a Ban on Intervention for Spatially Foreign Powers: A Contribution to the Concept of Reich in International Law (1939–1941)". In *Writings on War*, edited by Carl Schmitt and translated by Timothy Nunan, 75–124. Cambridge: Polity Press.

Schmitt, Carl. 2015a. "Dialogue on New Space." In *Carl Schmitt, Dialogues on Power and Space*, edited by Andreas Kalyvas and Federico Finchelstein, translated by S. G. Zeitlin, 51–83. Cambridge: Polity Press.

Schmitt, Carl. 2015b. *Land and Sea. A World-Historical Meditation*, translated by S. G. Zeitlin. New York: Telos Press Publishing.

Schmitt, Carl. 2017. *Ex Captivitate Salus: Experiences, 1945–47*, translated by Matthew Hannah. Cambridge: Polity Press.

Scudder, Harold H. 1928. "Melville's 'Benito Cereno' and Captain Delano's Voyages." *PMLA* 4 (2): 502–32.

Sollors, Werner. 2020. ""Better to Die by Them than Die for Them": Carl Schmitt Reads Benito Cereno." *Critical Inquiry* 46 (2): 401–20.

Sundquist, Eric. 1987. "Suspense and tautology in Benito Cereno." In *Herman Melville's "Billy Budd", "Benito Cereno", "Bartleby the Scrivener" and Other Tales*, edited by Harold Bloom. 81-106. Modern Critical Interpretations. New York: Chelsea House.

Thomas, Brook. 1987. *Cross Examination of Law and Literature: Cooper, Hawthorne, Stowe and Melville*. Cambridge: Cambridge University Press.

Tripp, Colleen. 2017. "Beyond the Black Atlantic: Pacific Rebellions and the Gothic in Herman Melville's 'Benito Cereno'." *Journal of Transnational American Studies* 8 (1). http://dx.doi.org/10.5070/T881022879 Retrieved from https://escholarship.org/uc/item/5k00f4gh

Chapter 4

Unlearning, (un)naming, cohabiting

Karin van Marle

Introduction

The notion of "unlearning" is pivotal when reflecting on possibilities to respond to the complexities of transformation, postcoloniality and decoloniality. Gayatri Spivak (1993) has explained that where initially she referred to unlearning in the context of being a "subject of knowledge within the institution of neo-colonial learning" she later shifted to the question of ethics, asking:

> How is it possible to imagine as the subject of ethics – that is to say, the human being who thinks of doing the right thing (and therefore is capable of doing the wrong thing) for the other person? How is it possible to think such a subject outside of the monotheist Judeo-Christian tradition and its critique?
>
> (25)

I draw on both notions of unlearning referred to by Spivak – the unlearning of certain privileged knowledges that disallowed others but also what it might mean to act in an ethical way.

I am interested in thinking about "unlearning" within the context of land appropriation as constitutive of *nomos* (Schmitt 2003, 78), but also within the context of epistemic violence and related to it, language. To what extent is the right to land, ownership and property inherently linked to a certain system of knowledge and with that the imposition of a certain language? How does language relate to the idea of *nomos* as fundamental, as constitutive? Central to Spivak's notions of unlearning is the unlearning of privilege that includes also the unlearning of certain knowledge that should result in the giving up of power and privilege relating to the knowledge itself, but also the language in which theories, concepts and methods manifest themselves. What must be unlearned, then, relates to the occurrence of the epistemic, linguistic and territorial violence that accompanied conquest. In this chapter, I tentatively argue that spatiality as a relation is bounded to epistemology and language; that to think about spatial justice involves thinking about epistemic justice and language.

DOI: 10.4324/9780203712771-4

The project linked to this collection focusses on the work of German scholar Carl Schmitt – notorious for his support of Nazism but rediscovered by crits[1] a number of years ago – in *The Nomos of the Earth* (1950). Significant for my consideration is his writing on naming (Schmitt 2003, 336–50). Naming stands central to the relation between epistemology, language and spatiality. In other words, naming underlies what we know about land and property as well as how we think about it; which theories inform and guide our views; in what language we speak about it.

Henri Lefebvre's (1996) distinction between habitat and inhabitance, and Chris Butler's (2012b) careful reflections on this distinction are of importance for my argument. A concern with habitat can be taken to refer to a mere functionalist approach to housing provision, whereas inhabitance encompasses so much more: over and above the actual structure it opens possibilities for how one lives, for political engagement and for affect. This distinction is helpful for me in exploring and thinking about spatial and epistemic justice, but also language and naming. My argument is that to enjoy inhabitance, one's knowledge and language should be valued. I consider what it could mean to read inhabitance with cohabitance, Hannah Arendt's notion of sharing the world with others (Arendt 1994; Butler 2012). Inhabitance includes not only "the right to the city" but also the right to difference (Butler 2012, 133) that could open the possibility of sharing the world with others. Related to the notion of inhabitance and cohabitance is the question of belonging. Important for my reflection is how epistemology and language affect inhabitance, cohabitance and belonging. I draw on Stewart Motha (2018), who in his recent work, *Archiving Sovereignty*, reflects on the notion of belonging.

The connection between language and land is central to literature and poetry in South Africa. Not only has the traditional farm novel filled many libraries over the years, the subversion of this genre has become prominent. I reflect on some of the writings by JM Coetzee and Antjie Krog as attempts to respond to what Coetzee (1992, 97) aptly calls "the failure of love". I consider whether through unlearning, alternative knowledges, languages, other approaches to language and ultimately to land and property could be disclosed by engaging Walter Mignolo's (2000) notion of "'border thinking', Boaventura de Sousa Santos" (2007) call for "post-abyssal thinking" and "subaltern cosmopolitanism", and Magobe Ramose's (2012) embrace of reconfiliation and the African ethic of Ubuntu. I consider these towards the end of the chapter but want to situate all of these ideas within Mignolo's (2011, xvi) reframing of the Cartesian notion of "I think therefore I am" to "I am where I think" or "I am where I do and think".

(Un)naming

In this section I recall Schmitt's view on the relation between naming and appropriation, whereafter I consider Mignolo and de Sousa Santos's views on Western epistemology and thinking. I explore the link between naming (and for my purpose naming is always already a manifestation of epistemology and language) and spatial injustice. I discuss a case on naming, or rather "unnaming" in which a minority rights organisation challenged the City Council of Pretoria/ Tshwane for changing a number of street names.

Schmitt (2003, 336) tells us that there are three "powerful statements about power". Firstly, that power has an impulse to secrecy, no rules can say no to the temptation to hide. A second feature is the centrality of power and the dialectics that it creates where the ruler, in order to remain in power should constantly organise new ways through which he can access power that involves more secrecy and eventually isolates the rules from the world he rules. It is the third feature of power that is most significant to the issue of naming and appropriation, namely the way in which the power to secrecy relates to a countertendency, namely to be visible and to be public (337). Power is articulated often by way of "archy" and "cracy". The former means from the source, while "cracy" relates to "power through superior force and occupation".

Added to "archy" and "cracy" is a third category, *nomos*. Schmitt explains how *nomos* is inherently part of "archy" and "cracy" to the extent that not one of them can exist independently without *nomos* (Schmitt 2003, 338). He shows also the difference between words combined with *nomos* and those with "archy" or "cracy". He explains that monarchy is for example the form of domination by which one rules – "monos" both carries and bears domination or power. In the case of the word "economy" the "oikos" becomes the object and the material of public housekeeping and administration. The crux here is that "A word bound to *nomos* is measured by *nomos* and subject to it …" (338). He goes back to the sixth century when *nemein*, to administer or to govern, was the verb for *nomos* (339).

Many changes have taken place over many years in the meaning and use of the word *nomos*. The most important shift was the transition from the nomadic age to the fixed household, because this shift occurred along with land appropriation that came along with a certain finality in contrast to the habits of nomads (Schmitt 2006, 341). However *nomos* is not limited to the idea of stability that might come with land appropriation, but rather displays its constitutive power by way of becoming law, *lex*. Notable is that *nomos* originates from the word *nemein*, which means to appropriate (Schmitt 2003, 345). *Nemein* could refer to both division (*teilen*), distribution (*verteilen*) and pasturing (*weiden*). Schmitt explains that the fact that *nomos* carries all three meanings shows the deep relation between them. What happens is that *weiden* (pasturing) becomes producing that is preceded by distribution. Distribution and division is then "the original constitution, the concrete primal norm, the beginning of law and property" (345). Schmitt explains that the idea of time immemorial or the legal concepts of prescriptive right and negative prescription could not establish a legal order on its own. The main point here is that appropriation comes first – "not division – not the *divisio primaeva* " (345). But what is the relation between appropriation and naming, *nomos* and *Nahme*; and, connected to naming, the relation between *nomos* and learning?

Schmitt uses the example of marriage to elaborate on the relation between *Nahme* and name – power and name-giving. A man takes a wife and gives her his name; the woman takes his name and so do their children. Similarly in the context of land, the appropriation of land is constituted only "when the appropriator is able to give the land a name" (Schmitt 2003, 348).

After the institutional dismantling of apartheid, the constitutive relationship between *nomos* and naming played out in South Africa in a very concrete way in a case on the naming of streets in the City of Tshwane/Pretoria. A right-wing organisation, Afriforum, challenged the City Council of Pretoria's decision to change the names of a number of streets (City of Tshwane 2016). In the majority judgement, delivered by Chief Justice Mogoeng, the Constitutional Court allowed the City to proceed with changing street names. Mogoeng starts his judgement by recalling South Africa's historical past as reflected in the preamble of the Constitution. The gist of his narrative is how apartheid as a system of institutionalised oppression based on an irrational differentiation between black and white that depicted black people as intellectually inferior and lesser beings, resulted in a situation where there was hardly any city, town, street or institution named after black people's historical leaders. Virtually all recognition and honour was given to white people and the history of white people. In this regard, Mogoeng remarked that "South Africa still looks very much

Figure 4.1 Renaming of streets in Pretoria 1. Source: the author.

like Europe away from Europe" (City of Tshwane 2016, para 12). Afriforum's main argument ironically rested on the contention that their sense of belonging was being infringed by the removal of the old street name signs.

The case raised technical issues – whether an interlocutory order may be appealed or not as well as issues concerning separation of powers, and proper consultation – that I will not address in this chapter. For my purposes it is important to reflect on the notion of belonging: the Chief Justice – rightly to my mind – challenged Afriforum's reliance on belonging, by invoking the sense of belonging of black South Africans living in Tshwane. The majority judgement speaks to how epistemic violence coincided with spatial injustice. Black people in Pretoria were not only forcibly removed, evicted from their houses and given space only on the outskirts of the city, but their history, memories and humanity were simultaneously denied. In Lefebvre's terms, they were thus not only forcibly denied habitat but also inhabitance.

The minority judgement (City of Tshwane 2016, paras 79-162), delivered by Justices Froneman and Cameron, raises a number of complexities in questioning the majority's claim that each and every invocation of white history inevitably will amount to racism. This judgement beckons deeper thinking about what Arendt (1994, 279) calls "wanting to share the earth" interpreted by Butler (2012b 151) as cohabitance and Spivak's questions about ethics. I return to this below. For now, the main aim of referring to this case is to

Figure 4.2 Renaming of streets in Pretoria 2. Source: the author.

relate the issue of street names (and in particular the invocation of a sense of belonging, or home in this context) to language and, precisely, to naming and appropriation. The case demonstrates the power that goes with naming and the slipping away of power that occurs when what one has named, is unnamed and, accordingly, what one knows is demanded to be unlearned.

The case demonstrates also for me something of what inhabitance entails. Henri Lefebvre (1996) lamented the shift from inhabitance to the functionalist concept of habitat, which to him was central to modernism, in particular technological modernism (Butler 2012a, 105). Habitat in this sense, was focused only on economic and technical questions of housing provision (2012, 115–16). In the context of the city of Pretoria/Tshwane one could argue that with the formal end of apartheid and with legislation like the notorious Group Areas Act 41of 1950 repealed, habitat was made possible to all who live in the city, although given the vast homelessness in the city even that claim would be merely theoretical. Inhabitance, on the other hand captures far more and is focused on active and meaningful participation in social life. Inhabitance invokes the struggle for home and for belonging as manifested in the street name issue. It speaks also to epistemology, what we know and the struggle to unlearn.

The question that comes to the fore here is whether inhabitance extends to all who live in a city – how do we respond to a colonial, apartheid, racist past in a way that discloses new ways of engagement and not mere repetitions? This question is related to the notion of unlearning and in light of Schmitt's insight on naming, also to (un)naming. When we confront epistemic violence that occurred with conquest, the need for inhabitance as an insistence not on mere habitat, housing provision or land reform or reparation, comes to the fore. For my purposes, inhabitance goes hand in hand with the call for Western knowledge to be decentralised, for Europe to be provincialised (Chakrabarty 2000), for both understandings of unlearning as explained by Spivak to occur.

Walter Mignolo (2000) has unpacked the inevitable relation between colonialism and modernity. This is important for the purposes of my chapter, because he exposes the complicity between land appropriation and the appropriation of ideas, history and knowledge. Mignolo (Delgado and Romero 2000, 8) explains how the "modern/colonial world" is a product of very specific histories. Imperial Spain made Christianity central, whereas imperial England, together with the French Enlightenment, displaced Christian designs with "secular civilising" ones. The United States, on its part, displaced the "civilizing mission" of the former with a global design of development and modernisation. Mignolo (Delgado and Romero 2000, 8) calls for a "border-thinking", which ties the border to epistemology. He argues that there are a number of macro-narratives guiding how we interpret certain events, from Christian cosmology to the Greeks, to narratives of natural history, not to forget liberal and Marxist cosmologies. The main point here is that all of these are existing Western macro-narratives.

With reference to Spivak, Mignolo (Delgado and Romero 2000, 9) discusses the extent to which the subaltern can't speak for herself, because of the pervasiveness of Western macro-narratives. He argues that not only did both neoliberal and neo-Marxist macro-narratives come to the fore at the height of the building of the nation-state in Europe, but these nation-states were at the same time involved in the "second-wave of colonial expansion" (10). The underlying point here is, as Mignolo rightly argues, that the expansion of capitalism happened simultaneously with the expansion of "concepts, methods and theories". He refers to a "hegemonic 'right' discourse" and asks "[s]hall the world continue to think and speak from the hegemonic models of thinking, from the rights and from the left that emerged in Europe under capitalism?" (10). For Mignolo, "border thinking" is a way to "imagine possible futures". I return to this notion below and read it in conjunction with what de Sousa Santos (2007) calls "post-abyssal thinking" and "subaltern cosmopolitanism"; and Ramose's (2012) support of "reconfiliation". Can these notions disclose possibilities for cohabitance and unlearning – for living differently and ethically in the postcolony?

But let's first look at how Mignolo (Delgado and Romero 2000), like Schmitt, makes the connection between territory and language. He holds that history has shown us "that language is the companion of the empire and a unifying factor of the nation" (12). Language is of course also part and parcel of epistemology. Mignolo illustrates how a certain purification of epistemology happens at the same time as a purification of language. "Furthermore, language is engrained in epistemology and the defense of the purity and hegemony of a language goes hand in hand with the defense of the purity and hegemony of an epistemology" (Delgado and Romero 2000, 13).

The South African example of how a certain standard of white Afrikaans was asserted during apartheid to exclude coloured Afrikaans speakers comes to mind (See for example Grundlingh & Huigen (eds) 2008, in particular the chapter by Willemse 2008, 27). The exclusion of coloured Afrikaners from the standard of Afrikaans as an aspect of the politics of racial separation peculiar to them made spatial exclusion (for example forced removal from places like District Six) and political exclusion (removal from voters' lists) much easier.

Part of Mignolo's notion of border-thinking is the idea of "languaging" (Delgado and Romero 2000, 16) that he contrasts with how the state deals with language. In the case of the latter, language processes become an object, something that can be owned. Grammar, language, epistemology and the law are inextricably intertwined and they are, moreover, powerful instruments controlled by the state. I return to languaging and border thinking as alternatives below, but first turn to the continuation of politics over language in recent times, after which I reveal the link between power, language and land.

Longing for the same

In this section, I reflect on the issue of Afrikaans and how from one strand of Afrikaans speaking people, the insistence on upholding the status quo of the language goes hand in hand with the insistence on the status quo relating to land and property. The campaign that was again led by Afriforum, this time in 2018, against the African National Congress's proposal, to amend the property clause in the Constitution (1996), stands in the guise of a longing for the endurance of colonial spatial organisation.

The student protests at South African universities underscored how the issues of epistemology and language are inextricably linked to the issue of spatial justice – not only at South African universities but also beyond. I have written about this elsewhere and will not repeat my arguments here (Van Marle 2018). However, I want to recall briefly one of the cases in which language policy was tested, namely the case heard by the High Court in Pretoria on the language policy adopted by the University of Pretoria. The case of the University of the Free State's language policy was decided subsequently in the Constitutional Court. The latter case in particular, when read with the street name case referred to above, opens up some of the many complexities and challenges of living together in the postcolony that lie also beyond the focus of this chapter. Here, I focus on the High Court case in Pretoria and read it against what Andrew Nash (2000) calls "the new politics of Afrikaans".

The challenge against the new language policy adopted by the University of Pretoria, similar to the challenge of the change of street names, displays for me a fear that perhaps comes with the insight that losing the power of naming and losing the power of asserting one's own language come also with another loss, the loss of the power over territory. It is exactly this territorial power, the endurance of spatial injustice, that stands in the way of both inhabitance and the possibility of cohabiting.

The case of *Afriforum and another v Chairperson of the Council of the University of Pretoria and others* (Afriforum 2017) was decided in the context of an issue of language that has been prominent in the history of South Africa for many years. The date 16 June 1976 will be remembered as a day when black youth rose up against being forced to learn Afrikaans at government schools all over the country. Over the past few years, language in tertiary education has become contentious. In particular, at formerly white Afrikaans universities, the continuance of Afrikaans as language of tuition has been challenged.

The University of Pretoria (UP) adopted a new language policy in the middle of 2016, doing away with undergraduate tuition in parallel streams of English and Afrikaans and replacing it with English-only tuition. It immediately faced a challenge by Afriforum in court. The UP case was different to other cases brought by Afriforum, challenging for example language policies adopted by the University of Stellenbosch and the Free State, because unlike the latter two, the procedure of adopting a new language policy was not contested. Here, rather, what was contested was the substantive issue of adopting English as the main language of tuition.

In his judgement, Judge Kollapen refers to language as being "considerably more than simply a means of communication; it has been recognised as central to human development and an inextricable part of the construction of human identity" (Afriforum 2017, para 1). He argues that, while language could play a positive role in affirming identity throughout history, there were many occasions in the past where those in power used language to dominate, subjugate and exclude (para 2).

The court had to decide on three issues: (1) whether the newly adopted language policy infringed section 29(2) of the Constitution (the right to mother tongue instruction where reasonably practicable); (2) whether it infringes section 9 (the equality clause) by discriminating unfairly on the basis of language; and (3) whether the newly adopted policy constitutes a breach of existing rights. The court decided against Afriforum on all three challenges, underscoring the role that the university can play in "advancing social cohesion and in providing an important intellectual space where South Africans, in their bewildering diversity, can together reflect on the kind of issues and debates that a young and vibrant society such as ours must confront" (Afriforum 2017, para 73). The distinction between habitat and inhabitance, or more relevant in this context, structural accommodation versus meaningful participation and belonging in university life, is crucial. The main question is not whether the university has the infrastructure (venues and lecturers that can teach in both English and Afrikaans, to link it with what was said above about whether "habitat" is provided), but what the continuous division of classes and students means and does to the search for intellectual spaces in which inhabitance, social cohesion and cohabitance can be strived for. To what extent does the university engage also in the process of unlearning?

I want to refer here to a notion that I reflected on formerly, namely that of the university as a heterogenous public space that underscores Kollapen's judgement (Van Marle 2000; Van Marle 2010). Drawing on Iris Marion Young's (1987, 1990) notion of "street life" together with Jacques Derrida's (1997) reflections on friendship, I contemplated an understanding of democracy that could create the possibility for the university as a truly heterogeneous space and not a space of continuing hegemony. The notion of the university as a heterogeneous public space emphasises the need for plurality and difference, multiple voices and clashing values to be not only protected but actively pursued in the context of the university. Of course, in the sometimes fierce language debates that took place on former Afrikaans campuses the position to hold on to Afrikaans was justified by a call for multi-linguism and against the hegemony of English only. However, the actual implementation of dual-medium language policies prevented exactly the possibility of plural and heterogenous university spaces by dividing Afrikaans and English students and in effect dividing students on racial lines. The holding on to Afrikaans was a call for purity, not plurality or heterogeneity, for maintaining a status quo of spatial privilege and separateness.

Let us look at Andrew Nash's (2000) Marxist analysis of language politics. Nash traces meticulously the way in which the ANC, most notably Thabo Mbeki, dealt with Afrikaners and Afrikaans in the mid-1990s and onwards.

Part of Mbeki's plan was to replace Afrikaans with English. Nash argues that the "elevation of English to de facto language of power, do[es] not benefit the majority of South Africans" (360). For him, such an intervention does not challenge the legacy of apartheid necessarily, and In some instances even continues it. However, it does make it easier for members of the black elite to enter the work place and the economy, but also public life, the media, education and elsewhere.

Nash discusses the views of people like Breyten Breytenbach, Johan Degenaar and André du Toit as examples of prominent Afrikaans dissenting voices against apartheid under apartheid. Breytenbach in 1976 said that "For Afrikaners to live on, Afrikaners must be prepared to 'become compost, decomposing in order to compose other forms'" (Nash 2000, 344). Sadly, Breytenbach's position since the 1990s concerning the protection of Afrikaans as minority language has altered radically. Nash invokes the view of Degenaar, who within the context of Elsa Joubert's *Die swerfjare van Poppie Nongena*[2] said that Afrikaners should show solidarity with people who have been wronged, "whoever they may be" (345). A similar sentiment was echoed by du Toit, with the added dimension that Afrikaner survival was inextricably linked to them having the "political and moral courage to act in solidarity with oppressed people" (347). For Nash, it is precisely here where the new politics of Afrikaans and its supporters fail. For all their reliance on republican politics, their defence of Afrikaans is one that falls squarely in the conception provided by liberal constitutionalism and the capitalist market (348). But more than that, for our purposes here, it is the ongoing appropriation of space through language that matters. As with the street name case the insistence on Afrikaans as a main language of tuition at South African universities is one that echoes and continues previous appropriation.

This continued assertion of space through naming and language stands in direct contrast to Magobe Ramose's call for "reconfiliation" in his critique of the Truth and Reconciliation Commission (Ramose 2012). I return to this notion and consider it together with Mignolo and de Sousa Santos below. Added to the failure of showing solidarity referred to above, the new politics for Afrikaans, based on a postmodern philosophy, negated all blame for the past. Nash explains that the context in which postmodernism came to the fore in other places in the capitalist West was quite different from South Africa. Not only did it arise within a context in which the project of modernity was at an advanced stage; it also came after Marxism (Nash 2000, 348–349).

The main claim against the new politics for Afrikaans and how it connects for me also with the issue of land, law and spatial justice is that it never developed into a "larger programme of social reform" or engaged in any sustained way with "actual historical struggles" (Nash 2000, 352). Even though its supporters offer a critique of capitalism and globalisation, their concern does not lie with the majority of people who suffer under the continuance of systemic inequality, but rather a "cultivated minority, defined by their cultural values, philosophical premises and aesthetic sensibilities" (2000, 353). At the heart of the problem lies the unwillingness to unlearn.

Nash's article was published in 2000 and over the past 18–19 years there have been some shifts. However, the recent brutal fights for Afrikaans in strong racial terms confirm many of his views. Nash predicted that the new politics for Afrikaans will turn out to be a protection for Afrikaans supported by

> people who have a strong material interest in defending the fruits of oppression and exploitation, even if they no longer defend apartheid itself, and opposing any struggle for liberation which goes beyond formal equality to ensure that all South Africans can participate equally in the making of their future.
>
> (2000, 361)

Nash also warned that this process will "forfeit the most valuable parts of the legacy of Afrikaner dissent in South Africa and leave all South Africans the poorer" (2000, 362). The recent court cases around the introduction of new language policies at tertiary institutions and the fierce battle for Afrikaans that surrounds these cases confirm this warning.

As indicated earlier, in 2018 the ANC-led government started the process to amend the property section in the 1996 Constitution to make it clearer that expropriation without compensation should be possible in cases where it is needed for justice to prevail. The response by Afriforum confirms what I regard as their longing to preserve the status quo and pertinently for this chapter, the status quo of colonial and apartheid spatial arrangements. Afriforum released a report dramatically titled "Expropriation without compensation. A disaster in waiting" (Afriforum 2018), in which they amongst other things deny that land was taken from blacks by whites and blame the government's land reform policy as the obstacle in the way of land reform.

Afriforum applied to obtain an urgent interdict against the adoption of the Constitutional Review Committee's first report into land expropriation. The application was dismissed for lack of urgency (Gerber 2018).[3] Afriforum's contestation of both language policy and the recommendation on the amendment of Section 25 make the relation between power, language/naming and land all too apparent.

In the section below, I turn to how, in the novels of JM Coetzee, the issue of language and its relatedness to land comes to the fore. I recall also Antjie Krog's reflections on land and language. There are glimpses and hints of the possibilities of alternative ways to relate to land and language in both Coetzee and Krog.

Crisis and subversion

In this section I consider Coetzee's apt identification of "a failure of love" (Coetzee 1992, 97) and Krog's of the relation between mastery and land as crucial obstacles to the possibility of living together and sharing the world, the land. What alternatives to living together are suggested in their works?

Scholars have commented on how Coetzee in a number of novels, for example *In the heart of the country* (1982), *The life and times of Michael K* (1985), and most notably *Disgrace* (1999) reworked the traditional farm novel (*plaasroman*) (See Smit-Marais and Wenzel 2006, 25). The traditional farm novel treats the relation between farmer and his farm as natural, the reader encounters "an unquestioned right to land" that "express[es] the very soul of the Afrikaner's being" (25). Coetzee, in writing what is called an anti-pastoral farm novel challenges the "dream topography" of the legacy of patriarchy, power and ownership in conjunction with black labour found in the traditional farm novel. What we find in Coetzee's anti-pastoral farm novel is the farm not only as lonely and desolate but also as "a contested space inscribed within a history of violence and dispossession" (26).

I want to focus on three aspects raised by Rita Barnard (2003, 199) in her reflection on Coetzee and in particular *Disgrace*, namely the failure to love; the crisis of linguistic structures and language; and a possible alternative vision of or relation to land. In terms of the failure to love, Barnard contrasts Coetzee's musing in his memoir *Boyhood* on his love for the Karoo farm Voëlfontein, with his acceptance speech of the Jerusalem Prize. In *Boyhood* (Coetzee 1997, 22) he writes: "There is not enough time in a single life to know all of Voëlfontein, know its every stone and bush. No time can be enough when one loves a place with such devouring love". In his acceptance speech, however, he says:

> At the heart of the unfreedom of the hereditary masters of South Africa is a failure of love. To be blunt: their love is not enough today and has not been enough since they arrived on the continent; furthermore, their talk, their excessive talk, about how they love South Africa has consistently been directed toward *the land*, that is, toward what is least likely to respond to love: mountains and deserts, birds and animals and flowers.
>
> (Coetzee 1992, 97)

For Coetzee, for the land to become a place of freedom it needs a different kind of love, one that is more reciprocal (Barnard 2003, 200). He names this love "fraternity" and connects it with liberty and equality and argues that this kind of love will be enjoyed only if the structures of the apartheid state were dismantled. In his view, the "settler's love" will be no more than a "sentimental yearning" "and any aesthetic appreciation of the African landscape" nothing but a "more fundamental hard-heartedness and inhumanity" (200).

Secondly, let us turn to the issue of linguistic structures and language – what Barnard calls "a crisis of definitions, relationships and responsibilities" that plays out on the level of "fundamental linguistic structures" (2003, 206). She recalls the exposure of the limitations of both English and Afrikaans in *In the heart of the country* that was originally published in bilingual form, with interior monologues and descriptions in English and the dialogues in Afrikaans (208). Similar to contemporary views of English as a new *lingua franca*, English is also the language in the novel that provides access to "metropolitan and international thought". However, it is also the language of alienation. Afrikaans, on the other hand, makes communication in the novel easier, but it "entraps the would-be radical intellectual in a grammar of deference and domination that instantly undermines any hope of establishing more reciprocal relations" (208–209). Barnard notes also one peculiarity of Afrikaans, namely the way in which the second-person pronoun, "you"/"jy" is avoided when speaking to a superior. The language of the traditional farm novel in general expresses social relations in a rigid way.

Coming to *Disgrace*, sociolinguistic processes in relation to transformation are raised. Barnard argues that the spatial location of the farm, that the farm is placed in the Eastern Cape, is significant. In contrast to *In the heart of the country*, *The life and times of Michael K* and *Boyhood*, situated in the Karoo where the linguistic choice is between English and Afrikaans, in the Eastern Cape the linguistic choices include English, Afrikaans, isiXhosa, as well as the nonstandard English of the isiXhosa speakers (2003, 210). The various transformations and challenges that the characters in the novel are confronted with come to the fore in terms of linguistic competence or failure. Barnard cites the following passage from the novel when Lurie is unable to protect his daughter from attack and rape: "He speaks Italian, he speaks French, but Italian and French will not save him here in the darkest of Africa. He is helpless …" (2003, 211). Barnard observes: "At this moment Lurie's failure to translate is complete …".[4]

We could recall also an interview with Coetzee in which he was asked to reflect on the "failure of landscape literature to find a language that is authentically African". Barnard notes how Coetzee responded rather impatiently that there is a "plenitude of languages available to the poet in Africa…languages devoid of a European past and undeniably embedded in African experiences". He continued by adding that since African languages don't have a scenic tradition landscape writers who wanted "to move into [African] languages and make use of them…would probably have lost their scenic ambitions as well" (2003, 213–214). Barnard observes that even though one might be left with the impression that the issue of what languages are "fitting" in Africa has been dealt with by Coetzee in this interview, it seems as if *Disgrace* returns to these complexities. She quotes from the novel:

> More and more he is convinced that English is an unfit medium for the truth of South Africa. Stretches of English code whole sentences long have thickened, lost their articulations, their articulateness, their articulatedness. Like a dinosaur expiring and settling in the mud, the language has stiffened. Pressed into the mould of English, Petrus' story would come out arthritic, bygone.
>
> (2003, 214)

Thirdly, I want to reflect on the extent to which Coetzee offers an alternative vision of rural life and relationship with the land. Barnard (2003, 222) notes that in *Disgrace* there is a hint of "giving up" that albeit "disconcerting and morally ambiguous" could offer something different from "a settling of accounts and the paying of a price". It could be noted that one of Ramose's (2012, 33) main critiques of the Truth and Reconciliation Commission is the extent to which it followed a "bookkeeping model" of reconciliation. Barnard reads Lurie's refusal to save one special dog as an acceptance of "perhaps helplessly, perhaps resolutely, the claims of an infinite number of creatures with whom he has no special connection" (222). These creatures are not his own kind and also do not fall in the easy category of "historical victims" (222). Is Lurie opening himself to the possibility of unlearning?

Lurie, when faced with an ethical question of how to act undergoes an experience of unlearning. In giving up the dog that he has grown to love, Lurie is acting in a way that can't be related to "kinship, labour, ownership, or debts – or anything that can be made sense of in the moral economy of the colonial or postcolonial pastoral" (Barnard 2003, 222). However, Barnard warns that the final scene of the book should not be forced into a moral answer or way forward – "It remains strange: unexpected, unpredictable…Coetzee…reminds us that the radically new, both in literature and society, will be impossible to predict and difficult to welcome" (223). The character in *Disgrace* that could be read to present an alternative relation to land is Lucy, Lurie's daughter. She has no desire to ownership, and therefore no desire to mastery. Her wish is to work the land, to grow vegetables. Lucy can be read as refusing (unlearning) what is expected from her; she has started the process of unlearning (see also Van Marle 2009).

Antjie Krog, within the context of land reform, argues as follows: "We require a fundamental shift – a new kind of literacy in systemic thinking through relationships, context, patterns and processes relating to land: not extracting from land but in fact learning from it" (2015, 207). What Krog calls the "problematic and dubious relationship with land" in South Africa is central to my argument. We need to recall that historically, the conflation of land and a certain idea of freedom that relates to mastery and ownership of land go back to the beginning of colonialism in the original land appropriation. Krog notes for example the connection between owning a farm and having "uncontested power" (2015, 210). She explores these relationships and connections by addressing a number of poetic traditions and poems on land and discovers these relations and connections of mastery in many South African cultural groups. An obvious example is the relation between mastery over land and patriarchy in a poem that says that when a man owns a farm he owns also a wife and children and slaves. (We can recall here Schmitt's (2003, 347) invocation of the institution of marriage in which 'man *took* a wife').

Commenting on the farm novel Krog (2015) draws on Coetzee in *White writing* (1998) who responded to the "unreal idyll in Afrikaans farm novels" by asking

> Was there no time before the time of the forefathers, and whose was the land then? Do white hands truly pick the fruit, reap the grain, milk the cows, shear the sheep in these bucolic retreats? Who truly creates wealth? (210)

Krog finds in a poem by St J Page Yako a relationship between land and a culture of humaneness and care being built every day. The central message of the poem is that it is the land that makes "the naturalness of caring possible" (212). The main idea is that doing things like sowing, planting and harvesting allows one to be humane. Krog finds in one of Thabo Mbeki's speeches an example of a "radical embeddedness with the land", a certain "interrelatedness that speaks 'both an epistemological and ontological dynamic' – a way of knowing and being that is *relational*" (219) in the sense that humans are all related to each other, but at the same time also related to the land.

Krog (2015) is concerned about what she sees as an inability "to map a new ethos of being land-owned as opposed to being landowner" (219). She explains what being land-owned as opposed to being a landowner might mean by drawing on Václav Havel's notion that ethics derives from a sense of belonging. For Krog there possibly lies a different ethics towards land in the notion of being owned by the land instead of owning the land that will bring about a "radical decentering" (219). Krog's vision is for a relationship with land where no one is master, "baas", where farming is "for all of us, for the sake of the land" (219). No one is free, no one claims the land. For her there is a sign of landowners being confronted by "a 'radical discontinuity' between their bourgeois private life and what one can described as an 'unimaginable' decentering of white political and cultural power" (220). It is in this context that Krog thinks that one can start to imagine the relations of power, mastery and patriarchy to be split up, displaced, fragmented.

Unlearning

> "It is part of morality not to be at home in one's home…Wrong life cannot be lived rightly".
>
> (Adorno 2005, 39)

The specific interest for this chapter was to start to reflect on how claims to land intersect with naming, claims to language and calls for epistemic justice and unlearning. Drawing on Schmitt's writing on naming and Mignolo's critical engagement with Western modernity and its imposition of epistemology I unpacked the entanglement between epistemic and spatial injustice. What we get from Coetzee is how the "love for the land" failed to extend to a love for people. The main concern underlying this chapter is how spatial and epistemic injustice manifest in a "failure to love" that makes living together, cohabitance and belonging impossible. Is it possible through unlearning and unnaming to disclose possibilities for such cohabitance?

Above I have referred to Mignolo's notion of "border thinking" and "languaging"; de Sousa Santos' call for "subaltern cosmopolitianism" and Ramose's (following Anthony Obina) call for the notion of "reconfiliation". Let me start with the latter, "reconfiliation" refers to the bringing together of sons and daughters. For Ramose this invokes granting, effecting, regaining and reclaiming and is intimately connected to the African ethical dimension of community (2012, 35). The latter refers to the notion of Ubuntu as the way in which humans are related to other living people but also to those who have left this world and those who are yet to be born. Ubuntu in this regard has a specific temporal dimension that challenges Western linear understandings of time as linear and chronological. I am interested also in the spatial dimensions of Ubuntu – if people are always already related to each other, this relation takes place in a specific space; it is not an abstract idea but one that is materially grounded.

This understanding of relationality also speaks to the relation between thinking and being; Mignolo's "I think where I am and do" comes to mind. Drawing on Levinas, Ramose argues for a way of living together in South Africa that might allow the "epiphany of the face" (2012, 35). Referring to living in poverty he says: "This is the living experience of reconfiliation in South Africa. It is the face that has come into being not by legal fiat but born out of existential necessity to recognize the other as a brother or a sister and promote their well-being instead of killing them softly or instantly" (36). This notion of reconfiliation could also link with Spivak's notion of unlearning as an ethical question – how to respond to others in a moral way?

I have referred above to Motha's (2018) engagement with belonging. He sees in Ramose's philosophy of Ubuntu "a fluidity – the possibility of movement toward another, more just dispensation" (129). However Motha cautions against what he sees as an "anticolonial longing for the recovery of the 'lost' sovereignty of the indigenous people of South Africa" (132) that stands in tension with the possibility of "postcolonial becoming" that he reads as central to the philosophy of Ubuntu and, as indicated above, the notion of reconfiliation. Motha notes that Ramose doesn't subscribe to a fixity of being, but rather sees it as an ongoing process that opens possibilities for becoming including unlearning.

Mignolo (Delgado and Romero 2000, 11) argues for border-thinking from where we can explore the possibilities to "imagine possible futures". With border-thinking he means that we should engage with colonialism and Western epistemologies from the position of the subaltern. Border-thinking underscores that we should change the terms and not merely the content of the conversation. Mignolo is asking for "the space for an epistemology that comes from the border and aims toward political and ethical transformation" (11). Linked to the idea of border-thinking is what he calls "languaging", namely to understand language as a process rather than a mere object or technical instrument to make communication possible (17). Language from this perspective is an integral part of life.

De Sousa Santos (2007, 63) resonating with Mignolo, holds that "subaltern cosmopolitanism" urges one to ask who needs cosmopolitianism? For him, the answer to this question is simple as it includes all victims of intolerance and discrimination, whose dignity is denied, whose citizenship is denied. Subaltern cosmopolitanism stands in opposition to hegemonic conceptions of cosmopolitanism. He insists on the relation between social and cognitive justice and says that there can be not one without the other. An important connection between his notion of subaltern cosmopolitanism and that of Ubuntu is the sense of incompleteness attached to both. As Ubuntu opens up to a continuous becoming, what de Sousa Santos calls "post-abyssal thinking" comes from the idea that "the diversity of the world is inexhaustible" and that "the epistemological diversity of the world does not yet have a form" (65)

What could border-thinking, reconfiliation, ubuntu and subaltern cosmopolitanism mean for cohabitation, for living together and sharing the world? Butler in her engagement with Arendtian cohabitation explains that cohabitation would ask for a "personal and societal shift" in how disadvantaged groups are treated. She invokes the question of "what it might mean to live together" within a context of certain histories of dispossession and violence (Filar 2014; Butler 2012). Following Hannah Arendt's call for cohabitation as an "ethical demand", she observes: "People who expect enmity to suddenly convert into love are probably using the wrong model. I think what Hannah Arendt meant when she said that 'we cannot choose with who we cohabit the world' is that all of those who inhabit the world have a right to be here by virtue of their being here at all" (Butler in Filar 2014, 3)

By unlearning, by re-thinking the border from the border, or from the position of subaltern cosmopolitanism, and by postcolonial becoming we will not reach the "love" that Coetzee asks for. Given the fraught history of postcolonial dispossession and disregard of all epistemologies not Western, sudden conversion will not be possible. Maybe all we can hope for is what de Sousa Santos (2007, 79) calls a "deep self-reflective undertaking" that might bring to the fore "solidary participation in the construction of a personal and collective future, without ever being sure that past mistakes will not be repeated".

Notes

1 I refer here to scholars working in critical theory in general, for example amongst others Chantal Mouffe and Ernesto Laclau who engaged with the ideas of Schmitt in their reflections on democracy (See Mouffe (1997)) but also scholars working in a critical legal tradition turning to Schmitt to reflect on sovereignty, liberalism and more (Arvidsson, Brännström & Minkkinen 2016).

2 The novel was translated by the author herself in 1980 as *The Long Journey of Poppie Nongena.*
3 Because the application was dismissed simply for lack of urgency a written judgment is not available.
4 There are also more subtle failures of the inability to make meaning possible in a multilingual environment in the novel. Barnard recalls a conversation between Lurie and Petrus after the attack on him and Lucy in which the gap in understanding is underscored.

References

Adorno, T. 2005. *Minima moralia. Reflections on a damaged life*, translated by EFN Jephcott. London: Verso.

Arvidsson, Matilda, Brännström, Leila & Minkkinen, Panu. eds. 2016. *The Contemporary Relevance of Carl Schmitt: Law, Politics, Theology*. Abingdon: Routledge.

Afriforum vs Chairperson of the Council of the University of Pretoria. 2017. 1 All SA 832 (GP) Case no 54451/2016.

Afriforum. 2018. *Expropriation Without Compensation: A Disaster in Waiting.* https://afriforum.co.za/wp-content/uploads/2021/11/AfriForum-Memorandum_Expropriation-without-Compensation_A-disaster-in-waiting.pdf

Arendt, Hannah. 1994. *Eichman in Jerusalem. A report on the banality of evil.* New York: Penguin.

Barnard, Rita. 2003. ""JM Coetzee"s "disgrace" and the South African pastoral." *Contemporary Literature* 44 (2): 199–224.

Butler, Chris. 2012a. *Henri Lefebvre. Spatial politics, everyday life and the right to the city.* New York: Routledge Glass House.

Butler, Judith. 2012b. *Parting ways. Jewishness and the critique of Zionism.* New York: Columbia University Press.

Chakrabarty,Dipesh. 2000. *Provincialising Europe.* Princeton, NJ: Princeton University Press.

City of Tshwane Metropolitan Municipality vs Afriforum and Another. 2016. (6) SA 279 (CC) *City of Tshwane Metropolitan Municipality vs Afriforum Case* CCT 157/15.

Coetzee, Carli. 1997. "The Afrikaans farm novel and idealised sons: CM van den Heever"s farm novels as narratives of the nation." *Alternation* 4 (2): 114–122.

Coetzee, James. 1982. *In the heart of the country.* Harmondsworth: Penguin.

Coetzee, James. 1985. *Life and times of Michael K.* Harmondsworth: Penguin.

Coetzee, James. 1992. *Doubling the point: Essays and interviews*, edited by Atwell, David. Cambridge, MA: Harvard University Press.

Coetzee, James. 1997. *Boyhood. Scenes from provincial life.* New York: Penguin.

Coetzee, James. 1998. *White writing: On the culture of letters in South Africa.* New Haven, CT: Yale University Press.

Coetzee, James. 1999. *Disgrace.* London: Secker and Warburg.

Danius, Sara, Jonsson, Stefan and Spivak, Gayatri. 1993. "An interview with Gayatri Chakravorty Spivak." *Boundary 2.* 20 (2): 24–50.

Delgado, Elana and Romero, Rolando. 2000. "Local histories and global designs: An interview with Walter Mignolo." *Discourse* 22 (3): 7–33.

Derrida, Jacques. 1997. *Politics of friendship.* London: Verso.

Filar, Ray. 2014. "Willing the impossible: An interview with Judith Butler." www.opendemocracy.net/transformation/ray-filla/willing-impossible-interview-with-judith-butler

Gerber, Jan. 2018. "Court dismisses Afriforum's urgent bid to interdict parliament's land expropriation report." https://www.news24.com/SouthAfrica/News/court-dismisses-afriforums-urgent-bid-to-interdict-parliaments-land-expropriation-report-20181130

Grundlingh, Albert and Huigen, Siegfried (Eds.). 2008. *Van Volksmoeder tot Fokofpolisiekar. Kritiese opstelle oor Afrikaanse herinneringsplekke*. Stellenbosch: Sun Press.

Krog, Antjie. 2015. "Baas van die plaas/Izwe lethu: Essay in fragments and two villanelles exploring different relationships to land in some indigenous poetic texts." In *Land divided land restored. Land reform in South Africa for the 21st century*, edited by Ben Cousins and Cheryl Walker, 206–231. Sunnyside: Jacana Press.

Lefebvre, Henri. 1996. *Writings on cities*, edited by E. Kofman and E. Lebas. Oxford: Blackwell.

Mignolo, Walter. 2000. *Local Histories /Global Designs: Coloniality, Subaltern Knowledges, and Border Thinking*. Princeton: Princeton University Press.

Mignolo, Walter. 2011. *The darker side of Western modernity*. London: Duke University Press.

Motha, Stewart. 2018. *Archiving sovereignty. Law, history, violence*. Ann Arbor, MI: University of Michigan Press.

Mouffe, Chantal. 1997. "Carl Schmitt and the paradox of liberal democracy". *The Canadian Journal of Law and Jurisprudence* 10(1): 21–33.

Nash, Andrew. 2000. "The new politics of Afrikaans." *South African Journal of Philosophy* 19 (4): 340–364.

Ramose, Magobe. 2012. "Reconciliation and reconfiliation in South Africa." *Journal on African Philosophy* 5: 20–38.

Santos, Boaventura de Sousa. 2007. "Beyond abyssal thinking. From global lines to ecologies of knowledges." *Review* XXX: 45–89.

Schmitt, Carl. 2003. *Nomos of the earth in the international law of the Jus Publicum Europaeum*. Translated by G. L. Ulmen. New York: Telos Press.

Smit-Marais, Susan and Wenzel, Marita. 2006. "Subverting the pastoral: The transcendence of space and place in JM Coetzee"s Disgrace." *Literator* 27 (7): 23–38.

Van Marle, Karin. 2000. "Universities as heterogeneous public spaces." *Codicillus* 41(1): 32–44.

Van Marle, Karin. 2009. *Refusal, transition and post-apartheid law ed*. Stellenbosch: SUN Media.

Van Marle, Karin. 2010. "Jurisprudence, friendship and the university as heterogeneous public space." *South African Law Journal*, 127(4): 628–645.

Van Marle Karin. 2018. "Life is not simply fact: Aesthetics, atmosphere and the neolibeal university." *Law and Critique* 29 (3): 293–310.

Willemse, Hein. 2008. "'n Kleurlingkenner se kleurling." In *Van Volksmoeder tot Fokofpolisiekar. Kritiese opstelle oor Afrikaanse herinneringsplekke*, edited by Albert Grundlingh and Siegfried Huigen, 27–37. Stellenbosch: Sun Press.

Young, Iris Marion. 1987. "Impartiality and the civic public. Some implications of feminist critiques of moral and political theory." In *Feminism as critique: On the politics of gender*, edited by Seyla Benhabib and Drucilla Cornell, 56–76. Cambridge: Polity Press.

Young, Iris Marion. 1990. *Justice and the politics of difference*. Princeton, NJ: Princeton University Press.

Chapter 5

Inventaris van my bankrotskap as digter/Inventory of my poetic bankruptcy

Antjie Krog

inventaris van my bankrotskap as digter

1. ruimtes elf mense snags en 'n kind wat wakkerlê
   (geluide vleesgulsigs)
2. ruimtes bespiedende werklose mans voorvaders ou vrouens
   (iemandslot geflans)
3. ruimtes fetusbloed kleinkinders weeskinders aidssterwendes
   (opdagende sakke breekgoed)
4. ruimtes iets om te eet 'n beker water 'n rustige ontlas
   (heeldagvergend)
5. ruimtes die streel wat somer sing kristallarinks populier
   (oë opaakstollend)
6. ruimtes dertig woorde Zulu vier woorde Engels hengel
   (daaglikse aardbewings)
7. ruimtes oorvuld garsdors in barre klaskamers
   (each one leech one)
8. ruimtes verkragters met name dwelms met kennis
   (by watter rib die mes hart-in glip)
9. ruimtes hoe liefgehê gehoop gevreug ge-innig omgegee
   (generasies wangehoop)
10. hoe huis straat omgeur raak met die uitvoer van hoop
    (ligtheid lagtheid uitmunt dié gebéúr)
11. ruimtes hoe om my verbeelding hierin te stort?
    ek weet nie hoe leef in hierdie ruimtes leef nie

inventory of my poetic bankruptcy

1. spaces eleven people at night and a child lying awake
   (sounds of lust)
2. spaces spying unemployed men ancestors old women
   (someone's patched fate)

DOI: 10.4324/9780203712771-5

3. spaces foetus blood grandchildren orphans people dying of aids
   (bags of broken ones turning up)
4. spaces something to eat a mug of water a peaceful defecation
   (calls for help all day)
5. spaces the caress of summer's song crystal larynx poplar
   (eyes clotting opaquely)
6. spaces thirty words of Zulu four words of English angling
   (daily earthquakes)
7. spaces overflowing barleydry in barren classrooms
   (each one leech one)
8. spaces rapists with names drugs with knowledge
   (below which rib to slip the knife into the heart)
9. spaces how loved hoped rejoiced in brought close cared about
   (generations despaired)
10. how a house a street are perfumed by hope
   (lightness laughter surpassing this happens)
11. spaces how to plunge my imagination into this?
   I don't know how life in these spaces lives

Chapter 6

The ground beneath our feet

Black feminist geography in South African literature

Barbara Boswell

Introduction

More than 20 years after South Africa's transition from white supremacist theocracy to a Black majority democracy, spatial justice has remained elusive for the majority of its citizens. For those dispossessed from land they may have lived on or owned – first by the Native Land Act of 1913; then by apartheid forced removal law, the Group Areas Act of 1950 – redress for this dispossession has been slow in coming, if not impossible to attain.[1] The idea of *nomos*, Carl Schmitt's (2003) formulation of the law, or order, of the materiality of space as being rooted in the ways in which European colonial conquest spread across territories considered "free" space, is one way of making meaning of the intractable problems of access to land and the failure of democratic South Africa to redistribute land as a means of redressing colonial and apartheid spatial injustice.

This essay deploys the concept of Black feminist geography, as articulated by Katherine McKittrick in the monograph *Demonic Grounds: Black Women and the Cartographies of Struggle* (2006), to explore how Black South African women writers, through their fiction and poetry, have articulated a critical Black feminist geography, countering the idea of a colonial/apartheid *nomos* as the taken-for-granted instantiation of South African spatial order. It examines the discursive place-making of Black South African women through literature, starting with the novels of Miriam Tlali and Lauretta Ngcobo, whom I position as the first writers to produce a critical Black feminist geography through their fiction, and concluding with contemporary poetry by Koleka Putuma and Diana Ferrus, who have most recently written about the exclusion of Black bodies in public space, and the ways in which slave geographies are the palimpsest on which the South African landscape rests.

First, I discuss the work of Lauretta Ngcobo and Miriam Tlali, the first Black South African women to publish written novels in English, to examine how they critically explored space in their pioneering novels that depict the experiences of African women under the system of apartheid. This essay argues that Tlali and Ngcobo were the literary pioneers of a type of Black feminist

DOI: 10.4324/9780203712771-6

geography which made visible the spatial injustices of apartheid. I trace how this strand of feminist Black geography shows the fault lines of continued spatial injustice under post-apartheid power regimes, papered over by ideologies of non-racialism and "rainbow nationalism". In examining two poems: Koleka Putuma's "Mountain", and Diana Ferrus's "My Naam is February/My Name is February", this chapter concludes by arguing that contemporary Black feminist poetry about place constitutes a form of feminist geography that makes visible the continued exclusion of Black bodies from contested space.

On *nomos*, Black feminist geography and space

For Schmitt, *nomos* can be understood as the "terrestrial fundament" (2003:47) – the literal and figurative grounding from which law, in any given territory, springs. Articulated as a theory of the interaction between law and space by Schmitt in 1950, *nomos* is, inter alia, "the immediate form in which the political and social order of a people becomes spatially visible" (2003:70). *Nomos*, while translated as "law", holds additional meanings when its etymology is parsed. Mitchell (2006:4–5) decodes its multiple meanings as follows:

> Rather than a simple noun, the word is a *nomen actionis*, which indicates an action as a process whose content is given in the verb. The action and process of *nomos* is given by the Greek verb *nemein*, meaning to take, to allot and to assign, which in turn is the root of the German words, *nehmen* and *Nahme*.

Nomos is thus that which orders global spatial politics and has its genesis in the expansion of global colonisation and the concomitant seizure of land by European nations:

> In [Schmitt's] clearest definition of the term, *nomos* is rooted in a primary moment of land-appropriation as the basis for justice, sovereignty and distribution in a given community. For Schmitt, therefore, the global spatial order goes beyond mere geography: it is something more akin to an unconscious archetype, albeit fixed in concrete knowledge and practice.
>
> (More 2014)

Nomos thus constructs, in Cover's (1983:4) famous formulation, "a normative universe". Ritu Birla (2011) brings Judith Butler's theory of performativity to bear on Cover's version of *nomos*. For Birla as for Cover, law as *nomos* implies "law as convention, what is done and what is accepted" (2011:91). Yet, at the same time, *nomos* as convention exposes a problem of agency: "who is the agent of convention?" (Birla 2011:91). Birla, however, continues to "draw attention to the temporal and spatial situatedness of convention" (2011:91) and, in so doing, she shows that *nomos* as convention frames subjects as always-already acted upon by spatial formation, without accounting sufficiently for how subjects and space mutually constitute each other – an aspect of *nomos* that, for Schmitt, is fundamental. By emphasising the spatiality of nomos, Birla unearths the dialectical constitution of *nomos* as the 'unity of order and emplacement' (Schmitt 2003; Chryssostalis 2013). This, in turn, allows Birla to read *nomos* through the lens of Butler's theory of performativity, which opens up a discursive space to destabilise the naturalisation of *nomos* as simply the given material, "conventional" order of things.

It is within this discursive space of performativity, as opposed to given normativity, that I position the four writers' work I examine in this essay as performing a Black feminist geography which deconstructs the normativity of South African *nomos*. Black feminist geography (McKittrick 2006) (McKittrick and Woods 2007) has been conceived of as a heuristic tool for mapping the place-making practices of Black subjects who inhabit the margins of discursive and geographical space. McKittrick and Woods (2007) posit oppositional Black geography as a set of theories for analysing both the spatiality of race and the ways in which Black subjects respond to and resist the oppressive geographies produced through racialisation. Such resistance can thus be read as resisting colonial-apartheid *nomos*, which, in upholding the normative order of space in a settler colonial and apartheid society, South Africa, produces racialised space and racially inequitable access to space. McKittrick and Woods argue that Black human geographies can be read as ways to determine "how the lives of these [black] subjects demonstrate how the "common-sense" workings of modernity and citizenships are worked out, and normalised, through geographies of exclusion" (2007:4).

McKittrick further examines the ways in which Black women reconfigure space through Black, womanist geographies. Geographies here mean not only the social science of geography, but also the art Black women make that accounts for the ways in which domination becomes spatially entrenched in landscapes. For McKittrick, Black women's art and activism form a feminist standpoint informed by their experiences of oppression on the grounds of their gender, race, and often, class positions. This positionality provides fertile ground from which to push back against the seemingly intractable oppressive structures produced by *nomos*.

> Black women's histories, lives, and spaces must be understood as enmeshing with traditional geographic arrangements in order to identify a different way of knowing and writing the social world and to expand how the production of space is achieved across terrains of domination.
>
> (McKittrick 2006:xiv)

Such feminist Black geography asks and answers questions around what it means when a Black feminist consciousness critiques the taken-for-grantedness of the way spaces are configured. It accounts for women's agency in resisting nomos, and makes visible the ways in which such agencies remake space. Through refusing to remain in those physically and intellectually demarcated spaces deemed "their place", Black feminist geographers such as the writers examined in this chapter, are engaged in a form of critical Black geography, deploying their art as activism which seeks, ultimately, to reconfigure space as a social justice project.

Writing Black space during apartheid: Miriam Tlali and Lauretta Ngcobo

Elsewhere I have written about Tlali and Ngcobo as the first South African writers who produced a critical Black feminist geography with which to counter apartheid domination (Boswell 2020). Tlali's novel, *Muriel at Metropolitan* (1975), later republished as *Between Two Worlds*, was the first novel in English to be published by a Black woman within the South African nation-state. The novel portrayed the life of Muriel, an educated African woman who works as a debtors' clerk in the fictional Metropolitan furniture store in Johannesburg, reflecting the daily gross and petty humiliations of apartheid spatiality as it plays out in the store.

The novel was banned upon publication, and the author endured police raids, being beaten and detained as a result of the attention it garnered. At the height of her persecution by apartheid police's notorious "Special Branch", she even resorted to burying her work-in-progress in plastic bags in her backyard every night as a way of preserving her manuscripts.

In *Muriel at Metropolitan*, Muriel's race positions her as a liminal figure both in the city of Johannesburg and the store in which she works, which are both spatially racialised as belonging to white South Africans. Within these racially codified spaces, Muriel embodies abjection. Yet, like countless other Black bodies, she is also that which is needed: her labour is indispensable for the smooth functioning of Johannesburg and the store. Muriel's presence in the city and on a shopfloor that simultaneously needs and rejects her works as a critique of apartheid spatiality and points to Tlali's production of an oppositional Black geography, which makes visible the "unknowable" and figuring these unknowable bodies into the "production of space" (McKittrick and Woods 2007:4).

In contrast to *Muriel at Metropolitan*, Ngcobo's *And They Didn't Die* is set against the sweeping backdrop of an impoverished reserve to which the main character, Jezile, is banished. Published in 1990, *And They Didn't Die* was Ngcobo's second novel, written and published in England, where Ngcobo was in exile. Ngcobo's lauded second novel offers an epic narrative including the experiences of three generations of African women, confined to the spatial desert of an apartheid Bantustan. Focalised through the chief character, Jezile, the novel produces a unique point of view from the perspective of the rural African woman, showing the cruel, dehumanising effects of the 1913 Land Act on African women and their families.

Set in the small, rural reserve of Sigageni, the novel explicates the effects of apartheid on the most dispossessed group in South Africa: Black rural women, confined to the Bantustans through apartheid law. Separated from her husband, a migrant worker in Durban, by the Pass Laws which prohibit her from entering and living with him in the city, Jezile is forced to live with her mother-in-law in abject poverty. Because apartheid prohibits her from working in the city, she ekes out a living as a subsistence farmer. The novel graphically illustrates the impact of the 1913 Land Act, which devastated Africans by removing them from ancestral land. It also highlights the brutally exploitative migrant labour system operated by the apartheid government.

Like Tlali's novel, *And They Didn't Die* is pioneering in its portrayal of the experiences of Black women, giving its main characters' textured and complex lives, intellectual curiosity and voices unparalleled in South African literature at the time of their publication. Its analysis of Jezile's life constitutes a complex representational matrix, making it one of the first South African texts to use intersectionality to theorise African women's lives, pointing to the ways in which both apartheid white supremacy and African patriarchy oppressed African women.

Both Tlali and Ngcobo's characters, through their critical consciousness of apartheid spatiality, demonstrate how "practices of domination, sustained by [white hegemony's] unitary vantage point, naturalize both identity and place, repetitively spatialising where non-dominant groups 'naturally' belong".

Muriel and Jezile's unique oppositional vantage points, their questioning of their "place" within the spaces that dehumanise them, serve to interrogate the natural order of apartheid spatiality, drawing into question the idea that space "just is" (McKittrick xi). In writing characters who question the belonging or unbelonging bestowed by their social order, Tlali and Ngcobo succeed in separating their characters' identities from the oppressive spaces in which they find themselves, denaturalising these respective racialised spaces. Ngcobo, like Tlali, shows the inhumanity of apartheid spatiality, highlighting the inconsistencies and failures of logic in white supremacy's ordering of space.

In examining Putuma and Ferrus's poems, I draw on the intersectional feminist theorising of space produced by Tlali and Ngcobo in these respective novels. I position Ferrus and Putuma as writers who have not only had their path as writers cleared by the pioneering work of Tlali and Ngcobo, but also as Black feminist writers who continue the tradition of critical spatial geography started by Ngcobo and Tlali.

Black feminist geography and *nomos* in Koleka Putuma and Diana Ferrus's poetry

Writing decades after Tlali and Ngobo, Putuma and Ferrus are producing literature from within a nation-state that is now a constitutional democracy, with a much-lauded constitution regarded as one of the most progressive in the world.

One would imagine that in a constitutional democracy stripped of legislated discrimination, the actualisation of basic human and socioeconomic rights of all citizens would have, by now, rendered obsolete the need for a critical Black geography. Yet even with pernicious laws such as the Population Registration Act and the Group Areas Act expunged from the legal system, the inherent promise of spatial justice held out by the transition to democracy has failed to materialise. Here it is possible to discern the continuation of the *nomos* of apartheid and the persistence of already existing spatial arrangements that are entrenched as normal. Whereas during apartheid, law bounded movement, access to cities and access to land, the economic policies adopted by the democratic state has instituted a new, but similar order that has extended and, in many cases, exacerbated, apartheid's inequality and legacy of spatial injustice.

Complicit in this shift of political power without a material shift in economic and spatial configurations, is the ideology of what I call "rainbow nationalism" (Boswell 2020) – an ideology which has its genesis in the nationalism produced by the South African Truth and Reconciliation Commission (TRC). Rainbownationalism is a unificatory, nation-building ideology which seeks to heal a deeply divided nation after 50 years of human rights abuses, dislocations and displacement of Black citizens under the apartheid system. The ideology obscured emerging forms of inequality, no longer explicitly predicated on race, but by a glaringly apparent, widening economic divide. Rainbow nationalism, for example, papered over cracks formed after an unheralded transition from an economic shift which favoured reconstruction and redistribution, to a macro-economic policy in favour of GEAR (the Growth, Employment and Redistribution Strategy) which liberalised trade (Bond 2000).

Spatial and economic justice deferred has led to a profound anger in younger Black South Africans, which has been the catalyst for movements like RhodesMustFall at the University of Cape Town (UCT) in 2015 and the national FeesMustFall movement, which also started in 2015 and has procured – at least on the face of it – free, government-sponsored tertiary education for eligible South Africans. At the heart of both of these movements sits contestations about the right to access space – space which ideologically "others" and economically excludes young Black South Africans who should have access to these spaces for the actualisation of their socioeconomic rights.

Two poems which are products of this political moment are Diana Ferrus's "*My Naam is Februarie* / My Name is February" and Koleka Putuma's "Mountain". Diana Ferrus, while not directly linked to the FeesMustFall or RhodesMustFall movements, is a poet whose work has had significant historical and political impact in South Africa and abroad. A self-identified descendant of the Khoisan and those enslaved at the Cape, Ferrus has made it a political and cultural aim to educate slave descendants and the larger citizenry about the practice of slavery at the Cape, as well as its enduring reverberations.

Ferrus is most well-known globally for her poem "Saartjie will be Home" which she wrote in 1998 while a Master's student at Utrecht University in the Netherlands. In this poem, Ferrus directly addresses Sarah Baartman, the Khoisan woman lured to England under false pretences of work in 1810, who was then paraded to Victorian audiences as a freak in a cage because of her physiology. Upon her death in 1815, Baartman's body was dissected and her skeleton, brain and genital organs preserved as cultural artefact at the Musée de l'Homme in Paris. Ferrus's poem was found on the internet by a French senator and is widely credited with expediting the repatriation of Baartman's remains to South Africa in 2002 for burial. Ferrus's *oeuvre* deals largely with issues of enslavement in Southern Africa, and "*My Naam is Februarie* / My Name is February" is no different.

The poem was commissioned by the Smithsonian Institute of the USA, and performed at a ceremony at Clifton beach in June 2015, to acknowledge the discovery of the slave ship the São José, which had run aground and sunk near that beach in 1794, drowning about 300 enslaved Mozambicans who were being transported to Brazil, and were shackled on board. A total of 150 people who escaped the ship and swam to shore were recaptured and sold as slaves at the Cape. The poem is unique in its bilingualism: though Ferrus performed it for an international audience at the ceremony of acknowledgement for the enslaved lives lost, she insisted on writing and performing the poem in both English and Afrikaans, the latter being her mother tongue. Ferrus's insistence on writing in Afrikaans is part of her activism to recuperate Afrikaans from its perceived status as a language of the oppressor, and historicise its origins as a creole language created by the enslaved at the Cape. Moreover, the poem switches between Afrikaans and English, but the different stanzas are not translations. English speakers are thus given only provisional access to the poem's full content, a literary strategy that places speakers of the dominant language at a disadvantage, inverting the hegemony of that language.

In "*My Naam is Februarie* / My Name is February", narrated from the point of view of one of the enslaved persons on the ship, Ferrus (2015) practises a critical Black geography that refuses to leave buried South Africa's slave past. The poem's narrator, named February, narrates not only his death and dismemberment at the site of the drowning, but also becomes a ghost that haunts the contemporary moment – much like the practice of slavery itself.

The poem starts: *My naam is Februarie. / Ek is verkoop – / my borste, privaatdele, my oë, / my brein / is nog nie myne – / soos die Sao Jose / loop ek opgekap, / word ek telkens gesink deur 'n ander storm.* ("My name is February / I was sold – / my breasts, private parts, my eyes / my brain / are not yet mine – / like the Sao Jose / I walk dismembered / often being sunk by another storm.") (Translation provided by this author).

February thus narrates their own drowning and bears witness to the deaths of countless other enslaved on the ship; but is also the enslaved worker at the Cape. February has drowned off the Cape coast, but their subjectivity still lingers there, still being sunk by other, contemporary storms. Ferrus affords the drowned slave personhood, a place from which to voice a claim long after their demise – a strategy which brings history into the present, to signify slavery's effects on the current citizenry.

A few stanzas into the poem, February's narration switches to English, as they relate the ways in which their labour built the Cape: "I reshaped this landscape / my hands wove the patterns of these vineyards / my feet pressed the grapes / and I was paid in wine / I carry Alcohol-Foetal Syndrome children on my back". In this way, February makes visible the labour that defined South Africa's economy and on which its economy still turns. Bringing this labour out of the shadows of history is a way of challenging the *nomos* of colonialism/apartheid, the naturalisation of the landscape and its cultivation as springing from the ingenuity and enterprise of those with dominion over it – i.e., land and slave owners. The poem could also then be read as a claim to the land and a belonging to the nation, since the hands that shaped and reshaped the landscape concretely "made" the country.

The submerged slave, first erased from the narrative of South Africa, enters history and haunts the present, refusing to remain submerged under the sea. Ferrus thus brings the spatial politics of enslavement – captivity, the slave ship, forced migration across oceans – into the present. February states "Two hundred years after the Sao Jose I was given the vote / they said I was free / But do you see how often I am submerged / weighed down? / I am the sunken, the soiled / forgotten / and yet memory will not leave me". Memory, or the imaginative practice of rememory, here invokes the ocean floor as a space which has to surface and be reckoned with in order for the descendants of February to know justice.

The poem closes with a stanza that calls for such surfacing: "My name is February / I will be resurrected, / brought to the surface / unshackled, unchained, unashamed!" It links the resurfacing of submerged history as the only way for slave descendants to find freedom from the metaphorical shackles that still oppress them. Such liberation would also encompass a new relationship to the space of Cape Town, a city where February "still march[es] on the eve of December First" in an attempt to have erased slave history remembered. "I walk the cobblestones of this city / when I cry in desperation / 'remember the emancipation of the slaves!'"

In this stanza, Ferrus links the suppressed memory of enslavement, and the emancipation of slaves, with the spatial layout of the city. The city is the space which contains the annual slave emancipation march, the space through which descendants move as they strive to recreate memory. However, the repetitious nature of the march – it occurs annually – implies that the cries for recognition of the city's foundations – the cobblestones that produce the space upon which its denizens are grounded, and which were laid by slaves; the very ground beneath our feet – remain unrecognised. Words, and specifically, poetic articulation, is the deconstructive tool Ferrus's feminist geography deploys in order to unravel the narrative which positions white settlers as bringing the civilising, productive capitalist order to the city; and that this development was a positive development for indigenous and enslaved peoples.[2]

The final poem that I examine as performing the work of Black feminist geography is Koleka Putuma's "Mountain" (Putuma 2016). Putuma was a student at UCT during the period leading up to the RhodesMustFall movement, and maintains close ties with student activists involved in it. Putuma's "Mountain", published in February 2016, tells the story of a group of Black hikers in Namaqualand, trying to scale a mountain, but who cannot get access to it because the mountain is hemmed in at its slopes by private estates.

One hiker laments that: "every entrance (we see) is fenced / the dogs bark at the sight of our footsteps / The dogs want to jump the fence / the dogs look on defence / I feel on defence / I feel ready for a fight, / Guarded against a fight I do not yet see". Even the act of navigating the land makes the narrator of this poem feel "on defence". Because of the spatial markers of fences and guard dogs blocking off access to the mountain – a public space – the narrator, before encountering anyone, already feels guarded. The space surrounding the mountain is designed and demarcated in such a way as to expel outsiders before they can even attempt to gain entry. To access the mountain, they have to travel through private property, thus trespassing and invoking the ire of these property owners. The poem narrates in some detail the hikers' encounter with one such property owner, who forbids them access through her property, effectively rendering the mountain out of bounds.

The group is confronted by an "old white lady" who berates them for trespassing "on private property": "'You can't go up the mountain, without going past my property' / she says / I ask if she owns the mountain / she says she owns the land / Namaqualand? / I think she is implying she built the mountain / erected it stone by stone / Imagined its existence before her birth". The narrator of this poem makes visible here the *nomos* of the spatial arrangement, where white land ownership implies ownership of a public space – the mountain – with the white land owner imagining the mountain into existence even before her birth. The mountain's existence is so tied to the personhood of the white woman who owns land on its slopes that the whole mountain becomes part of her everyday lived experience. For the white woman guarding her parcel of land from Black trespassers, the dogs, the fences and the very mountain structures her experience of dominion over territory, producing a taken-for-granted ownership of this domain. Her act also represents a doubling of the colonial appropriation of land – reinstating, by repetition the act of re/claiming her patch of land.

The very presence of the Black hikers, however, destabilises this *nomos*. The Black narrator's refusal to accept these spatial relations produces a critical Black geography which shakes the very foundation of the *nomos* of Namaqualand. The property owner tells them that she owns the mountain, and tells them to leave. The poem riffs on the idea of "private property", repeating this phrase several times to emphasise the way in which public space, and Black people's bodies, become the property of whites, through the appropriative logic of colonial-apartheid *nomos*. This appropriative logic can be apprehended in Schmitt's (2003:325) tracing of the way in which an original land-appropriation creates an original title to which all subsequent proprietary entitlements can be legitimised:

> Concretely speaking, *nomos* is, for example, the chicken in every pot that every peasant living under a good king has on Sunday, the parcel of land every farmer cultivates as his property, and the car every American worker has parked in his garage.

At this point, the narration changes point of view from the hiker to the white woman, whose interior monologue shows her ideology in relation to land as private property:

> I'm not making it about race, It's not personal / it's just her mountain in Namaqualand / It's just private property / In the way your thoughts are private property / in the way your freedom is private property / In the way your obsessive partner thinks you are his / her private property / In the way your body is private property / In the way private property was lynched and sold back in the day / It's not personal, this private property thing / It just does not belong to you.

Creating a continuum of property rights, stretching from the contemporary moment, where part of the mountain is carved up for property, right back to the period of enslavement, when Black bodies were property to be bought and sold, makes visible the link between these types of ownership: white supremacist domination. The trade in Black bodies as a form of ownership of property was a proprietorship predicated on race – only whites could "own" Black bodies in this way, in the same way that ownership of the land in Namaqualand is accessible only to whites in the contemporary spatial arrangement in South Africa.

The poem's narrator reflects on

> This current native land act / tells us so / move, if we can't afford it / move, if the neighbourhood is hostile / move, because our guests are too loud / move, because the neighbours have been complaining / move, because the three dogs on a leash need more space on the pavement / move, because I will bump you out of the way because I do not see colour / move the last two syllables of your name off your ID, so I can swallow who you are / Move your child to another school, ours is full.

This litany of moves indicates the ways in which Black citizens are constantly manipulated around and out of spaces naturalised as white space – spaces where their presence is as unwelcome as the body of Muriel in Metropolitan at the height of apartheid. The effect is to discursively disrupt the *nomos* that enables white entitlement to and ownership of the land.

Conclusion

Like Ferrus, Putuma brings history into the present, naming these forms racialised forms of aggression "this current native land act". Within this line also, lies the difference between apartheid and post-apartheid Black feminist geography: whereas during apartheid the structure that was opposed was tangible, measurable law – a clear enemy of justice – in the contemporary period the ideological construct of the unified, constitutionally protected nation, the rainbow nation tends to the wilful forgetting of political injustice, the appropriation of land through colonisation, the further disavowal of Black citizens via apartheid law and *nomos*, and the denial of continued racial oppression as the price of belonging. While Ngcobo and Tlali's work challenge the morally reprehensible legal edifice of apartheid and its *nomos* – a noble form of activism, given the acknowledgement of apartheid as a "crime against humanity" by the United Nations in 1966, the contemporary writers' poetics of space pick away at the seams of the ideologies that work to continue racial and economic spatial inequality in post-apartheid South Africa, ostensibly a democracy. Ferrus and Putuma's poetry make visible the deferment of racial, gender and spatial justice (and the intersections of these forms of justice), producing a post-apartheid, oppositional *nomos* that points to the limitations of the law in providing restorative justice to citizens who have, through legal regimes, been born into centuries-old systems of injustice. Their work shatters the myth of rainbow nationalism, teasing out the tensions between a *nomos* that continues to disavow and displace certain racialised and gendered subjects through legitimised and legal economic land exclusion.

Notes

1 Though the Restitution of Land Rights Act 22 was promulgated in 1994, establishing a Commission on Restitution of Land Rights and a Land Claims Court in 1995, land restitution in South Africa has moved at a glacial pace. By 2017, only 21 percent of 81759 million hectares of freehold farmland had been transferred from white to black ownership in South Africa (Sihlobo and Kapuya 2018).

2 See, for example, the Democratic Alliance's former leader Hellen Zille's recent tweet: "For those claiming legacy of colonialism was ONLY negative, think of our independent judiciary, transport infrastructure, piped water, etc." This tweet led to Zille being rebuked by her political party, as well as charges being brought against her by said organisation. It caused a media and social media outcry, with many South Africans accusing Zille of racism.

References

Birla, Ritu. 2011. "Performativity Between *Logos* and *Nomos*: Law, Temporality and the Non-Economic Analysis of Power." *Columbia Journal of Gender and Law* 21 (2): 90–113.

Bond, Patrick. 2000. *Elite Transition: From Apartheid to Neoliberalism in South Africa*. London/ Sterling/Virginia: Pluto Press.

Boswell, Barbara. 2020. *And Wrote My Story Anyway: Black South African Women's Novels as Feminism*. Johannesburg: Wits University Press.

Cover, R. M. 1983. "The Supreme Court, 1982 Term—Foreword: Nomos and Narrative." Faculty Scholarship Series. Paper 2705. http://digitalcommons.law.yale.edu/fss_papers /2705.

Chryssostalis, Julia. 2013. "Reading Arendt 'reading' Schmitt: Reading *nomos* Otherwise?". In *Feminist Encounters with Legal Philosophy*, edited by Maria Drakapoulou, 158–184. Abingdon: Routledge.

Ferrus, Diana. 2015. "My Naam is February/My Name is February" as mentioned in personal communication with me from Diana Ferrus, June 5, 2015.

McKittrick, Katherine. 2006. *Demonic Grounds: Black Women and the Cartographies of Struggle*. Minneapolis, MN: University of Minnesota Press.

McKittrick, Katherine, and Clive Woods. 2007. *Black Geographies and the Politics of Place*. New York: South End Press.

Mitchell, Dean. 2006. "A Political Mythology of World Order: Carl Schmitt's Nomos." *Theory, Culture & Society* 23 (5): 1–22.

More, Ana. 2014. "From Lines to Networks: Carl Schmitt's Nomos in Africa and the Early Atlantic System." *Politica Comun* 5. Online publication. https://doi.org/10.3998/ pc.12322227.0005.004.

Ngcobo, Lauretta. 1990 [1999]. *And They Didn't Die*. New York: The Feminist Press.

Putuma, Koleka. 2016. "Mountain (Water's Cousin)" posted to Facebook on February 18, 2016.

Schmitt, Carl. 1950 [2003]. *The Nomos of the Earth in the International Law of the Jus Publicum Europaeum*. Translated by G. L. Ullmen. New York:Telos Press.

Sihlobo, Wandile and Tinashe Kapuya. 2018. "Special Report: The Truth about Land Ownership in South Africa." *Business Report*, July 23. Online publication. https:// www.businesslive.co.za/rdm/politics/2018-07-23-special-report-the-truth-about-land -ownership-in-south-africa/.

Tlali, Miriam. 1975. *Muriel at Metropolitan*. Johannesburg: Ravan.

Chapter 7

(Un)making Annie

Black female subjectivity, the normative (white) suburban South African home and land repossession

Victoria J. Collis-Buthelezi

Of Annies and Nonnas: locating Ngcobo's *And They Didn't Die*

Lauretta Ngcobo's second novel, *And They Didn't Die*, documents the migration from the rural to the urban and back of its black female protagonist, Jezile Majola, in 1950s South Africa. In Jezile, Ngcobo offers us a complex representation of black female subjectivity; Majola is a woman with her own dreams and desires. She is a wife, a mother and an activist in her own right. In Jezile, Ngcobo offers us a counter to the "nameless, shadowy, 'woolly Kaffir maids'" of much of South African fiction that appeared before her novel (Ngcobo 1991:190). *And They Didn't Die* follows the protagonist Jezile Majola from her rural village of Ixopo to Durban as a young bride eager to conceive her first child with her husband, a migrant worker in Durban. It takes us along too as Jezile returns to back to Ixopo then to the suburban home of the Potgieters and finally back home again. We see the desires, failed dreams and contradictions behind the appellation of "meid"/"kaffir meid" as the Potgieter home makes Jezile an *Annie* (a generalised name for black maids/domestic workers in apartheid South Africa) to Mrs. Potgieter's *Nonna* (madam as she crosses the threshold of the Potgieter home).

As scholars such as Desirée Lewis and Barbara Boswell have shown, Ngcobo's novel is not "poverty porn", but makes clear the strength, endurance and beauty of black women who lived under apartheid, both in its cities and in its villages (Lewis 1992; Boswell 2016). Ngcobo underscores that black women did not die, but lived rich and joyful lives, despite the erasure of personhood that they endured in the white spaces of apartheid's *nomos*. Yet in Jezile Majola, Ngcobo also makes visible the particular forms of oppression faced by black women under apartheid. I argue that in so doing, she offers a feminist recounting of systemic productions of South African black female subjectivity(ies) under the *nomos* of apartheid.

In 1990, Lauretta Ngcobo's second novel, *And They Didn't Die*, appeared in print for the first time. It was nine years after the publication of her debut novel, *Cross of Gold*. The year 1990 was also the year in which Nelson

DOI: 10.4324/9780203712771-7

Mandela was released from prison by the apartheid state. Mandela's release was considered the start of grand apartheid's dismantling; as such 1990 is often understood as the start of the transition to full democracy in South Africa, if not the start of the post-apartheid era. *And They Didn't Die* is thus both a late apartheid and a post-apartheid (whatever post- means)[1] novel. At once it is a document of the rapidly unravelling racial dispensation that upheld whites as citizens, and those 'who [we]re not known as white'[2] to be varying degrees of "pariah" in South Africa, as Sol Plaatje famously argued in *Native Life in South Africa* in 1916 (Plaatje 1919 [2007]:17).[3] Ngcobo's novel is a harbinger of the unfinished business of the social, spatial and economic contracts and coercions that came with such a "formalis[ation]" through colonialism, segregation and ultimately apartheid, particularly for black women. In an interview with Brian Worsfold in 1993, Ngcobo herself offered some insight. The end of apartheid had been authored in largely legal and political terms, but while "political willingness" was a key component, Ngcobo maintained that, "[t]here is no freedom without the economy and there is no freedom for a people whose culture has been decimated the way ours has" (Worsfold 1995:190). The political end of apartheid, she said, did not give South Africans the opportunity to "debate between [themselves]". Yet, Ngcobo contended, "the raging storms of the last 30 years have not once given us[,] the opportunity for a debate" (186).

For Ngcobo, the negotiated settlement that brought about the end of apartheid did not address some of its residual effects. These effects include the persisting inequities of the economy, on the one hand, and patriarchy and white cultural hegemony, on the other. In what follows, I read Ngcobo's novel as not only plotting out what would likely remain after a colonial/segregationist/apartheid *nomos*, but also how these "remains" emplaced onto black women's bodies in such a land. Though juridically a full person post-apartheid, I argue that the South African economic order continues a kind of non-personhood of black female subjectivity. If the *nomos* of the white SA *oikos* appropriated (and incorporated) black female subjects by completely depersonalising them, the post-apartheid economic order, or *oikonomia*, continues to deny black female subjectivity full personhood. In other words, if the Schmittian use of *nomos* was/is spatial "as original and originary land appropriation" (Chryssostalis 2013:165), Ngcobo points to the ways in which this can and did, in South Africa, extend to understandings of the black female body as appropriate-able sexually and in terms of its reproductive capacity and its labour. This appropriation of the black female body as reproductive capacity and as labour meant that it was also subject to the combination of order and emplacement that Schmitt identifies as at the centre of *nomos*. In other words, it was not just the land appropriation (as Schmitt argues) that represented the combination of order and emplacement at the heart of colonial-apartheid's logic, but also very much central to colonial-apartheid was the appropriation of the black female body (and attempted appropriation of black female being). In addition, if the appropriation extends to the black female body/being, then the black female body/being was also subject to the other two subsequent processes of *nomos*, namely distribution (black bodies were literally spatially distributed by the pass laws, etc) and (re)production.

Blackness under colonial-apartheid

Almost since the Union of South Africa in 1910, the main protagonists in the story of colonial-apartheid's appropriation of the black body (reflected in intra- and inter-national black migration to South Africa's mostly urban, mining centres) have been largely black men. In large numbers black men were conscripted and coerced to serve as labour for the mines. Therein lies the figure of "the [black, heteronormative male] migrant worker" (Peberdy 2009). The *nomos* of colonial-apartheid worked to consolidate South African cities as white spaces. At the same time, with the discoveries of diamond, gold and other mineral resources, cheap labour was needed to retrieve these from underground (Scully 1997).[4] Black men were accordingly recruited from South Africa's villages, rural and peri-urban areas, to which legislation like the Native Land Act had relegated black African life in an effort to "re-tribalize" black Africans and remove "black spots" from the country's cities. The notorious pass laws resulted as part and parcel of the spatial normative order of colonial-apartheid and these made it difficult (though not impossible) for whole black families to legally move to cities and settle there.[5]

By the 1950s, the hostel was a major centre of black male urban life, a site of black male emplacement that had directly resulted from the pass laws. Many black men living and working in the cities often had a "village wife" minding the children and the "tribal" home, who fulfilled the role of *makoti* (daughter-in-law) in the homestead of her husband's family. While in the city there was the *squeza*, who sometimes knew, and other times did not know of her partner's other family in his village of origin. It is not that black women did not move to South Africa's cities, but rather that since the 1910s, black women's movement – and thus their *emplacement* – was state regulated in such ways that reconfigured domestic relations in black (heteronormative) families so that a wife (or wives) were not required to move with her (their) husband; in fact, she was often barred from doing so by law. Black women had to apply for their own passes to travel to urban centres. To have long-term legal permission to stay there, they needed to work. As black male labour migration became more and more a cornerstone of South Africa's extractive economy, black families were often restructured and strained.[6]

The home in South African literature

The close reading of Ngcobo's *And They Didn't Die* that I offer here, is a part of and a rupture in a longer literary genealogy. This genealogy includes

Sol Plaatje's *Mhudi* (1930), Olive Schreiner's *The Story of an African Farm* (1883), Zakes Mda's *Madonna of Excelsior* (2008) and Imraan Coovadia's *High Low In-Between* (2009). Such a genealogy reveals the South African (white largely suburban) home as a site in which a particular (South African) black female subjectivity is produced or at least is meant to be produced – that of the "meid". Love, (mostly white) home, intimacy and friendship are enabled by interracial economic relations. We could broaden this to the "middle-class" or aspirant home, but there is something about whiteness that we need to tease out and to which we need to attend, and reading these relations only in terms of class would not allow this. I do not mean that black middle-class homes do not require "meids" and make "Annies" in contemporary South Africa, but that historically this specific category of black female subjectivity emerged and is maintained in service of South African whiteness from the colonial era into apartheid, whether invoked in black homes or not. Further, there is a way in which the production of "meids" is not only a *specific category of black female subjectivity* but is meant to reorganise black female subjectivity in general.

In other words, in the making and ordering of South Africa as geopolitical space, white South African (suburban) homeliness/domesticity becomes a kind of machine that produces (or at least hopes to produce) black female subjects/subjectivities. I am thinking of the home in South Africa as a site of subject-making in line with Antonio Benítez-Rojo's notion of the Plantation in *La Isla que se repite* or *The Repeating Island*; that is, a kind of machine that produces the Caribbean/the Caribbean subject. Benítez-Rojo argues that the islands that comprise the Caribbean are not all the same, but what they share is the system of production/making subjects and space (Benítez-Rojo 1997). In other words, the South African home is a site of production of black female subjectivity. Its purpose is to make Annies, black female caregivers who reproduce and nurture whiteness. Black women in this order come to exist only in the service of reproducing and securing whiteness.

Schmitt argues that as a word *oikonomia* (or order of the household) "presents a synopsis of such concepts as organization, order, and economy that are important for the whole semantics of the root *nem*" (Schmitt 2003,339). After all, *oikonomos* appears in the sixth century BC, when *nemein*, the verb for *nomos*, "customarily meant to administer or to govern" (*ibid.*), does too. Thus, the *nomic* in the oiko-nomic, is significant in two ways, one could argue:

(1) it signals that the household is an order-formation, a political, juridical, symbolic and economic system of administration and governance of people and things;
(2) it signals the grounding of the domestic order into the physical space of the house. Or as Schmitt puts it, it is the linking of house and *nomos* that marks the overcoming of the nomadic way of life (Schmitt 2003:340). From this point onwards, in other words, the order of the household, the *nomos* of the *oikos*, ceases to be nomadic and becomes sedentary.

> Rather, it is housed in a specific site. As such, one could argue, the home is not any domestic order but a concrete order, located on the specific site it occupies, its spatial arrangement corresponding to its normative architecture. In fact, the spatialisation of the South African suburban home under apartheid typically included the backrooms – separate outbuildings from the main family home – in which the *meid* typically slept, kept her belongings and "lived" when not tending to the white family.

Emerging as apartheid was drawing to a formal legal and political end, Ngcobo's novel not only reveals the ways in which black female subjectivity was expected to codify itself and be visible during the apartheid era and before, it also lays bare the intractability of such expectations on black womanhood beyond the political, legislative end of formal apartheid. This is the case precisely because (the production of) black female subjectivity was so tied to spatialised affective structures that persist well beyond apartheid as part of the new democratic dispensation, namely the home and domesticity as normatively configured during colonial-apartheid. The latter represents a dimension of the continuation of the *nomos* of apartheid that we cannot afford to ignore.

When grand apartheid ended it did not mean the end of intimacies of the home, but rather their extension. If Nelson Mandela became the "father of the nation" who could finally bring about the full entrance of all South Africans into the famed rainbow nation, not only was a "mother" of the nation needed who could be accepted as more homely than his second wife, Winnie Madikizela-Mandela, but that national metaphor of South African home and domesticity could also not quite dismantle the domesticity that prevailed before, which required a majority of black women to enter it as caregivers, not necessarily to their own children, but to the children of others.

My argument is not so much that all black women in South Africa are "meids" or that "meids" in South Africa are one and the same, mere objects of production. As forms as varied as the academic monograph to the comic strip have shown us, what is presumed to be the interiority of black women in domestic service or their motivations is often unknown and at times, black women in service engage in their own practices of self- and space-making in direct contradiction and resistance to what may be expected of them (Cock 1980). *And They Didn't Die* is itself an example of black women's subversion of apartheid's racial and gendered taxonomies. My claim is perhaps overly simple – that under the sign of South Africa (from the colonial era into apartheid) a particular type of black female subjectivity has been most desired and produced as part of the South African *nomos*; when apartheid ended, rather than shift that order, the new dispensation made attempts at ameliorating it, but never quite dislodged it. *And They Didn't Die* bears witness not only to black women's conscription into such black femininity, at times playing the part, but never fully accepting the role; at the same time, it calls for post-apartheid efforts at constructing a new South Africa to attend to the limits of black female subject-formations with which we have been bequeathed.

Schreiner's daughter

Ngcobo once said that she saw herself as Schreiner's descendant as a writer, writing in response to her (Ngcobo 1991:189–199). It was not an uncritical or uncomplicated sense of relation; *And They Didn't Die* was in part an attempt to break down the "barriers" between white and black women as madams and "meids", respectively, as fictionalised in Schreiner's *The Story of an African Farm* (1883). A (proto-)feminist novel about the coming of age of the white woman-child protagonist, Lyndall. *The Story of an African Farm* also, perhaps despite itself, reveals the ways in which, from quite early in the country's history, South African (white) domesticity depended upon and "formalized into a distant ... exchange" white and black women's interactions (Ngcobo 1991:199).

If we look at Schreiner's novel, we notice at least one textual moment in which interracial friendship is asserted. That is, when the farm's German overseer appeals to his "friendship" with one of the "kaffir *meids*". Tant'Sannie, the Boer wife, throws the German off the farm in retaliation for the German's supposed belief that she is incapable of evicting a "kaffir *meid*" because of Tant'Sannie's own desire for the German. This hint of her powerlessness as a woman and failed sexuality because of the "kaffir *meid*", pushes Tant'Sannie to evict the German (Schreiner 1883, 1982:89). The black woman/white woman friendship is impossible here because black and white women can only exist in triangulation with white men. Black and white women's friendship in this triangulation threatens the assertion of a complete white female sexuality. When he is being sent away, the German asks another "*meid*" why he is being treated this way by Tant'Sannie, the "*meid*" laughs and he is left hurt by his friend's rejection. The German had insisted throughout their exchange that they, he and the "*meid*", were friends. What does this exchange tell us? Why does she laugh and mock him as he asks for help and declares their friendship? I am not sure that what transpires within the pages of the novel enables us to comprehend the exchange between the German overseer and the "*meid*".

By way of answering this question, let us turn to Sol Plaatje's *Mhudi*. Written alongside *Native Life in South Africa* in the 1910s, Plaatje's novel would only be published in 1930 as something of a for-posterity project by Lovedale Press.[7] The novel follows its eponymous character, a Tswana woman, her family and her friends during the mfecane[8] in the 1830s and their response to their dispersal as a result of the mfecane. Interestingly, the female native does not really emerge in *Native Life in South Africa*, but she does emerge in *Mhudi*. In the novel, and not in the ethnography, the native woman is the central figure. Set in nineteenth-century southern Africa, *Mhudi* is a kind of *Odyssey* in reverse – it follows its female protagonist, Mhudi, on her journey around the region in search of her husband, Ra-Thaga.

It is Mhudi who sees the Boers not as a fulfilment of the Barolong dream to be able to fight the Matebele, but as more dangerous than the Matebele because at least the Matebele "w[ould] spear you to death and put an end to your pains", whereas the Boers torture their "offenders" (Plaatje 1930:102). The violence of the Mzilikazi's attempt to consolidate black Africans into one nation under the Matebele is preferred to the violence of the Boers, which Mhudi sees as an attempt to push the Barolong into servitude. The Barolong make an attempt at friendship with the Boers but even as they help them fight the Matebele, by the end of the novel the promise of interracial friendship is reduced to an unequal economic entanglement. When the women of Mhudi and her husband, Ra-Thaga's, village learn of the Boer couple's torture of their Hottentot maid, they extend to the Boers the title of "Ra-Thaga's friends" to distance their relation to them. Rather than the Barolongs' friends, friends of the nation, they become only Ra-Thaga's friends, but the Boers take this to mean that they "had made a fresh impression of friendliness among their hospitable black benefactors" (Plaatje 1930 [2007]:102). The Barolong hospitality in giving the Boers Moroka's Hoek is nearly met with Ra-Thaga's death when he drinks from the Boer's water vessel on a visit; and 'were he not a Marolong he would be paid for his presumptuous act with a lacerated back' (103).

Interracial friendship, for the Boers, is not one of equality. This is perhaps why Mhudi prefers the Matebele; she contends that if your men surrender to the rule of the Matebele you become their equal, surrendering to the Boer means perpetual inequality. When it is time to negotiate the terms of dividing the land they will capture from the Matebele, the Boers strive to institutionalise this inequality suggesting that they get the land and the Barolong the cattle (125). In the end the interracial friendship modelled here makes the share of resources and power inequitable, and results in the betrayal of fellow black people (represented by the Matebele). While friendships emerge between Ra-Thaga and the Afrikaans Phil-jay and Mhudi and Annetje, Phil-jay and Annetje instrumentalise the friendship in economic terms. She has come to care deeply for Mhudi, Annetje explains at the novel's end; thus Mhudi and Ra-Thaga must come live with her and Phil-jay. Mhudi must be their children's "ayah" (or Annetje's "*meid*" and her children's Annie) and Ra-Thaga Phil-jay's farmhand.

Mhudi reveals not only the types of unequal interracial relations formalising in the 1830s, but also the kinds of white and black subjectivities this system of racial inequity required of South African domesticity; to be friends, black women (and men) had to provide their labour in service of white "friends". If we reread the exchange between the German overseer and the "meid" in Schreiner's novel with this in mind, the meid's laughter seems related to Mhudi's own refusal to "work" for Annetje. The "meid" in *The Story of an Africa Farm* is of course already inside of the systems of relation that make up the South African domestic scene that Annetje and Mhudi's exchange portends. But *Mhudi* reveals what may have existed before the "barriers" (to which Ngcobo refers in her 1991 essay (Ngcobo 1991)) went up to manifest the distance necessary for the profound intimacy of care by black women of white families and the denial of black women as members of their own families and therein humans. Such barriers were actualised in suburban homes across the country with meid's quarters in the backyard – a room separate from the main house.

Or as one of Antjie Krog's unnamed friends, whose "meid" lives in such a room in her backyard, explains in *Country of My Skull* (1998), "[m]aids don't feel like other people about their children. They like to be rid of them. Anyway, [Annie] likes me now" (Krog 1998:250). Interestingly, the subtitle of Krog's non-fiction book is "Guilt, Sorrow, and the Limits of Forgiveness in the New South Africa". The book explores the South African Truth and Reconciliation Commission (TRC) and Krog's own journey of self-exploration as an Afrikaans woman and journalist tasked with covering the TRC. But neither *Country of My Skull* nor the TRC attend to the roots of South African domesticities or attempt to reimagine them. Despite Krog's references to the ways in which "meids" are treated differently or the Commission's debates about how to define rape, most of the book speaks to the Krog's interpersonal relations with her family and the larger political questions of the time as well as the more well-known instances of violence that transpired under apartheid, including the work of the apartheid death squad Vlakplaas and the murder of Amy Biehl. Important topics to address, but Krog never quite attends to the forms of black female subjectivity that apartheid demanded.

The "barriers" of Ngcobo's 1991 essay are made visible and rendered farcical in *And They Didn't Die*. Such barriers erupt from the pages of Krog's prose poem to the new South Africa as loudly as from Schreiner's *The Story of an African Farm* or Plaatje's *Mhudi*. In *And They Didn't Die* we are given access to the *meid*'s quarters as well as her employers'. Such access is not only physical. It also makes available to the reader the life story that leads the novel's Annie to her meid's quarters as well as her life there and beyond. In other words, the reader can see the making of the Potgieters' Annie. Ngcobo reveals the supposed inscrutability of Annies as a strategy of managing South African (white) domesticities and the uncomfortable questions they must pose. What of the day when a white child realises that the care s/he receives comes at the expense of his caregiver's children? What of the day s/he realises that the heater s/he has does not have a facsimile in the room of the woman caring for her/him, nor in the home in which that woman grew up or he one in which her children are raised? Such exchanges as offered to Krog by her friend above attempt to make black women in service something other than human – human enough to act as fonts of care and love for white homes, but not so human that difficult questions about what they are sacrificing warrants answers that evoke their sameness.

Jezile goes to work for the Potgieters in Johannesburg in order to support her children in rural KwaZulu-Natal after her husband is arrested for stealing a chicken to feed their children. (After being a migrant labourer in Durban, the authorities force him to return to the rural areas because his wife tries to stay with him without a pass.) Although, Mr. Potgieter is initially the nicest of the couple, Jezile/Annie comes to live for Mrs. Potgieter. She receives meat bones like the family's dog. Interestingly, Olive Schreiner's intended "Introduction to A Vindication [of the Rights of Woman]" also presents the metaphor of the "kaffir meid" as "dog", though it was only published in 1994 along with an introduction to it by Carolyn Burdett (1994) entitled "A Difficult Vindication" (Schreiner 1994:193). Jezile/Annie is refused access to the food cupboards unless under Mrs. Potgieter's surveillance. She cannot eat in the kitchen at table except on rainy days, and then she has to get permission. The family refuses to electrify her room (Ngcobo 1991:200–1). But more than anything, through Mrs. Potgieter's renaming of Jezile, she "los[es] her name, her past, her friends and relatives, her language, her initiative" and as Annie, Jezile becomes "just a shell of her former self" (201). As Schmitt argues (2003, 336) "[a] land-appropriation is constituted only if the appropriator is able to give the land a name". For Schmitt naming is key to appropriation, to the *nahme*, the taking in other words that is at the basis of *nomos*, for naming involves the "unequivocal publicity" (Schmitt 2003, 347) of the appropriation and the *nomos* that it institutes. Crucially, such taking is not only the taking of land. Interestingly, for our purposes, Schmitt gives the example of marriage, and what it means for a man to "*take* a wife and give her his name" (347–48). It is interesting here that it is Mrs. Potgieter who renames Jezile, and therefore initiates the depersonalisation of Jezile that her husband completes with sexual abuse.

Then one day both women (white wife and black "*meid*") are revealed to be victims of white male abuse. Mr. Potgieter beats Mrs. Potgieter one evening, leaving her on their bedroom floor "crying disconsolately with blood all over her face" (204). It is Jezile who enters the house in time to stop Mr. Potgieter's further abuse of his wife. Later that night Jezile/Annie returns to her room in the backyard to find Mr. Potgieter lying on her bed, where he rapes her. "I love you. I've loved you for a long time and you know it", he tells her. As he tightens his grip on her arm he says "I said I won't hurt you. You know I don't love her … Now calm down I'll be good to you" (204). He twists her arm, puts her on the bed and "pin[s] her down" (204–5). Jezile screams "[b]ut in that isolated backyard it was like whistling against thunder"; as if becoming Annie made her cry for help and of pain inaudible to her white madam. When Potgieter finishes he "d[oes] not leave the room" but tries to "plea[d] with her to understand. He was sorry it happened that way, he said. For a long time he had had visions of a beautiful time with her" (205). "If it wasn't for the law", he says, "I would love you openly; I would even marry you. I loved you when you were with your people in Umzimkulu. I brought you here because I love you; I could not bear not to see you ever again …" (205). Thus in "taking a *maid*", the white house-owner takes her labour, her care, her affection and humanity, takes her presence and attention, takes her body, takes everything in short and gives nothing but the bare minimum. Food is rationed, electricity refused, comforts denied, and a name that is generic, a name as good as any, a name in fact that indexes her status, her place, generic function and replace-ability, not her person and its singularity. It is no accident that her cries "cannot" be heard. For having the capacity to be heard, means a certain standing, the minimum perhaps of personhood.

Potgieter laboriously endeavours to make his violent abuse of Jezile/Annie an expression of love. He takes her in his arms and "loves" her. He pledges his willingness to commit to her, although she is already married. When Potgieter beats his wife, Jezile hears it from her room in the backyard and enters the house and effectively stops it. Although Mrs. Potgieter is in her bedroom when Potgieter rapes Jezile in the same room in the backyard from which she heard her "madam's" cries, Mrs. Potgieter does not hear it that night or on the countless other nights that follow.[9] She remains so deaf to Jezile's repeated violation at the hands of her husband that when Jezile becomes pregnant and bears Mr. Potgieter's child all she can ask is "who is the father?"

Unspeakable things unspoken

To return to Schreiner's *The Story of an African Farm*, I want to suggest that we understand the German's "friendship" with the "meid" in that novel in line with Mr. Potgieter's violent and repeated rape of Jezile in Ngcobo's. Ngcobo's making visible and audible to her readers the different acts of violation that often enact interracial "friendship" and "love" in South Africa calls us to reread the silences of Schreiner's novel in this way.

What is a declaration of friendship and love for a black woman when expressed through violence and coercion and when the very conditions of black female subjectivity are oppressive? Ultimately, Jezile/Annie's presence in the house as domestic labourer (physically and sexually) alleviates Mrs. Potgieter's position within the home as wife and mother and allows her to "begi[n] to ease her way out of the house and its drudgery … often out during the day … [and] look[ing] happier" (204).

This kind of female interracial friendship involves the amelioration of the white woman's situation at the expense of the black woman's domestic and sexual labour. She must be reconstituted into a shell or ghost, a metaphysical abstraction – a "meid". Ngcobo's novel reveals the black woman as "meid" as a fact of the built domesticity of the South African (white) home in which black female subjectivity is produced.

While many backyard *meid*'s rooms have been decommissioned since 1990, many remain. They stand as repositories of "unspeakable things unspoken"

(Morrison 1989:1–34). They beg us to extend the project of transformation and (in today's terms) of land repossession, to the repossession of the body. Such a reconstruction would not only involve extending the political dispensation to all of South Africa's citizens as happened in April 1994 with the first democratic election. It does not only require the economic reconstitution of the South African economy. It necessitates that we break down structures of affect that continue to perpetuate white supremacy and patriarchy in the continued commodification of black female subjectivity in South Africa as "*meid*". With *And They Didn't Die*, Ngcobo bequeaths us this work – unmaking Annies.

Notes

1 As Carli Coetzee argues in her opening to Accented Futures, neither 1990 (with Mandela's release) nor 1994 (when the first democratic elections were held in South Africa) spell the end of apartheid as much as they signaled that it 'is ending' (Coetzee 2013: ix). Rather, she continues, they gave rise to a process that we might deem South African apartheid's 'long ending' and the 'new beginning' of something that may not yet be articulable (Coetzee ix).

2 This is the term used to describe people of colour (Black African, Coloured, and Indian) in the statement of purpose of 'The Coloured People's Vigilance Society'; started in 1901 in Cape Town, the society was started in response to the rising vulnerability of people of colour in South Africa as a result of the South African War (1899–1902) and the forced removals brought on by the Bubonic Plague. See Peregrino, F. Z. 1901: 8. For more on the response to the Bubonic Plague and its effects on people of colour in South Africa (specifically Cape Town) see Swanson 1977:387–410.

3 The book was Plaatje's attempt to document the effects of the Native Land Act of 1913, itself a "formalis[ation]" of the land appropriation and disposition begun from the 17th century through European conquest and colonialism in southern Africa. Also see Lungisile Ntsebeza, 'Land redistribution in South Africa: the property clause revisited', The Land Question in South Africa: The Challenge of Transformation and Redistribution ed. Lungisile Ntsebeza and Ruth Hall, 2007:108.

4 Scully also explores attempts to keep female workers out of cities that predate mineral extraction.

5 I refer to the Native Land Act of 1913, the Urban Areas Act (1923) the Minimum Wages Act (1925), the Population Registration Act (1950), and the Separate Amenities Act (1953) amongst others.

6 For more on colonialism and families of colour post-emancipation in the Western Cape, South Africa see Scully 1997. For more on apartheid-era family structure and experience, see Moodie, Ndatshe, and Sibuyi 1988. For more contemporary scholarship on women in mining settlements post-apartheid, see Benya 2015.

7 Lovedale press was the printing press of the mission school Lovedale. It would later become the University of Fort Hare, an institution that many of Africa's liberation leaders attended; these include not only Nelson Mandela, but Robert Mugabe, Julius Nyerere and Kenneth Kaunda.

8 The mfecane (translated as the crushing) refers to various violent dispersals of several black African ethnic groups in southern Africa as wars were waged amongst several of these groupings and with Dutch and English settlers. Often the mfecane is associated with the consolidation of the Zulu state under Shaka (Zulu) and the flight of leaders

such as Mzilikazi that it precipitated. Mzilikazi is at the centre of the potential dispersal of the Barolong about which Mhudi is concerned. Some historians dispute the mfecane and Shaka existence. See Hamilton 1998.

9 There are thus essential differences between Ngcobo's rendering of the relations of domestic abuse and that of Marlene van Niekerk's much later *Agaat* (2004), where the main character, Milla (through whose eyes the narrative exclusively unfolds), is also abused by her husband, Jak, but in which there is no hint of sexual abuse by Jak of Agaat. Further, the novel is at pains to point to Milla's constant intervention to prevent or end Jak's verbal abuse of Agaat and the other farm workers, as if to redeem Milla's otherwise brutal subjugation of *Agaat*. At the same time, there are numerous instances in the novel, where Agaat intervenes, subtly but effectively, to prevent or stop Jak's abuse of Milla.

References

Benítez-Rojo, A. 1997. *The Repeating Island: The Caribbean and the Postmodern Perspective*. Durham, NC: Duke University Press.

Benya, A. 2015. "The Invisible Hands: Women in Marikana." *Review of African Political Economy* 42 (146): 545–560.

Boswell, B. 2016. "Rewriting Apartheid South Africa: Race and Space in Miriam Tlali and Lauretta Ngcobo's Novels." *Gender, Place and Culture: A Journal of Feminist Geography* 23 (9): 1329–1342.

Burdett, C. 1994. "A Difficult Vindication: Olive Schreiner's Wollstonecraft Introduction." *History Workshop* 37: 177–187.

Cock, J. 1980. *Maids and Madams: A Study in the Politics of Exploitation*. Johannesburg: Ravan Press.

Coetzee, C. 2013. *Accented Futures*. Johannesburg: Wits University Press.

Chryssostalis, J. 2013. "Reading Arendt 'reading' Schmitt: Reading *nomos* Otherwise?". In *Feminist Encounters with Legal Philosophy* edited by Maria Drakapoulou, 158–184. Abingdon: Routledge.

Coovadia, I. 2009. *High Low In-Between: A Novel*. Cape Town: Umuzi.

Hamilton, C. 1998. *Terrific Majesty: The Powers of Shaka Zulu and the Limits of Historical Invention*. Cambridge, MA: Harvard University Press.

Krog, A. 1998. *Country of My Skull: Guilt, Sorrow, and the Limits of Forgiveness in the New South Africa*. Johannesburg: Random House.

Lewis, D. 1992. "Myths of Motherhood and Power: The Construction of 'Black Woman' in Literature." *English in Africa* 19 (1): 35–51.

Mda, Z. 2008. *The Madonna of Excelsior*. Oxford: Oxford University Press.

Moodie, T. D., V. Ndatshe and B. Sibuyi. 1988. "Migrancy and Male Sexuality on the South African Gold Mines." *Journal of Southern African Studies* 14 (2): 228–256.

Morrison, T. 1989. "Unspeakable Things Unspoken: The Afro-American Presence in American Literature." *Michigan Quarterly Review* 28 (1): 1–34.

Ngcobo, L. 1991. "A Black South African Woman Writing Long after Schreiner." In *The Flawed Diamond: Essays on Schreiner*, edited by V. Itala, 189–199. Denmark: Dangaroo Press.

Ntsebeza, Lungisile. 2007. "Land Redistribution in South Africa: The Property Clause Revisited." In *The Land Question in South Africa: The Challenge of Transformation and*

Redistribution, edited by Lungisile Ntsebeza and Ruth Hall, 107–131. Cape Town: HSRC Press.

Peberdy, S. 2009. *Selecting Immigrants: National Identity and South Africa's Immigration Policies, 1910–2008*. Johannesburg: Wits University Press.

Peregrino, F. Z. 1901. "The Coloured People's Vigilance Society". *The South African Spectator*, 8.

Plaatje, S. T. 1919 [2007]. *Native Life in South Africa*. Northlands: Picador Africa.

Plaatje, S. 1930 [2007]. *Mhudi*. 4th ed. London: Penguin Classics.

Schmitt, C. 2003. *The Nomos of the Earth in the International Law of the Jus Publicum Europaeum*. New York: Telos Press Publishing.

Schreiner, O. 1983 [1982]. *The Story of an African Farm*. New York: Penguin Classics.

Schreiner, O. 1994. "Introduction to the Life of Mary Wollstonecraft and the Rights of Woman." *History Workshop* 37: 188–193.

Scully, P. 1997. *Liberating the Family?: Gender and British Slave Emancipation in the Rural Western Cape, South Africa, 1823–1853*. Cape Town: David Philip.

Swanson, M. 1977. "The Sanitation Syndrome: Bubonic Plague and Urban Native Policy in the Cape Colony, 1900–1909." *The Journal of African History* 18 (3): 387–410.

Van Niekerk, M. 2004. *Agaat*. Cape Town: Human en Rousseau.

Worsfold, B. 1995. "In Conversation with Lauretta Ngcobo." *BELLS* 6: 183–192.

Chapter 8

"Space is space"

The *nomos* of apartheid, "the coloniser who refuses" and uncolonial spatiality in JM Coetzee's *Waiting for the Barbarians*

Jaco Barnard-Naudé

> "Spatial justice is a chasm, an empty space that cannot be colonized by any political position"
>
> (Philippopoulos-Mihalopoulos 2011, 14)

> "colonization, this exotic, regressive form of the master's discourse, in the face of the capitalism called imperialism"
>
> (Lacan 2007, 92)

Introduction

I begin with the words of Nadine Gordimer in a review of JM Coetzee's *Life and Times of Michael K*:

> [Coetzee] chose allegory for his first few novels. It seemed he did so out of a kind of opposing desire to hold himself clear of events and their daily, grubby, tragic consequences in which, like everyone else living in South Africa, he is up to the neck, and about which he had an inner compulsion to write. So here was allegory as stately fastidiousness; or a state of shock. He seemed able to deal with the horror he saw written on the sun only – if brilliantly – if this were to be projected into another time and plane. His *Waiting For the Barbarians* was the North Pole to which the agitprop of agonized black writers (and some white ones hitching a lift to the bookmart on the armoured car) was the South Pole: *a world to be dealt with lies in between.*[1]
>
> (Gordimer 1984, 3 as quoted in Jolly 1989, 69–70 (emphasis added))

Rosemary Jolly (1989, 70) remarks in response to these words – in which, of course, spatial metaphor abounds – that Gordimer raises "the larger question of what literature can, or in this case, even should, be expected to do; what kind of *territory* it undertakes to explore" (emphasis added). And this is the question that I, with reference to Coetzee's "North Pole", *Waiting for the Barbarians* (1980), would like to explore in what follows.

DOI: 10.4324/9780203712771-8

Taking its cue from Gordimer, the chapter contends that the "world to be dealt with", "lies in between" and here I would like only to explore that in-between as a liminal space in the novel. This liminal space comes into its *becoming* in what I call the ministration scenes in *Waiting for the Barbarians*. These are the scenes in which the magistrate describes how he washes and cares for, without exploiting, the body of a blind barbarian girl that he takes into his rooms after he founds her in a street of his town, subsequent to his release of the barbarian prisoners captured by the character that embodies the *nomos* of Empire, Colonel Joll, the imperial torturer and murderer.

The novel stages the *nomos* (Schmitt 2003) of Empire as pervasive, as indeed the order of its imperial day. That the frontier town functions as an allegory of South Africa under apartheid, although not exclusively so, has been noted by many commentators (most recently and elaborately, by Attwell (2015, 105–106, 113–15).[2] For Schmitt (2003, 81), colonialism is, in its "entirety", the history of land-appropriation, of "spatially determined processes of settlement" in which order and emplacement are combined in a unity from which they cannot be separated. All subsequent processes of colonial, imperial and apartheid distribution and production thus follow from the original land-appropriation, "the line in the soil, the furrow in the field" (Chryssostalis 2013, 166), and the essence of the *nomos* of colonialism, of "the capitalism called imperialism" (Lacan 2007, 92), consists in this precedence of appropriation before distribution and production (Schmitt 2003, 334).

In the course of elaborating my argument that the ministration scenes function as the rudimentary figuration of an *un*colonial spatial justice after apartheid, I will have recourse to the psychoanalysis of Jacques Lacan and specifically his four discourses as elaborated in Seminar XVII (Lacan 2007) and elsewhere. It is important for my purposes to emphasise that for Lacan, "discourse" is not "merely" linguistic relations, but rather the designation of the social bond that underlies the linguistic relation (Bracher 1988, 32). In this regard, I claim that the ministration scenes displace the magistrate's master's discourse, grounded as it is in the spatial injustice of the imperial *nomos*.

In *Seminar XVII*, Lacan repeatedly characterises the master's discourse as "the other side" (2007, 136) of psychoanalysis. The claim, then, that the ministration scenes displace the master's discourse, implies a reading of these scenes as inaugurating analytical discourse and this is precisely the wager of the present chapter. Implicit and explicit in my argument, then, is that spatial justice after apartheid critically depends on the emergence of a discourse of the analyst – a discourse that cannot be other than embodied and, as such, spatial. With reference to Chryssostalis's (2013, 158) reading of Arendt's account of *nomos*, I argue that such an emergence will, as it does in the novel, turn on a relation and a relationality that re-imagines "the spatiality of *nomos* in non-territorial terms" and on "emplacement without the priority of appropriation".

Ultimately, I read *Waiting for the Barbarians* as the story of an incomplete discursive (and thus socio-spatial) transformation[3] for which literature creates the space. If, as Derrida (1992, 36) claims, literature is "the institution which allows one to say *everything*, in *every way*", then Coetzee narrates both the violence of what Derrida calls the "instituted fiction" (here, the instituted fiction of the *nomos* of apartheid/"Empire") as well as the dream of what he calls the "fictive institution" (the institution of spatial justice after apartheid). In *Acts of Literature,* Derrida goes on to argue that literature is "subject to an imperative: to give space for singular events" (55). The law of literature, then, the one that it institutes as well as the one that it is instituted by, gives space for singular events. I argue that in the ministration scenes Coetzee brings the law under the jurisdiction, as it were, of literature, by giving space to the singular events between the magistrate and the barbarian girl. In so doing, Coetzee dares both to read and write *nomos* otherwise (Chryssostalis 2013, 158).

The focus of the incomplete discursive transformation is, of course, the magistrate who, I argue, becomes in the course of the novel what Albert Memmi (1974, 63) calls "a coloniser who refuses". For Memmi, the coloniser who refuses represents an "impossible historical situation" (83). But it is this very impossibility that comes to stand as the condition of possibility of the incipient spatial justice that the ministration scenes spatialises as a discourse of the analyst. In other words, the novel delivers the magistrate to the "impossible historical situation" that comes to function as the condition of possibility of transformation. To be sure, after the ministration scenes nothing is ever the same again for the magistrate, not simply because these scenes hystericise his master's discourse (as all analytic discourse must do), but also because through these scenes we come to glimpse the emergence of what Lacan (2007, 176) calls "another style of the master signifier" and thus of a *nomos* that – through reading and writing otherwise – may at last also be lived otherwise.

"Space is space": the "global historical process" in *Waiting for the Barbarians*

Most of the action in *Waiting for the Barbarians* takes place in a "colonial town at the frontier of a larger colony designated as the Empire". As the late Stephen Watson (1986, 370) puts it: *Waiting for the Barbarians* is "a novel of an imaginary empire, of an imperialism which is merely an extension of colonialism". Coetzee's insistence throughout the novel on these signifiers of generality, however, has to be read both in light of the fact that the book was written by a South African author during apartheid, and in light of Gordimer's assertion that Coetzee "chose allegory for his first few novels".

It is, accordingly, impossible to miss that *Waiting for the Barbarians* is also specifically a novel about apartheid – that "colonialism" which the liberation movements famously described as of "a special type" (Bozzoli and Delius 1990, 14). How can one fail, for instance, to see the parallels between the sadistic Colonel Joll's detentions, torture and murder of the barbarians, and the detention, torture and murder of political activists under apartheid?

Moreover, as David Attwell (2015, 107–113) has noted, the fact that specific events in the history of apartheid – such as the death of Steve Biko in police detention in 1977, together with the outrage that it generated amongst white liberal South Africans at the time – inexorably found their way into the novel via the voice of its protagonist (who the reader comes to know only as "the magistrate"), means that *Waiting for the Barbarians* is also a novel about a specific time during apartheid and, by extension, one could argue, about the specific spatiality of apartheid. Stated in explicitly Schmittian terms, *Waiting for the Barbarians* is ultimately a novel about the *nomos* – the spatialised normativity and the normativised spatiality – of "grand" apartheid as colonialism of a "special type".

In his article on colonialism in Coetzee's novels up to *The life and times of Michael K*, Watson (1986, 370) quotes a 1978 interview in which Coetzee remarked that he was inclined "to see the South African situation [today] as only one manifestation of a wider historical situation to do with colonialism, late colonialism, neo-colonialism". Watson further draws attention to Coetzee's underlining of "his sense that South Africa's situation was bound up with a global historical process" when he added, "I'm suspicious of lines of division between a European context and a South African context, because I think our experience remains largely colonial" (370).

These remarks bring us back to the criticism of *Waiting for the Barbarians* for its "mimetic inaccuracy" and its refusal of historical determinacy. Whiteson argued, for instance, that the "heart of the novel is not darkness but mush" (Jolly 1989, 69) and Irving Howe in *The New York Times Book Review*, that a more "specified historical place and time" may have provided the novel with more "bite and pain" (69).

But at least one critic insists that the novel's "ambiguities of time and place" "are clearly deliberate" and, moreover, that the indeterminate geography "indicates that the setting of the novel is something of a key to the working of the narrative" (Jolly 1989, 70). "To reject the strange geography of the novel, to desire it to be immediately recognizable, is to reject the narrative itself, to diminish the fiction" (71). Such a reading, Jolly goes on to suggest, "indicates a refusal on the part of the reader to take the fiction as itself" (71). It stems from a "desire to change the fiction into something that it cannot or will not be" (71).

As though he is taking his cue from these later published words, Watson (1986, 372) draws attention to how Coetzee's first novels impose "with a seeming disregard for all historical veracity, an eminently twentieth-century voice and academic intelligence onto a historical period seemingly remote from it in both time and space". But whereas Gordimer deplores this technique in Coetzee, Watson celebrates it. With reference to Crewe's argument that Coetzee became the first South African author to break consciously, even self-consciously, with "the conventions of realism" in his first novels by candidly announcing their "own fictionality", Watson writes:

> to those who had been brought up on an unrelenting diet of South African liberal realism, with its studious commitment to depicting everything from the flattened vowels of the English South African accent to the contents of the laundry basket, and having as its controlling center some bewildered nobody beating his or her moral wings in vain – to such people JM Coetzee's first novel had something of the liberating, clarifying force of a genuine revelation.
>
> (372)

On the whole, Watson's argument amounts to a contention that something important about the *level* at which Coetzee aims his critique, is lost in advance through the compulsion to bring liberal realism in its form as the historically specific *nomos* of apartheid to bear on the novel. It is, rather, the *specificity* of the fiction in its deliberate use of generality or indeterminacy in relation, especially, to space that should detain us here, because these are the keys to a door that open onto a universalist critique, literally, not simply a critique of one apartheid amongst others, one colony amongst others, or, precisely, one Empire amongst others, but of Empire, colonisation and apartheid as generalised and generalising processes of modernity as such.

If, as Schmitt, contends, the history of colonialism is in its "entirety" the history of land-appropriation and if our experience at the level of the planet or the globe is "largely colonial" (Watson 1986, 370), as Coetzee calls it in 1978, then we cannot avoid Schmitt's contention that the *nomos* of the Earth is land-appropriation and that the collective victim of the inscription of bare life into the unity of order and emplacement that it founds, is precisely Frantz Fanon's "wretched of the Earth" (Fanon 1963). Indeed, Fanon's *Wretched of the Earth* reads as the bio-/thanato-/necro-political dangerous supplement to Schmitt's *Nomos of the Earth*.

However, I would extend this to argue that the critical target of *Waiting for the Barbarians* is possessive spatial appropriation in general. Shortly after it becomes clear that the magistrate has lost his jurisdiction over the frontier town – as a result of the declaration of an emergency in the Empire and with the arrival of the ominous Colonel Joll in his town – he makes an extraordinary statement: "The space about us here is merely space, no meaner or grander than the space above the shacks and tenements and temples and offices of the capital. Space is space, life is life, everywhere the same". In these words, it seems that the signifiers of spatial generality in the novel ("the Empire", "the capital" and "the frontier") and indeed of existential generality ("magistrate", "barbarian", "prisoners", "the nomads") are pushed to the utmost limits of what they can encompass – space in general and life in general – to conclude that it is simply what it is, "everywhere the same".

In what follows, I will suggest that we take the magistrate at face value *and*, simultaneously, that we do not take him at face value when he utters these words. In terms of taking him at face value, I am interested in teasing out the consequences of the fact that the statement above is indeed the statement of a magistrate in a frontier colonial town who has lost his jurisdiction. Stated differently, my sense is that it is of enormous interpretive significance that these are the words of a coloniser who is becoming unmoored from the master-signifier – the Lacanian "S1" – of Empire.

It is precisely for this reason that I also suggest that we do not take the magistrate at face value. What this entails at the interpretive level is that we read his statement that "space is space" "otherwise" (Chryssostalis 2013, 158) and I will do so by bringing Slavoj Žižek's reading of tautologies to bear on the magistrate's tautology about space. This manoeuvre will reveal that the tautology, far from signifying nothing, in fact confirms that Coetzee's target in *Waiting for the Barbarians* is spatial appropriation in general. My reading of the tautology holds that the statement not only conceals the contradictions at the very heart of modernity's approach to space, but also conceals the void at the heart of modern Cartesian subjectivity. It is this void – and the proclivity for possessive spatial appropriation to cover it up – that lies at the centre of colonialism and its *nomos*.

The coloniser who refuses

Coming now to the subject of the utterance and to taking him at face value, Coetzee's novel is at pains from the start to narrate that the magistrate is a cipher of colonial agency gone awry, veritably recoiling on itself. Time and again, the magistrate is opposed to Colonel Joll who is installed from the start as the cipher of unequivocal, resolute colonial agency. Colonel Joll is the Sadean hangman who pathologically follows his duty to Empire as the Lacanian Big Other, the ubiquitous third on the scene of his tortures.

The magistrate, on the other hand, to borrow Watson's use of Albert Memmi's (1974, 63) term, is "a coloniser who refuses". Watson (1986, 378) notes that all of Coetzee's protagonists up to but not including Michael K, "are colonizers who wish to elude at almost any cost their historical role as colonizers". As such, they are "wrought to a pitch of desperation in their efforts to escape the intolerable burdens of the master-slave relationship" (378). There are many indications in the novel that the magistrate, in the course of the novel, progressively *becomes* just such a coloniser – from the way in which he responds to Joll's killing and torture of the barbarian prisoners, to his release of the prisoners that Joll sends to the town, to his care, in the ministration scenes, for the barbarian girl who is left behind after the prisoners are released, to his ultimate outright revolt and condemnation for treasonously consorting with the enemy.

What, may we ask, is the symptom of the magistrate as a coloniser who refuses, if that of the Sadean Colonel Joll – to whom he becomes opposed – is pathological compliance with duty to Empire? In his reading of Memmi, Watson (1986, 378) argues that in the case of the coloniser "who does not (or perhaps cannot)" return to his "home country" (i.e. cannot leave the space that he inhabits), and who, nevertheless, does not accept colonisation, "the specter of contradiction of multiple contradictions confronts" him "at every turn" so that, in Memmi's words "he lives his life under the sign of a contradiction which looms at every step, depriving him of all coherence and all tranquility".

As a coloniser who refuses, the magistrate's symptom, then, is contradiction. Now, Watson (1986, 373) remarks that Coetzee is, against the custom of realism, with his eye on the coloniser who refuses, at pains to "register the impact of colonialism" at the basic level of language and this "impact of colonialism" on language is that it contradicts itself. Instead of conveying meaning through signification it "fails to signify, to mean at all": "The only tongue the colonialist can speak is the circular one of tautology", Watson (373) writes.

It should hardly surprise us, then, that our magistrate so casually announces the tautology that "space is space". But what would it mean, in the end, to take *this statement* at face value, as the word of a coloniser who refuses? My wager in this regard is as follows: the very fact that the magistrate is, at this point in the novel, already in the process of becoming a coloniser who refuses, means that we must read his tautology "otherwise". Of course, he is still the coloniser who speaks the circular tongue of tautology, but, in a certain sense, he does not know what he is saying. His tautology signifies nothing only at the level of the enunciation. At the level of the enunciated content, things are entirely different. At the level of the enunciated content, the tautology takes the form of the statement of a contradiction not simply at the heart of the coloniser who refuses, but indeed at the heart of modern spatial consciousness in general. How so?

Let's begin with a resonance: the assertion "space is space" immediately recalls the much more frequent, typically positivist, assertion that "law is law" (a tautology that, one could argue, was by and large indeed the primary symptom of apartheid's adjudicators, its magistrates and judges (see, for instance, Dugard 1971). Slavoj Žižek (2005, 103) has drawn attention to the fact that tautologies of this type – another prevalent one of course being "God is God" – "functions precisely in the Hegelian sense, as one's identity which reveals the supreme contradiction". To assert, then, that "space is space" is, at one level, no more than our magistrate's way of asserting the contradiction at the heart of his identity as "a colonizer who refuses". It is no coincidence that the chosen category of the understanding (to resort to the Kantian term) is space, for the magistrate's ontological contradiction as a coloniser who refuses is ultimately a spatial one.

But the tautology itself can also be read as the assertion of a fundamental contradiction in relation to the "ontology" of space itself. To see how this works, let's look closer at Žižek's analysis of the "law is law" tautology as harbouring a contradiction. Žižek (2005, 119) writes: "the tautology 'law is law' shows the illegal and illegitimate character of the establishment of the reign of the law". In essence, "law is law" is a tautology in which one term represents the presentation of positive legality and the other its alegal origin. Asserted in the form x is x, the statement is a contradiction.

Far from the authoritarian resonance of these assertions, Žižek (2005, 119) argues that these tautologies are "scandalous":

> they subvert the foundations of power, of its authority, at the very moment when they give the impression of supporting them. The illegitimate violence by which law sustains itself must be concealed at any price, because this concealment is the positive condition of the functioning of law. Law functions only insofar as its subjects are fooled, insofar as they experience the authority of law as "authentic and eternal" and do not realize 'the truth about the usurpation' [...] The whole of classical politico-philosophical thought rests on the refusal of an overturning of law.
>
> (119–20)

But how exactly does this logic work in the context of space? We have to follow Žižek (2005, 125) to the end here in his explication of the structure of a contradiction masking as a tautology. A contradiction, he argues, is not an opposition. An opposition is the statement of two positive facts which he designates as + and -. This is not the structure of the contradiction. The structure of the contradiction must be stated as + and 0 or, in Žižek's Lacanian idiom, as "presence" and "lack". Žižek's example of a contradiction is the relationship between Good and Evil: "Evil is not a positive entity. It is only the lack, the absence of Good" (125).

What, then, is the structure of the contradiction in relation to, or inherent in, space? It is necessary to understand here that the revolution in the modern understanding of space for which Kant is responsible is that space "in itself" or "as such" is, for the understanding, unrepresentable, because space is subjective and as such always already represented. The essence of the Kantian revolution in relation to space, then, can itself be stated as a tautology: we cannot represent space without representing space. Space, argues Kant, is a non-empirical, a priori intuition (1998, 175). This, argues Kant, means that "one can never represent that there is no space, though one can very well think that there are no objects to be encountered in it" (175).

The empty space is, of course, defined as a void, but what is interesting here is that Kant thinks that we can think the void but that we cannot represent it. In a very particular sense, there *is* no such thing as the void. The void, then, is pure negativity or, put differently, it is positivised lack, it is not a positivity in itself. And here we have the contradiction: space is both contained in and by matter and its relations *and* space *is also* the lack of this very matter and their relations.

A case can, therefore, be made that the magistrate's assertion that "space is space", literally conceals the profound contradiction at the heart of our modern understanding of space – a contradiction which can also be stated as "space is everything but space". It remains, however, to bring our findings in relation to space back to the agent of the contradictory utterance, our magistrate as a cipher of "the colonizer who refuses".

I take my cue again from Watson (1986, 375) here, where he writes that the rendering of colonialism in Coetzee is primarily that of a "projection of a certain mental aberration located exclusively in the divided consciousness that is a special feature of Western humanity" and that

> the colonizing project of the West was set in motion when this same man embarked upon his Cartesian project of separating subject from object, self from world in a dualism which privileged the first of the two terms and thereby assured his domination of nature and any other obstacle he might confront.
>
> (375)

From this observation, Watson (1986, 376) deduces that the voracious, limitless appetite of the cogito's will to power is attributable to the "unbudgeable void at the very heart of it" and that colonialism is "perhaps the most significant expression" of this void. In short, it is not surprising, then, that "the metaphysics of power" (389) at the very basis of the modern era "should appear as the greatest threat" (389) – modernity is an era of a "continuing colonialism" (376). In fact, it will be seen that Coetzee, in Watson's reading at least, deconstructs Conrad's notion of the coloniser discovering "at the heart of Africa a void which would seem to penetrate every level of existence" (371). The void is relocated, both spatially and temporally, and found lurking in the very heart of European consciousness well before colonisation.

Rachel Langford (2003 116) has argued that the colonial representation of space is ultimately a utilitarian one and that, as such, it follows the attributes of "abstract space" as defined by Lefebvre: "[T]he space of the colonies is envisioned in thoroughly objectified terms, as unmodified by human intervention, as transparently knowable and as consumable, both as knowledge and as material resource". She continues:

> The emphasis in the spatial discourses of colonialism on territorial homogeneity, and on the colonies as a *tabula rasa* unincorporated into any human's social practice, betrays the extent to which there lies embedded within colonialism's discourse this violent ideology of space as abstract space.
>
> (117)

It is therefore not difficult to see that the representation of space as abstract space – as unoccupied, undifferentiated and for that reason appropriable, ownable, void space – is the representation most suited to the will to power as the driving force of colonialism, not simply in a historical sense but indeed in an ideological and even pathological one. It is such a representation of space that clears the way for the clearings that are such a persistent accompaniment to the *terra nullius* principle in colonialism (Pottage 2019, 165). And it is through such a representation of space, then, that Schmitt's insistence on *nomos* as a land-appropriation and as the "spatially determined processes of settlement in which order and orientation are combined", become fully appreciable.

Against this background, stands our magistrate's position as one in a series of Coetzee's protagonists who are characterised by "insatiable hunger" "for ways of escape from a role which condemns them as subjects to confront others as objects in interminable, murderous acts of self-division" (Watson 1986, 378). But Memmi argues that this position is untenable, it is an impossible historical situation and its ultimate effect is impotent stasis. Watson (1986, 385) writes that the coloniser who refuses is a type of person only "half in the world of being" and "only half in the world of becoming" and that it would not be unusual for people who find themselves in this dilemma "to begin succumbing to the attractions of a world of being as opposed to a world of becoming and to place a higher value on the former rather than the latter" (Watson 1986, 384). Watson continues:

> It would seem to be part of the essence of their position that they often cannot decide in favor of one or other mode of being. If they choose contemplation, history will not cease to remind them of their irresponsibility and guilt. If they decide to act, to enter history, the world of being that they have necessarily left behind will continue to be present to them in the form of an inner hollowness.
>
> (385)

Ultimately, the coloniser who refuses "wants to preserve both being and becoming. He does not want to give up either" (388).

Unlearning empire? The ministration scenes

We have come a long way from our unruly magistrate who so boldly asserts the tautology that space is space at the beginning of *Waiting for the Barbarians*. In the previous section, we have tracked why and how the magistrate is best described as a coloniser who refuses, having read the "space is space" tautology as paradigmatic/symptomatic speech of a coloniser who refuses. In this concluding section, I will argue that a critical instance of the magistrate's spatial orientation/emplacement in the novel, works as something of a key when it comes to the question of overcoming the *nomos* of colonial-apartheid towards spatial justice.

The point in this section is that the conditions of possibility of the impossible confrontation with the void at the heart of colonialism, are and must be spatial and that it is the very in-between emplacement of the coloniser who refuses *with* the colonised that functions as the condition of possibility of such an impossible confrontation. It is from this impossible confrontation with the void that something like spatial justice, contingent and transient, emerges.

And this, I contend, is what takes place in the ministration scenes of *Waiting for the Barbarians*. A becoming *un*colonial, as opposed to decolonial becoming, is perhaps a good description for that which is embarked upon, but never quite completed, in fact left radically incomplete, by the magistrate in this novel. Becoming uncolonial has obvious links to what Van Marle discusses under the heading of "unlearning" in her chapter for this collection (Van Marle 2022). Becoming uncolonial, then, could be described as a form of abandoning the certitudes of imperialism as colonialism/apartheid, of unlearning both its proclivities and reflexes, both its will to power and its unconscious drive for power. Unlearning imperialism, argues Ariella Azoulay (2019, 8) entails attending to the "conceptual origins of imperial violence, the violence that presumes people and worlds as raw material, as always already imperial resources". Those conceptual origins lie in the psyche of the coloniser and given, as Langford makes clear, that this imperial violence is profoundly spatial, becoming *un*colonial, then, and as unlearning, is the encounter of psychic space with the spatial injustice of imperialism.

There are a number of indications in *Waiting for the Barbarians* that the magistrate, as a coloniser who becomes, in the course of the narrative, a coloniser who refuses, has begun the difficult task of unlearning empire, even before he takes the blind girl off the street and into his rooms. First of all, there is the magistrate's choice of residence. Early on, he tells the reader that he does not reside in the "official lot" of the civil magistrate which he describes as being on the "quietest street in the town", "an attractive villa with geraniums in the windows" (Coetzee 1980, 22). Instead of taking his place amongst the props of this bucolic scene, he has made a conscious decision to occupy "the rambling apartment over the storerooms and kitchen intended for the military commandant we have not had for years" (22). The magistrate's private space could accordingly be described as a liminal one. Stewart Motha (2012) has pointed to the importance of liminality in the postcolonial context, arguing that a "character of being in the postcolonial setting", which he describes as a liminal one, "might provide another range of political possibilities" (142). Motha points specifically to the spatial aspect of liminality as the occupation of the "space in-between".

The magistrate's rooms as a liminal space/place facilitates another range of political possibility, a range that has been foreclosed by Empire. For example, after Colonel Joll's return with the barbarian prisoners, the magistrate begins "to see the disadvantages of living" in this apartment: "the noises coming from the yard below", the yard that has now been turned into a "permanent prison yard", disturbs his peace, confronts him anew with the tyranny of Empire – and it does so by infiltrating the most private of the spaces that he occupies. In other words, the space facilitates an encounter with his conscience as a coloniser. Yet, although he could move to the villa at any point, he refuses to do so; he endures the becoming discomfiting of the liminal space that he has chosen to occupy. This points to a range of political possibility in which the private sphere no longer shuts out the destructive politics of Empire, but in fact allows itself to be affected and troubled by it.

Motha (2012) also suggests that liminality might "be the resistant or emancipatory flipside of in-finite sovereignty" in that it might open the possibility of a non-sovereign subjectivity" (143). It is precisely to the possibility of such a non-sovereign subjectivity that *Waiting for the Barbarians* opens up when the magistrate brings the blind barbarian girl, whose feet were broken during torture, into his rambling, liminal apartment. And it is in this liminal middle that he becomes able, first, to wash her feet (Coetzee 1980, 30), deformed by the Empire's torture, and, later, to attend to her entire pained body (31–2). Philippopoulos-Mihalopoulos (2015, 190) writes: "the middle can be thought of as the space of struggle. It is a space of encounters with other bodies, a space in which one's body affects and is affected by other bodies".

Because the middle is a space of struggle, the affect here is not mercy. The narrative evokes no mercy for the magistrate – he remains mercilessly guilty when he reports that "the distance between myself and her torturers, I realize, is negligible" (Coetzee 1980, 29). There is no suggestion of an absolution of this complicity by the action that follows (this is not the law performing its merciful double, à la Martha Nussbaum, in relation to the girl).

Instead, the narration that follows makes it clear that these ministrations *undo* the magistrate as a magistrate, as a man of the *nomos* of Empire. In other words, in and through these scenes the magistrate himself becomes what Motha (2012, 143) calls a "liminal being" (a name which I regard as another, amongst others, for the coloniser who refuses). In Lacanian language, these events represent an unmooring – if ever there was one – of the magistrate from the institutional master-signifier (the S1) of Empire. Lacan attributed an enormous significance to the role of shame in analysis and in Seminar XVII he says:

> Today I have brought you the dimension of shame. It is not a comfortable thing to put forward. It is not one of the easiest things to speak about. This is perhaps what it really is, the hole from which the master signifier arises. If it were, it might perhaps not be useless for measuring how close one has to get to it if one wants to have anything to do with the subversion, or even just the rotation, of the master's discourse.
>
> (Lacan 2007, 189)

My sense, therefore, is that the ministration scenes confront the magistrate, more than anything, with the shame of Empire, with the hole, the void, from which his master-signifier arises, with the spatial injustice of *nomos*. This shame is, for the magistrate, *embodied* in the blind barbarian girl with her feet broken by torture, lost to her people; and it is in attending to this body broken by Empire that the magistrate finally becomes undone.

The narrative is at pains to remain consistent with regard to the way in which the ministration scenes undo him. There is, for instance, no verbal communication between him and the girl during the repeated performances of this ritual: "it is a week since words have passed between us", writes the magistrate at the beginning of the episode (Coetzee 1980, 32).

To this absence of verbal communication we must add the fact that, during the performance of the ritual, the magistrate literally struggles to stay awake: "I lose myself in the rhythm of what I am doing [...] There is a space of time which is blank to me: perhaps I am not even present" (30). This passage should be read with what the magistrate says later on: "in the very act of caressing her I am overcome with sleep as if poleaxed, fall into oblivion sprawled upon her body, and wake an hour or two later dizzy, confused, thirsty. These dreamless spells are like death to me, or enchantment, blank outside time" (33).

In his *The Fall of Sleep*, Jean-Luc Nancy (2009, 1) writes that sleeps sums up all our falls: "Sleep is proclaimed and symbolized by the sign of the fall", "the more or less swift descent or sagging, faintness". What emerges in such a reading, then, is that the narration is concerned to register not only the fall of a certain language, but indeed the fall of a certain consciousness and, perhaps most importantly, the fall of a certain force of *nomos*. This is the fall of *nomos* as appropriation, of *terra nullius* as performing a clearing. In these scenes, the "land" is no longer empty, the "barbarian" is no longer cleared away. Instead, she is attended to, encountered without conflict, ministered, not administrated.

Without ever saying as much, it is clear that Coetzee is gesturing at the practical unlearning of Empire in these profoundly spatial, profoundly intimate scenes. This unlearning in the form of the ministrations takes place despite the magistrate, in spite, even, of himself (which is why Attwell's (2015, 106) description that *Waiting for the Barbarians* is a novel about "baulked desire", is so appropriate). This aspect becomes clear, when the magistrate, in a moment of "rational" consciousness, suffers fits of self-resentment "against my *bondage*" (Coetzee 1980, 44 (emphasis added)) not to the girl, but to "the ritual of the oiling and rubbing, the drowsiness, the slump into oblivion" (44).

From the point of view of the link between possessive appropriation and *nomos,* the novel cannot be more explicit that, whatever takes place between the magistrate and the girl, it is precisely not possessive appropriation, it is precisely not *nomos* in territorial terms, it is "emplacement without the priority of appropriation" (the version of *nomos* that Chryssostalis (2013, 158) retrieves from Arendt's reading of *nomos*). This is not simply the case because the magistrate cannot decide whether he desires the girl sexually ("angry with myself for wanting and not wanting her" (35)), but indeed also because he does not "know what to do with her, no more than one cloud in the sky knows what to do with another" (36).

The "spatial justice" of the analyst's discourse

This un-nomic *im*propriety, as we might call it, carries on until it reaches its apogee when the magistrate's desire becomes so frustrated that he asks the girl "speaking thick and muffled into her ear" (43): "And why do I want you here?" and she replies: "You want to talk all the time."

As "improper" as this itself might sound, one cannot but ask at this point if this is not precisely the reply that a psychoanalyst – if pressed by the analysand – would be forced to give? To be sure, we have gone, as the repetition of the ritual progressed, from a magistrate who could barely stay awake, let alone talk, to one who wants to "talk all the time". What if we were, on this basis, then, to suggest that the space that is being inaugurated here is the space of the analyst's discourse; that it is in fact the girl who functions as an analyst for the magistrate in these scenes and not the magistrate who is an analyst (as has been elsewhere suggested (Yuan 2000, 79))?

From the point of view that Lacan (2007) argued that the discourse of the analyst is the inverse of that of the master it would appear that it is not so inappropriate in the context to suggest such a reading. Through this lens, it becomes, for instance, possible to see that discursively the position of the girl corresponds to that of the agent in the analyst's discourse, "addressing" by making visible, finally visible to the magistrate, his divided subjectivity, the "unbudgeable void" at the core of his consciousness.

Lacan insisted that the relationship between the analyst as agent and the analysand as other is impossible "because it turns the other into the cause of desire of the other" (Verhaeghe 1995, 96), eliminating her subjectivity. Yet it is precisely this impossibility that functions as the condition of transference through which the subject becomes able to "encircle his object", an ability to which the magistrate does eventually accede when he, confused and angry as he is about it all, finally admits that the presence of the girl has forced him "to interrogate" his desire and, even further, that she has forced him to look into himself and "see only a vortex and at the heart of the vortex oblivion" (Coetzee 1980, 51) – in other words, *that* void.

In this sense, then, the space between the girl and the magistrate functions analytically and, as such, it is an irreducible disruption of the master's discourse. I would not describe these scenes as spatial justice in the sense of ordinary liberal or social justice, but rather as approximating the kind of spatial justice of which Philippopoulos-Mihalopoulos (2015, 175) writes; a spatial justice that demands "a rearticulation of justice as something that might – just might – emerge from within the spatiolegal operations".

Philippopoulos-Mihalopoulos (2015) argues that this notion of spatial justice manifests in the "embodied gesture" of withdrawal: "the only way in which a body can question the emplacement of itself as well as other bodies [is] by withdrawing from an atmosphere of fixed positions" (175). This withdrawal is precisely what the magistrate enacts: he withdraws himself and the girl from their "fixed positions" in the atmosphere of Empire, when he takes her into his liminal rooms and does not treat her as a coloniser would ordinarily, nomically, treat the colonised.

Philippopoulos-Mihalopoulos also writes that spatial justice can only emerge as "an ontology that resists pre-formed hierarchies and boundaries" (177). In our context, such resistance means resistance to the *nomos* and the *logos* of Empire – and what happens in the magistrate's rooms begins to resemble the rudiments of something like a spatial justice after Empire/apartheid. Of course, this is not a full and final justice; rather it is a justice which is incompletely, transiently attended to *there* in his rooms to *that* body *and* a justice which is forever still to come, still to be done – universally so. It is thus no coincidence that Coetzee renders the character of the barbarian girl as blind – the allusion to the classically blindfolded lady Justice is impossible to miss. It is only much later in the novel that the magistrate expresses this justice in the form of a question when he asks: "*Justice*: once that word is uttered, *where* will it all end?" (Coetzee 1980, 118 (emphasis added)).

The fleeting, liminal *un*colonial spatiality between the girl and the magistrate thus does not offer us a "final" solution in the form of Soja's (1996) thirdspace, rather, its strangeness, its uncanny texture, takes the form of a question mark (Philippopoulos-Mihalopoulos 2015, 178) – as all analyses do. But it is a question mark that changes everything.

One can be forgiven for thinking at least initially, that socially, spatially speaking, nothing changes or is changed after the ministration scenes – the magistrate is still the magistrate and the girl is still a blind barbarian girl who now works in the kitchen (there is, thus, a return to the humdrum reality of Empire as the "manoueuvering space of the lawscape" (Philippoppoulos-Mihalopoulos 2015, 175). However, the unshakeable feeling that everything is different and is radically changing is soon confirmed when the magistrate hosts a dinner for the leader of a relief detachment from the capital in the course of which he ends up condemning the vacuity of the logic of Empire, openly wishing for a barbarian triumph and thereby sealing his fate as a traitor (Coetzee 1980, 54–6).

According to Lacan, the end result of the analytical process is radical difference (Verhaeghe 1995, 96). And, in accordance with this logic, the paradoxical upshot of the impossible "objective" positioning of the girl as analyst in the discourse is that the magistrate does come to see her in her irreducible otherness, first, in a dream that has "taken root" (Coetzee 1980, 57). In it he sees the girl as herself, "herself as I have never seen her", he says, "a smiling child, the light sparkling on her teeth and glancing from her jet-black eyes" (57). Much later, this dream transforms into reality. Having taken the girl back to her people, as she says good-bye, he sees her as "a stocky girl with a broad mouth and hair cut in a fringe across her forehead staring over my shoulder into the sky; a stranger; a visitor from strange parts now on her way home after a less than happy visit" (79).

Lacan also argued that it is "impossible to *be* an analyst, the only thing you can do is to function as such for somebody during a limited time" (Verhaeghe 1995, 96). To this Verhaege adds that "the greatest danger is that of reducing each discourse to one concrete implementation" (98). We should, finally then, not be surprised that shortly after the incident where the magistrate seals his fate, the space of analysis begins to give way to the space of another kind of discourse when, at the end of Chapter 2, the girl begins sexually to encourage the magistrate and he declines – to her bitter chagrin (Coetzee 1980, 59). The magistrate's refusal here of course has everything to do with the subjective transformation that is taking place, the giving way of his own discursive position as master. What is clear is that the power dynamic that has sustained the relationship between coloniser and colonised has profoundly come undone by virtue of the liminal space that facilitated an encounter of a different order – and it is this undone nature of the relationship that ultimately leads to the magistrate returning the girl to her people (77–9).

Conclusion

To conclude, my wager has been that to read *nomos* otherwise would be to read the ministration scenes for what they so achingly are: acts, however modest, however transient, of an upheaval that has no end, of an undoing of the magistrate through which a certain confrontation with the void of the Real at the heart of *his* colonial subjectivity begins to function as the pre-condition of an as yet unrealised "empire in which there would be no more injustice, no more pain" (Coetzee 1980, 26).

"This is *the beginning* of spatial justice then, right in the middle", writes Philippopoulos-Mihalopoulos (2015, 186, emphasis added). For Philippopoulos-Mihalopoulos, this is the middle between striated and smooth (186). In the contextual space of the novel, it is the liminal space – between the striated official residence of the magistrate and the flattened space of the prison yard – which facilitates this beginning of spatial justice after apartheid.

There is certainly no *arrival*, no *realisation* of that *nomos* (if it would have been one) in this literature, only the dogged persistence of a man who "lost his way long ago but presses on along a road that may lead nowhere" (170): "This is not the scene I dreamed of" (170), remarks the magistrate in closing. But in the ministration scenes and in what they unleash, he is *reading nomos* otherwise (Chryssostalis 2013); finally, "here", because literature's "giving" law takes place "here", in its giving space, as Derrida remarked long ago, "for singular events".

Notes

1 The original reference for Gordimer's piece is Gordimer 1984. I am well aware that the allegorical reading of Coetzee's novels has been challenged, notably by Attridge 2004's

proposal for a "literal" or literary reading. Yet Attridge himself acknowledges the validity and value of the allegorical reading when he concludes at the end of his chapter entitled "Against Allegory", that "I am not against allegory, then, in spite of this chapter's title; allegorical readings of many kinds have been and will continue to be of the greatest significance" (Attridge 2004, 63–64). The "allegorical" reading on which this chapter relies to a great extent, will hopefully at least contribute to the significance of the allegorical strategy in relation to reading Coetzee. I am placing "allegorical" in scare quotes, because I believe that the reading that I embark upon here both is and is not a classically allegorical reading. For one thing, my attempt to show that Coetzee's literature creates the space for what Derrida calls "singular events" finds itself closer to Attridge's concern for the literary mode which can reveal to us the alterity of literature. Differently put, the "allegorical" reading that I embark upon here, ultimately stands in the service of a return to the singularity (and thus Attridge's "literality") for which literature creates the space.

2 It should be noted here that Attwell's point is that specific events during apartheid, such as the torture and murder, in 1977, of Steve Biko in police detention, found their way into the novel (2015, 113) by way of allegory. Implicit, then, in Attwell's description of the milieu of *Waiting for the Barbarians* as "a historically vague, Manichaen, allegorical landscape" (115) is that the novel is an allegory of a *specific time* during apartheid. I would, however, suggest that, regardless of the fact that events relating to a specific time during apartheid found their way into the novel by way of allegory, *Waiting for the Barbarians* is *also* an allegory of the *spatiality of apartheid in general.* In other words, the "vague", "allegorical landscape" is meant to function as a representation of the *general space* – the condition, as it were – of apartheid throughout its time.

3 In reading *Waiting for the Barbarians* as a novel about an incomplete discursive transformation, I am thus at the same time in agreement and in disagreement with Attwell's description of the novel as one about "the failure to imagine a future, a novel about baulked desire, too" (2015, 106). Insofar as I read the novel as thematizing incomplete transformation, I disagree that it is necessarily a novel about the failure to imagine a future. As this chapter sees it, the point is that the novel leaves open the question of imagining a future – it does not necessarily fail to imagine a future. On the other hand, the idea of a "baulked desire" is central to this chapter's concerns and in this respect it concurs with Attwell that a "baulked desire" plays a critical role in *Waiting for the Barbarians.*

References

Attridge, D. 2004. *J.M. Coetzee and the Ethics of Reading: Literature in the Event.* Chicago, IL: University of Chicago Press.

Attwell, D. 2015. *J.M. Coetzee and the Life of Writing.* Auckland Park: Jacana.

Azoulay, A. 2019. *Potential History: Unlearning Imperialism.* London: Verso.

Bozzoli, B., and P. Delius. 1990. "Editors' Introduction: Radical History and South African Society." *Radical History Review* 1990(46–47): 13–45.

Bracher, M. 1988. "Lacan's Theory of the Four Discourses." *Prose Studies* 11: 32–49.

Chryssostalis J. 2013. "Reading Arendt 'Reading' Schmitt: Reading Nomos Otherwise?" In *Feminist Encounters with Legal Philosophy*, edited by M. Drakopoulou, 158–184. New York: Routledge.

Coetzee, J. M. 1980. *Waiting for the Barbarians.* London: Minerva.

Derrida, J. 1992. *Acts of Literature*, edited by D. Attridge. New York: Routledge.

Dugard, J. 1971. "The Judicial Process, Positivism and Civil Liberty." *South African Law Journal* 88: 181–200.

Fanon, F. 1963. *The Wretched of the Earth.* Translated by Constance Farrington. New York: Grove.

Gordimer, N. 1984. "The Idea of Gardening." *The New York Review of Books*, February 2. https://www.nybooks.com/articles/1984/02/02/the-idea-of-gardening/#:~:text=The%20Idea%20of%20Gardening%20%7C%20by,New%20York%20Review%20of%20Books.

Jolly, R. J. 1989. "Territorial Metaphor in Coetzee's "Waiting for the Barbarians"." *A Review of International English Literature* 20(2): 69–79.

Kant, I. 1998. *Critique of Pure Reason.* Translated by P. Guyer and A. W. Wood. New York: Cambridge University Press.

Lacan, J. 2007. *The Seminar of Jacques Lacan, The Other Side of Psychoanalysis: Book XVII.* Edited by Jacques-Alain Miller and translated by Russell Grigg. New York: W. W. Norton.

Langford, R. 2003. "Challenging the Colonization of Space: Exteriors and Interiors in the Films of Ousmane Sembène and Souleymane Cissé." In *Francophone Post-Colonial Cultures: Critical Essays*, edited by K. Salhi, 114–125. New York: Lexington.

Memmi, A. 1974. *The Coloniser and the Colonised.* London: Souvenir Press.

Motha, S. 2012. "Colonial Sovereignty, Forms of Life and Liminal Beings in South Africa." In *Agamben and Colonialism*, edited by M. Svirsky and S. Bignall, 128–151. Edinburgh: Edinburgh University Press.

Nancy, J. 2009. *The Fall of Sleep.* Translated by Charlotte Mandell. New York: Fordham University Press.

Philippopoulos-Mihalopoulos, A. 2011. "Law's Spatial Turn: Geography, Justice and a Certain Fear of Spaces." *Law, Culture and the Humanities* 7(2): 1–16.

Philippopoulos-Mihalopoulos, A. 2015. *Spatial Justice: Body, Lawscape, Atmosphere.* New York: Routledge.

Pottage, A. 2019. "Holocene Jurisprudence." *Journal of Human Rights and the Environment* 10(2): 153–175.

Schmitt, C. 2003. *The Nomos of the Earth in the International Law of Jus Publicum Europaeum.* Translated by G. L. Ulmen. New York: Telos.

Soja, E. 1996. *Thirdspace: Journeys to Los Angeles and Other Real-and-Imagined Places.* Oxford: Blackwell Publishers Inc.

Van Marle, K. 2022. "Unlearning, (Un)naming, Cohabiting." In *Spatial Justice After Apartheid: Nomos in the Postcolony*, edited by Jaco Barnard-Naudé and Julia Chryssostalis. Abingdon: Routledge.

Verhaeghe, P. 1995. "From Impossibility to Inability: Lacan's Theory on the Four Discourses." *The Letter: Lacanian Perspectives on Psychoanalysis* 3: 76–99.

Watson, S. 1986. "Colonialism and the Novels of J. M. Coetzee." *Research in African Literatures* 17(3): 370–392.

Yuan, Y. 2000. "The Subject of Reading and the Colonial Unconscious: Countertransference in J.M. Coetzee's *Waiting For the Barbarians*." *American Journal of Psychoanalysis* 60(1): 71–84.

Žižek, S. 2005. *Interrogating the Real*, edited by R. Butler and S. Stephens. London: Continuum.

Chapter 9

Queer states

Beyond the *nomos* of the closet in Tendai Huchu's *The Hairdresser of Harare*

Derrick Higginbotham

Introduction

First published in 2010, Tendai Huchu's novel, *The Hairdresser of Harare*, depicts the fraught friendship between two hairdressers, Vimbai and Dumisani, sometime in the late 2000s, as various policies of the Mugabe government had a deleterious impact on the national economy and lives of those living in Zimbabwe.[1] Even as it captures the unravelling of the formal economy, the novel explores the socio-political meanings of space, with special attention to gender, sexuality and citizenship. The events the novel portrays likely occur sometime after 2005, since Vimbai, the narrator, mentions a government action when describing Sam Levy's Village, the "premier" mall in Harare:

> During Operation Murambatsvina, when thousands of structures were declared illegal and arbitrarily demolished, Sam Levy's was discovered to have been built without proper planning permission. There was some talk about demolishing the whole structure, but how could they, since it provided a comfort zone for the new elite, an imaginary place of civilization? (Huchu 2010, 139)

From May to June 2005, armed police and public security officers destroyed informal settlements and markets within the city, claiming that it was "cleansing" Harare of "slums" and curbing the purportedly illegal commercial activities that occurred in such informal spaces (Musoni 2010, 301–3; see also Harris 2008, 44–6). The legal pretext for this government action was that vendors did not obtain the proper permits to build workshops and produce goods, and as Vimbai observes, the authorities also targeted Sam Levy's, a well-to-do shopping mall, precisely because its builders apparently did not follow government regulations. In the novel, the authorities ultimately refuse to destroy Sam Levy's because it is a "comfort zone" as well as, in more lofty terms, a "place of civilization". Such a description is apparently attributable in part to the fact that Sam Levy's caters to the wealthy and in part because it is much more English

DOI: 10.4324/9780203712771-9

than Zimbabwean, both in its architecture and the goods it proffers, when compared to the informal markets that dotted the city.

Operation Murambatsvina illustrates the government's capacity to classify individuals, groups and spaces as criminal, as not belonging within the boundaries of the nation. The government officially declared that its war against informal settlements and markets would enable it to establish better housing and reorganise smaller and medium enterprises to increase commercial success. This action, the government claimed, would bring "dignity, order and prosperity to stakeholders and the nation at large" (as quoted in Musoni 2010, 308). However, between 2002 and 2005, in the lead up to this operation, hundreds of companies had shut down across the country, and in Harare, deindustrialisation took hold, which, in turn, encouraged substantial growth of the informal economy.[2] Operation Murambatsvina, rather than creating prosperity, devastated a key sector of the economy, and created a moment of internal migration, uprooting communities within the city as well as the country at large, transforming citizens, even if only temporarily, into outsiders. Internal migrants like these have a status akin to foreigners since their location in geographic and political space becomes provisional; they are thereafter vulnerable to further displacement. Such a government action, moreover, echoes the spatial arrangements found in different colonial contexts like those of the apartheid government in South Africa with its repeated forced removals of Black citizens into separate "homelands" (Musoni 2010, 303). I contend that Huchu situates the events in the novel as occurring after Operation Murambatsvina because it underscores the state's power to reorganise a country's *nomos*, its spatialised normative and legal orders (Schmitt 1950, 47; Chryssostalis 2013, 163–6). Under the twin banners of preserving collective dignity and establishing social order, the state transforms groups of citizens into aliens, which, I argue, dovetails with Huchu's depiction of sexual minorities, specifically gay men, in contemporary Zimbabwe.[3]

The state constitutes such groups – whether of informal traders or sexual minorities – as part of a socio-juridical process aimed at fortifying national boundaries. From the point of view of the state, these groups acquire the status of an "included exclusion", to use Jaco Barnard-Naudé's phrasing (2017, 31). That is, the government's sense of political and legal community congeals through an exclusion from that community of those who do not meet its criteria. Such an inclusion of the exclusion is always already *nomic* in that it involves both an ordering and an order; after all, it implies a specific spatial normativity, according to which spaces are arranged and individuals placed inside or outside of them, as well as recurrent acts of ordering, which enforce the boundaries and normalise spaces, creating – sometimes metaphorically and sometimes not – an "interior" space for the "included" and an "exterior" space where those "others" (are to) reside. When thinking about the constitution of the *polis* as a polity, Hannah Arendt contends that the law functions like a wall, establishing a firm boundary between those inside and those outside, thus securing a space for those inside to act; without the "wall-like law", she insists, the city itself would not achieve permanence ([1958] 1998, 64; 194–5; and 197–8). To put it differently, the space that the law as *nomos* establishes affords those inside the potential to make history and be remembered. Drawing on Arendt, Hans Lindahl proposes that *nomos* is both physical because the law engenders space, partitioning it in specific ways like the establishment of the nation and its borders, and normative in that it "concerns a claim about the common interest of the polity" (2006, 886).

Huchu's novel intricately engages with both senses of *nomos*. It does so by focusing on Dumisani, a gay man, and the consequences he faces once his sexual identity becomes public. Little has been written about *The Hairdresser of Harare*, although the scholarship that exists mostly concentrates on its representation of homosexuality. While Mtenje's recent article does not consider the politics of space, it does highlight the ways that masculinity, sexuality and national belonging are central issues in the novel (2019, 173–5). Chitando and Manyonganise as well as Gibson's (2016, 567–71; 2013, 72–3) analyses grapple with the novel's depiction of political homophobia in similar ways, but they also do not link the representation of sexuality and gender to the politics of space. By contrast, Ncube (2016, 14–19) employs the notion of the closet to interpret the text, yet he does not consider the spatial dimension of the closet. Rather than ignore that dimension of the closet like Ncube or endorse Warner's (2005, 52) declaration that the closet is a "misleading spatial metaphor", my argument returns our attention to the way that the closet engages with a spatial politics. Still, my use of closet as a concept does not construe exit from it as "the sole basis" for the identities and agencies of sexual minorities (Ross 2005, 161). It aims, rather, to capture the intricate ways in which people navigate heterosexism and the homophobias it produces. By attending to notions of the closet and the significance of the different kinds of silences around sexuality and sexual practices, this chapter emphasises the need to emplace our studies of the closet, without rejecting the importance of visibility politics to different iterations of sexual liberation.[4]

Space, law and queerness

My reading of *The Hairdresser of Harare* contends that the closet marks a taking of space from sexual minorities, which occurs concurrently with the exclusive appropriation of public space by heteropatriarchal authority, expressed in manifold ways. This process of appropriation is typical of how *nomos* establishes itself, certainly for Schmitt ([1950] 2006, 69–71). Schmitt's definition of *nomos* refers to the "first land-appropriation" when the "political and social order of a people becomes spatially visible" (69 and 70). Positive law might ratify this appropriation, but *nomos* signifies that initial act of appropriating land, and this emphasis on the materiality of land as it transforms into the space of a people proves provocative when thinking about what the closet can signify. Using

Schmitt's sense of *nomos*, I stress that the closet marks sexual minorities' loss of physical, public space since the closet implies displacement from the world outside it. It thus negatively marks the space where sexual minorities cannot, or at least should not *be*, confirming their status as outlaws, in a literal sense, with laws in Zimbabwe and other locations prohibiting same-sex activity.

Nations can strengthen and/or imitate the logic of apartheid by legally fortifying the closet. As Eric C. Christiansen (2000, 1021) contends, the South African government refined the Immorality Act in the 1960s to target sexual minorities specifically, so that they had the status of "unapprehended felons", fortifying separateness based on sexual identity. However, its democratic Constitution rejected "apartheid legal norms", and it has since dismantled much of the *nomos* of the closet, eliminating the legal "apartness" of sexual minorities, a socio-legal transformation that did not occur in Zimbabwe after the end of colonial rule (1046).[5] In the former Rhodesia, colonial rulers established laws against same-sex activity in 1891, and, since independence, the Mugabe government has only added to those regulations by enshrining, for instance, a ban on same-sex marriage within the country's constitution in 2013, which is one example of how the government reinforced the *nomos* of the closet in Zimbabwe (Constitution of Zimbabwe 2013, § 78(3)). Moreover, the taking of space by the heteropatriarchal state appears more pronounced in places like Zimbabwe because, as part of the decolonisation process, nations must reconceptualise the scope and practice of freedom within the renewed nation, a reconceptualisation that does not always match the promise of liberation attached to decoloniality. During and immediately after Zimbabwean independence in 1980, for example, lesbians and gays enjoyed public space in new ways, with the formation in 1982 of the first lesbian organisation, gay men's use of Harare's Cecil Square for cruising, and even some media articles defending sexual minorities (Epprecht 2004, 175–176). While such changes suggested that the state would formally include sexual freedoms as a part of decolonisation, by 1983, the government began limiting the freedom of sexual minorities, insisting that gay men were not allowed on Cecil Square, for instance (176–7).

This exclusion of those who were once briefly included marks the beginning of a pattern of political homophobia that would intensify in the 1990s and 2000s, with the government adamantly insisting that sexual minorities were not a part of the nation. Several factors converged to create these conditions. First, by the mid to late 1990s, Mugabe's government and his supporters could no longer define themselves as morally superior compared to South Africa since its transition to democracy meant it endorsed a radically different set of ideals compared to apartheid rule; as well, South Africa no longer existed as an external military and economic threat against which Zimbabwe could define itself as a nation (Phillips 1997, 481). Simultaneously, in 1991, the International Monetary Fund and the World Bank, at the invitation of the Mugabe government, launched the country's Economic Structural Adjustment

Program, embarking on a large-scale deregulating of the economy that over the coming years generated unemployment, bankrupted local businesses, increased inflation and created food insecurity. These events precipitated the crash of the Zimbabwean dollar, which, in turn, eroded political support for Mugabe and the ZANU-PF (Zimbabwean African National Union – Patriotic Front), his political party (Epprecht 2013, 134–6).

With Mugabe and his government losing political power, they sought an enemy against which the nation could rally, and without South Africa as that adversary, the government utilised homophobia – a homophobia informed by pre-existing religious and cultural norms – in order to generate a threatening other (Epprecht 2013, 134–137). In a 1995 parliamentary debate on sexual minorities, for instance, Aeneas Chigwedere, an MP and ZANU-PF member, contended that supporting sexual minorities would mean that the government would want its people to be "unchaste", to be "animal-like and immoral" and in response to this danger to the dignity of the Zimbabwean people, sexual minorities should be "eradicated" from the nation, like a weed excised from a garden (as quoted in Phillips 1997, 471). With the economy in tailspin, the Mugabe government and its supporters engaged in what Sylvia Tamale calls "the politics of distraction", diverting people's attention from the state's mismanagement of the economy and focusing people's anxieties and ire, instead, on the supposed dangers that sexual minorities posed to the family and, by extension, the nation (Tamale 2014, 167; see also Mtenje 2019, 176).

Huchu's novel ultimately proposes that where sexual freedoms are not part of decolonisation, sexual minorities invariably find themselves in a queer[6] state, betwixt and between nations. My argument contends that such queerness – a queerness that is never quite comfortable or fully at home – could be a model for thinking *nomos* "otherwise" (Chryssostalis 2013), as grounded in the experience of the displaced, of those whose identities are complexly manifold, instead of in the moment of geopolitical appropriation and constitution, a moment when governments and communities fortify borders and boundaries, creating a monocultural vision of "the people" that can be imagined, and can imagine themselves as "pure". This queer state, which Huchu's novel links to the immigrant experience, destabilises any sense of "belonging", especially any belonging defined by an untroubled identification amongst people that functions as the foundation for a polity; this queer state, by contrast, points to the creation of a polity not constituted by reductive forms of othering, one characterised by a capaciousness that embraces others without erasing differences (see also Cohn 2005, 33).

The heteropatriarchal *nomos* of the postcolony

As Primorac and Chan note, *The Hairdresser of Harare* demonstrates the ways that "heterosexuality, patriarchy and social violence" interlink, which illuminates that a specific iteration of heterosexual masculinity rules public space in the city, delimiting its normative borders and thus defining who can speak and act within that sphere (2010, 720). By unpacking the novel's depiction of men's deployment of heterosexism to establish who should have the freedom to be in public space or to head a household, I show the way that it creates a limited parallel between Vimbai and Dumisani's experiences in the city, which further underscores the ways that they are both alike as outcasts. The final section of this chapter will demonstrate that while the heteropatriarchal order marginalises both Vimbai and Dumisani, only Dumisani becomes a pariah, which signals the more alarming predicament that sexual minorities face within this order.

The moment of engendering the "space of appearance" (Arendt 1998, 199) that constitutes the public realm involves gendering that space so that it appears predominantly heteropatriarchal. The novel dramatises the outcome of this gendering process via repeated scenes in which Vimbai encounters men on the streets of Harare who expect her to respond affirmatively to their sexual solicitations. When she rejects them, these men verbally humiliate her. For instance, after Mrs Kumalo awards the management of her salon to Dumisani and not to Vimbai, who expects this promotion, Vimbai feels disappointment, so she leaves work early, without Dumisani joining her as he usually does. Finding herself alone on the city streets, she describes the following interaction with a stranger:

> 'You must be a hell of a thief because you stole my heart just by the way you walk.' He was trotting, trying to catch up with me. 'Girl, talk to me, just for a minute and I will be happy for the rest of my life … hell, baby you are hard to get but let me be your Romeo and I'll treat you like the princess you are.'
>
> 'Go away,' I say, increasing my pace.
>
> 'Baby just give me a chance, I'm a great guy, I have a good job, my own house and a nice car. It's just at the garage today and that is why I am walking'.
>
> (Huchu 2010, 79–80)

When Vimbai rebuffs this man's solicitations, she faces verbal threats that make visible the ways in which the public realm is not available to single women; it is the space for heterosexual men to speak and act. After Vimbai adamantly rejects this man, he immediately tells her that she is ugly, and then he calls her a slut (80), an epithet that expresses the link between gender and public space. In this man's vision, Vimbai moves from the places that she could and should occupy – his car, his house, his bedroom – to the place of the slut, the disobedient woman who illicitly occupies public space.

A similar logic appears not only in the street but also occurs within Vimbai's home, suggesting that even in supposedly private space, a single women's presence can be regarded as a problem for male authority figures. As the narrative unfolds, Vimbai reveals that she had a short-lived relationship with a wealthy businessman, Philip Mabayo, who abandons her after he rapes her, and she becomes pregnant with their daughter, Chiwoniso (41). Because he periodically sends her envelopes of money, he arrives at her house one night presuming that she will be sexually available to him; her refusal results in his harassment: he declares that she is his "bitch and [he] can have [her] any time [he] want[s]" (41). In his mind, because he has "paid for her", he can have sex with her when he wishes. Vimbai's resistance to sexual harassment on the street and in her own home clarifies her stance with regard to heteropatriarchy since her interactions with men in these two different spaces overlap with one another in a manner that leaves her disenchanted with men entirely, making her an outsider to the heteropatriarchal order.

Moreover, Vimbai breaks from the heteropatriarchal rules that govern the family, which further exemplifies her deviation from its *nomos*. After her brother, Robert, dies while working in the UK, he bequeaths to Vimbai the home he bought in the better suburbs of Harare. At the reading of Robert's will, Vimbai's parents and her older brothers, Takesure and Knowledge, are shocked that Vimbai receives the house. Additionally, they are appalled by her decision to reject the gerontocratic and patriarchal *nomos* that would exclude her from the property, insisting that she should offer the house to her eldest brother, Takesure, who already voiced plans to live there with his family and to permit Knowledge and his family to have the cottage that is part of the estate (30–1). Her insistence that she occupy the house results in a conflict with her parents and older brothers that challenges traditional norms determined by age and gender, which govern those who possess authority over space and place, those whose voices and actions matter within the family and, by extension, within the city and the nation generally. Importantly, this incident illustrates the spatiality of heteropatriarchal normativity: who can rightfully appropriate, who can rightfully belong, who can rightfully be ousted, who has to defer, who can plan the future, and, ultimately, who has a future. Her younger brother, Fungai, later visits Vimbai in her home, and when they discuss this family conflict that estranges her, he insists that "in our culture a parent does not apologise to their child" (55). Even as Fungai maintains that the family order is inviolable, Vimbai thinks differently, claiming that "I made an effort to see them at the memorial and they turned me away like a dog", an animal metaphor that will echo later in the novel when Vimbai imagines sexual minorities as like animals (55). Such mistreatment means that she no longer considers her parents family, a break that signifies her alienation from yet another vital socio-political institution that governs the spaces of the city and the nation.

The novel juxtaposes this alienation with Dumisani's estrangement from his family because of his sexuality, making these two characters more similar than either of them appears to recognise. The novel emphasises this connection between Vimbai and Dumisani at a key moment when the church, yet another institution, valorises the *nomos* of the heteropatriarchal polity, reaffirming a line between proper citizens and errant outcasts. After Vimbai and Dumisani grow closer as friends, she invites him to attend church with her and Chiwoniso. Once at her Pentecostal church, they listen to the following sermon by Pastor Mvumba:

> Brothers and sisters, don't you see the signs [of sinfulness] in front of your eyes? Look at Zimbabwe. Ask why the Lord is punishing us like this. It's because the whole earth has become like Babylon or Sodom and Gomorrah. There are no more moral values in people's hearts. Just coming to the church this morning, I saw many young women wearing mini-skirts. Why do they do this? They do not know it, but it is because they are sent by the devil to entice men and to lead their hearts astray. They are harlots like Jezebel and if you cannot resist, then it is better for you to pluck your eyes out so you may not see. People are having sex outside of marriage and this angers the Lord. ...You must be on the lookout for homosexuals and sexual deviants. Perverts shall burn. How can a man and another man sleep together? God made Adam and Eve not Adam and Steve. Can a woman and a woman make a baby?
>
> (72).

Importantly, Vimbai's finds this sermon invigorating since she asserts that it "filled [her] with the power of the Holy Spirit" (72), an emotional state that points to the sexism and homophobia she harbours, but she does not recognise that she is not the pastor's primary audience. When Pastor Mvumba describes women who wear miniskirts, he addresses a "you" bound to be tempted by these women, which indicates that his chief audience is not women. Even though Mvumba begins this part of his sermon with a call to "brothers and sisters" as those constituting the nation of Zimbabwe, the target audience of his sermon is heterosexual men. He thus implies that heterosexual men are the legitimate and exclusive inhabitants of the polity, the proper citizens of the nation who are under threat from two groups of people: women in miniskirts and sexual minorities. They specifically threaten the dignity of these heterosexual men and the integrity of the nation that enables these men to actualise their freedom.

This pastor's focus on miniskirts is anything but arbitrary. When detailing the longer history of Black men's struggle against colonial rule in Zimbabwe, Epprecht (2004, 159) explains that nationalist leaders responded to their emasculation under colonial rule in a distinctive way. Their economic exploitation, for example, impeded men's capacity to fulfil their traditional role of financing marriages and their own households, and in reaction they invested in a hyper-masculinity that also could challenge white settlers' machismo. This hyper-masculinity forged in the struggle movement required the wholesale rejection of femininity, so that miniskirts, exemplifying both women's emancipated sexuality as well as Western modes of attire, became objects of heteropatriarchal contempt for many male nationalists. In Huchu's novel, the pastor's condemnation of miniskirts, then, signifies a repudiation of women, of femininity generally and of sexual intimacy outside of marriage, marking one of the ways in which a particular form of hypermasculinity was carried over from the nationalist struggle into the newly liberated state via religious institutions. Heteropatriarchy sustains this hypermasculinity and results in Vimbai's peculiar status as an included – after all, heterosexual men and women 'belong together' – exclusion because of the way in which her womanhood, her sexuality and status as single intersect.

Furthermore, as Barbara Boswell (2015, 52) argues, the efforts in 2014 to pass anti-homosexuality laws in Nigeria and Uganda intermesh with "decency" laws that target women's purportedly sexually explicit dress; efforts to establish both types of laws assume a "repudiation of the feminine", the same repudiation of a stereotypical femininity forged within the anticolonial struggle, linking sexism and homophobia in a distinctive manner. Ashly Currier (2010b) makes a comparable argument when analysing the homophobia that the South Western African People's Organization (SWAPO) deployed in governing a liberated Namibia. For instance, in early 1997, Alpheus Naruseb, the SWAPO Secretary for Information and Publicity issued an official statement in the newspaper, *The Windhoek Advertiser*, in which he states that "We made sacrifices for the liberation of this country, and we are not going to allow individuals with alien practices such as homosexuality to destroy the social fabric of our society" (119). Framed by the need to protect the space of the liberated "country", Naruseb imagines same-sex sexual practices – and, implicitly, sexual minorities – as "alien", as destructively seeking to undo "the social fabric" of the new-born nation. A related sentiment circulates within Pastor Mvumba's sermon as it appears in *The Hairdresser of Harare* since the pastor creates a parallel between the danger that women in miniskirts pose to heterosexual men and the "homosexuals and sexual deviants" that those men must be on the lookout for, presumably in both public and private spaces, because of their joint threat to the harmony of the heteropatriarchal nation (Huchu 2010, 72). This oppressive logic of the danger to the nation's moral status echoes the sentiments of Mugabe's government in its orders for Operation Murambatsvina, with its claim that this operation will restore the city and the nation's dignity, pointing to the ways that national unity forms through various forms of othering.

In this novel, Huchu thus documents another form of apartheid in Zimbabwe; this apartheid is not state racism but a spatialised state sexism and homophobia. Moreover, if Schmitt is right that the fundamental process of constituting *nomos* consists in the appropriation of space, then we can see how the novel allegorises a *nomos* of heteropatriarchal apartheid in the postcolony more generally. For example, when the state takes over and clears out the informal markets, what it does in nomic terms is to reinforce its entitlement to the public sphere of the street, to clear it of "undesirables" and reconfigure it in the way that it sees fit. None of the spaces in the book seem to escape this logic. The social sphere of the street and the church, as well as the supposedly private sphere of the household are set upon and ordered by heterosexual, male authorities so as to clear out those who appear guilty of "alien practices" (miniskirts, same-sex desire), either violently suppressing them, as in Vimbai's case, or displacing them *into* the closet, as in Dumisani's case. It is this heteropatriarchal *nomos* that constructs and then excludes them as outcasts, although only Dumisani must be expunged from the nation, registering the particular disgust that heteropatriarchal authority has for visible sexual minorities, if only because heterosexual men "need" women symbolically and materially to ratify their identities.

Between non-place (*ou-topos*) and placelessness (*a-topos*)

While the novel portrays institutions like the government, family and church as reinforcing a heteropatriarchal order that classifies unmarried, heterosexual women as part of the "included exclusion" necessary to secure the nation, it also stresses that the closet functions as a complex experience of included exclusion. Stated in spatial terms, the closet is *ou-topos* – a non-place – since it is a secret and liminal space that is both inside and outside the heteropatriarchal *nomos*, making figures like the closeted Dumisani safe but perpetually precarious, always potentially subject to displacement. This precarity of the closet appears at a key moment in the narrative: after Dumisani leads Vimbai to believe that they are a couple and after she begins to suspect him of having an affair, she reads his diary, discovering that he is, as Vimbai puts it, "A HOMOSEXUAL – Ngochani" (Huchu 2010, 166). Vimbai's shock is textually and linguistically stressed by the use of all capitals and the Shona word that can signify a homosexual. Vimbai, then, outs Dumisani, initially to herself and the reader but eventually also to others, with several consequences for Dumisani. In this section, I demonstrate that the metaphor of the closet evokes a specific spatial politics for sexual minorities, with the novel finally suggesting that there is no proper geographic place that they can occupy within the borders of the heteropatriarchal *nomos* of Zimbabwe. If someone exits the closet, then that person can be exposed to the annihilating violence of this *nomos*. Ultimately, Dumisani loses the spaces, places and relations that create belonging, and as a consequence, he dramatises the condition of *a-topos*, a placelessness distinctive to the immigrant and the displaced more generally.

The Hairdresser of Harare illuminates the closet's connection to the norms governing space when Vimbai interprets certain conversations, acts of interpretation that rationalise away other possible meanings. Late in the novel, for instance, after Dumisani and Vimbai begin to appear as a couple, he invites her to stay the weekend with him and his family, who are part of the economic and political elite of Harare. As they settle in for dinner, the following exchange takes place between the Ncubes and Vimbai:

> 'I hope you like the food,' Mrs Ncube said to me sounding a little nervous after she had said grace.
>
> 'It looks lovely,' I replied.
>
> 'Only the best for the girl who cured my son.'
>
> 'Come on let's get stuck in,' Mr. Ncube said rather abruptly. Dumi, sitting beside his father, maintained a somewhat stony expression.
>
> (116–17)

At first, Vimbai does not react to Mrs Ncube's remark that she had "cured" her son. Others in the scene, however, make readers amply aware that something is off kilter since Mr Ncube "abruptly" directs everyone's attention to the food. Moreover, Dumisani's expression is "stony", indicating that he has shut down emotionally in response to his mother's remark, which threatens to expose him and thus jeopardises his efforts to create an ostensibly heterosexual bond with Vimbai. Not long after this exchange, Vimbai explains to readers her interpretation of this remark: she presumes that Dumisani's mother means that Vimbai cures him of a broken heart (118). This presumption enables Vimbai to continue investing her affection in Dumisani and dramatises the closet as a delicate yet efficacious spatial marker, delimiting where knowledge should stop and where the will not to know secures heteronormativity.

Notably, both Vimbai and Dumisani appear economically invested in keeping him in the closet, which, in part, explains her reticence to ask questions when odd interactions occur like the one at the Ncubes' dinner table. Not only does Vimbai enjoy lavish food and other luxuries when visiting the Ncubes, which vividly contrasts with the scenes of food shortages that are staple to Vimbai's everyday world, but Dumisani's parents provide her with extravagant gifts, particularly when they underwrite her own hairdressing salon. Indeed, she retrospectively recognises that this material support reinforces her love for Dumisani. After the family subsidises her salon in the upscale Sam Levy's Village, Vimbai contemplates the Ncubes' generosity. She grasps that their generosity likely would not "outlast my relationship with their son", realising upon reflection that "it became blurry as to whether it [her relationship with Dumisani] would have gone this far if I had not found out about his privileged background" (158). Had she not discovered that Dumisani's family was wealthy, she remains unsure whether their relationship would have progressed, especially given aspects of Dumisani's behaviour that trouble her, like his refusal of sex and his secrecy about where he sometimes goes late at night. This uncertainty indicates her investment in maintaining a certain kind of unknowing about Dumisani, their bond and their household. A similar argument about economic investment can be made in relation to Dumisani because the novel makes it clear that he cultivates his bond with Vimbai not just because of his affection for her and her daughter. He, for instance, presents her to his family as his "girlfriend", a statement that equivocates upon the precise meaning of that word, with the result that his family renews his regular allowance, which they had cut off because of his affair with another man (94–5).

Furthermore, Huchu's novel stresses that the closet impacts one's place socio-economically, making it hard to succeed in the already precarious urban world of heteropatriarchal Harare. At one point, Vimbai observes that Dumisani opts out of the expected trajectory of a son since he refuses to be involved in the family business (121). Dumisani instead pursues his own ambitions to be a hairdresser, a story that Vimbai already knows. Still, she cannot appreciate that Dumisani probably refuses to be a part of his father's business so as to preserve a degree of sexual freedom. Had he committed to the family business, he undoubtedly would have attained a greater degree of wealth and status, but the pressure to conform to heteropatriarchal obligations like that of marriage would intensify. Huchu's novel thus implies that Dumisani's inability to be openly gay within his family as well as within the public world – a public world bounded by longstanding laws against same-sex activity – curtail his economic opportunities, putting him in a marginal social space, one comparable to that of a single, heterosexual, working-class woman like Vimbai, a marginality that is one of the costs of the *nomos* of the nation. The novel suggests through both characters that the closet and class intersect in intricate ways, implying that there are many different closets that can form depending on the choices that are socially available.

The question of who properly belongs in the post-liberation nation animates other conflicts in Huchu's novel since some of the formal aspects of decolonisation, in the end, prove unable to secure a public world defined by a capacious practice of freedom and inclusiveness. One such conflict occurs between, on the one hand, Trina, who is the best supplier of hair products for Mrs Kumalo's beauty salon and also a white Zimbabwean impacted by the government's fast-track land redistribution in early 2000, and, on the other hand, the unnamed Minister M__, Mrs Kumalo's most valuable client, who was a member of the struggle to liberate the country from colonial rule and also serves in the Mugabe government. Through her networks, Minister M__ discovers that Dumisani and Vimbai will do Trina's hair as thanks for her work as a consistent supplier for the shop (103–4). In response, the Minister arrives at the salon, fist in the air, chanting national slogans in support of the ZANU-PF. After those in the salon listlessly echo the Minister's slogans, she zeroes in on Trina, and the two women argue about the redistribution of Trina and her husband's farm. Dumisani tries to intervene, but the argument escalates, with the Minister commanding Trina to "Go back to Britain you white pig" and Trina insisting that Zimbabwe is her "home, and I have as much right as you to be here" (105). That the Minister highlights Trina's whiteness indicates the framework of her politics: for her, decolonisation ideally requires the banishment of whites.

The novel, however, complicates this straightforward formulation that implies an independent Zimbabwe is only for Black citizens. In an earlier scene, when readers first meet Trina, she arrives at the shop and greets everyone in Shona. Vimbai then reveals that "There was never a time when we spoke to her in English. For all we knew she might not have been able to speak the language. The freckles on her face said she was one of us and had been basking in the glory of the same sun for far too long" (44). Even though a descendant of white settlers, Trina appears to Vimbai and those in the shop as "one of us", a citizen of the same nation because of her exclusive use of a local tongue. By highlighting that no one knew whether Trina could speak English, the novel ensures that the Minister's later demand that Trina return to Britain sounds, at best, like empty rhetoric and at worst, like political absurdity. After all, if she only speaks Shona, Trina would be socially adrift, at best, in Britain. This incident, nevertheless, highlights the question of who belongs in Zimbabwe's political community.

In addition, the Minister specifically insults Trina by calling her a "pig", an important epithet in this novel because of its link to the political homophobia historically marshalled by the Mugabe government. When Vimbai discovers Dumisani's sexual identity by reading his diary, her sense of betrayal overwhelms her:

> My daughter had been the product of the union between man and woman. What could a man and a man ever hope to produce in a million years? Even the president had called them worse than pigs—I might have disagreed with a lot of what he has done to the country but I had to agree with him there.
>
> (167)

At this moment, Vimbai recalls a well-known incident in 1999 when, in a speech delivered to traditional chiefs to muster support for land redistribution, Mugabe offered a digression, claiming that even pigs and dogs know the difference between male and female, whereas gays and lesbians do not, a sign that they are not human and not bearers of the legal or political rights granted by the nation (Epprecht 2004, 181). Mugabe then urged the 200 chiefs to join the fight in respecting Zimbabwean culture, implying that gays and lesbians are not a part of the nation's cultural heritage. The novel makes a quiet but pertinent link between this moment when Minister M__ calls Trina a pig and Vimbai's sympathy for Mugabe's sentiment that gays and lesbians are, in fact, worse than pigs, which obliquely connects Trina's ambiguous status as citizen to Dumisani's ambiguous status as citizen. Vimbai, furthermore, seems to forget her own claim earlier in the novel that her family treats her "like a dog" (Huchu 2010, 55) by shunning her, a forgetfulness that impedes her capacity to be sympathetic to Dumisani's predicament and leads to the novel's finale. The novel deploys these animal metaphors to represent how the dominant order, in different ways, sets Trina, Dumisani and Vimbai apart from their fellow human beings and exiles them from the places, the *topoi*, where the bonds of humanity, civility and citizenship are forged: the street, the home, the church and, ultimately, the polity.

The queer state of *a-topos*

While Vimbai and Trina do remain in Zimbabwe at the novel's end, Dumisani cannot, especially after Vimbai outs him, underscoring the inability of visible sexual minorities to be included in the nation. When Vimbai discovers Dumisani's secret that he is gay and that he has been having an affair with Minister M__'s husband, she reveals the affair to the Minister, earning herself a favour (171–3). Then, the Minister arranges to have Dumisani beaten, with the intent to kill, although he, by chance, does not die; Vimbai, upon seeing Dumisani wounded, returns to the Minister to bargain for Dumisani's passport, which the Minister's men stole, so that Dumisani can travel to the UK with a promise to never return (186–7). The final scene in the book has Vimbai, Chiwoniso and Michelle, Dumisani's sister, at the airport – that emblematic "non-place" (Augé 1995, 94–102) of transit between domestic and international locations – seeing off a physically weaker Dumisani. Significantly, Huchu's novel does not offer the reader any sense of what Dumisani's life is like in the UK, which is contrary to Gilson Ncube's (2016, 16) assertion that *The Hairdresser of Harare* implies that countries of the global north are better for sexual minorities like Dumisani. Indeed, the only time that the novel represents the UK, it dramatises the dislocation and disappointment that Vimbai's brother, Robert, experiences as an immigrant, and that knowledge can cast a pall over a reader's interpretation of Dumisani's future. Even though Robert earns enough money to buy the house that he bequeaths to Vimbai, he does so by working in a nursing home because he cannot fulfil his dream of finding employment as a teacher. The image of the UK as a possibly difficult place for displaced persons hangs over Dumisani's departure, and it, combined with the knowledge that racism and homophobia still circulate in the global north, does not suggest he will belong in the UK in any simple sense.

The novel's refusal to give any clear sense of what Dumisani's life is like in the UK stresses that he ends up in a condition of *placelessness*, inhabiting that precarious 'space' of the immigrant, which is the flipside of the nowhereness he experiences in the heteropatriarchal *nomos* of the Zimbabwean polity. As Bourdieu (2004, xiv) contends, the immigrant is "neither citizen nor foreigner, not truly on the side of the Same nor really on the side of the Other". This suspension between citizen and foreigner makes Dumisani seem like someone who is, to use Bourdieu's term, *a-topos*, without a place, particularly because the current iteration of the Zimbabwean nation finds its foundations in the exclusive love of heterosexuals, especially middle-class and wealthy heterosexual men. Huchu's representation of Dumisani's predicament highlights the ways that the Mugabe government marshalled homophobias that circulate within different social locations and institutions to shore up the boundaries of the nation and to firm up the moral ground upon which the government justified its actions; Operation Murambatsvina indicates that this project of marginalising those who are socio-politically vulnerable does not solely focus on sexual minorities but can include any population that the state deems in violation of the culture's dignity, like the presence of the working poor in Harare's informal settlements and markets (see also Phillips 1997, 484).

The "diasporic, unhoused" character of a figure such as Dumisani, pained as he appears, can represent a queer state, one that refuses to distinguish rigidly between the self and other, between an "us" and a "them", precisely because such a state of being exists in the borderland, a state that, as Gloria Anzaldúa contends, contains multiplicity (Said [2004] 2014, 53; Anzaldúa 1999, 101–4).[7] In the contradictory space of the borderland, identities can be remade and new communities built, even though such creativity does not exclude suffering. Precisely because of his queer state, Dumisani signals a different ethics of living with others, one that refuses such homogeneity. Rather than relying upon bonds that find their foundation in notions of the "purity" of a traditional culture and/or national identity, this diasporic form of living, paradoxically, discovers the foundation of belonging in "modes of un-belonging" that are defined by plurality and the freedom of movement within as well as between borders, not by an inelastic monoculture that imagines others as moral and mortal threats to be contained and extirpated, which only enables states to practice necropolitics, as Mbembe defines it (Butler 2007; Mbembe 2003, 18). A figure like Dumisani indicates the need for individuals, civil society organisations, as well as politicians to struggle for a more expansive erotic politics of the state, an erotic politics that embraces diversity and necessitates the removal of colonial laws regarding same-sex practices as part of this social transformation. The ending of *The Hairdresser of Harare*, while not skirting the pain of placelessness, longs for a state that can reach over the "wall-like" law that enables its solidity, embracing a decoloniality that does not claim the legal and cultural inflexibility that historically belongs to *nomos*. Instead, a decolonial state could begin to think its *nomos* otherwise, from the position of those who have been rendered *a-topos* by the old *nomos,* from the space of the borderlands, where a fluid sense of community inheres, a community that is not beholden to the exclusionary love of a narrowly defined culture, people or nation.

Notes

1 I want to thank my research assistant, Trish Coetzee; while I was a Lecturer in the English Department at the University of Cape Town, she helped me to gather much of the scholarship that informs this argument.

2 Amanda Hammer (2014) outlines a variety of factors that together contributed to deindustrialisation, including the long term effects of the reduction in public spending that was part of the terms of the Economic Structural Adjustment Programme imposed in the 1990s, along with the economic disruptions that fast-track land redistribution in 2000 energised, because economic outputs in agriculture diminished with the break-up of large farms and the creation of smaller farms with different owners (See also Mlambo 2008).

3 Throughout this article, I use the phrase "sexual minorities" to refer to people invested in expressing their erotic desires with those of the same sex, a group that is statistically not the norm. Huchu's novel often uses the terms "gay" and "homosexual", and Mugabe, when he was speaking as a public figure, typically referred to "gays and lesbians", which suggests that these terms are a part of discourse about sexual identities in Zimbabwe. Still, such terms, as Notisha Massaquoi (2013, 39) puts it, "are not fixed identities and where there is a multiplicity of sexualities not yet uniformly defined", these specific terms are not necessarily the only ones available. "Sexual minorities" proves more capacious as terminology. On the complexity of naming, see also Matebeni and Msibi (2015).

4 Both Marlon B. Ross and Rinaldo Walcott warn that the closet can imply an individual and geographic progress that prioritises the visibility of sexual and gender minorities as these minorities appear in the global north, abetting a colonialising framework; instead, they demand a supple politics of visibility sensitive to differences across geographies and cultures (2005, 162–63 and Walcott 2016, 146–54). Carlos Ulises Decena, in his work on tacit expression of sexual identity in gay male Dominican immigrant communities in New York, and Marc Epprecht (2013), in his work on the history of sexuality in Zimbabwe, complicate our understanding of the closet by situating it in quite different sociocultural contexts without doing away with it as part of the politics of sexuality (Decena 2008, 354–55; see also Ahmed 2006, 175–76). In particular, Epprecht proposes that "cultures of discretion" (1998, 635–38) in Zimbabwe mean that until the 1990s when the government brought sexuality into public debate, there was very little overt discussion of sexual practice or identity, although there is much historical evidence of same-sex activity between men, specifically in legal records. Such approaches show that the line between what is tacitly known and what is a secret can be blurry precisely because the closet is a collaborative social formation that people negotiate within specific circumstances. Moreover, Ashley Currier argues in her study of LGBT organisations in Namibia and South Africa that visibility matters to any political struggle for the freedom of sexual and gender minorities; however, it is not a single passage from invisibility to visibility, but rather invisibility and visibility fluctuate as they are used strategically (2012, 10). Importantly, Currier's study focuses solely on organisations, not individuals, although her point about invisibility and visibility as changeable modes of presentation depending on the exigencies of the time and place holds true for both. In other words, the act of coming out is not a singular act of an individual; rather, as Sedgwick notes, one will come out repeatedly over time as one interacts with different individuals, groups and institutions, making it a continuous process for both individuals and collectives (1990, 68).

5 Focusing on a longer history of law and sexuality in the United States, William N. Eskridge, Jr. (2009) makes a similar case, positing that sexual minorities became the subject of legal restrictions throughout the 1940s and 1950s, with the result that by the 1960s, they were "smothered by the law" (98). This patchwork of different laws curtailed, if not entirely prohibited, sexual minorities from open participation in employment, in association, and citizenship, creating a legal and political separateness that Eskridge, Jr. characterises as an "apartheid of the closet". These laws, he insists, "enforce compulsory heterosexuality as a pervasive public policy" (7), and it is only

in recent decades that some of this legal framework has been undone. This notion of apartheid is not state racism, as it was for decades in South Africa, but a state sexism and homophobia.

6 My adjectival use of "queer" here is indebted to the theorising of Cathy Cohen, José Esteban Muñoz and Nadia Ellis, each of whom push queerness beyond identity in the same way that my understanding of "queer states" resists calcified notions of identity. Cohen (2005), for instance, contends that queer politics should be coalitional, finding its significance in a "shared marginal relationship to dominant power that normalizes, marginalizes, and privileges", not in a shared history or identity, so that difference becomes vital to the formation of community (43). Similarly, Muñoz posits that queerness is a perpetual departure, a feeling that "this world is not enough", and motivates a move from wherever here is to a there, which means that queerness never stabilises anywhere (2009, 1). It signifies hovering between here and there, the present and the future, holding differences together. Nadia Ellis picks up on the spatial metaphors in Muñoz's definition and reframes this queerness as specific to the Black diaspora and their habituation "to belonging where they should not, to connecting to people with whom difference is pronounced" (2015, 100). Similarly, William J. Spurlin, in an essay on national identity and sexual dissidence in postcolonial Africa, contends that "queer be understood as a kind of 'unstoppable alterity' that continually holds authoritative understandings of national belonging and citizenship in question" (2013, 71; see also Mtenje 2019, 178); this notion of queer as continually disrupting dominant notions of national belonging and citizenship dovetails with my own sense of queerness as resistance to purity and conformity.

7 B Camminga, in their book on transgender refugees in South Africa, also utilises Gloria Anzaldúa's notion of the mestiza to underscore both the discomfort and political possibilities that emerge from those who inhabit borderlands, whether physical, epistemological, or ontological. Importantly, Camminga recognises that the capacity to value social and individual ambiguities – the ethical premise for a more expansive erotic politics of the state, in my argument – can find its ground in the experience of those marginalised by national borders (although not exclusively so), and that the pain and difficulties of marginalisation are largely produced by powerful institutions that exert power over others. In other words, such suffering and struggles are not intrinsic to those who are marginalised or to their capacity to sustain ambiguity in their identities and experiences (Camminga 2019, 143–147).

References

Ahmed, Sara. 2006. *Queer Phenomenology: Orientations, Objects, Others*. Durham, NC: Duke University Press.

Anzaldúa, Gloria. 1999. *Borderlands/La Frontera: The New Mestiza*. 2nd ed. San Francisco, CA: Aunt Lute Books.

Arendt, Hannah. 1998. *The Human Condition*. 2nd ed. Chicago, IL: University of Chicago Press.

Augé, Marc. 1995. *Non-Places: Introduction to an Anthropology of Supermodernity*. Translated by John Howe. London and New York: Verso.

Barnard-Naudé, Jaco. 2017. "Law, Memory and Post-Apartheid Spatiality: 'Reading Nomos Otherwise' 'Mapping the Heterotopic'." In *Spatial Justice and Diaspora*, edited by Emma Patchett and Sarah Keenan, 10–50. Oxford: Counterpress.

Boswell, Barbara. 2015. "On Miniskirts and Hegemonic Masculinity: The Ideology of Deviant Feminine Sexuality in Anti-Homosexuality and Decency Laws." In *Contested*

Intimacies: Sexuality, Gender, and the Law in Africa, edited by Derrick Higginbotham and Victoria Collis-Buthelezi, 46–65. Cape Town: SiberInk.

Bourdieu, Pierre. 2004. "Preface." In *The Suffering of the Immigrant*, edited by Abdelmalek Sayad, xi–xiv. Cambridge: Polity Press.

Butler, Judith. 2007. "I Merely Belong to Them." *London Review of Books* 29 (9): 26–28.

Camminga, B. 2019. *Transgender Refugees and the Imagined South Africa: Bodies Over Borders and Borders Over Bodies*. New York: Palgrave Macmillan.

Christiansen, Eric C. 2000. "Ending the Apartheid of the Closet: Sexual Orientation in the South African Constitutional Process." *NYU Journal of International Law and Politics* 32: 997–1058.

Chryssostalis, Julia H. 2013. "Reading Arendt 'Reading' Schmitt: Reading *Nomos* Otherwise?" In *Feminist Encounters with Legal Philosophy*, edited by Maria Drakopoulou, 158–184. London: Routledge.

Cohen, Cathy. 2005. "Punks, Bulldaggers, and Welfare Queens: The Radical Potential of Queer Politics?" In *Black Queer Studies: A Critical Anthology*, edited by E. Patrick Johnson and Mae G. Henderson, 21–51. Durham, NC: Duke University Press.

Constitution of Zimbabwe Amendment (No. 20) Act, 2013 [Zimbabwe], 22 May 2013, available at: https://www.refworld.org/docid/51ed090f4.html [accessed 18 April 2022]. See specifically Chapter 4, Part 2, Number 78.3.

Currier, Ashley. 2010. "Political Homophobia in Postcolonial Namibia." *Gender & Society* 24 (1): 110–129. https://doi.org/10.1177/0891243209354275.

Currier, Ashley. 2012. *Out in Africa: LGBT Organizing in Namibia and South Africa*. Minnesota, MN: University of Minnesota Press.

Decena, Carlos Ulises. 2008. "Tacit Subjects." *GLQ: A Journal of Lesbian and Gay Studies* 14 (2–3): 339–359. https://doi.org/10.1215/10642684-2007-036.

Ellis, Nadia. 2015. *Territories of the Soul: Queered Belonging in the Black Diaspora*. Durham, NC and London: Duke University Press.

Eskridge, William N. 2009. *Gaylaw: Challenging the Apartheid of the Closet*. Cambridge, MA: Harvard University Press.

Epprecht, Marc. 1998. "The 'Unsaying' of Indigenous Homosexualities in Zimbabwe: Mapping a Blindspot in an African Masculinity." *Journal of Southern African Studies* 24 (4): 631–651. https://doi.org/0305-7070/98/040631-21.

Epprecht, Marc. 2004 [2013]. *Hungochani: The History of a Dissident Sexuality in Southern Africa Second Edition*. Montreal, QC: McGill-Queen's University Press.

Epprecht, Marc. 2013. *Sexuality and Social Justice in Africa: Rethinking Homophobia and Forging Resistance*. London: Zed Books.

Hammer, A. 2014. "The Paradoxes of Class: Crisis, Displacement, and Repositioning in post-2000 Zimbabwe." In *Displacement Economies in Africa: Paradoxes of Crisis and Creativity*, edited by Amanda Hammer, 79–104. London and New York: Zed Books.

Harris, Ashleigh. 2008. "Discourses of Dirt and Disease in Operation Murambatsvina." In *Hidden Dimensions of Operation Murambatsvina*, edited by Maurice Vambe, 40–50. Harare: Weaver Press.

Huchu, Tendai. 2010. *The Hairdresser of Harare*. Harare: Weaver Press.

Lindal, Hans. 2006. "Give and Take: Arendt and the *Nomos* of Political Community." *Philosophy & Social Criticism* 32 (7): 881–901. https://doi.org/10.1177/0191453706066979.

Massaquoi, Notisha. 2013. "No Place Like Home: African Refugees and the Emergence of a New Queer Frame of Reference." In *Sexuality Diversity in Africa: Politics, Theory, and Citizenship*, edited by S. N. Nyeck and Marc Epprecht, 37–53. Montreal: McGill Queens University Press.

Matebeni, Zethu and Thabo Msibi. 2015. "Vocabularies of the Non-normative." *Agenda* 103/29 (1): 3–9. https://doi.org/10.1080/10130950.2015.1025500.

Mbembe, Achille. 2003. "Necropolitics." *Public Culture* 15 (1): 11–40.

Mlambo, Alois. 2008. "Historical Antecedents to Operation Murambatsvina." In *Hidden Dimensions of Operation Murambatsvina*, edited by Maurice Vambe, 9–24. Harare: Weaver Press.

Mtenje, Asante Lucy. 2019. "'Something Radical': Problematizing the Masculine State in Tendai Huchu's The Hairdresser of Harare." *Journal of the African Literature Association* 13 (2): 172–187. https://doi.org/10.1080/21674736.2019.1576307.

Muñoz, José Esteban. 2009. *Cruising Utopia: The Then and There of Queer Futurity*. New York and London: New York University Press.

Musoni, Francis. 2010. "Operation Murambatsvina and the Politics of Street Vendors in Zimbabwe." *Journal of Southern African Studies* 36 (2): 301–317. https://doi.org/10.1080/03057070.485786.

Ncube, Gibson. 2016. "Deconstructing the Closet: A Sociological Reading of Tendai Huchu's Novel, *The Hairdresser of Harare*." *South African Review of Sociology* 47 (3): 8–24. https://doi.org/10.1080/21528586.1163288.

Phillips, Oliver. 1997. "Zimbabwean Law and the Production of a White Man's Disease." *Social and Legal Studies* 6 (4): 471–492.

Primorac, Ranka and Stephen Chan. 2010. "Postscript: Making Do in Hybrid House." *The Round Table* 99 (411): 719–722. https://doi.org/10.1080/00358533.2010.530415.

Ross, Marlon B. 2005. "Beyond the Closet as Raceless Paradigm." In *Black Queer Studies: A Critical Anthology*, edited by E. Patrick Johnson, Mae G. Henderson, 161–189. Durham, NC: Duke University Press.

Said, Edward. [2004] 2014. *Freud and the Non-European*. New York: Verso.

Schmitt, Carl. [1950] 2003. *The Nomos of the Earth in the International Law of the Jus Publicum Europaeum*, translated and annotated by G. L. Ulmen. New York: Telos Press Publishing.

Sedgwick, Eve Kosofsky. 1990. *The Epistemology of the Closet*. Berkeley, CA: University of California Press.

Spurlin, William J. 2013. "Shifting Geopolitical Borders/Shifting Sexual Borders: Textual and Cultural Renegotiations of National Identity and Sexual Dissidence in Postcolonial Africa." *Studies in Ethnicity and Nationalism* 13 (1): 69–79.

Tamale, Sylvia. 2014. "Exploring the Contours of African Sexualities: Religion, Law, and Power." *African Human Rights Law Journal* 14: 150–177.

Walcott, Rinaldo. 2016 *Queer Returns: Essays on Multiculturalism, Diaspora, and Black Studies*. London and Ontario: Insomniac Press.

Warner, Michael. 2005. *Publics and Counterpublics*. New York: Zone Books.

Chapter 10

Abstract space

Continuation, infestation and sanitation in the South African Lawscape

Isolde de Villiers

Introduction

In this chapter, I am particularly interested in how the language of sanitation and infestation in the colonial-apartheid and "post"-apartheid context, reflects a colonial approach to space as abstract in the Lefebvrian sense of the term (Lefebvre 1991, 50–1). Indeed, my argument proceeds from the view that the law-founding violence of colonialism, consisting as it does in the foundational act of land appropriation (Schmitt 2003, 80) which grounds the *nomos* both internally and externally, depended on a view of space as abstract. The main feature of abstract space, according to Lefebvre, is that it relates negatively to its inherent and underlying features, namely politics and history, while it relates positively only to its own implications namely "knowledge linked to power, applied sciences and technology" (Lefebvre 1991, 50–1). Abstract space is disembodied space and stands in contrast to differential, lived space or social space. It is space devoid of the complexity of bodies and relations, it is neatly ordered and structured Newtonian space (Butler 2012, 40).

Abstract space, because it is emptied out space, also neutralises race. For instance, the notorious colonial doctrine of *terra nullius* ("empty" land) rests on a conceptualisation of space as "sitting there statically, waiting to be 'properly' used" and the indigenous inhabitants of this "empty" space are regarded as simply part of the landscape to be colonised (Keenan 2015, 23). This Cartesian idea of space as an empty container in which bodies can be placed, as opposed to space as the product of interrelations (Butler 2012, 38; Massey 2005, 10), determines, by way of neatly demarcated borders, where law begins and ends. In jurisdictional terms, law is viewed as an ordered and rational system, while space is viewed as the "inert arena in which law is evenly applied" (Keenan 2015, 22; Valverde 2015).

The argument in this chapter is structured as follows. First, I expand on the notion of abstract space in Lefebvre's work. In this regard, I consider the link between the production of abstract space as capitalist space and the production of colonial space as racist space, with specific reference to Foucault's discussion of the power-knowledge of hygiene. Secondly, I draw a link between sanitation,

DOI: 10.4324/9780203712771-10

the production of colonial cities and abstract space, and illustrate how the law encompasses a view of space as abstract by turning to the work of Robert Home on how the "sanitation syndrome"[1] in racialised urban planning practices led to the production and continuation of colonial city governance (Home 2014). Home investigates sanitation as a metaphor and its link to racialised planning practices. It is this link between racist segregation, law, the technologies of city planning and how this connects to the metaphor of sanitation, that forms the central concern of this chapter.

I then shift the focus to the city of Tshwane/Pretoria to show how the language of sanitation was used in an ostensibly "post-apartheid" time-space to justify the evictions at Schubart Park in 2011. I refer to the modus operandi of the employees of Wozani Security, called "the red ants" (on account of the red overalls they wear during their eviction operations), to show that the difference between what is labelled as infestation and what is categorised as sanitation is often only a question of power.

Finally, I consider the performance artwork, *Chandelier* by Steven Cohen (2001) in Newtown to highlight the ways in which the eradication of shacks by the "red ants" is in fact also a form of invasion and infestation. This aesthetic intervention opens the possibility of lived space. Cohen places his (white) body in the scene of sanitation and in doing so challenges the disembodied production of abstract space. By inserting his body in that particular space, Cohen draws attention to the other bodies and therefore to the differential and lived space of Newtown.

A clean environment and sanitary living conditions are of course integral for dignified living and the argument in this piece is not that this can be disregarded or that all health and sanitation measures are exercises or remnants of colonial power. Instead, the question here is rather how the language of infestation, dirt and grime, when used as categories linked to abstract space, can be employed to both rationalise new acts of violent spatial production and to perpetuate existing ones.

Abstract space, the 'logic of separation' and hygiene as power-knowledge

For Lefebvre, abstract space consists in highly technicised and super bureaucratised space (Lefebvre 1991, 311), which is produced through analytical processes of abstraction that are entrenched in legal forms, institutional structures and social relationships. Abstract space is grounded in mathematical and scientific thinking, which regards space as an empty container, merely waiting to be filled with bodies (169).

The concept of space-as-container is ruled by separateness. In a container, separate, separated and separable entities collect in fragmented fashion. Lefebvre argues that this mode of separation is transferred to entities and their components: "fragmentation replaces thought, and thought, reflective thinking, becomes hazy and may eventually be swallowed up in the empirical activity of simply counting things" (1991, 170). Lefebvre calls this the "logic of separation" that both supports and is constituted by a "strategy of separation" (170).

Lefebvre does not discuss colonialism at great length in *The Production of Space*, with the exception of references to Spanish-American towns in Latin America.[2] Its preoccupation, rather, is the way in which capitalism and neocapitalism have produced abstract space, which includes the "world of commodities", its "logic" and its worldwide strategies, the power of money and that of the political state (Lefebvre 1991, 53). Yet, as pointed out in the introduction, the colonial doctrine of *terra nullius* (and the land appropriation which it justifies), relies on an understanding of space as container in the same way as abstract space is undergirded by such an understanding. By extension, the "logic of separation" is a common denominator in both the formation of abstract space as capitalist space and in the formation of colonial space as racist space.

Other processes of which Lefebvre writes in the context of abstract space, are also discernible in the production of colonial space, notably his argument that the abstract space of capitalism is marked by the demise of the body (Lefebvre 1991, 310). This demise is two-sided: both symbolic and concrete. It is concrete due to the violence[3] that bodies in abstract space are subjected to, but also symbolic due the compartmentalisation and fragmentation of the living unit of the body (Lefebvre 1991, 310–11).

In *Society Must Be Defended,* Foucault (2003) links the way in which technical knowledge such as medicine and hygiene, becomes a technique of political power applied to the body and the population:

> technical knowledge such as medicine, or rather the combination of medicine and hygiene, is in the nineteenth century, if not the most important element, an element of considerable importance because of the link it establishes between scientific knowledge of both biological and organic processes (or in other words, the population and the body), and because, at the same time, medicine becomes a political intervention-technique with specific power-effects. Medicine is a power-knowledge that can be applied to both the body and the population, both the organism and biological processes, and it will therefore have both disciplinary effects and regulatory effects.
>
> (Foucault 2003, 252)

Like the demise of the body in Lefebvre's idiom, the discourse of medicine as a discourse of power and knowledge, turns the body into an object. This objectality of the body and the way in which differences are turned into objects are well illustrated when Foucault argues that the reduction to objects, homogenisation and the eradication of difference drive the concept of the nation. Initially, nobility is the nation, one distinct from the other nations that circulate in the state. This notion of the nation then leads to the problem of the nation of the revolution, the latter the concept of the nationalism of the nineteenth century, which ultimately brings about the notion of race and finally the notion of class (Foucault 2003, 134).

Ultimately, abstract space diminishes social and spatial complexity to the "logic of profit and the rationality of social and spatial engineering" (Popke 2001, 745). It is, as such, "the space of the bourgeoisie" (Lefebvre (1991, 57), but Foucault's discourse on the power-knowledge of medicine and hygiene, read with Lefebvre's characterisation of the demise of the body, reveals a racial dimension to the production of abstract space. Along these lines, Popke (2001), writing in the context of industrial Durban's Cato Manor, draws attention to the role that race plays in spatial abstraction and the link between the market and race. He explains that "race became refigured as different kinds of body-machine, not unlike the many other kinds of useful machines being fabricated and applied to the benefit of industrial Durban" (742) and these machines were enlisted in the production of abstract space. Abstract space's uniformity is thus not only produced through the way in which plans are applied and how capital markets and property operates, but profoundly also through the objectification inherent in racialisation.

Infestation, sanitation and the production of colonial cities

In the previous section, I linked the power-effects of discourses of hygiene to racialisation as one form of the demise of the body in abstract space. In this section, I want to focus more closely on the specificities of the "sanitation syndrome" as an instance of the power-knowledge of hygiene and consider closely the role that it played in the production of the colonial city.

Colonial cities were initially created for the exclusive use of the colonisers. This was, for instance, evident in the justification of the local British officers when the secretary of the British colonies raised concerns in 1931 over the potential for racial discrimination in the new settler colony in Kenya:

> In view of the fact that Government has set aside large areas of land for the use and benefit of the native tribes of the Colony, it is only proper that the townships, which were primarily established for occupation by non-natives, should be reserved for those who should properly reside there.
>
> (Memorandum on Legislation (1931), quoted in Home 2014, 76)

The colonial project fundamentally entailed the building of the coloniser's idea of a town in a newly conquered area, either in the form of new settlements in open territories or by displacing existing towns through superimposing new models upon existing frameworks. Carlos Vainer (2014) has shown how this process initially started out under pretexts of beautifying and was initially about an art or a style, but with the turn to hygiene the "modern" town was initiated and old neighbourhoods were demolished to make way for "wide boulevards of a clean, disciplined and disciplinary town with sanitation" (48).

In the context of British colonial town planning, one of the main proponents of sanitation was William Simpson, a medical doctor. Simpson was an influential figure during the 1890s and became a professor at the then new London School of Hygiene and Tropical Medicine after he rose in prominence because of his work in Calcutta (80). In this position, he wrote several textbooks and acted as an advisor for British colonies on racial segregation planning policies. Part of this advice entailed creating building-free areas around European-only residences which marginally exceeded the distance that the average mosquito was deemed to be able to fly (80).

This meticulous, yet bizarre and often unfounded, obsession with health, or at least with what was deemed to be health, echoes the sanitary order proclaimed by the formal legal system in the way in which it juxtaposes itself against a more robust, rogue and unpredictable sphinx (Wilson 1991, 129). Simpson became infamous for blaming the "dirty native" and "Asians" for causing various illnesses in India, where he initially worked, but also in Britain's colonies more generally (Home 2014, 80). Urban growth and intercommunal tensions in the colonies were managed through racial segregation (for instance in Kenya and Palestine) via different planning acts, which were chiefly based on English legislation (80). In 1932, the English Town and Country Planning Act presented the option of comprehensive physical planning, which was then transplanted and adapted for Britain's colonies. The recommendations of Simpson (and those who followed him) provided a justification for the separation of people *that was disguised in* professed dangers of the spread of malaria, the plague and other illnesses.

It is thus no coincidence that Home locates the historical origin of the sanitation syndrome at the same time as the rise of "town planning" (Home 2014, 80). To illustrate the spatial effect of the sanitation syndrome in the production of the colonial city, Maynard Swanson (1977), on whose article Home (2014) draws, explains the effect of the metaphor of infectious diseases in the creation of colonial towns. The years around 1900 in South Africa were marked by public authorities and medical administrators who were devoted to the powerful "imagery of infectious disease as a societal metaphor" (Swanson 1977, 387). This metaphor of disease greatly influenced policy and led to the racial segregation laws of that period. Swanson also shows how the sanitation syndrome formed an ostensibly contradictory, but ultimately, close bond with the need for and primacy of cheap labour to be close to the city. Although from different angles, both of these aspects played a crucial role in the development of locations and mentality around South African cities that are prevalent today.

The creation in South Africa of "locations" on the outskirts of the city between 1900 and 1904, can be attributed to the bubonic plague and the mass removal of Africans from the city centres on the advice of medical officers and other government authorities (Swanson 1977, 388–390). Swanson shows that the Cape Colony's responses to the smallpox epidemic during 1882–1883, on the one hand, and the bubonic plague of 1901, on the other, were different (1977, 392–393). He attributes the difference in response not only to the fact that public health administration and the powers of government had developed from the smallpox epidemic to the plague, but also to the "readiness by the 1900s of Cape authorities to turn to territorial segregation in dealing with the black presence in urban areas" (Swanson 1977, 393).

The first response of the government of the Cape Colony to the bubonic plague was to move for a mass removal of all Africans from Cape Town and it therefore made haste to create a native location under the Public Health Act (Act 4 of 1883) (Swanson 1977, 393). This location, ironically named Uitvlugt (meaning exodus), was established (also ironically) on a sewage farm on the Cape Flats (Swanson 1977, 393). Approximately 7000 Africans were moved around this period. Uitvlugt later became known as Ndabeni, which is currently an industrial area in Cape Town (Swanson 1977, 393). This mass removal could not be carried out under the provisions of any other legislation applicable to municipalities at the time.

From the 1880s and onwards in South Africa, the emergent policy with respect to cities was cemented into legislation and administration as a result of the bubonic plague episode, specifically in the Cape Colony. Emergency provisions were put in place and legislation governing health issues relied on to justify the hasty establishment of locations (Swanson 1977, 410). In the Transvaal province of South Africa at the time, the sanitation syndrome was captured in the Transvaal Law 5 of 1885, which deprived "Asiatics" of the right to vote and to own property "except in such [...] locations as the government for purposes of sanitation shall assign them" (Swanson 1977, 391). Examples of this same approach can be found in the Cape of Good Hope colony's Public Health Act 4 of 1883, which provided, for instance, in section 15:

> In cases of urgent necessity arising from the prevalence or threatened outbreak in any district of infectious disease [...] it shall be lawful for the Minister to make and proclaim such regulations to be in force within such districts as may be required to prevent the outbreak, or check the progress of, or eradicate such disease.
>
> (Cape of Good Hope, Acts of Parliament 3741–70).

In a similar vein, the Public Health Act 36 of 1919 of the Union determined the powers of the Minister in section 69(1)(d) as follows:

> The Minister may make regulations [...] providing for the effective enforcement of this Chapter *as regards persons of particular races or different*

classes of persons and assigning, where deemed desirable, responsibility in connection therewith to local authorities or employers of labour.

(Public Health Act 36 of 1919 in Union Gazette Extraordinary, 24 June 1919, emphasis added)

Local authorities were defined in section 7 of the Public Health Act of 1919 and included rural and urban local authorities. Urban local authorities were furthermore defined as follows:

> (3) An urban local authority includes any municipal or borough or town [...] which is constituted in accordance with any law and which under any law is endowed with *sanitary powers for safeguarding the health of the inhabitants of its district* (Section 7(2) and 7(3) of the public Health Act of 1919, emphasis added).

The above excerpts from colonial legislation show how meticulously law has been complicit in facilitating the sanitisation that produced the colonial city. Sanitation projects are racialised and routinely facilitated and justified by law and legal instruments: court orders, legislation, by-laws. All these legal functions facilitate the production of the abstract space of the settler colonial city. The discussion above about the demise of the body and the drive for sanitisation and immunisation that marked the colonial laws of the sanitation syndrome could be read as denying the "bodiness" of bodies in space. This again surfaces the link between the denial of bodiness as a feature of abstract space and the racism of the sanitation syndrome as part and parcel of the production of colonial space.

The sanitation syndrome, even though premised on concepts of health and the preservation of the body, produces abstract space, where human bodies are infectious or infectable objects and not space as the complex collection of relations between bodies. In the sanitation syndrome, this abstraction is racialised. It is the black, native body (see Simpson 1908, 371–3) that is infectious and the white European body that is infectable. This logic of space and power of medical knowledge compartmentalises, fragments and ultimately separates these bodies, disregarding their interconnectedness. Bank and Minkley (1998/1999) show the persistence of the racist sanitation syndrome from colonial planning practices to the apartheid city:

> Planning in Cape Town in the twentieth century was deeply shaped by the ideas that the reckless behaviour and place of living of "the native" endangered the lawful and innocent [whites] instead of within the "poverty places" of the so-called transgressors themselves. In constructing *symbolic inversions of the formal body (and place) and the abstract space of colonialism,*

> planners sought to extend their power to inspect and regulate the personal conduct and social life of "the native",
>
> (Bank and Minkley 1998/1999, 12, emphasis added)

There is, accordingly, a close connection between the production of abstract space as colonial, racist space, violence and law (Butler 2012, 72). Butler (79) suggests, however, that the law is not pure abstraction, but instead should be thought of as an example of what Lefebvre calls a "concrete abstraction" (Lefebvre 1991, 69), because its logic of abstract relations has a material inscription that impacts on the practices of living bodies and on the social world (Butler, 2016). The purchase of this point is discernible in the ostensible abstraction of the sanitation syndrome which disguises its concrete segregating and fragmenting effect.

Despite the apparent totalising nature of the tendencies of abstract space (fragmentation, homogenisation, hierarchical ordering of space) Lefebvre still argues that abstract space generates and enhances internal contradictions that cannot be hidden or suppressed (Lefebvre 1991, 308–11). This acknowledgement of embodied and lived space along with the permeability of bodies complicates, in the context of this discussion, the distinction between infestation and sanitation, vermin and exterminator, and opens up abstract space to the radical uncertainties of relationality (Massey 2005). It is through this that the possibility of an alternative, differential and lived space emerges. Towards the end of this contribution, I shall discuss a concrete instance of how just such a complication has played out in the context of the "post"-apartheid city's attempts to produce abstract space through the "clean up" operations of the employees of Wozani Security, who have become known as the "red ants".

In the next section, I focus on the City of Tshwane/Pretoria to show how the sanitation syndrome and the continuation of the proclivity for abstract space are still at work in present-day South Africa. In present-day Tshwane, it can be detected in the various injustices that have been perpetrated under the guise of the above-mentioned "cleaning-up" drives in the city. But I begin with apartheid era Pretoria and the forced removals from Lady Selborne, which was one of the few places where black people could hold title during apartheid. I then move to the "post-apartheid" era and the "evacuations" that took place at Schubart Park in 2011, in order to trace the continuation of abstract space in the Pretoria/Tshwane lawscape.[4]

Forced removals and "evacuation": the continuation of the sanitation syndrome from Lady Selbourne to Schubart Park in Pretoria/City of Tshwane

Lady Selborne

Because Lady Selborne was one of the few urban places outside the so-called "homelands",[5] where black people could hold full title during apartheid, the government saw it as a threat to white people, not least because the property prices in the area were higher than those in the adjacent, white suburb of Hercules (Mojapelo 2009, 37). Attempts to demolish Lady Selborne already started in 1950 after the introduction of the Group Areas Act 41 of 1950. Maserole KgariMasondo (2008a and 2008b) draws the link between the Lady Selborne removals in Pretoria in 1961 by the apartheid government and the strategies underlying the formation of Ndabeni in the Cape Colony in 1901, when she highlights the role that the "health hazard stereotype" played in the forced removals. The National Party government vowed to abolish Lady Selborne and sketched a picture of the township as a health hazard due to its overpopulation (Kgari-Masondo 2008a, 135). Kgari-Masondo draws on the 1949 "Report from the departmental Committee – Statement embodying particulars and survey of the affairs of Lady Selborne" to make this claim. The conditions of overpopulation were, however, not disputed at the time. The Joint Council of Europeans and Non-Europeans, which was sympathetic to the cause of the inhabitants of Lady Selborne, in a 1952 submission

> conceded, of course, that at present there is deplorable congestion in the township, but undoubtedly the proposed extension and development of Attridgeville and Saulsville will attract many who are now paying exorbitant rentals for the dubious privilege of living in extreme discomfort
> (Proposal by the Pretoria Joint Council of Europeans and non-Europeans 1952, 3)

Instead of evicting the inhabitants of Lady Selborne based on the dire conditions, they therefore suggested another way of dealing with the overpopulation, namely that "European-occupied land to the west of Lady Selborne be purchased and made available for decongestion purposes" (ibid.). The government, however, tasked the Pretoria city council with the eradication of Lady Selborne and justified this with reference to the overcrowding (Kgari-Masondo 2013).

Predictably, just like in the case of Ndabeni, the overpopulation and health hazards of Lady Selborne can actually be placed at the door of the city council. Lady Selborne was incorporated into the City of Pretoria in 1949 and at that stage consisted of almost 2000 registered properties (Mojapelo 2009, 38–40). While residents complained about high municipal rates and the underdevelopment of infrastructure, their grievances were ignored (Mojapelo 2009, 40). At the same time, the city council overvalued the prices of the properties in Lady Selborne (Kgari-Masondo 2008b, 74–5, 2008a, 134). Because of these inflated prices, landlords were forced to lease out their homes, or to construct additional rooms that could be rented out. This gradually led to further overcrowding. If the city council had responded to the consistent complaints of the inhabitants and attended to their concerns, the health issues as well as aspects of overpopulation could have been addressed.

John Mojapelo, who lived in Lady Selborne as a young child and who is one of the inhabitants who has returned after a successful land-restitution claim, captures the story of Lady Selborne in his book *The Corner People of Lady Selborne* (2009). Mojapelo's family home in Lady Selborne was demolished in 1963. This followed proclamations in 1958 which declared that Lady Selborne would be subject to forced removals and the final proclamation of 1961, which declared Lady Selborne a white area (Mojapelo 2009, 198–9). The book describes the forced removals as a drawn-out process. It was only in 1973 that all black people were removed from Lady Selborne and the area renamed to Suiderberg with street names also changed (Mojapelo 2009, 222). It took the municipality a long time and several amendments to Acts and proclamations, but they finally got rid of the inhabitants of Lady Selborne. The use of the machinery of law over a long period of time along with neglect are also evident in the story of Schubart Park.

Schubart Park

The apartheid Government's National Housing Board commissioned the construction of the Schubart Park housing complex in the early 1970s. The complex comprised four high rise apartment blocks with a total of 813 units and was located in the heart of the inner city. The building started in 1976 to make subsidised accommodation available to civil servants who were working in the administrative capital of the apartheid state. The buildings were constructed in a modernist style, influenced by Le Corbusier and rather impressive for its time (Du Toit 2009; Schutte 1984; Swart 2011). The fact that they were so centrally located, close to most government offices, was integral in aiding, bureaucratically, the law's project under apartheid of racial segregation through spatial control.

After South Africa's transition to democracy in 1994, the Pretoria City Council took control of the buildings in 1999 (Du Toit 2009, 161). This change in management also inaugurated a change in the demographics of the building's residents. Whereas the city centre (and also Schubart Park) used to be a space occupied mainly by white South Africans, with black South Africans relegated to the fringes of the city, the advent of democracy witnessed the so-called "white flight" from the city centre to the suburbs (Du Toit 2009, 160–2). The same is true for Schubart Park. The council started to privatise some of their services and a municipal entity, Housing Company Tshwane, was formed in 2001 which took over the management of the Schubart Park complex in 2005 (Du Toit 2009, 165).

The problems associated with the delivery of basic municipal services, rental lords and a generally strained relationship between the inhabitants and the municipal council, were already evident in 1999 when the city council took ownership, but after the Housing Company Tshwane was put in charge of the complex, these problems became more pronounced (Du Toit 2009). The complex increasingly deteriorated. Necessary maintenance work was not done, control over the collection of rent slipped and service delivery was reduced over the course of the years following 2005 (161). The downward spiral of refuse piling up and ongoing water and electricity cuts, followed by protest action of the inhabitants, came to a head on 21 September 2011. Two localised fires broke out in one of the apartment blocks due to the protest action (*Schubart Park v City of Tshwane,* para 3, Van Marle, De Villiers 2013, 132). The police, on the instruction of the city council, then evacuated all the residents (*Schubart Park v City of Tshwane,* para 3–4).

As a result, an estimated number of between 3000 and 5000 people were left homeless (*Schubart Park v City of Tshwane,* para 8). Because the city council claimed that it was an evacuation and not an eviction, they skirted the constitutional obligation to provide alternative accommodation (Van Marle, De Villiers 2013, 143). Only some residents could be accommodated in temporary shelters. Several urgent challenges to the evacuations followed in the North Gauteng High Court, but that court found in favour of the city council. A year later, when the matter was heard in the Constitutional Court, the judgment found that it was indeed an unlawful eviction and not an evacuation (*Schubart Park v City of Tshwane,* para 20–1). Therefore, section 26 of the Constitution of the Republic of South Africa, 1996, which prohibits arbitrary eviction,[6] was applicable and the Court ordered that the residents had to be reinstated in their homes.[7]

The heads of argument of the City of Tshwane in the Constitutional Court raised the "unhygienic and unhealthy" conditions in Schubart Park as one of the conclusions reached after the investigation of structural engineers (SCIP Engineering Group), which was appointed by the City of Tshwane after the proceedings in the North Gauteng High Court (*Schubart Park v City of Tshwane* (2013), Respondent's Heads of Argument in the Constitutional Court para 30.4). The City furthermore claimed in the Heads of Argument that because of these unsanitary conditions, the building "cannot be occupied in its current state" (para 30.4). It additionally relied on the regulations of the National Building Act (these regulations had been issued in terms of section 17(1) of the National Building Regulations and Building Standard Act 103 of 1977), submitting that the inhabitants of Schubart Park "cannot be allowed to live in unhealthy, unhygienic, dangerous and uninhabitable conditions, particularly given the history of fires and fatalities that followed the outbreak of fire within the residential complex" (para 59).

The "fatalities" that are cited here must be the fatalities that followed a fire that broke out in Kruger Park (the complex across the street from Schubart Park) in 2008 in which six people died, two of them after jumping from the windows of their flats (Anon. 2008). The context of the 2008 Kruger Park fire is that some inhabitants of Schubart Park were, in a prelude of what was to come in 2011, evicted by the "red ants" (see further discussion below) without the necessary court order as required by section 26 of the Constitution. In solidarity with their neighbours, the inhabitants of Kruger Park set alight the rubbish chutes of their block in protest.

Tracing the media coverage on the Schubart Park case of 2011 and reading the final judgment of the Constitutional Court, it becomes clear that the conditions in Schubart Park were such mainly due to a lack of maintenance and a failure to provide the necessary basic services. Throughout the pleadings there is evidence of the city council's grossly negligent disposition towards the residents and the way in which it utilised and relied on the suggestive power of sanitation in order to evict the residents from their homes.

Indeed, I would argue that the North Gauteng High Court's decision in favour of the "evacuation" is steeped in a larger proclivity for the production of the inner city as post-apartheid abstract space, in other words, as the space of postcolonial, neocolonial capitalism, reserved for the post-apartheid bourgeoisie. The Court's decision relies on well-established tropes of the sanitation syndrome. When initially deciding on the urgent interdicts, the Court was easily convinced by the arguments for safety and sanitation presented by the municipal council. Without bothering to order an inspection of the premises, the Court (also located in Pretoria, in fact only a few street blocks away from Schubart Park) uncritically accepted both the metaphor of sanitation and the actuality of infestation that the council claimed existed.

Figure 10.1 Skeleton of block D. Source: Herman Verwey.

Figure 10.2 The city moving into Schubart Park. Source: Herman Verwey.

Yet, the alleged infestation, that necessitated the sanitation measures carried out by the council was caused by its own failure to properly maintain the apartment complex. On the day of the evictions, Schubart Park was emptied out: inhabitants were evacuated, belongings were carried out onto the street by the metro police and later, as the images above show, the buildings were raided for scrap metal and many of the walls removed in the process. The buildings are now hollow structures on the cityscape. As the circumstances surrounding the 2008 Kruger Park fire shows, this hollowing out did not start on the day of the evictions – it was a slow process in which the city council increasingly viewed the inhabitants of Schubart Park as vagrants and nuisances and the block as unsafe and unhygienic. The city council chose to overlook the fact that there were (also) mothers and children and families living in the apartments, and generally lumped all the inhabitants together as troublemakers to get rid of. This hollowing out, driven as it was by the sanitation drive and its concomitant conceptions of infestation, affected the everyday lives of those who wanted to make the city their home. It is a concrete manifestation of an attempt to produce abstract space – space as emptied out, space as an empty container or blank canvas prepared for capitalist appropriation, where scientific logic and formal law can rearrange structures without acknowledging the bodies or the relations between the bodies as space. Despite the finding against the City of Tshwane in the Constitutional Court, the empty skeletons that remain of Schubart Park stand as the ruins of a realised production of abstract space.[8]

The "red ants" as infestation

As mentioned in the introduction, the "red ants" are security guards employed by Wozani Security (Manda 2017). Wozani Security is frequently contracted by municipal councils in the Gauteng Province to carry out eviction operations. During these operations, they wear red overalls, red helmets and red shields. The modus operandi of the "red ants" is callous and efficient, calculated, meticulous and violent. They simply deal with the task at hand, ostensibly ignoring the inhabitants, usually destroying structures and removing belongings in the presence of the desperate inhabitants. Those who are lucky, manage to bribe some of the "red ants", after which their property is treated with a little more care.

Figure 10.3 *Chandelier*, 2001, C-print. Image size: 90 x 71cm. Paper size: 100 x 81cm. Photo: John Hogg. Source: © Steven Cohen. Courtesy of Stevenson, Cape Town and Johannesburg.

In April 2001, in Newtown, Johannesburg performance artist Steven Cohen coincidentally arrived on the same day as the "red ants" were destroying the informal settlement under the M1 highway in order to make way for the Nelson Mandela Bridge; now a distinct landmark of the city without which one can hardly imagine the cityscape of Johannesburg. Cohen was there to record his performance entitled *Chandelier*. For the performance he is painted completely white. He is dressed and decorated in a white corset made from an extravagant chandelier of which the lights are battery-powered and were turned on as the sun was setting over Newtown. With this exaggerated costume, I propose that Cohen relies on whiteness to disrupt whiteness.[9] By placing a white body in that space, the artist powerfully draws attention to the racial politics at play in the eviction. This is important, especially because most of the "red ants" are black employees of a white-owned company. The destruction can therefore easily look like black people breaking down the shacks of other black people. But Cohen illuminates the racial undertones of the eviction and, for purposes of this chapter, how eviction is driven by a racialised logic of sanitation.

Through other performances such as *Ugly Girl* in 1998 at Securicor Loftus (a rugby stadium in Pretoria) and *Patriotic Drag* in the same year, when Cohen, as Princess Menorah, attended a white, right-wing commemoration of the South African War at Fort Klapperkop in Pretoria, Cohen exposes the hypermasculinity of these spaces. In an interview, he also mentions that his work is exaggerating whiteness, purposefully drawing attention to its otherwise normalised and silent presence in South African spaces (Du Plessis 2006, 19-21). It is not surprising that Cohen arrived in Newtown on the day of the performance without having knowledge of the "red ants"' operations. Their demolitions take place without any prior notice to the inhabitants whose homes are destroyed. In the video footage and photographs of Cohen's performance artwork, he moves amidst the destruction wrought by the "red ants"; one woman shakes his hand, another chases him away, an inebriated man brings him a copy of the Hustler magazine and amidst the chaotic soundtrack of the video, one of the residents is heard singing the national anthem of South Africa, *Nkosi Sikelel'iAfrika*.

Part of the intention of the *Chandelier* project was to shed light on what is seldom seen, namely the subhuman conditions of those who live under the city's bridges. As it turned out, the performance also powerfully shed light on the brutality of the "red ants" eviction style. Cohen is, however, keenly aware of the problematic nature of romanticising informal settlements and the possible symbolic violence of his presence as a racially white subject in that space. He writes: "It was hard for me to set myself up as, in part, a privileged white luxuriating among the despair" (Cohen 2002). The project thus also forced the artist himself to acknowledge the privilege that inevitably attaches to his white, albeit queer, body (Sizemore-Barber 2016, 207).

I propose nonetheless that Cohen shines the dangling chandelier crystals on a space that the city council, assisted by the "red ants", once again attempted to produce as abstract space. Cohen insists on inserting his body into the space, one that feels out of place, and in doing so, he not only obstructs the drive to "sanitise" the space, but also exposes both the underlying whiteness and the overt hypermasculinity of eviction operations or "cleaning-up missions" in urban South Africa.

Importantly, this provocative performance art piece also brings to the surface the manner in which the operation executed by the "red ants" can itself be read as an infestation. In his artist statement, Cohen (2002) writes as follows about the "red ants":

> Like the red ants they are nicknamed after, they invade a settlement and violently destroy it. I have never before seen the red ants swarming over shacks with crowbars swinging, and the flying tin and ripping plastic and falling boards and scraps that were a shelter being so easily unthreaded.
>
> (Cohen 2002)

Martin Murray, in *Taming the disorderly city: The spatial landscape of Johannesburg after Apartheid* (2008, 90), writes extensively about the "red ants" and their removal operations when he draws attention to the "disposable people at the peri-urban fringe" (90), the struggle for survival in the inner city, the revitalisation and displacement in the inner city and the banality of indifferent urbanism. Wozani Security can mobilise roughly six thousand troops at a time. This is a substantial force with the functional capacity of a small army.

The colloquial name ("red ants") of these private security guards, already opens them up to the reading that they are, in fact, themselves an infestation from the point of view of the evictees and those in solidarity with their plight. Despite the fact that the "red ants" perform a clearing that can be read as a continuation of the colonial sanitation syndrome, their designation by their victims as an infestation signals a resistance that is grounded in turning back the terms of stigmatisation on the sanitary order itself.

As mentioned, the "red ants" are employees of the white-owned Wozani Security, which in turn is contracted by the municipal council or, in some instances, private land owners. After evictions that took place at RNS House in Pretoria in 2016, the "red ants" were explicitly accused of racism (Versluis 2016). The Deputy Director of Wozani operations, Koos Van Rhyn, responded to these allegations by saying that the claims were hard to contemplate seeing that "he was the only white person on the scene while all the red ants are brown and black" (translated from Versluis 2016). Clearly, Van Rhyn missed the blinding irony of the fact that he was not just any white person, but indeed the white Deputy Director of Wozani Security on the scene. Needless to say, the lingering and lurking whiteness of the "red ants" operations would have totally passed him by. While Cohen could not have known it at the time of his performance, his chandelier and his exaggerated white make-up on that day in Newtown amongst the "red ants", powerfully exposed the fact that this security company is predominantly white-owned and that their claim to a diverse board was disingenuous.

That there can be real consequences to the labelling of Wozani Security's "red ants" as an infestation, was borne out when in February 2005, the Johannesburg Metropolitan Council ended its multimillion-rand contract with Wozani Security after charges of bribery and corruption, as well as allegations that Wozani fraudulently misrepresented its black economic empowerment status (Murray 2008, 215). In 2014 the Gauteng Human Settlement MEC Jacob Mamabolo and Wozani Security CEO Johan Bosch reached an agreement that the "red ants" would bring an end to their violent evictions. One of the undertakings of the agreement was also that the "red ants" would not act upon fraudulently obtained court orders (Mamabolo 2014). It is clear that this agreement did not bring an end to the violent evictions effected by the "red ants", because more recently they were suspended by the Private Security Industry Regulatory Authority from executing any eviction orders after two people died in Lenasia in September 2019 (Evans 2019).

Conclusion

The inextricable link between law and its spatial dimensions is emphasised in Schmitt's reference to *nomos* as both the land appropriation and the subsequent processes of distribution and pasture (production) (Chryssostalis 2013, 163). In this chapter, I have shown how the fear of the spread of the bubonic plague and other diseases was used to justify racialised urban planning practices that produced (and reproduced) colonial cities. A single example was the creation of Uitvlugt location in the Cape Colony in 1901. The language of the sanitation syndrome, which led to racial segregation and the exercise of spatial power in colonial South Africa, continued in apartheid South Africa. The forced removals in Lady Selborne in the Transvaal province during the 1960s aptly illustrated this. In the "post-apartheid" time-space, I illustrated the continuation of the sanitation syndrome in the 2011 Schubart Park evictions.

Underlying this continuation of the drive to sanitise at any and all cost, from colonial to contemporary South Africa, is a proclivity for the production of abstract space as the space of capitalism and thus of the bourgeoisie. This approach to space informs what becomes categorised as infestation and sanitation. In the colonial and apartheid era, the language of sanitation, as illustrated above, is a racialised discourse that naturalises both the city as colonial product and the production of the city as colonial.

The production of abstract space in South Africa has taken place throughout its history, from segregation in the colonial South African city, to the configuration of white exclusivity in the apartheid city, to "clean-ups" in the contemporary South African city. The racialised basis of the sanitation syndrome persists in all these arrangements, albeit that it takes the dramatic performance art of Steven Cohen to surface the lingering whiteness in the sanitation drives of contemporary South African municipal councils and reveal how the *nomos* of apartheid persists on the ground.

Notes

1 Home derives the concept of the sanitation syndrome from the work of Maynard Swanson, who was a historian at the University of Miami at the time when he wrote the article entitled "The Sanitation Syndrome: Bubonic Plague and Urban Native Policy in the Cape Colony, 1900–1909". His research also covered Durban and Port Elizabeth.

2 Thanks to Chris Butler who has drawn my attention to the fact that Lefebvre does discuss colonialism extensively in later works such as *De l'état* (1976), and also, for pointing me to the work of Stefan Kipfer, who addresses the blind spots in Lefebvre's recognition of colonialism. See in this regard Kipfer and Goonewardena 2013.

3 Lefebvre's (1991, 57) assertion that abstract space "depends on consensus more than any space before it" is thus immediately qualified by the statement that violence "does not always remain latent or hidden" within this space.

4 The notion of the lawscape is derived from the work of Andreas Philippopoulos-Mihalopoulos (2007). The term captures the way in which law and the city are intertwined: 'The facetious question, therefore, whether the law dictates the city or the city dictates the law is to be answered with a stentorious circularity' (9). He refers to a similar question posed by David Harvey (in Harvey (2000)) – Harvey formulates the question with society instead of law, i.e. whether society dictates the city or the city society.

5 The homelands were designated geographical areas reserved for inhabitancy by black people during apartheid. The creation of these homelands exacerbated the gross inequality of land distribution in South Africa that was begun during colonialism. They were created through a series of legislation such as the Bantu Authorities Act of 1951, the Promotion of Bantu Self-Government Act 46 of 1959 and the Black Homeland Citizenship Act 26 of 1970. The central aim of the apartheid government with the homelands (also called reserves or Bantustans) was to grant the homelands independence as separate nation states and in doing so give black people citizenship of the homelands while depriving them of their citizenship of South Africa. This was one of the crucial spatial steps towards producing a white South Africa. The apartheid government presented these racist geographical demarcations as a noble endeavour to allow "the 'black man' to develop at his own pace and according to his own custom" (Van der Westhuizen 2007, 41). The inequality inaugurated by colonisation was hereby continued and cemented through Apartheid's spatial legislation. The homelands that were granted independence were however never acknowledged as states by any other country (Harris 2002, 71). Muriel Horrell (1956), who worked at the Institute of Race Relations during the enactment of the Group Areas Act and Amendment Acts, captured some of the debates at the time in her 1956 report *The Group Areas Act: Its Effect on Human Beings,* which has been published as a booklet with useful maps and diagrams included. Her report is useful for showing the effects of the Group Areas Act on urban areas.

6 Section 26(3) of the Constitution, provides that "no one may be evicted from their home, or have their home demolished, without an order of court made after considering all the relevant circumstances. No legislation may permit arbitrary evictions.". The Constitutional Court, in cases such as *Grootboom* 2001 and *Port Elizabeth Municipality* 2005, has interpreted the section to mean that no eviction may be carried out without a court order and no order will be granted without meaningful

engagement between the parties, reasonableness and the provision of alternative accommodation.

7 The struggles of the residents and an alternative take on the inhabitants, which challenges the narrative of the City Council, are set out by Van Marle and De Villiers 2013.

8 In 2014, after obtaining permission from the metro police, photographer Herman Verwey took a series of photographs of the remnants of Schubart Park. The images included in this piece are reproduced with the artist's permission. The rest of the gripping photographs in the series can be viewed at http://hermanverwey.blogspot.com/2014/06/post-apocalyptic-schubart-park.html.

9 With whiteness I mean something more than the race classification categories of apartheid legislation, while acknowledging that these categories still reverberate in post-1994 South Africa. Whiteness relates to all the privileges and powers (symbolic, systemic and otherwise) attached to white supremacy. In the context of the sanitation syndrome, whiteness is problematically associated with cleanliness, health and sanitation, whereas black is connected to squalor and disease. With the disruption of whiteness I have in mind something that corresponds with the critique of whiteness of Yancy (2004, 107–108): 'whiteness masquerades as a universal code of beauty, intelligence, superiority, cleanliness, and purity', it is the 'signifier of purity, cleanliness and goodness'. These are the categories and associations that stand to be disrupted in a post-apartheid time-space.

References

Anon. 2008. "6 Die in Fire as Red Ants Evict Tenants." *Sowetan Live*, July 23. http://www.sowetanlive.co.za/sowetan/archive/2008/07/23/6-die-in-fire-as-red-ants-evict-tenants.

Bank, Andrew and Gary Minkley. 1998/1999. "Genealogies of Space and Identity in Cape Town." *Kronos* 25: 4–16.

Butler, Chris. 2012. *Henri Lefebvre: Spatial Politics, Everyday Life and the Right to the City*. New York and Abingdon: Routledge.

Butler, Chris. 2016. "Abstraction Beyond a 'Law of Thought': On Space, Appropriation and Concrete Abstraction." *Law and Critique* 27 (3): 247–268.

Chryssostalis, Julia. 2013. "Reading Arendt 'Reading' Schmitt: Reading *Nomos* Otherwise." In *Feminist Encounters with Legal Philosophy*, edited by Maria Drakapoulou, 159–184. New York and Abingdon: Routledge.

Cohen, Steven. 2001 *Chandelier*. https://vimeo.com/13098642?embedded=true&source=vimeo_logo&owner=2907442. Photographs of the performance can be found at https://steven-cohen.com/en/creations/2001-chandelier-en/

Cohen, Steven. 2002. Interview. https://youtu.be/nkwJ29fUQyk

Du Plessis, Rory. 2006. "Exhibiting the Expulsion of Transgression." In *Sex, Gender, Becoming, Post-Apartheid Reflections*, edited by Karin Van Marle, 19–40. Pretoria: Pretoria University Law Press.

Du Toit, Jacques. 2009. "Utopia on Trial Again: Perceived Resident Quality at Schubart Park in South Africa." *Journal of Architectural and Planning Research* 26 (2): 161.

Evans, Jenni. 2019. "Red Ants Back on the Eviction March as Court Lifts Suspension." *News* 24, October 29. https://www.news24.com/SouthAfrica/News/red-ants-back-on-the-eviction-march-as-court-lifts-suspension-20191029. Accessed 29 October 2019.

Foucault, Michel. 2003. *Society Must Be Defended: Lectures at the College de France*. New York: Picador.

Government of the Republic of South Africa v Grootboom. 2001. (1) SA 46 (CC).

Harris, Verne. 2002. "The Archival Sliver: Power, Memory, and Archives in South Africa." *Archival Science* 2: 63–86.

Harvey, David. 2000. *Spaces of Hope*. Edinburgh: Edinburgh University Press.

Home, Robert. 2014. "Legal Histories of Planning and Colonialism." In *Routledge Handbook on Cities of the Global South*, edited by Susan Parnell and Sophie Oldfield, 75–85. Abingdon: Routledge.

Horrell, Muriel. 1956. *The Group Areas Act: Its Effects on Human Beings*. Johannesburg: SA Institute of Race Relations.

Keenan, Sarah. 2015. *Subversive Property: Law and the Production of Spaces of Belonging*. Abingdon: Routledge.

Kgari-Masondo, Maserole Christina. 2008a. *"A Superstitious Respect for the Soil"? Environmental History, Social Identity and Land Ownership: A Case Study of Forced Removals from Lady Selborne and their Ramifications c1905–1977*. PhD thesis. Available at http://scholar.sun.ac.za/handle/10019.1/1215.

Kgari-Masondo, Maserole Christina. 2008b. "A Home Makes One Motho: The Idea of 'Humanness', 'Home' and History in Lady Selborne's Forced Removals, Circa 1905 to 1977." *Historia* 532: 70–97.

Kgari-Masondo, Maserole Christina. 2013. "Incomplete History Curriculum? Teaching Socio-Environmental History in South African High Schools from an Indigenous Perspective." *Yesterday & Today* 10: 101–123.

Kipfer, Stefan and Kanishka Goonewardena. 2013. "Urban Marxism and the Post-Colonial Question: Henri Lefebvre and 'Colonization'." *Historical Materialism* 21 (2): 1–41.

Lefebvre, Henri. 1991. *The Production of Space*, translated by Donald Nicholson Smith. Blackwell: Cambridge.

Mamabolo. 2014 "Red Ants Sign Eviction Agreement." *The Citizen*, July 14. http://citizen.co.za/category/news/newsnational/.

Manda, Sihle. 2017. "Metros Pay Millions to 'Red Ants'." *Mail and Guardian*, June 13. https://mg.co.za/article/2017-06-13-00-metros-pay-millions-to-red-ants.

Massey, Doreen. 2005. *For Space*. London: Sage Publications.

Mojapelo, John Seakalala. 2009. *The Corner People of Lady Selborne*. Pretoria: Unisa Press.

Murray, Martin. 2008. *Taming the disorderly City: The Spatial Landscape of Johannesburg after Apartheid*. New York: Cornell University Press.

Philippopoulos-Mihalopoulos, A, ed. 2007. *Law and the City*. Abingdon: Routledge.

Popke, Jeffrey. E. 2001. "Modernity's Abject Space: The Rise and Fall of Durban's Cato Manor." *Environment and Planning A* 33 (4): 737–752.

Port Elizabeth Municipality v Various Occupiers. 2005. (1) SA 217 (CC).

Proposal Submitted by the Pretoria Joint Council of Europeans and non-Europeans on the Proclamation of Group Areas: Pretoria, Witwatersrand, Vereniging Region. 30/10/1952. Available at http://www.historicalpapers.wits.ac.za/inventories/inv_pdfo/AD1715/AD1715-5-27-3-3-001-jpeg.pdf.

Schmitt, Carl. 2003. *The Nomos of the Earth in the International Law of Jus Publicum Europaeum*. Translated by G. L. Ulmen. New York: Telos.

Schubart Park Residents' Association and Others v City of Tshwane Metropolitan Municipality and Another. 2013. (1) SA 323 (CC).

Schutte, C.D. 1984. *Social Interaction and Place Perspective Experienced by Residents of Schubart Park, a High-Rise Complex in Pretoria*. Pretoria: Human Science Research Council.

Simpson, W.J.R. 1908. *Principles of Hygiene as Applied to Tropical and Sub-tropical Climates*. London: John Bale. https://archive.org/details/b2135991x/page/n11. Accessed 18 May 2019.

Swanson, Maynard W. 1977. "The Sanitation Syndrome: Bubonic Plague and Urban Native Policy in the Cape Colony, 1900–1909." *The Journal of African History* 18 (3): 387–410.

Swart, Johan. 2011. *Urban Church. Re-developing Space within Pretoria's Schubart Park Complex*. Thesis for a Master's degree in Architecture completed at the University of Pretoria.

Sizemore-Barber, April. 2016. "A Queer Transition: Whiteness in the Prismatic, Post-Apartheid Drag Performances of Pieter-Dirk Uys and Steven Cohen." *Theatre Journal* 68: 191–211.

Vainer, Carlos. 2014 "Disseminating 'Best Practice'. The coloniality of urban knowledge and city models" in *Routledge Handbook on Cities of the Global South* edited by Susan Parnell and Sophie Oldfield, 48–56. Abingdon: Routledge.

Valverde, Mariana. 2015. *Chronotopes of Law: Jurisdiction, Scale and Governance*. Abingdon: Routledge.

Van der Westhuizen, Christi. 2007. *White Power & the Rise and Fall of the National Party*. Cape Town: Zebra Press.

Van Marl, Karin and Isolde de Villiers. 2013. "Law and Resistance in the City of Pretoria: Space, History and the Everyday." *Australian Feminist Law Journal* 38 (1): 129–145.

Versluis, Jean Mariè. 2016. "Bottels vlieg by uitsetting in Pta." *Netwerk 24*, March 9. http://www.netwerk24.com/Nuus/Algemeen/bottelsvliegbyuitsettinginpta20160309?mobile=true

Wilson, Elizabeth. 1991. *The Sphinx in the City: Urban Life, the Control of Disorder, and Women*. Berkeley, CA: University of California Press.

Yancy, George. 2004. "A Foucauldian (Genealogical) Reading of Whiteness: The Production of the Black Body/Self and the Racial Deformation of Pecola Breedlove in Toni Morrison's The Bluest Eye." In *What White Looks Like: African-American Philosophers on the Whiteness Question*, edited by George Yancy, 107–42. London: Routledge.

Chapter 11

Unequal scenes

Johnny Miller

Inequalities in our social fabric are oftentimes hidden, and hard to see from ground level. Visual barriers, including the structures themselves, prevent us from seeing the incredible contrasts that exist side by side in our cities. Racial segregation was cast in concrete and iron during apartheid; barriers which still exist. Maps from the census, taken in 2011, show each major South African city as a patchwork of distinct colours – a representation of the racial groups which are still divided, to this day.

The beauty of being able to fly is to see things from a new perspective – to see things as they really are. Looking straight down from a height of several hundred metres, incredible scenes of inequality emerge. Some communities have been expressly designed with separation in mind, and some have grown more or less organically. Some informal settlements in these photographs did not exist during apartheid; they are fully modern creations, of a poisonous environment of fear and exclusion which continues to entrap our cities. They represent the frustrations, the setbacks, the fear and the desires of millions of South Africans who live in similar situations.

These images were taken 22 years after the end of apartheid in South Africa's largest metro urban areas: Johannesburg, Cape Town and Durban. All the locations were researched using census data and mapping software to find highly unequal locations, which were then photographed and recorded using a DJI Inspire drone. They were not Photoshopped or modified in any way, except for basic cropping, exposure and colour corrections.

The images speak to the issues of inequality in our society in an unambiguous, objective way. I deliberately focused on economic inequality by attempting to find visual metaphors, and an aesthetic which would be extremely powerful and easily shared in today's media-saturated world. By providing a new perspective on an old problem, I hope to provoke a dialogue which can begin to address the issues of inequality and disenfranchisement in a constructive and peaceful way.

DOI: 10.4324/9780203712771-11

Figure 11.1 Alex Sandton Bridge. Source: the author.

Figure 11.2 Bloubosrand Kya Sands. Source: the author.

Figure 11.3 Durban Phoenix Area. Source: the author.

Figure 11.4 Hout Bay Imizamo Yethu. Source: the author.

Figure 11.5 Johannesburg Primrose. Source: the author.

Figure 11.6 Masiphumelele Lake Michelle. Source: the author.

Figure 11.7 Papwa Sewgolum Golf Course. Source: the author.

Figure 11.8 Vukuzenzele Sweet Home. Source: the author.

Chapter 12

Sense of place, virtual displacement and a *nomos* beyond apartheid

What value for a rights-based approach?

Loretta Feris and Jaco Barnard-Naudé

Introduction

People are frequently displaced as a result of development projects and forced to sever ties with their home, their community, their ancestral lands, the natural landscapes in which they reside and the relationships that bind them to their environment. Consequently, involuntary displacement resulting from development projects has been recognised in the literature for its negative human rights impact (McDowell 1996; Clark 2002; Downing 2002). However, this literature has recognised such a negative human rights impact almost exclusively on the basis of physical displacement.

Displacement, however, cannot be limited purely to physical displacement. Often, people are not physically relocated and, instead, continue to live in close proximity to the newly developed road, coal-fired power plant, mine etc. As a result of this close proximity, however, they are privy to the myriad of impacts (air pollution, waste, land degradation, noise etc) caused by these developments and the profound ways in which these activities alter the natural environment. Furthermore, they are themselves impacted, because they bear the brunt of, for instance, fumes, dust and noise emanating from such developments. In addition, they are often made to bear witness to sacred cultural sites becoming altered or even ruined and to the destruction of livelihoods as arable agricultural land is turned into industrial and commercial spaces in which they have no stake.

Consequently, the lived experience of such people's relationship with the environment changes and their "sense of place" is altered – to the point of an experience of displacement. Following the work of Glen Albrecht (2005, 2007), who has identified the distress caused by environmental change as psychological stress, we consider in this chapter whether this form of virtual displacement, as we would like to call it, should, much like physical displacement, require a human rights response and in particular a response that resides in the sphere of environmental rights, in a postcolonial/"post"-apartheid era. Indeed, our argument will be that "virtual" displacement fundamentally disrupts traditional notions of displacement and that what we characterise as "virtual" displacement should be placed on an equal footing

DOI: 10.4324/9780203712771-12

with physical displacement to the point that no distinction between the two should be normatively justifiable.

We will begin with a brief review of the literature on sense of place, which we go on to consider in the context of Carl Schmitt's reading of *nomos* as a "unity of order and orientation" (Schmitt 2003, 42) or, as Julia Chryssostalis has translated it, "order and *emplacement*" (Chryssostalis 2013, 165 (emphasis added). We read Chryssostalis's translation as providing the conceptual and discursive link, through the concept of "emplacement", between sense of place and the spatial dimension of law as *nomos*. As regards the distinction, or relation, between space and place, we follow Doreen Massey's (1994, 3) suggestion that space refers to the multiplicity and simultaneity of configurations of "social relations" as they are experienced and lived in time, and that place can be conceptualised in terms of the specific and dynamic "social interactions" that are tied together in a locality (Massey 1994, 155). In this regard, Massey (1994, 156) writes of a "specificity of place which derives from the fact that each place is the focus of a distinct *mixture* of wider and more local social relations". Along these lines, we will continue to consider virtual displacement – as a particular mixture of "wider and more local social relations" that are present in a locality – in relation to sense of place. Finally, we assess the extent to which an environmental rights-based approach can offer value in such a reimagination of displacement.

Sense of place, nomos and virtual displacement

The concept of "sense of place" was first proposed by geographers in the later decades of the twentieth century (Lynch 1960; Relph 1976; Tuan 1974, 1975, 1977) to describe "the emotional significance that geographic spaces are able to take on in human experience" (Giuliani 2003, 146) thus transforming them into places. Yi-Fu Tuan (1980, 4) distinguished "sense of place" from "rootedness" by arguing that "sense of place" implies, unlike "rootedness", "a certain distance between self and place that allows the self to appreciate a place". In its most general definition, then, "sense of place" refers to "an emotional connection with place via understanding its symbols and meanings" (Najafi and Shariff, 2011, 188). Datel and Dingemans (1984, 135) defined "sense of place" as "the complex bundle of meanings, symbols, and qualities that a person or group consciously and unconsciously associates with a particular locality or region".

Today, it is generally accepted that "sense of place" consists of a combination of two complementary components: place attachment and place meaning (Kudryavtsev, Stedman and Krasny 2012, 230). Whereas place attachment refers to the "extent to which an individual values or identifies with a particular environmental setting" (231), place meaning "refers to the symbolic meanings", such as cultural values, "that people ascribe to settings" (232).

The first aspect of place attachment that is of relevance for the purposes of this chapter, is place-specific dependence, expressed as the "degree to which occupants perceive themselves to be strongly associated with and dependent on a particular place" (Moore and Graefe 1994, 19). This association is typically based on the fulfilment of specific needs, such as being close to sources of livelihood (Cross 2001, 8). In more recent work, the sense of place is directly linked to environmental quality (Giuliani 2003, 148–9). This link allows for an acknowledgement of the psychological complexity of the relationship between individuals and their environment as well as the complex interplay between environmental quality and the emotions that are felt in relation to a place. In this regard, Giuliani makes a strong argument for the recognition of place attachment as a bond that goes beyond simple affection for a particular place. Rather, it is a relationship with an enduring quality, directed toward a specific place, not interchangeable with another that has merely the same functional quality (Giuliani 2003, 148–9) and arguably not interchangeable with one in which the specific environmental quality associated with the sense of belonging, has been significantly deteriorated.

The "place meaning" aspect of the sense of place is often also expressed as place identity (Steele 1981, 12). Cultural practices, ancestry, symbolic meanings and heritage all form part of a place's identity and a person's sense of belonging: people see their identity as intrinsically connected to that particular place. Time, history and space are encoded and contextualised by way of interpersonal, community and intercultural relations in a specific environment (Oliver-Smith 2001, 64) and, in turn, individuals are emplaced in this environment in particular ways. The relationship between biophysical space and cultural identity is eloquently captured in the words of First Nations Chief Seattle (Sealth), Chief of the Suquamish, Duwamish and other Salish tribes in the latter half of the nineteenth century on the occasion of the sale of two million acres of the tribe's land to the United States government:

> Every part of this country is sacred to my people. Every hillside, every valley, every plain and grove has been hallowed by some fond memory or some sad experience of my tribe. Even the rocks that seem to lie dumb as they swelter in the sun along the silent seashore in solemn grandeur thrill with memories of past events connected with the fate of my people, and the very dust under your feet responds more lovingly to our footsteps than to yours, because it is the ashes of our ancestors, and our bare feet are conscious of the sympathetic touch, for the soil is rich with the life of our kindred.
>
> (Windsor and McVey 2005, 146–65)

A consideration of the sense of place provides an opportunity to focus specifically on how spatiality is localised in the context of land and landscapes, whether they be rural, urban, developed or untouched by development. It also allows us to consider the many different social and cultural connections we have to a particular place through physical connections, psychological connections, livelihood connections, spiritual connections, ancestral connections and well-being connections. Perhaps most significantly, sense of place compels us to reflect on who occupies places, how places are utilised and the extent to which we are emplaced (Chryssostalis 2013, 165) by social conditions.

At the level of the letter or of the literality of the law, its relationship with spatiality and, specifically, with place and sense of place appears to be peripheral. Attempts to find an acknowledgement of the significance that a sense of place has in people's lives by way of a simple survey of laws and regulations, for instance, amounts to a needle in a haystack exercise (Feris 2016) – reference to it is limited and, where it occurs, it is devoid of any attempt to define it or interrogate it in a meaningful way. Yet law has the power to regulate our places in ways which not only profoundly change those places, but also alter our own experience of place in radical ways (Bennett and Layard 2015).

Carl Schmitt's (2003, 42) reading of *nomos* as the "unity of space and law, of order (*Ordnung*) and orientation (*Ortung*)" can, however, help to foreground both the spatial dimension of law and the normative dimension of spaces in the context of developing our understanding of a postcolonial sense of place. While Giorgio Agamben's (1998, 19) translation of Schmitt's "orientation" as "localization" comes close to the concept of place inherent in *Ortung*, Chryssostalis (2013, 165; 178) translates it both as "localisation" and as "emplacement", the latter evoking not only that order is always already localised, but also that order always already "takes place", not just in the sense of occurring but also in the sense of order as always already not simply order in general but indeed as the order of a locality. *Ortung* is always already concrete, situated and, therefore, in its "unity" with order, thoroughly (em)placed. As Lindahl (2004, 22 (emphasis added)) remarks: "legal power is essentially spatialising, or more properly, placialising: *to ascribe rights and obligations is also always to assign a legal place to persons – to emplace them and vice versa*". The unity of norm and space implied in Schmitt's concept of *nomos* thus always already implies that specific (and dynamic) mixture of social relations that defines a place.

For Schmitt, (67–9), all law is grounded in land-appropriation as the first "partition and classification of space" (67) and *nomos* is the Greek word that captures this fact. The translation of *nomos* as "law", or the Roman "lex", does not reflect that law as order is always already concretely emplaced, nor the fact that place is always already ordered/normativised. As Hans Lindahl (2006, 887) remarks: "A space of action is a legal space of action to the extent that it reveals places as ought-places [...] abiding, in the twofold sense of abiding by the law and abiding in a place, is one of the spatial modes of appearance of legal validity".

The activities that are today characteristically the causes of displacement in the postcolony, such as mining or the construction of dams, highways and power plants, are activities that are pervaded by land reappropriation which is facilitated by legal regulation. That is to say, these activities are as highly ordered as they are specifically emplaced. A particular aspect of such legal regulation of land reappropriation that is of relevance for the purposes of this chapter, is that it allows law to be enlisted to legitimise *dis*placement. In this way, post-apartheid displacement becomes as politically "normative" as it so overtly was during the apartheid era, for instance, in forced removals and its adjacent brutal forms of (dis-)ordering and (dis-)emplacement. Ostensibly, today's normativity of displacement differs substantially from the overtly racialised political normativity of the past, yet the outcome in terms of placial normativity is by and large alarmingly similar to that exacted during the apartheid era, since displacement in the postcolony has not failed to take place along racialised lines that continue to be as pronounced as they were during apartheid.

Thinking sense of place after apartheid thus requires that we remain particularly vigilant in terms of recognising the nomic/normative dimension of the law's involvement in displacement. When law in the "post"-apartheid era – pervaded as it is by the infiltration of global neoliberalism not only as political economy but as political normativity – either expressly authorises, or silently fails to prevent, displacement, taking account not simply of its spatiality but of its *placiality* necessitates a focus on the abundance of literature that has meticulously delineated the negative consequences of "development-induced displacement" (The World Bank 2004, xviii), the impacts of which are felt in the realm of the economic, the social and the environmental. Examples of this include: the dismantling of production systems; the impoverishment due to the loss of productive assets or income sources; the relocation of people to environments where their productive skills may be less applicable or where the competition for resources are greater; the weakening of community institutions and social networks; the dispersion of kin groups; and finally, the loss of people's cultural connection to land and, often within this, the loss of cultural identity, traditional authority and the potential for mutual help (The World Bank Group 2001).

Displacement erodes the way in which time, history and space are "encoded and contextualized" by way of "interpersonal, community and intercultural relations" (Oliver-Smith 2001, 64). It thus fundamentally touches on the relationship not only of a particular individual but indeed of a particular community with their environment. As such, as Fried (1963) has argued, the forced transfer of people from their place of residence represent an interruption in the individuals' sense of continuity, because it involves the fragmentation of two essential components of identity, namely spatial identity *and* group identity which are associated with strong affective attachments (Fried 1963; Guliani 2003, 144). Displacement thus erodes the sense of place in individual and collective identity formation.

However, activities which lead to large-scale loss of the environmental quality of a place do not necessarily entail physical displacement. A recognition of the wider reach of involuntary displacement is evident in the World Bank's acknowledgement that resettlement affects not only those physically displaced but also those who stay behind and feel the impact of losing their neighbours and resources (World Bank 2001. In these cases, people remain in close proximity to, for instance, industrial development projects such as coal-fired power plants and mining. These projects are characterised by their impacts on the physical environment: air pollution, water pollution, land degradation, heritage disturbances. Such activities thus create conditions in which the environment is transformed to such an extent that it becomes an unfamiliar or alien place to those who remain there. What takes place in these cases is what Lindahl (2006, 889) describes in a different context as the "irruption" of a strange place from within an own place. The "own" place thus itself becomes strange and those who used to belong to the place experience a sense of alienation so profound that they feel foreign in their own place.

These environmental impacts profoundly affect people's health and well-being, their livelihood and the social cohesion of communities (Madihlaba 2002, 156–7). In other words, they have a direct and profoundly concrete effect on how people are emplaced in their place. Those who live with and within such a transformed place suffer a sense of loss, similar to what would have occurred if they had actually been displaced. They are, in fact, virtually displaced, because the transformation of the place carries the consequence of fracturing cultural identities and community bonds. This fracturing can be seen, for example, in the case of the proposed titanium mining in Xolobeni on the Wild Coast of South Africa, where Australian mining company, Mineral Commodities Ltd and the government's battle with the community has given rise to sporadic violence and allegations that the government is holding out on service delivery to the Xolobeni community in an attempt to force it to consent to the titanium mining (Washinyira 2016; Ngcukana 2018).[1] In addition, when a place is faced with the prospect of significant and sudden change, it alters the basis of place-specific dependence. In the context of the possibility of hydraulic fracturing in the Karoo region, for example, the potential threat to water sources in a predominantly agricultural region marked by severe water scarcity may mean that the basis for livelihood and well-being will be eroded to the point where it could be argued that while communities have remained in a particular locality, they have nonetheless been displaced by virtue of the profound loss in environmental support.

Moreover, it is now clear that the worldwide increase in ecosystem distress syndromes is matched by a corresponding increase in human distress syndromes (Albrecht 2007, 15). People are emotionally affected, often quite severely, by negative impacts on their immediate physical environment. In fact, there is growing evidence of a connection between global-scale environmental challenges, such as climate change, and psychological distress (Afifi and Jäger 2010, 57–69).

Yet, at the same time, one can argue that modern law also provides for ways to mitigate the losses referred to above and a human rights framework can potentially play a critical role in outlining processes that will ensure fair relocation. Once again, the involvement of a human rights framework to procure fair relocation necessarily implies that the law's normativity invariably has spatial consequences and specifically in terms of how such displacement is concretely emplaced. Procedural rights and in particular rights to access to information, to participation and access to justice, have been emphasised in an effort to ensure some form of environmental justice in the context of displacement (Adeola and Viljoen 2018, 335–50).

However, while law and a rights-based approach have provided mechanisms to mitigate the worst consequences of displacement, or for one or the other form of redress in the context of involuntary resettlement, the concept of involuntary displacement has been narrowly defined as "actual physical relocation from land" (Gebre 2003). Thus, legal recognition of involuntary displacement is limited to those instances where "the decision of moving is made and imposed by an external agent and when there is no possibility to stay" (World Bank 2001). Below, we make the case that the time has come for the human rights framework to recognise and aid in mitigating, the loss of sense of place as a full-fledged form of displacement to which the same (and possibly additional) legal resources should be available as in the case of physical displacement. To be sure, below we argue that any hierarchical distinction between "virtual" displacement and "physical" displacement is untenable when it comes to considering the normative consequences – both forms constitute a displacement from which should follow similar considerations of legal protection.

"Solastalgia"

Focusing on the intersection between ecosystem and human health, Glen Albrecht (2007) has studied the effect of environmental change or ecosystem change on one's emotional well-being. In documenting the changes to the Upper Hunter Region of New South Wales in Australia, brought about by coal mining, Albrecht observed that the emotions of the residents were similar to displaced populations, even though they weren't displaced.

In the face of the severe changes in environmental quality and in the natural landscape, the inhabitants experienced the violation and loss of their sense of place, in all of its dimensions, a feeling which Albrecht called "solastalgia" (Albrecht 2005, 44), coined as a neologism that combines the Latin *solacium* (comfort) and the Greek *algos* (pain). The concept of solastalgia is intended to give "greater meaning and clarity to environmentally induced distress" (Albrecht et al. 2007, S95). In direct contrast to the dislocated spatial and temporal dimensions of nostalgia, it captures "a form of homesickness one gets when one is still at 'home'" (Albrecht 2005, 45), "the pain or sickness caused by the loss or lack of solace and the sense of isolation connected to the present state of one's home and territory" (45). Albrecht (2010, 227) further elaborates the notion of solastalgia as follows:

> It is the 'lived experience' of negative environmental change manifest as an attack on one's sense of place. It is characteristically a chronic condition tied to the gradual erosion of the sense of belonging (identity) to a particular place and a feeling of distress (psychological desolation) about its transformation (loss of wellbeing).

Albrecht's work was recognised in an Australian Court ruling in which the Land and Environment Court of New South Wales (LECSNW) overturned a decision by the Minister for Planning and Infrastructure to grant the expansion of an open cut coal mine that was to be located almost adjacent to the town of Bulga (*Bulga Milbrodale Progress Association Inc v Minister for Planning and Infrastructure and Warkworth Mining Limited* 2013 NSWLEC 48 (Bulga 2013)). The Bulga Milbrodale Progress Association, who appealed the Minister's decision to approve the expansion application, contended that:

> as a direct result of impacts from noise and a deterioration in air quality from the existing operations, Bulga residents are experiencing substantial negative impacts on health and wellbeing, including stress, anxiety, sleep deprivation, impacts on family relationships and friendships, solastalgia (a feeling of loss of place), and impacts on their socialising and recreational activities in the community.
>
> (Bulga 2013, para 256)

The Association further contended that the social impact on Bulga village had been underestimated in the environmental assessment and that the project would ultimately result in the destruction of the village (Bulga 2013, para 404).

The court accepted as evidence a survey of the community of Bulga to assess the levels of distress already experienced by the community (Bulga 2013, para 429), previous research in the area and the expert opinion of Albrecht.

In a judgment which was upheld on appeal (*Warkworth Mining Limited v Bulga Milbrodale Progress Association Inc* 2014 NSWCA 105), the LECSNW recognised that the expansion's "impacts in terms of noise, dust and visual impacts and the adverse change in the composition of the community" would "exacerbate the loss of sense of place, and materially and adversely change the sense of community, of the residents of Bulga and the surrounding countryside" (Bulga 2013, para 18).

This recognition of virtual displacement by the court not only shows that there is room for the positive law to engage with the concept of virtual or simulated displacement (and the issues that it raises) in a real and meaningful way – it also reveals how centrally *nomos* – as spatialised normativity – determines place. In fact, the decision amounts to a refusal by the court to extend a *nomos* that would profoundly alter, through virtual displacement, the place known as Bulga. The decision not only elaborates the profoundly spatial consequences of a court's decision, it also indicates that an existing *nomos* – like the walls of the city (Arendt 1998, 198) – can work to protect, or at least prevent the further loss of, a community's sense of place. Indeed, one could argue that in the Bulga judgment, the *nomos* functions precisely in the way that Arendt contemplated, namely to protect and preserve the "organised remembrance" (198) of the community, for to protect sense of place, as the court did, is invariably to protect the memory of a place. Moreover, the court's acknowledgement that environmental quality – the concrete and physical space of Bulga as a place – plays a critical role in the community's sense of place, means that the court (rightfully) treated place attachment and place meaning as the mutually co-constituent aspects of sense of place.

Central to any understanding of sense of place should, however, be the recognition that it is determined subjectively. Any landscape evokes multiple experiences of that place, informed by the landscape itself, but also our relationship to that place as expressed by culture, identity and heritage. Thus, not every loss of sense of place would lead to an experience of virtual displacement. One can probably imagine a type of sliding scale in which the stronger a person or community's affective and material connection to a particular state/condition of their land, the stronger the place attachment and the role of the place in the construction of identity. This would translate as a strong place dependency and the conclusion that the more change occurs in relation to the place, the higher the chance of psychological displacement will be. In Bulga, the very fact that the community litigated the Minister's decision, implies a strong place dependency for a critical mass of that community.

Loss of sense of place may, of course, be experienced differently within the same community – for some there may be trade-offs: while the proposed development may bring loss of sense of place, some people may be willing to accept economic benefits as the trade-off. The court in Bulga acknowledged the limited evidentiary weight of Albrecht's use of the interview technique to evidence solastagia (Bulga 2013, para 429), yet it nonetheless held that the subjective views of the Bulga residents who were interviewed could not be discounted (Bulga 2013, para 429), because it was "part of the larger picture of evidence from the community" demonstrating the negative social impact and loss of sense of place that was likely to occur.

Sense of place as part and parcel of the right to the environment

When it comes to the protection of vulnerable communities from virtual displacement – as part and parcel of spatial justice after apartheid – the question that invariably arises within the context of South Africa's Bill of Rights is whether loss of sense of place can be articulated in the normative terms of these rights so as to ground protection from virtual displacement constitutionally. The first question is thus whether loss of sense of place can be translated into a substantive constitutional right. From the point of view of *nomos* in the postcolony, this becomes the question of the connection between concrete space and abstract norm. If South Africa's Bill of Rights represents the posited, albeit aspirational, norms of the constitutionally democratised postcolonial polity, then this is in fact a question as regards which of these norms fall to be spatialised (or further spatialised) in the context of protecting sense of place.

Here, we briefly consider the call for a "right to place" (Imbroscio 2004). The focus of this section is primarily on the possibility of conceptualising virtual displacement in the context of an existing right such as the environmental right in South Africa's Constitution. A second and related question extends to the utility of a rights framework. Why should we couch loss of sense of place or virtual displacement in the language of fundamental rights? What are the advantages of such a rights-based approach, as opposed to, say, grounding sense of place solely in a private law property rights claim based in the law of nuisance? Below we consider whether the call for a right to place understands place in such a way that it can also accommodate a "right" to sense of place.

Calls for a right to place have been articulated in a variety of ways. In some instances, it has indeed taken the form of a call for extended recognition of property rights, land reform and security of tenure (see, for example, Blomley 2004). Others have framed it as claims to place-making with respect to the power relationships at play in the context of citizenship and urban places and spaces (Lepofsky and Fraser 2003). As regards fundamental constitutional rights, citizenship has also been used to consider granting a right to place as an entitlement of citizenship (in an American context) that would afford people the capacity to live in the "place communities" of their own choosing (Imbroscio 2004, 575–609). This would include the "right to stay put" and could also be used to challenge barriers such as access to employment, access to state subsidies, racial discrimination and economic discrimination (Imbroscio 2004, 583).

With respect to displacement and loss of place, the right to place has been invoked in the context of urban land and scholars and activists have used the concept to decry the demolition of public housing in American cities (Samara et al. 2013, 319–26). This work focuses on the loss that occurs when homes are torn down and people are displaced (Samara et al. 2013) and frame this as a struggle over the collective right to place.

Yet, the right to place has been formulated as a claim beyond the right simply to housing. Rather, housing is considered to be "one aspect of a broader social context in which low-income urban populations work to create homes and communities that sustain them in the face of social welfare austerity and, often, public hostility" (Samara et al. 2013, 319). In this, the right to place literature has followed Henri Lefebvre's distinction between habitat and inhabitance and has, in its own terms, emphasised that the right to place extends to inhabitance, rather than to the protection merely of habitat (Lefebvre 1996, 79). As Karin van Marle (2022,) writes in her chapter in this volume:

> A concern with habitat can be taken to refer to a mere functionalist approach to housing provision, whereas inhabitance encompasses so much more: over and above the actual structure it opens possibilities for how one lives, political engagement and affect.

The emphasis within the right to place literature on the socio-spatial aspects of the right to place resonate strongly with both the place dependency and the place meaning aspects of sense of place and this has accordingly opened the way for the accommodation of sense of place as part and parcel of the right to place.

While the right to place remains, at best, in the advocacy stage in all of the above mentioned fields of the positive law, it seems to us that the environmental right – as a right that is capable of wide construction – holds the most potential for accommodating a rights claim in relation to loss of sense of place. Whilst it is true that the right to the environment, like the right to place, has not been recognised in any international human rights treaty, it is nonetheless a right that is legally at a far more advanced stage of development vis-à-vis the potential legal protection of sense of place. It has been recognised in a number of regional agreements, such as the African Charter which recognises the right to an environment in Article 24: Right to a General Satisfactory Environment. The Article states that: "All peoples shall have the right to a general satisfactory environment favourable to their development" (OAU 1981). The Additional Protocol to the American Convention on Human Rights in the Area of Economic, Social and Cultural Rights "Protocol Of San Salvador" (OAS 1988) similarly protects the right to environment. Article 11 guarantees everyone the right to live in a healthy environment and to have access to basic public services.

In terms of domestic legal recognition, Boyd (2011) demonstrated in his pioneering work that almost 200 constitutions around the world have adopted some form of environmental rights, including substantive environmental rights. In the South African Constitution (Constitution of the Republic of South Africa 1996 (the Constitution)), section 24(a) provides that "everyone has the right to an environment that is not harmful to his or her health or well-being". The right is expressed as encompassing protection against infringements on the environment which would harm human health, on the one hand, and well-being, on the other. This is in contrast to most constitutions that simply use the word "environment", such as the Korean Constitution where the environmental right in Chapter II, Article 352 merely states that "the substance of the environmental right shall be determined by law" (Korea (Republic of) 1948 (rev. 1987)).

It is in the concept of "well-being" as part of the environmental right, that sense of place is likely to find/found its legal protection. This would be in line with a more general link between human well-being and environmental impacts and the idea that well-being is embedded in the concept of sustainability (Dietz et al. 2009, 114–23;).

As a concept, well-being has been accused of being elusive in nature. In *HTF Developers (Pty) Ltd v Minister of Environmental Affairs and Tourism* (2006, 132) the court commented on the vague nature of the concept and noted that "the term 'well-being' is open-ended and manifestly [...] incapable of precise definition" (para 18). However, the term has now gathered a considerable amount of scrutiny in South African literature and to a more limited degree in jurisprudence (see, for instance, *Hichange Investments (Pty) Ltd v Cape Produce Company (Pty) Ltd t/a Pelts Products, and Others* (2004, 393). An overview of these sources point to the fact that an array of meanings can be distilled from the concept. These range from the subjective, emotional to the more objectively construed socioeconomic.

Sense of place has been very explicitly expressed as being connected to well-being. It has been noted that "well-being" implies that the environment has not only an instrumental value, but also an inherent worth (Glazewski 2002, 176). In this respect, Glazewski argues that "the environment can be likened to many cultural objects such as a Pierneef painting, a Herbert Baker building, or San rock art. These objects certainly have instrumental value in so far as they generate tourism, for example, but they also have intrinsic value and are worthy of conservation for that reason alone" (176). From this point of view, one could argue that a particular area may be deserving of legal protection simply because of the sense of place that it provides and regardless of its other "instrumental" values.

Kotzé and Du Plessis (2010, 166) suggest that well-being implies that people must be protected against environmental harm which may have an impact on their ability to be content and at ease. Van der Linde and Basson (2012, 50–16) take the view that in addition to mental and physical health, well-being also captures aesthetic considerations. The aesthetic dimensions of the right was considered in *Paolo v Jeeva NO & Others* (2002, 406) in which the applicant argued that proposed alterations to a neighbour's properties would drastically impair one of the major attributes of the property, namely the view which can be enjoyed from it, and as such the alterations would diminish its value. However, the Court dismissed this argument.

Van der Linde and Basson (50–16) have criticised this decision, pointing out that the reduction in the value of the property that would result from the applicant's inability to enjoy the magnificent views from his property, forms part of the field of protection of the applicant's right to an environment which is not detrimental to his well-being. The decision in the court a quo was overturned on appeal to the Supreme Court of Appeal which accepted the argument that impairment of a view would lead to diminished market value, but decided the matter on the basis of the unlawful nature of the approval of the extension plan. In subsequent decisions, the courts have refused to acknowledge a so-called right to a view (*Muller NO and Others* 2006, 415 and *De Kock v Saldanhabaai Munisipalitieit and Others* 2006, 56).

In the *Bulga* case, on the other hand, the court dealt with the loss of scenic views and, more generally, with the "visual impact of the mine" (Bulga 2013, para 434) as part of its adverse social impacts and held that the proposed extension of mining would have "adverse visual impacts of sufficient magnitude and on a sufficiently large number of properties as to have social impacts on the residents of Bulga" (2013, para 439). In this way, the court acknowledged that the visual impact of a proposed development has a bearing on its sense of place and that the loss of scenic view, especially where that scenic view includes a view of an important cultural heritage site (as it did here), can contribute to a loss of sense of place. This determination was part of the overall determination that the project's impacts were unacceptable, the mitigation strategies inadequate and that it could therefore not be approved.

The refusal by South African courts to acknowledge what some would consider the aesthetic dimensions of well-being, however, does not mean that sense of place cannot legally be incorporated in the concept of well-being. Instead, to reduce sense of place to aesthetics incites one to fall into the trap of conceptualising sense of place simplistically as something that is simply visual, rather than as indeed fully engaging the full meaning of "aesthetic", namely the conditions of sensuous perception as such. It is the kind of trap that is often reflected in specialists' reports, compiled as part of the Environmental Impact Assessment (EIA) process in contemplation of a site's development, in which sense of place is often essentialised as an expression of the visual. Such a view denies the complex nature of sense of place and, with it, the range of complex emotions and relationships that come into play when sense of place is lost as a result of environmental degradation.

A consideration of sense of place as part of the well-being component of the environmental right must necessarily also encompass the social and economic dimensions of well-being (Van der Linde and Basson 2012, 50–1–50–16; Feris and Tladi 2005, 201; Du Plessis 2011, 279). Kidd, for instance, argues persuasively that well-being is a critical component of the study of poverty and poverty alleviation and that poverty is, in fact, the absence of well-being (Kidd 2013, 516–21). In this context three dimensions of human well-being are foregrounded: material deprivation, relationships and subjective experiences (Kidd 2013, 516–21) – dimensions that clearly resonate very strongly with the conceptual content of sense of place. It is important to note in this context that, as both the Xolobeni and the Amulsar examples show, it is often poor communities that are most vulnerable with respect to the social and economic impacts of a development, including workers with a strong place dependency, living in close proximity to polluting activities and who do not have the financial means to relocate out of reach of those activities.

Elsewhere, notions of economic and social comfort have been included in attempts to legislate on well-being, most notably in Scotland and more recently in Wales. The Local Government in Scotland Act of 2003 provides local authorities with the authority to advance well-being (Local Government in Scotland Act 2003, section 20). Here, well-being is construed as the inclusion of:

- Economic factors such as the availability of suitable and high quality jobs, measures to encourage local small businesses, efficient and effective transport links, lifelong learning, training and skills development, the provision of infrastructure and new information and communication technologies, etc;
- Social factors such as the promotion of good quality and affordable housing; safe communities; the encouragement of the voluntary sector; looking after the needs of children and young people, particularly the most vulnerable; access to the arts or leisure opportunities; access to education, etc;
- Health related factors such as the promotion of good physical, social and mental health and developing and promoting policies which have a positive impact on health outcomes, especially on health inequalities;
- the removal of objects considered hazardous to health, removal of disfiguring or offensive graffiti from buildings, protecting communities against the threat of climate change, freedom from a high risk of flooding, improving and promoting biodiversity and accessibility to nature

(Scottish Executive 2004, 2).

Here, well-being is not only clearly connected to the legal discourse on the environment, it is also seen as encompassing wider social and economic conditions similar to those that are relevant in terms of sense of place. The Wales Social Services and Well-being (Wales) Act of 2014 similarly defines well-being in addition to physical and mental well-being as social and economic well-being (Wales Social Services and Well-being (Wales) Act of 2014, section 2).

In his early work on environmental rights, Glazewski argued that environmental well-being encompasses a sense of environmental integrity and explains that it is "a sense that we ought to utilize the environment in a morally responsible and ethical manner. If we abuse the environment we feel a sense of revulsion akin to the position where a beautiful and unique landscape is destroyed, or an animal is cruelly treated" (Glazewski 2000, 86). This view emphasises the emotional connections that we may hold with respect to the biophysical space in which we find ourselves and the ways in which we find our identity as part thereof. Thus, environmental care itself becomes not only part of well-being, but indeed part of the spiritual and cultural dimensions of place identity (Feris and Tladi 2005, 201).

In the context of the displacement of indigenous communities, the loss of the spiritual and cultural dimensions of well-being are often most strongly felt.[2] In a decision (*Yakye Axa Indigenous Community v. Paraguay* 2005) in the Inter-American Court of Human Rights, concerned with the displacement of an indigenous community in Paraguay, from lands that formed part of the community's traditional territory, the Court in relation to the Article 21 right to property (Organization of American States 1969), emphasised "the special meaning of communal property of ancestral lands for the indigenous peoples, including the preservation of their cultural identity and its transmission to future generations" (Organization of American States 1969, para 51).

The Court found that property in this context "must take into account the close ties of indigenous peoples with their traditional territories and the natural resources therein associated with their culture, as well as the components derived from them" (Organization of American States 1969, para 137). Significantly, the Court noted that property includes intangible value. This is a very important recognition of the relationship between communal land ownership and indigenous traditions, customs, rituals, values, art and relationships with nature. These relationships to land speak to a community's sense of place and the well-being inherent to it.

What this overview suggests is that while well-being is capable of being widely construed, its meaning is not necessarily elusive. Donald proposes that a teleological and interdependent approach to constitutional interpretation allows for the normative content and goals of the rights in the Bill of Rights, along with the underlying constitutional values, i.e. freedom, equality and dignity, to inform the content of well-being. As such expanding the possibilities for linking well-being to multiple intersections of disadvantage which may not be directly addressed in the Bill of Rights (Donald 2020, 78). Well-being is, therefore, clearly understood as embracing a wide range of dimensions, including those equated with sense of place and that, conversely, loss of sense of place without physical displacement (i.e. virtual displacement), may profoundly impact on well-being and, accordingly, may constitute – in the context of the South African Constitution – an unjustifiable limitation on the right to the environment.

What value does a rights approach offer?

Once one establishes that sense of place can find accommodation within the context of environmental rights, the question remains as regards the value that can be derived from viewing loss of sense of place specifically through the lens of a human rights framework and the environmental right that such a framework protects. What value does such an approach offer for spatial justice after apartheid and for a *nomos* beyond apartheid?

Increasingly, the physical displacement of people by development projects has been recognised as a human rights concern. The United Nations Basic Principles and Guidelines on Development-Based Evictions and Displacement notes that displacement resulting from environmental destruction or degradation often takes place without any regard for the human rights violations that ensue as a result (Human Rights Council and Kothari 2007, para 9; Downing 2002, 3). Forced evictions "constitute gross violations of a range of internationally recognized human rights, including the human right to: adequate housing, food, water, health, education, work, security of the person, security of the home, freedom from cruel, inhuman and degrading treatment, and freedom of movement" (Human Rights Council and Kothari 2007, para 6). In conveying the duties of States with respect to displacement and evictions, the Guidelines make it clear that

> States shall: refrain from violating human rights domestically and extraterritorially; ensure that other parties within the State's jurisdiction and effective control do not violate the human rights of others; and take preventive and remedial steps to uphold human rights and provide assistance to those whose rights have been violated.

The value of these guidelines is that they spell out the duties of States vis-à-vis physical displacement; in particular the notion that States must ensure that it is carried out in accordance with international human rights law (Human Rights Council and Kothari 2007, para 21).

International human rights tribunals have also recognised the human rights impacts of development projects that lead to displacement and the African Court on Human and Peoples' Rights (2004) has found that physical displacement may violate rights under the African Charter to: enjoyment of cultural and traditional values; protection before the law; integrity of person; property; and economic, social, and cultural development (*The African Commission on Human and People's Rights v Kenya* 2012, para 20). The African Commission on Human and Peoples' Rights similarly found that the government of Kenya had violated various rights of the African Charter on Human and Peoples' Rights in creating the Lake Hannington Game Reserve and forcibly removing the Endorois pastoralist community from their ancestral lands.

If the argument is accepted that loss of sense of place without physical displacement can cause virtual displacement, then such virtual displacement would be subject to human rights protection in ways that are similar, *mutatis mutandis*, to physical displacement, thus placing an obligation *on the State* vis-à-vis the virtually displaced. First and foremost, procedural or what is known in international environmental law as Principle 10 rights (United Nations 1992) must be adhered to. Principle 10 sets out three fundamental rights: access to information, access to public participation and access to justice. These rights play a vital role in environmental governance and serve to promote transparency, inclusivity and accountability in decision-making processes.

However, procedural safeguards provide at a minimum, adherence to these processes, but do not necessarily lead to substantive outcomes. For example, public participation in no way equates to participation in, or even the influencing of the final decision-making with respect to the activity that is assessed. Public participation is not decision-making in consultation with, but decision-making after consultation, which does not ensure that comments reflecting the interests of those that are affected will play an integral part in the final decision.

Also, public participation processes are not implemented in ways that acknowledge and address structural inequalities of participants and the presence of predetermined positions of power (social power, political power and economic power) that are part of this process. The production and perpetuation of spatial inequalities remains an important part of the inability of law to achieve environmental justice. It is the production, ownership and use of power in a post-apartheid South Africa, for example, that continues to define and weaken opposition to activities such as mining.

This leaves the question open as regards the value of relying on a substantive environmental right with respect to virtual displacement. In the South African context, it has become apparent that there is very little scope in constitutional jurisprudence for direct enforcement of the environmental right. As a rule, courts avoid constitutional remedies and, instead, remedies are found in legislation or in the common law (Currie and De Waal 2013, 207). This position seems to be in line with the approach of the European Court of Human Rights which held in *Kyrtatos v Greece* (2005, para 52) that "severe environmental pollution may affect individuals' well-being and prevent them from enjoying their homes in such a way as to affect their private and family life adversely, without, however, seriously endangering their health", but went on to state that the European Convention on Human Rights is not "designed to provide general protection of the environment as such" and that "to that effect, other international instruments and domestic legislation are more pertinent in dealing with this particular aspect".

Yet, as Glazewski (2002, 178) has noted in the South African context: "[b]y including an environmental right the constitution makers have put environmental justice issues squarely into the realm of government responsibility". It is in this context, too, that Glazewski makes reference to "apartheid's environmental legacy". This legacy is surely part and parcel of the general legacy of the *nomos* of apartheid which the Constitution sets out to transform. It could thus also be argued that the notion of "well-being" can only be properly interpreted against the backdrop of apartheid's environmental legacy and that this may well mean – given the history of *physical* forced removals that was so fundamental to this legacy – that "well-being" must serve as the constitutional vehicle through which protection from virtual displacement can be legally secured.

At the level of regional tribunals, there has been more appetite for the substantive approach and the African Commission on Human and Peoples' Rights has found oil development practices in the Ogoni region of Nigeria to be in violation of the right to a general satisfactory environment (*Social and Economic Rights Action Centre (SERAC) and Another v Nigeria* 2001), as guaranteed under Article 24 of the African Charter (Organisation of African Unity 1986).

Human rights litigation has some clear advantages, in particular the fact that it can lead to systemic change. Drawing attention to an environmental rights framework and couching sense of place within such a framework can, however, also be useful in other ways. Importantly, it influences the making and implementation of policy. It plays a role in the drafting of policy, legislation, regulations, plans and guidelines. It requires adherence in respect of the implementation of these policy and regulatory instruments. It also offers guidance for courts when scrutinising the regulatory framework and/or the implementation thereof. There is, for example, a growing call for mandating a human rights impact assessment as part of or in addition to the EIA process (Center for International Environmental Law 2010, 1–2). With respect to the environmental right, policy and legislation mandating an environmental assessment should adhere to the requirements of such a right. At the implementation stage, an overarching standard in the assessment process should be whether an activity or project may lead to an infringement of environmental health and well-being. Where the right is interpreted to include sense of place protection as part of well-being, such an assessment would have to seriously take account of the possible loss of sense of place. Finally, the court as arbiter would have to ensure that the EIA adheres to these requirements.

In many jurisdictions, a tool like EIA already includes an assessment of the impact that a particular development might have on the inhabitants' sense of place. However, sense of place is very often not defined (the South African regulatory framework, for example, is absent of any such definition). In addition, as suggested earlier, it is inadequately captured as "social impact assessment" or "visual impact assessment" in the absence of a comprehensive assessment of the key economic and social factors determining sense of place and, perhaps more importantly, in the absence of guidance as to how these factors should be assessed. The environmental rights mandate thus serves to emphasise the need to articulate and define sense of place much more specifically and with reference to the many dimensions thereof.

More profoundly, by recognising the human rights dimensions of loss of sense of place, it elevates the substantive importance of the concept itself. It stresses the importance of devising a legal process that would more effectively assess sense of place so as to capture the multiplicity of connections to place and space. This may require, for example, a deeper, more substantive and multifaceted engagement with affected communities and groups, using methods such as empirical data gathering, psychological assessments and storytelling. A more nuanced assessment of the loss of the sense of place experienced by people would open up the opportunity to consider the extent to which loss of sense of place may lead to virtual displacement and to actively consider options beyond mitigation, including the "no go" option.

Conclusion

Law sanctions the displacement of people, while simultaneously buffering the effects thereof, inter alia, by requiring that it takes place within the dictates of a human rights framework. The law similarly allows for the radical altering of the spaces in which humans find themselves, to the point that they experience a loss of sense of place – in these different ways *nomos*, as spatialised normativity, *takes place*. The virtual displacement we write of here, needs to be protected by human rights, acknowledging the ways in which loss of sense of place impacts on the environmental right, especially if we are interested in overcoming a historic *nomos* of apartheid and colonialism which so profoundly violated, in physical and virtual ways, the colonised's sense of place. In essence, a human rights approach to virtual displacement can shape the way in which we view sense of place and provide a framework that allows for engaging with it in a more meaningful, yet nuanced manner, while working to overcome the *nomos* of apartheid.

Recognising sense of place as part of the constitutionally protected environmental right can significantly affect the coming into being of a post-apartheid *nomos*, especially because protecting sense of place in this way (i.e. by way of an obligation on the State), can significantly disrupt the routinely sharp dissymmetry in power between developers and local communities, as so clearly illustrated in the Xolobeni case. If the task of spatial justice after apartheid includes thinking *nomos* beyond the repetition of land-appropriation – which development projects that cause loss of sense of place arguably are – then the spatialisation of the environmental right in the Constitution cannot afford to neglect sense of place, especially in light of apartheid's inexorable and enduring environmental legacy.

Notes

1 There are striking similarities between the Xolobeni case and the case of Armenia's Amulsar gold mine (see Ellis 2019). In both cases, the community has demonstrated that the mining activities will cause a widespread loss of sense of place and in both cases they have been at loggerheads with both government and the mining company in an effort to prevent the loss of sense of place. The similarity goes to show that communities as far removed from each other as South Africa and Armenia, are facing similar environmental challenges in relation to the preservation of sense of place and it demonstrates that the legal recognition of virtual displacement is, in the age of the Anthropocene, a pressing need that is all but specific or unique to South Africa.

2 While this chapter does not endeavour to engage in depth with the concept of indigenous people it should be noted that in an African context the concept of "indigenous people" is somewhat controversial. However in the Kenyan Endorois case the court condemned the expulsion of the indigenous Endorois people from their land in Kenya and thus this case is seen as a major victory for indigenous peoples across Africa. (*Centre for Minority Rights Development (Kenya) and Minority Rights Group International on behalf of Endorois Welfare Council v. Kenya, 276/2003, African Commission on Human and Peoples' Rights 4 February 2010*)

References

Adeola, R., and F. Viljoen. 2018. "Climate change, development projects and internal displacement in Africa." *Journal of African Law* 62 (3): 335–350. https://doi.org/10.1017/S0021855318000219.

Afifi, T., and J. Jäger. Eds. 2010. *Environment, forced migration and social vulnerability*. Berlin, Heidelberg: Springer.

Agamben, G. 1998. *Homo sacer: Sovereign power and bare life*. Stanford, CA: Stanford University Press.

Albrecht, G. 2005. ""Solastalgia": A new concept in health and identity." *Philosophy Activism Nature* 3: 41–55.

Albrecht, G. 2010. "Solastalgia and the creation of new ways of living." In *Nature and culture: Rebuilding lost connections*, edited by S. Pilgrim and J Pretty, 217–234. London: Earthscan.

Albrecht, G., G. M. Sartore, L. Connor, N. Higginbotham, S. Freeman, B. Kelly, H. Stain, A. Tonna, and G. Pollard. 2007. "Solastalgia: The distress caused by environmental change." *Australasian Psychiatry* 15 (1): 95–98. https://doi.org/10.1080/10398560701701288.

Arendt, H. 1998. *The human condition*. 2nd ed. Chicago, IL: University of Chicago Press.

Bennett, L., and A. Layard. 2015. "Legal geography: Becoming spatial detectives." *Geography Compass* 9 (7): 406–422. https://doi.org/10.1111/gec3.12209.

Blomley, N. 2004. *Unsettling the city: Urban land and the politics of property*. New York and London: Routledge.

Boyd, D. 2011. *The environmental rights revolution: A global study of constitutions, human rights and the environment*. Vancouver, Canada: University of British Columbia Press.

Bulga Milbrodale Progress Association Inc v Minister for Planning and Infrastructure and Warkworth Mining Limited. 2013. NSWLEC 48.

Center for International Environmental Law. 2010. *EIAs in practice: Potential lessons for human rights impact assessment*. http://www.ciel.org/wp-content/uploads/2015/04/EIA_Brief_Jun10.pdf.

Centre for Minority Rights Development (Kenya) and Minority Rights Group International on behalf of Endorois Welfare Council v. Kenya. 2010. African Commission on Human and Peoples' Rights 276/2003.

Chryssostalis J. 2013. "Reading Arendt 'reading' Schmitt: Reading Nomos otherwise?" In *Feminist encounters with legal philosophy*, edited by M. Drakopoulou, 158–184. New York: Routledge.

Clark, D. L. 2002. "The World Bank and human rights: The need for greater accountability." *Harvard Human Rights Journal* 15: 205–226.

Constitution of the Republic of Korea. 1948. Consolidated text, English translation. Available through World Constitutions Illustrated via Hein OnLine, https://heinonline-org.uow.idm.oclc.org/HOL/Page?handle=hein.cow/zzks0002&collection=cow

Constitution of the Republic of South Africa. 1996. https://www.gov.za/documents/constitution-republic-south-africa-1996

Council of Europe. 1950. *European convention for the protection of human rights and fundamental freedoms, as amended by protocols nos. 11 and 14, ETS 5*. https://www.coe.int/en/web/conventions/full-list?module=treaty-detail&treatynum=005

Cross, J. E. 2001. "What is sense of place?" Conference Paper uploaded on Researchgate.net. Accessed December 2016.

Currie, I., and J. De Waal. 2013. *The bill of rights handbook*. 5th ed. Cape Town: Juta.

Datel, R. E., and D. J. Dingemans. 1984. "Environmental perception, historical preservation, and sense of place." In *Environmental perception and behaviour: An inventory and prospect*, edited by T. F. Saarinen and T. F. Seamon, 131–144. Chicago, IL: University of Chicago Press.

De Kock v Saldanhabaai Munisipaliteit. 2006. ZAWCHC 56.

Dietz, T., E. A. Rosa, and R. York. 2009. "Environmentally efficient well-being: Rethinking sustainability as the relationship between human well-being and environmental impacts." *Human Ecology Review* 16 (1): 113–122.

Donald, M. 2020. "Unlocking the potential of well-being in the environmental right: A teleological interpretation." *Stellenbosch Law Review* 31 (1): 55–79.

Downing, T. E. 2002. *Avoiding new poverty: Mining-induced displacement and resettlement.* London: International Institute for Environment and Development.

Du Plessis, A. 2011. "South Africa's constitutional environmental right (generously) interpreted: What is in it for poverty?" *South African Journal on Human Rights* 27 (2): 279–307. https://doi.org/10.1080/19962126.2011.11865016.

Ellis, G. 2019. "Mining vs the environment: The battle over Armenia's Amulsar gold mine." *Aljazeera*, January 31. https://www.aljazeera.com/blogs/europe/2019/01/mining-environment-battle-armenia-amulsar-gold-190130135537637.html.

Feris, L. 2016. "Making legal sense of a "sense of place" in the Karoo." In *Hydraulic fracturing in the Karoo: Critical legal & environmental perspectives*, edited by J. Glazewski and S. Esterhuyse, 395–408. Cape Town: Juta.

Feris, L. A., and D. Tladi. 2005. "Environmental rights." In *Socio-economic rights in South Africa*, edited by D. Brand and C. Heyns, 249–264. Pretoria: Pretoria University Law Press.

Fried, M. 1963. "Grieving for a lost home." In *The urban condition: People and policy in the metropolis*, edited by L. J. Duhl, 151–171. New York: Basic Books.

Gebre, Y. 2003. "Resettlement and the unnoticed losers: Impoverishment disasters among the gumz hosts in Ethiopia." *Human Organisation* 62 (1): 50–61.

Giuliani, M. V. 2003. "Theory of attachment and place attachment." In *Psychological theories for environmental issues*, edited by M. Bonnes, T. Lee, and M. Bonaiuto, 133–170. Hants: Ashgate.

Glazewski, J. 2000. *Environmental law in South Africa.* Durban: Butterworths.

Glazewski, J. 2002. "The rule of law: Opportunities for environmental justice in the new democratic legal order." In *Environmental justice in South Africa*, edited by David McDonald, 171–198. Cape Town: University of Cape Town Press.

Hichange Investments (Pty) Ltd v Cape Produce Company (Pty) Ltd t/a Pelts Products, and Others. 2004. 2 SA 393.

HTF Developers (Pty) Ltd v Minister of Environmental Affairs and Tourism. 2006. ZAGPHC 132.

Human Rights Council and M. Kothari, "Annex I" *Report of the Special Rapporteur on Adequate Housing as a Component of the Right to an Adequate Standard of Living, Miloon Kothari*, 2007. A/HRC/4/18. https://digitallibrary.un.org/record/600545?ln=en

Imbroscio, D. L. 2004. "Can we grant a right to place?" *Politics & Society* 32 (4): 575–609.

Kidd, M. 2013. "Environment." In *The bill of rights handbook.* 6th ed., edited by I. Currie and J. De Waal, 516–529. Cape Town: Juta.

Kotzé, L. J., and A. Du Plessis. 2010. "Some brief observations on fifteen years of environmental rights jurisprudence in South Africa." *Journal of Court Innovation* 3 (1): 157–176.

Kudryavtsev, A., R. C. Stedman, and M. E. Krasny. 2012. "Sense of place in environmental education." *Environmental Education Research* 18 (2): 229–250.

Kyrtatos v. Greece. 2005. 40 EHRR 16.

Lindahl, H. K. 2004. "Finding place for Freedom, Security and Justice: The European Union's claim to territorial unity." Constitutionalism Web Papers 1.

Lefebvre, H. 1996. *Writing on cities.* Cambridge, MA: Blackwell.

Lepofsky, J., and J. C. Fraser. 2003. "Building community citizens: Claiming the right to place-making in the city." *Urban Studies* 40 (1): 127–142. https://doi.org/10.1080/00420980220080201.

Lindahl, H. 2006. "Give and take: Arendt and the Nomos of political community." *Philosophy & Social Criticism* 32 (7): 881–901. https://doi.org/10.1177/0191453706066979.

Local Government in Scotland Act. 2003. https://www.legislation.gov.uk/asp/2003/1/enacted

Lynch, K. 1960. *The image of the city*. Cambridge, MA: MIT Press.

Madihlaba, T. 2002. "The Fox in the Henhouse: The environmental impact of mining on communities in South Africa." In *Environmental justice in South Africa*, edited by D. A. McDonald, 156–167. Athens, OH: Ohio University Press.

Massey, Doreen. 1994. *Space, place and gender*. Minneapolis, MN: University of Minnesota Press.

McDowell, C., ed. 1996. *Understanding impoverishment: The consequences of development-induced displacement*. Providence, Oxford: Berghahn Books.

Moore, R. L., and A. R. Graefe. 1994. "Attachments to recreation settings: The case of rail-trail users." *Leisure Sciences* 16 (1): 17–31. https://doi.org/10.1080/01490409409513214.

Muller NO v City of Cape Town. 2006. 5 SA 415 (C).

Najafi, M., and M. K. B. M. Shariff. 2011. "The concept of place and sense of place in architectural studies." *International Journal of Human and Social Sciences* 6 (3): 187–193.

Ngcukana, L. 2018. "Mining project will destroy us, say Xolobeni villagers." *City Press*, October 1. https://city-press.news24.com/News/mining-project-will-destroy-us-say-xolobeni-villagers-20181001.

Oliver-Smith, A. 2001. *Displacement, resistance and the critique of development: From the grass roots to the global. Final report prepared for ESCOR R7644 and the research programme on development induced displacement and resettlement*. Oxford: Oxford Refugee Studies Centre.

Organization of African Unity (OAU). 1981. *African charter on human and peoples' rights "Banjul charter"*, CAB/LEG/67/3 rev. 5, 21 I.L.M. 58.

Organization of American States (OAS). 1969. *American convention on human rights, "pact of San Jose"*, Costa Rica.

Organization of American States (OAS). 1988. *Additional protocol to the American convention on human rights in the area of economic, social, and cultural rights "protocol of San Salvador"*, OAS Doc. OAS/Ser.L/V/I.4 rev. 13.

Paola v Jeeva NO. 2002. 2 SA 391 (D).

Relph, E. 1976. *Place and placelessness*. London: Pion.

Samara, T. R., A. Sinha, and M. Brady. 2013. "Putting the "public" back in affordable housing: Place and politics in the era of poverty deconcentration." *Cities* 35: 319–326.

Schmitt, C. 2003. *The Nomos of the earth in the International Law of the Jus Publicum Europaeum*. Translated by G. L. Ulmen. New York: Telos.

Scottish Executive, 2004. Local Government in Scotland Act 2003: 'Power to Advance Well-Being Guidance' (April). https://www.webarchive.org.uk/wayback/archive/20150220071351/http://www.gov.scot/Publications/2004/04/19276/36157

Social and Economic Rights Action Centre (SERAC) & Another v Nigeria. 2001. AHRLR 60 (ACHPR).

Social Services and Well-being (Wales) Act. 2014. https://www.legislation.gov.uk/anaw/2014/4/contents/enacted

Steele, F. 1981. *The sense of place*. Boston, MA: CBI.

The African Commission on Human and Peoples' Rights v Kenya. 2012. ACHPR 6.

Tuan, Y. F. 1974. *Topophilia: A study of environmental perception, attitudes, and values*. Englewood Cliffs, NJ: Prentice-Hall.

Tuan, Y. F. 1975. "Geopiety: A theme in man's attachment to nature and to place." In *Geographies of the mind*, edited by D. Lowenthal and M. Bowden, 44–56. New York: Oxford University Press.

Tuan, Y. F. 1977. *Space and place: The perspective of experience*. Minneapolis, MN: University of Minnesota Press.
Tuan, Y. F. 1980. "Rootedness versus sense of place." *Landscape* 24: 3–8.
United Nations. 1992. *Rio declaration on environment and development*. Report on the UN Conference on Environment and Development, Rio de Janeiro, 3–14 June 1992, UN doc. A/CONF.151/26/Rev.1 (Vols. 1-III).
Van der Linde, M., and E. Basson. 2012. "Environment." In *Constitutional law of South Africa*. 2nd ed., edited by S. Woolman and M. Bishop, 50-i–50-68. Cape Town: Juta.
Van Marle, K. 2022. "Unlearning, (Un)naming, Cohabiting." In *Spatial Justice After Apartheid: Nomos in the Postcolony*, edited by Jaco Barnard-Naudé and Julia Chryssostalis. Abingdon: Routledge.
Warkworth Mining Limited v Bulga Milbrodale Progress Association Inc. 2014. NSWCA 105.
Washinyira, T. 2016. "We will die for our land, say angry Xolobeni villagers as dune mining looms." *Mail & Guardian*, February 12. https://mg.co.za/article/2016-02-12-we-will-die-for-our-land-say-angry-xolobeni-villagers-as-dune-mining-looms-1.
Windsor, J. E., and J. A. Mcvey. 2005. "Annihilation of both place and sense of place: The experience of the Cheslatta T'En Canadian first nation within the context of large-scale environmental projects." *Geographical Journal* 171 (2): 146–165. https://doi.org/10.1111/j.1475-4959.2005.00156.x.
World Bank. 2001. "Operational policy on involuntary resettlement (OP 412)." *World Bank*, Washington, DC: World Bank, December. https://policies.worldbank.org/sites/ppf3/PPFDocuments/Forms/DispPage.aspx?docid=1572&ver=current.
World Bank. 2004. *Involuntary resettlement sourcebook: Planning and implementation in development projects*. Washington, DC: World Bank.
Yakye Axa Indigenous Community v. Paraguay. 2005. ICHR (ser. C) 125.

Chapter 13

Memory Card Sea Power

Photographs by David Southwood

Text by Sean Christie from 'Under Nelson Mandela Boulevard: Life Among the Stowaways' and photographs by David Southwood from 'MEMORY CARD SEA POWER'

Stowaway subcultures have existed in the Tanzanian port cities of Dar es Salaam and Tanga since the mid-1970s, from which they spread to the major ports of Mombasa, Lamu and as far north as Djibouti (integrating with existing stowaway subcultures in those ports). Any southwards spread of this subculture was blocked by civil war in Mozambique and racial apartheid in South Africa, but by the mid-1990s these obstacles had fallen away, and young Tanzanian stowaways – men in their late teens and twenties – migrated to South Africa in significant numbers, establishing communities on the fringes of all the major port cities. They found the conditions in these places ideal for their purposes. Harbour security, untested for decades, was primitive. The CBDs verging on the ports were in varying phases of collapse, as wealthy residents and business owners continued to move out to the suburbs, a process that had started in the 1980s with the breakdown of apartheid-era influx laws. The stowaways found they could melt into the shanty towns that had sprung up under city bridges, alongside railway lines and in vacant plots. Incredibly, their presence went virtually unnoticed for 15 years.

In Cape Town these "Beachboys" camped under the flyover bridges of Nelson Mandela Boulevard (then Boulevard East) and in the railyards of Cape Town's Foreshore, a 194 ha area reclaimed from the ocean in the 1940s as part of the port expansion works. The architecture that has grown up in this space, including two unfinished Freeway bridges, is often described as "inhumane", and as City planner Lisa Kane argues, the development of Foreshore freeways, "was an inherently political exercise", given The Eastern Boulevard's "dubious distinction of being the cause of the first large scale demolitions in District 6, starting in 1960". And yet this architecture has for 20 years functioned as refuge for undocumented migrants, the undisputed undesirables of the post-apartheid period, who risk, when they cross into South Africa, becoming enmeshed in the continent's most elaborate detention and deportation system.

The presence of the Beachboys provides an extraordinary bridge between Cape Town's present and its past, and simultaneously challenges

DOI: 10.4324/9780203712771-13

predominant representations of the city as well as understandings of how city space is used and what politics are imbued in roads, railways and vacant lots. The multi-nodal nature of the Beachboy world also exposes the complex ways in which Cape Town is connected to other South African and African cities, drawing Cape Town into the wider context of continental torsions and conflicts.

For a city so often described in terms of its cultural distinctions, its political and geographical exceptionalism, this is a timely angle of exploration, and a satisfying one.

In "Writing the city after apartheid", one of 39 essays in *The Cambridge History of South African Literature*, Michael Titlestad points out that, "The simultaneous transformation of apartheid cities and their vestigial divisions have made these concatenations (cities) primary sites for literary engagements with the simultaneous utopian promise and crippling contradictions of contemporary South Africa" and yet looking back over post-apartheid writing about cities he concludes that "the post-apartheid city is too immoderate and unresolved to be mapped".

"Haiyo Dave", said the distant figure.

"Adam!"

"Yeah is me, Dave, I've been in Russia since I last saw you man, in Saint Petersburg". "You know, Dave, we beach boys call this place 'The Freezer' because it's so cold," he said, a gold-plated incisor glinting in his mouth.

"I take it you're not carrying?"

Adam opened his mouth and rolled a white plastic cube around with his tongue.

"Coke?"

"Heroin".

"Don't swallow".

"It's no problem. I'll just throw it up later".

Reaching into a small blue rucksack he pulled out a large faux-leather 2010 diary, the corners of which had swollen with moisture and burst. This he opened first at the pastel-coloured continental maps that large diaries have at front and back. He pointed out Dakar, Jakarta, Singapore, Dubai – some of the cities he had travelled to. On almost every other page he had drawn cargo and container ships in pencil and pen. He began jabbing at them with his callused fighters' fingers, pointing out the engine room, the lifeboats, the tonnage hatches, even the bulbed area above the rudder – all established Beachboy hiding places. Lastly he pointed out the portal to the anchor chain locker, and waved his hand to indicate danger.

"Fire".

"Fire?"

"Anchor out, fire in", he clarified, and to demonstrate what a gigantic anchor chain rapidly paying out through a small portal would do to a human body caught up in the action he scooped up a handful of dirt from between his feet, and threw it out over the start of the N1.

"Tha's not Swahili, Dave, tha's Bob Marley", said Adam, in the tailings of what I'd have said was a Brummie accent if the likelihood of his having ever lived in Birmingham wasn't so infinitesimally small.

"Baby don't worry, about a thing. Because every lil thin, goabe orite", he croaked, and the three sitters cracked wide grins.

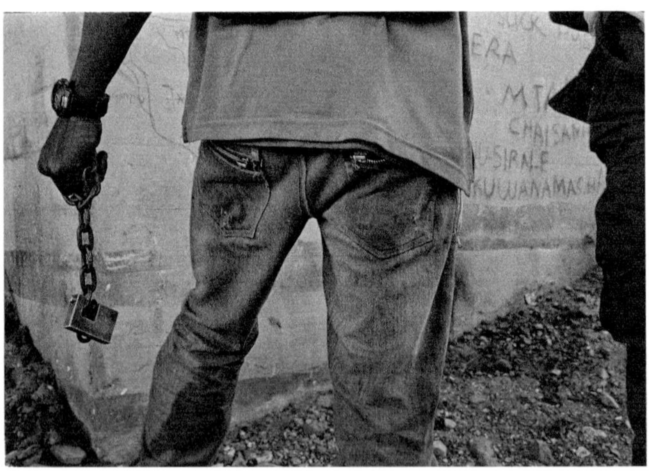

Adam felt like a smoke so we headed for The Freezer, and here ran into a 19-year-old called Daniel-Peter, who pointed to a vessel with a flag of Jamaica painted on the smokestack.

Beach Boy Graffiti

sea power

kibiki reno-hope to sea
hope to sea niga swaily
kipaka memory card
easy to die, tough to get
tanal life god bless
corder sailor, never big up
opportunity never come twise
wa beach
waa hop 2 sea
god yucken bless mi
don't west your time

balti more

ndongosh from mapipa area kimakavezi, pelea house
sad boy say time will tell
today africa, tomorrow yurope

the power of sea, forever and ever
fuck you dog stowaway
one day 2c
kacho lee i'm 2 the rop

some lost, some die, some win
bremen
to stavanga
junior was here smoking weed 2006
pray's the lord
ohio states miami new york city
junior no more
god bless da sea
rashidi mwanza to sea neva afrika again

professor ngaribo
i like ship no like pussy
sea never dry
escape from cape
manigar swahili don't sleep too much
hope to disappear
to cry isn't solution. you can cry till jesus will come back. bater to get ship. faster.
no pain to spain
sex man chateka, from vingweta

life goes on
easy to die tuff to get. beter to die young.
some win. some lost. some die
seaman life no story only action
who to trust now?
in god we trust
in thug we trust
days goes on
no way to escape my life without ship
more time to get catch me if can fine
don't trust a woman because a woman is a snake and a snake is a dangerous animal
things never be the same

im two ameca

time will tell life is going on
god bless my people we pray for you to get good time

jesus fails
thuff to get easy to die. one time you gonna die
push life to sea
sherney tmk hate all wizzard
stiff necked fools
die or save, seamanlife is not story. action
try to make friend not enemy you never no
nothing is tough. accept tough is yourself

"Haiyo Sean", said Adam, sauntering over a moment later.
"I take it you're not carrying?"
Adam opened his mouth and rolled a white plastic cube around with his tongue.
"Coke?"
"Heroin".
"Don't swallow".
"It's no problem. I'll just throw it up later".
Adam felt like a smoke so we headed for The Freezer, and here ran into a 19-year-old called Daniel-Peter, who pointed to a vessel with a flag of Jamaica painted on the smokestack.

"The boy says it's a good ship because it's low in the water. That means it's loaded and ready to go", Adam explained.

"We're going to try to stow that ship tonight, me and this boy. I love this boy", he said paternally. "He's not scared of anything. He's a little boxer from Keko in Dar es Salaam. All Keko boys are little boxers".

"It lasts me maybe ten days".

He also had a torch, a short length of tubular metal and five or six empty plastic packets.

"The best place to hide is inside the cargo hold", he explained.

"The only problem is they lock the hatch and don't open it again. It's dark down there so you need a light".

The length of metal had a more vital function.

"When your food and water run out you need to use a small iron like this to hit the hatch, so that the sailors can hear and let you out. Otherwise you die".

"Yoh i m going last night i jup on ship name bluu sky. pls keep on touch with me family. fhone my daughter mum pls. pls tell her what is hapen. Memory Card. sea power".

Chapter 14

Rewriting type

Writing *nomos* otherwise

Iain Low

Introduction: colonial overwriting and writing *nomos* otherwise

South African cities are colonial constructs. They have evolved through a series of deliberate but protracted impositions on a found indigenous landscape. These impositions have taken the form of "over-writings" of the landscape and effect the erasure of the pre-existent and substitute a new order – a *nomos* grounded in a constitutive land appropriation (Schmitt 2006, 67) – in the service of the coloniser. Through time, this practice has produced a South African urbanism that is spatially hierarchic in that it racially set people apart through its exclusive service to a predominantly white minority power base. The consequent marginalisation effected by this *nomos* dispossessed indigenous people of both land and culture. Accordingly, the single most enduring legacy of colonial-apartheid – the "master" legacy of the master's legacy – is the spatial one. Space is the construct that most effectively realised and maintained apartheid's grand plan and continues to ensure the endurance of its legacy.

In April 1994, subsequent to democratic election, the new African National Congress (ANC) government inherited a nation wherein most of its inhabitants were effectively landless, homeless and economically disempowered. After apartheid, the Truth and Reconciliation Commission (TRC), the then unique South African mediation instrument, designed to confront and resolve the legacy of apartheid, constructed the issue of reconciliation as a primarily experiential exercise. Effectively absolving the perpetrators of any punitive consequence, trauma and nominal material compensation were consequently the outcome for victims participating in the TRC.

It is thus not surprising that the failure to deal strategically and substantially with land and shelter has been at the forefront of the perceived failures of the South African postcolony. As the ongoing debate about expropriation without compensation and the amendment to Section 25 and the right to property in the 1996 Constitution has illustrated, land redistribution and its concomitant reordering, whether urban or rural, continue to be central to contemporary settlement practice and is fundamental to the South African quest for reconciliation and "normalcy"(Low 2003). My argument in this contribution is that, for architecture,

DOI: 10.4324/9780203712771-14

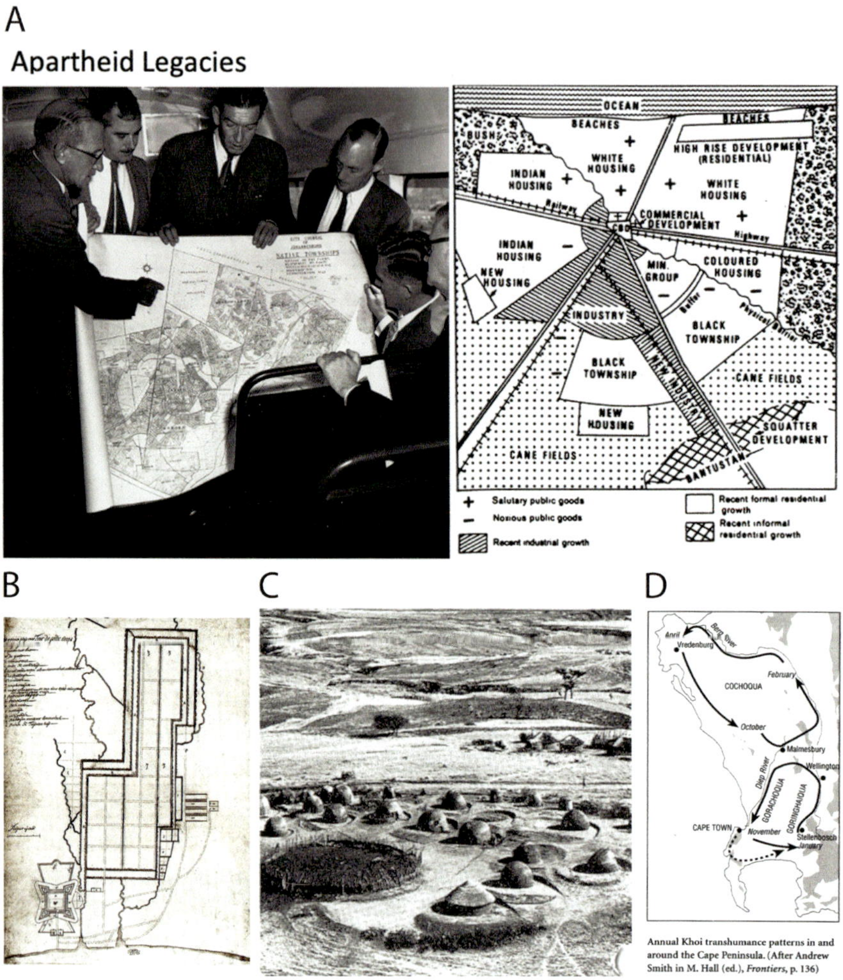

Figure 14.1 The *nomos* of apartheid. The legacy of apartheid has been inscribed through the competing spatial practices of, on the one hand, bantu and colonial settlement which set apart, and on the other, those of the indigenous *san* and *khoe* whose spatial practices are predicated on nomadism with their "unsettled" temporal relations toward land. (A) NBRI Apartheid planned segregation. (B) VoC Cape Town. (C) Bantu settlement patterns. (D) San nomadic routes.

this quest turns not only on the reading of *nomos* "otherwise" (Chryssostalis 2013) but also on the responsibility and capability of architects to consciously deploy their agency in *writing nomos* otherwise (Low 2004, Awan et al. 2011).

Carl Schmitt's (2003) reading of *nomos* as encompassing both order and emplacement (Chryssostalis 2013) is founded in a thorough understanding of the intimate connection between space and power. While power may be temporal, its spatial consequence is more permanent and remains as overwritten on the landscape with the consequence that continues to effect human relationality within the built environment long after political change (Judin and Vladislavic 1998). Despite the change in power, apartheid's spatial legacy remains firmly etched in its urban landscapes. The physical characteristics of radical separation and the extreme inequalities that typified apartheid planning continues to identify our cities and townships as exploitative colonial constructs. Apart from an exceptionally minor black elite, the previously marginalised remain predominantly marginalised. The continuity of apartheid spatiality is, in other words, at least in part a consequence of a disinterested elite who control the levers of power, yet possess minimal agency whereby to effectively engage in the exigency of spatial transformation. The spatial transformation attempted through the introduction of new legislative instruments has predominantly failed – unsurprisingly, given its confinement within a liminal space of policy and planning, largely commanded by politicians and planners who possess remarkably little or no spatial literacy. As a result, the unacceptable failure of transformation remains "written" in the continuity of spatial inequality experienced by the majority of poor black citizens.[1]

Against this backdrop, *rewriting architectural type* (Low 2004) and *writing the city* (Bremner 2010), have become common tropes in contemporary discourse of the transforming city. Paralleling Bremner's notion of writing the city into being I would posit that the responsibility of an architect, in a country that aspires toward the post-apartheid, must be thought of in relation to a notion of *becoming* which I characterise as both *writing the city into being otherwise* and *writing the city otherwise into being*. These two notions of writing otherwise are inextricably intertwined. They necessarily imply a fundamental, transformative rewriting, but whereas the first gestures at an outcome – the city otherwise – the second emphasises the transformation we need at the level of imaginative architectural thinking, through practice and resultant material. Thus, in order for the city to become otherwise, we need, as architects to *write the city otherwise*. Simply put, spatial transformation depends to a great extent on how we do and do not *practise* architecture. As regards the latter, I will demonstrate that the rewriting of type has been a consistent, although liminal, intentional practice in those post-apartheid architectures that can be characterised as having brought into being the signs of a city otherwise, or of an otherwise city, that is, a city critically "conscious" of the Other which it has denied for so long. In so doing, these projects have begun the immense task of writing the South African *nomos* beyond that of apartheid.

Architecture as a measure of transformation

Eighteen years ago, Lesley Naa Norle Lokko, in her 2002 Vivienne Japha and Len and Gunnel Hicks Memorial Lecture at the University of Cape Town's School of Architecture Planning and Geomatics, identified the need for a transformed understanding of the interrelationship between race and architecture as being intrinsic to the transformation of space (unpublished lecture; Lokko 2002). Constructing her lecture as ten tales, she related the narratives of different architectures that have been produced in relation to the specificity of local situations. In the context of a past defined by a racist spatial order, such an architecture, which places race and the undoing of racist injustice at its centre, may be understood as *the* informing precondition of writing the South African *nomos* otherwise – Social Justice and Spatial Equity then become synonymous in the quest for spatial reconfiguration.

Most recently in South Africa, the concept of land appropriation has come to reside as a form of redistributive justice through restitution by the return transfer of ownership and, as previously inferred, land expropriation without compensation has been mooted as one potential way of accelerating land reform in South Africa (Malema/EFF 2018). However, in the absence of any conceptualisation of the potential of a radical reconfiguration of the spatial order of settlement, the re-establishment of societal unity remains remote. In other words, the failure to grapple with the *nomos* of the earth *in loco* at critical moments of political change, renders continuity of a pre-existent norm, thereby ensuring the exchange of one hegemony for another (Memmi 1965, 5, 6, 165).

In the major South African metropolises – Johannesburg, Cape Town and Durban – the spatial transformation requires of architects and built environment professionals that they engage the structural tension that exists between the racially constructed traditional centre, exemplified by old white Central Business Districts (CBDs) and their peripheries in the form of apartheid's black townships. This disparity also mimics the contradictions within the new global/local economic order. These above-mentioned cities each entertain definite aspirations to global relevance, with tourism and international convention centres, as well as local economic growth, specifically informing and driving urban development. However, through reasons of economic base, geography, climate and ethnicity each city is also particular with a necessity to attend to local imperatives with local resources driving local responses. The need to compete with the market, both nationally and globally, adds undermining complexity to these initiatives.

A developer-driven architecture of neo-Tuscan and pseudo-Victoriana is ubiquitous in our emerging suburban landscapes. This is evident in the shopping malls and gated housing estates that proliferate at the urban periphery of major South African city centres. Fortified buildings, gated communities and mega malls characterise the residential and working environments of a new minority of upper/middle class employed. In attempting to delve beyond their surfaces, one is soon confronted by their intrinsic nature. These projects are qualified by a radical privatisation and loss of the public realm, further elevating the pseudo-status of a superficial understanding of transformation and the prospect of rebuilding the city in a postcolonial context. At the other end, despite the introduction of new legal regimes and ambitious regulatory environments, the Reconstruction and Development Project (RDP) type dwelling unit – multiplied through delivery across vast areas of land across the length and breadth of country, as a debased replica of apartheid's NE51/9 (Non-European

9th prototype of 1951) house, at distances still further along the periphery of South African cities – thereby remaining a predominant form of monofunctional settlement development "after" apartheid. The "new" National Development Plan (NDP 2013), whilst the first plan to directly address spatial change at a state level, remains largely unimplemented.

Yet, although these conditions seem to predominate, there do, however, also exist alternative architectural cultures that are attempting to define a new identity for building in the post-apartheid era. In this regard, two polarities seem to have emerged: first, the neoconservative approach, which largely falls within the "category" of a stylised postmodernism; and, in contrast, a post-structural approach, which seems genuinely to be attempting to construct a situated local response, and consciously addresses the exigencies of our current milieu.

The neoconservative approach may be identified by a propensity for mimicry, or that blatant pastiche associated with early postmodernism and the alliances of developers with "entrepreneurial" architecture. At the one end, there seems to be a prevalence of the Eurocentric "steel and glass" imagery associated with the "designer" lifestyle. This is evident in an emerging building typology or image that may be found in any urban setting. It belies any building type or functional tendency and may be associated equally with the domestic setting and car showrooms and even with some of our new public institutions. Simply put, it seems to participate in a "global" style or brand that originates in a tectonic sensibility in response to innovation in construction products and materials. However, embedded within this response, there also exists the parallel and complementary tendency or nostalgia for exoticised mud, thatch and gum poles!

While the buildings that emerge from this approach display a proficiency in detail and a compelling "aesthetic", they seem in fact to produce "pseudo-African" buildings. Their design frequently trivialises the prospect of design as a discursive pursuit by resorting to the thinness of a classical-material practice. Albeit unintentional, these buildings project a predilection for external appearance, as opposed to the interiorisation and the concomitant lived spatiality of everyday user needs whilst belying the more complex aspects of the corporeal nature of the social and tectonic modes of production inherently associated with the vernacular and indigenous African spatial configuration as Other cultural practice.

Consequently, one result of this neoconservative approach to spatial design is that the more phenomenological and experiential dimensions of architecture and its concomitant discourse become subsumed in the security of "familiar forms" – forms both reminiscent of but also repetitive vis-à-vis the *nomos* of colonial-apartheid. The predilection for form seems to have come to predominate design development and consequently almost guarantees an architecture that is derivative. This form of writing the city into being after apartheid is, I would suggest, not a writing otherwise, but rather reflects a formal continuity of form. And yet, from my observation, it is often these kinds of buildings that seem to become recognised by the architectural profession in rewarding buildings and projects through its merit awards.

The spatial contestation of apartheid's boundaries of form and thought is not a clear one. It has, however, begun to initiate the production of hybrid urban conditions and respective planning responses. In certain instances, these are not only capable of incorporating other histories, but more so, of producing spaces for new lived experiences and memories for a new, transforming

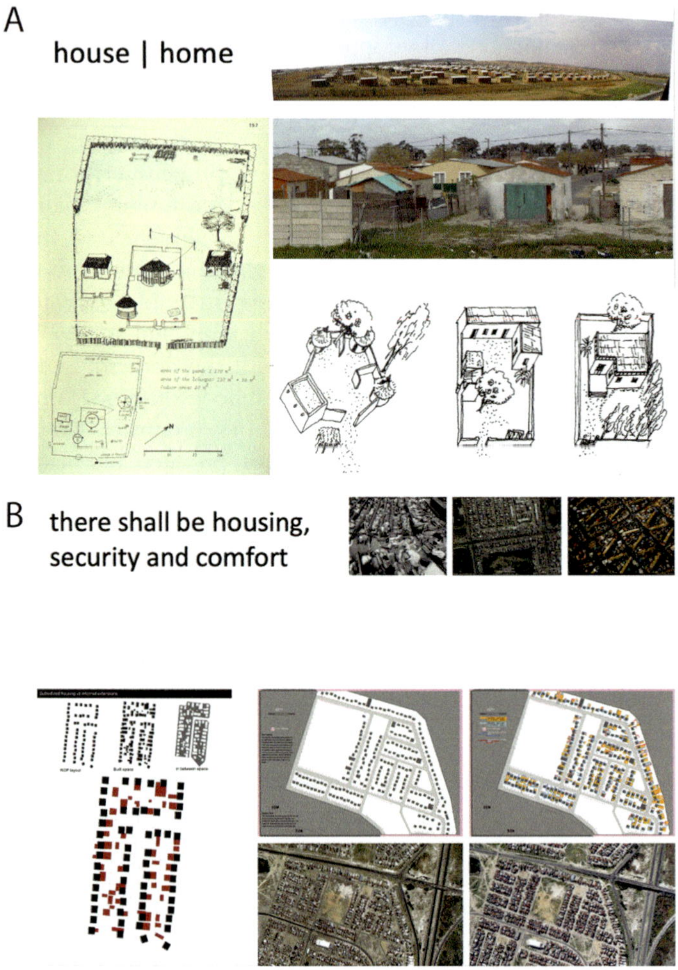

Figure 14.2 House/Home Settler colonialism served to destroy the homestead, promoting the house over that of the home – and the investment above that of the dwelling. The practice of "backyarding" has become a logical response to the under provision of both shelter and the production of humane settlements through the significant failure of the state's Reconstruction and Development Project RDP House RDP type. (A) African Homestead Outside to inside—Modern control RDP adaptations. (B) Delft backyard growth. Cape Town.

society. Thus, beyond the "comfort hegemony", the RDP type dwelling and the neoconservative approach, there does exists evidence of numerous small efforts – animated through a post-structural design approach – that effect counter movements in which the city is written otherwise.

Rewriting type, writing *nomos* otherwise

My sense is that if architecture in South Africa is to rise fully to the occasion of transformation, it will require the establishment of a critical framework through which to engage difference through the projects we, as architects, design. Globally, the typological categorisation whereby buildings were identified through their function has been replaced by an emerging questioning which has occasioned a rewriting of type (Low 2004).

In parallel, alternative approaches to the design process have begun to evolve. The traditional design strategy which favours "creative problem-solving" in relation to a set of predigested approaches has been superceded in both critical schools of architecture and leading practices. Space is open to new forms of innovative design production, through confrontational situations such as issues informed by sociopolitical history, whereby "siting" and "programming" may be actively thought of in terms of design-making. One of the primary benefits of this has been the displacement of rational objectification and the validation of a more subjective but critical engagement within the design process. To ask after "what is possible under a *given* set of circumstances?" prompts the imagination to speculate about architectural design, or, in other words, to re-question by asking the deeper question: "What might inform form?" (Low 2014)

The first impetus in the rewriting of architectural type(s) should thus be the exercise of the human imaginary. This, I would contend, is the entry prerequisite in writing *nomos* otherwise. A new, transformed identity for architecture needs to be predicated on an architect taking a stand on the side of imagination and of the possible. Primarily this demands a form of thinking that exists beyond the bounds of the rational programmatic, the developer formulaic, the economic utilitarian and any recently evolved new normatives. To be imaginative implies to speculate, to postulate and to take informed risks. In South Africa this necessarily means engaging in the unknown, with the Otherness that has ensured our divides for so long. It requires the exercise of a capacity for critical reflection that locates our imagination in between the local and the global. In this way, when ethically informed, we might begin to reclaim new identities for architecture and contribute to meaningful production of spatial transformation and writing the city otherwise into being (Bremner 2010, 48) – toward a *nomos* beyond apartheid. Without an ideological reorientation of design, through the critical reformulation of our thinking and making, we are "condemned" and architecture will become subsumed within the ranks of the African postcolonial demise.

Today, the failure of the post-apartheid state resides not simply in state capture, but in the failure of the ANC and its various macro-economic policies to prioritise the transformation of apartheid spatiality at the forefront of its implementation agenda. In fact, in the absence of any radical change or rupture, a (new) *nomos* of the post-apartheid postcolony has evaded South Africa. Consequently, such a new *nomos* is at present only measurable through the evidence of small but significant projects, locally produced, which contribute toward spatial transformation under the sign of writing the city otherwise into being.

A common feature of these projects lies in their provocation of a distinctive difference in shifting our gaze from (building) type to that of (building) authorship. Rewriting type, as a design process, is not necessarily a new phenomenon. While cutting against the grain of the modernist ideal, this process may be considered to simultaneously fulfil the modernist project by resurrecting its social programme. Narrative method presents another way of thinking through the project of architecture (Bremner 2010), one which incorporates the imagination and returns us to the origins of orally based vernaculars, thereby relocating traditional principles ahead of modernism. This infers great potential for constructive engagement with the differences that apparently continue to maintain our sociocultural and political divides. In attending to and developing this method, architecture stands poised to participate in the work of nation-building and hopefully in the production of "great South African buildings" that are reflective of the values contained within the Constitution, the spirit of the so-called African Renaissance (Mbeki 1998) and the more recently articulated project of "decolonisation" (#RMF 2015), and their concomitant tropes of socioeconomic transformation, through inclusive African cohesion.

The rewriting of type has not necessarily yet become a conscious and collective design act. However, when its pursuit is constructed by way of coproduction between competing interests, be they political or disciplinary, the result appears more resilient and appropriate to both state and community aspiration. Despite the paucity of its manifestation, concrete evidence of built interventions, whose spatiality contests that of apartheid's colonial segregation, is therefore liminal but not unapparent. These projects, however, do not necessarily constitute *nomoi*, nor even collectively a *nomos*, but rather, are representative of diverse emerging attempts to write the otherwise city by engaging with innovative inclusionary practices through the production of alternative local spatialities.

Often emerging from within the non-government sector, this series of interventions are discernable across South Africa and positively reflect on instances where project implementation has broken with the past and begun to deliver on alternative models of spatial formation. Connecting with people's needs, rather than reflecting scientific norms and standards, these projects emanate from a form of design-thinking whose translation directly reflects on and interprets local conditions. Here, careful reconsideration of a topical issue with a building's siting and programming, and its modes of production, interface with the pre-existent conditions of community practice and highly specific needs on the ground.

In many of these instances a predominant trope is evident in the dialectic between house | home – the *house* as a discreet quantifiable unit of economic measure has been qualitatively challenged to resolve a *home*, supportive of human need and of dwelling in comfort. Responding to the absence of socioeconomic opportunity within poor communities, a live/work model has sought to incorporate private needs with "public" commercial opportunity, contesting the historic condition of mono-functionality. Commonly recognised as "cross-programming", this form of development builds on practices already long evident and evolved through counter practices endemic within the informal sector of postcolonial settlements across the African continent and in other postcolonial contexts such as in Latin America. Contesting the nuclear family structure of the Western family, these responses redefine the house as a *homestead* capable of accommodating the temporal and changing nature of a non-Western complexity evident in the emerging African *socius*.

Within the collective realm, complex emergent terrains of culture, public institutions, have also presented fertile ground for challenging past solutions and presenting new spatial configurations, capable of engaging the imagination of new community constituencies emerging most notably from within the previously marginalised. Embedded within apartheid's segregated areas, multiple micro institutions have afforded a sense of dignity and diversity within these previously mono-functional environments. Their representation often commemorates dispossession and related traumatic events from the past, but in a manner that contributes "ownership" to local communities, thereby enhancing their sense of belonging as newly constituted communities. Frequently these attend to questions of a newly imagined collective representation brought about by the rethinking of the public institution.

Despite that, we might not yet relate to these so-called emergent "architectures", some have been compelled to pause and take note, to observe and interrogate the origin and source of their difference. Whilst these projects have been completed in the past 25 years, and whilst others under design and construction demonstrate incremental progress in spatial transformation.

The early emergence of new building types

It should therefore be expected that cultural heritage interventions and the regularisation or "formalisation of the informal" predominate in informing these projects – as informants, these arguably present the most fertile ground for rethinking the South African project of architecture and its re-identification. Early in the first decade after democracy, heritage was considered as an effective public medium through which to address the cultural genocidal tendencies of the past and project alternative identities for the so-called "new" South Africa. New museums emerged as sites of intense cultural experimentation. Furthermore, during this period competitions afforded pluriversal participation, engendering a sense of possibility for the role of space and architecture in the project of transformation. The competitions for the Apartheid Museum, implemented south of Johannesburg, the Constitutional Court in Braamfontein and the Provincial Legislative Assemblies for the Northern Cape and Mpumalanga, all provoked a genuine sense of public intrigue and critical engagement. Not only could they provide alternative cultural infrastructure, but their siting and open programming have actively encouraged movement by citizens across previous divides, thereby contributing to generating a further sense of participatory citizenship.

Often sited in areas of significance by virtue of historical conflict, the project's initially commissioning through open competition, encouraged the imaginative application of design agency in order to "rewrite" transformed building types (Low 2004). Cross-programming, between state and community, and urban connectivity, together with material and tectonic experimentation brought a new sense of the socio-physical tectonic to the fore. Peri-urban and rural areas enjoyed a similar attention, promoting experimentation in landscape urbanism and in what might constitute appropriate social programmes for healing both the land and its neglected communities.

Where these projects involve infrastructure provision, they do so in a way that recognises the cultural capacity of urbanism to contribute to economic and social revitalisation. Frequently generated by the grassroots movements, these efforts have been supported by the re-emergence of non-governmental organisations (NGOs) who operate at the interface between the State and Community, thereby hinting toward the necessity for the instruments of state power to shift and transform themselves, in order to foster genuine and sustainable change. One lesson that seems to be emerging, is that of the need for an intermediary agent in the mediation between seemingly irreconcilable power centres particularly between the State and Community (Watson 2002)

Most of these interventions are therefore highly specific and relate to the temporal exigencies of a plurality of situations. They are also representative of a phenomenon that concurs within what Arjun Appadurai has termed the *production of locality* (Appadurai 1996). Cutting against the grain of western hegemony and its rationality of economic utilitarianism, Appadurai's approach is predicated on the establishment of new relationalities as the precondition for locally produced change. For Appadurai, however, space and the scaler and material dimensions of that change are not considered central but simply as the physical manifestations of that change. Social infrastructure, or people as infrastructure, as Maliq-Simone (2004) has defined contemporary forms of community, therefore becoming the founding base of ruptured change. Ultimately the approach is constituted by processes of subversive hybridisation as evidenced in different strategies directed at so-called "formalising the informal"; reblocking and densifying of human settlements; the strategic introduction of economic opportunities within mono-functional domains; the memorialisation of past atrocities; and in providing cultural and utilitarian infrastructure to apartheid townships and cities. Each therefore contribute to establishing human relationalities and contributing toward the rebuilding of new post-apartheid communities or *socius*.

Below, I reflect on a few projects in which I discern attempts of post-apartheid architecture to write the city as critically different from the *nomos* of colonialism and apartheid and in relation to and with a certain practical wisdom or phronesis of the Other as different and difference (Douzinas and Geary 2005) – and thus otherwise. In each of these instances, space is the medium through which these interventions are manifest. In each precedent, imaginative spatial reconfiguration is a fundamental recurrence to the success of developing the particular intervention as a transformed type. Within the context of the current milieu, I argue that these projects should compel architecture to become more cognisant of the relational and contextual underpinnings that give rise to particular specificities. However, despite Appadurai's above referred disclaimer (1996) against form and scale as informants in the realm of the discourse on space, these are considered as highly significant informants of relationality for the production of locality, and the ultimate manifestation and measure of any emergent *nomos* in the postcolony.

Some examples

Johannesburg

The new Jeppe/Bree Taxi Rank in Johannesburg

One of the most vicious consequences of the system of apartheid lies in the impact of dispossession, forced removals and remote segregation of the lives of African people. One of the predominant reflections that emerged from South Africa's Truth and Reconciliation (TRC) hearings was the collective and individual trauma that resulted from these actions. Communities and families and their indigenous traditions were systematically dismantled and destroyed in what yet still requires formal recognition as a great cultural genocide. The brutality of that violence is in fact still evident in South African society in the sustained psychological damage to individuals, families and communities, but equally in the enduring necessitation of being constantly on the move.

In order to transform the fractured terrain, and in the absence of a viable state system of transport for black communities, a locally initiated mini-bus taxi system emerged early under the apartheid days. Connecting a peripherally located waged (black) labour class with urban (white) sites of employment entailed the development of an extensive system of interconnecting informal taxi routes. Operating intensively at peak morning and evening hours, the off hours saw drivers maintaining and cleaning their vehicles through innovatively appropriating at any open or free space.

Responding to the absence of support infrastructure for this imperative service, post-apartheid has experienced the emergence of a series of intermodal transit sites which act as both destination and transfer sites. The massive daily influx of commuters into and through Johannesburg from Soweto and the South of the city, saw the delivery of a number of strategically located new taxi ranks across the city. Implemented through the city's Johannesburg Development Agency (JDA) they have become vital landmarks for interconnecting people with home and work, thereby affording opportunity for multiple complementary programmes to attach themselves.

The Bree/Jeppe Street rank has become a market centre for informal trades whereby strategic spatial configuration has evolved a *suq* type market, organised through cross block pedestrian armatures connecting the urban fabric on the ground levels, with larger traditional food courts and support service at the upper levels. Not only has this intervention responded to a transit crisis that was created by apartheid spatial planning, but it has remarkably contributed in

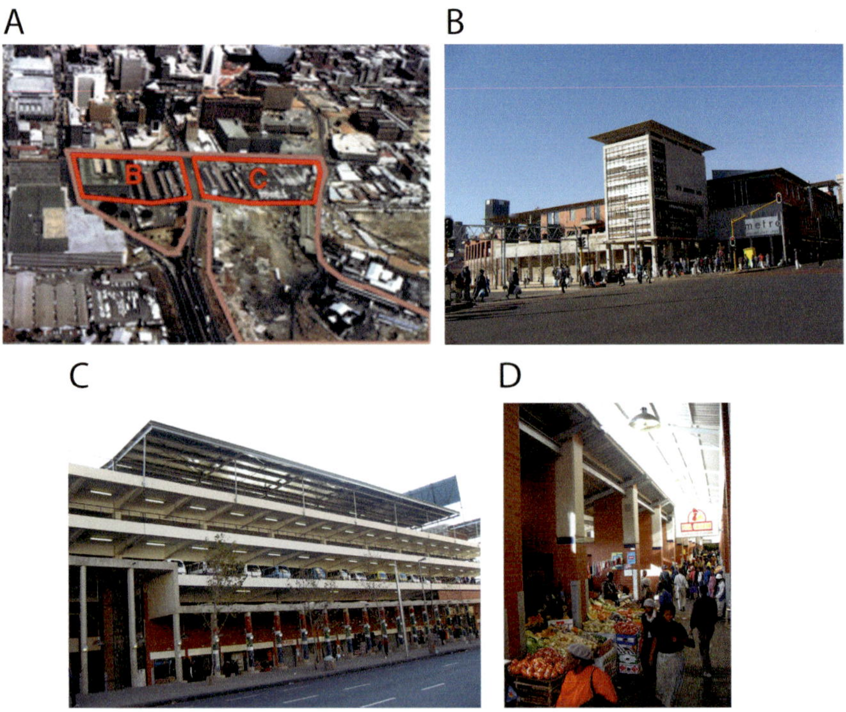

Figure 14.3 The new Jeppe/Bree Taxi Rank – downtown Johannesburg. Movement and mobility characterise everyday life in the (post-) apartheid city. In the absence of spatial transformation, urban segregation endures, forcing people to migrate across the metropolis on a daily basis. Large local taxi ranks perform as new public realms and accommodate necessary intermodality whilst supporting complementary programmes of shopping and entertainment as well as vehicle cleansing and repair. (A–D) Hybrid infrastructure for taxi and commerce, careering to those who still dwell on the apartheid periphery.

bringing the so-called "formal" into a constructive relation with the so-called "informal", thereby retaining most of the productive qualities of so-called informal trading. The taxi industry has become relatively more disciplined and the city has gained through a significant institution which sponsors the ordinary public and private dimensions of a city's everyday life.

Apartheid Museum and Hector Pieterson Museum

The Apartheid Museum in Johannesburg is a project that has captured the imagination of South Africans across the spectrum of cultural identities. Integrating a number of traditionally discrete design mechanisms, it has established a complex and interwoven experience for the user which enforces the visitor's body-mind labour and contests the comfort of the familiar. Despite its seeming linear unfolding of sequential time, the ambiguities between public and private, between casino and institution, between black and white, between mining landscape and built form and between inside and outside, provide a thoughtful series of powerful and contradictory confrontations to provide a discursive itinerary for the participant. Building and landscape, interior and exterior, past and present come to collaborate in a work of genuine merging that proposes the integration of a new cultural terrain in which South Africans with their multiple and emerging identities have been able to engage. This synthetic approach to reimagining a new integrative landscape/urbanism located the project cogently within contemporary global architectural discourse, without directly referring to any pre-existent type (Low 2004).

Close to the Apartheid Museum, in Orlando, Soweto, lies the site of the genesis for the 1976 SA township school riots. The events that lead to the death of Hector Pieterson have been memorialised through many reflections over time. However, the Museum named after him draws all these strands together to establish another unique intervention that demands active user participation. Whereas the Apartheid Museum collapses the separating distance between building and landscape, between Johannesburg CBD and its own siting, the Hector Pieterson Museum at Orlando employs a cinematic structure to locate our experience of Soweto within the history of events around the riots. The multiple surrounding sites of conflict have been carefully woven into the visitor's experience through their judicious incorporation as we move though this project.

Through the framing of critical views, historic moments are explicitly brought back into existence and interiorised within the museum. Space is collapsed, and perhaps more significantly, the temporal separation of events that occurred over a protracted time and geographic area have been brought into a single condensed experience. Not only does this create a unique museology, but, in approximating the very actions around that site, it also holds the potential to afford those previously separated by apartheid, a unique yet interpretive experience of those occurrences. Consequently, those caught on either side

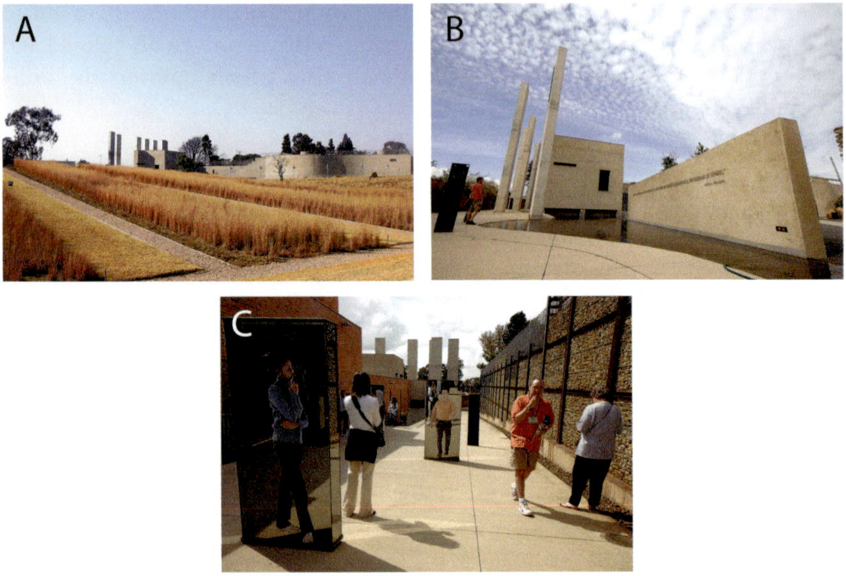

Figure 14.4a The Apartheid Museum, Xavier, Johannesburg. (A) Museum highveld landscape. (B) Entrance sequence.

of apartheid's cruel divide are brought into a spatial experience that has the potential to bridge and thus begin to overcome the past in a unique recognition, supported by critical programming and the unexpected yet associated experiences afforded. In this way, the museum participates in an incipient writing of *nomos* otherwise.

Durban

Durban has always been a vibrant city. It is subtropical and east facing and comprises a mix of cultures. Historically, it has enjoyed significant ethnic and physical diversity in its composition. This has afforded a richer cultural and urban fabric than other cities. Not dissimilar to Johannesburg under the post-1994 ANC provincial governance, Durban also enjoyed a somewhat progressive local authority – the Durban/Ethikweni Metropolitan Municipality (Metro) which until 2008 seemed committed to a series of strategic interventions. While these interventions may be considered locally specific and experimental, they are responsive to both local need and the larger Metro agenda to integrate and transform the city simultaneously. The City Architect's department distinguishes itself from other Metros in that it has consistently submitted new, experimentally progressive projects to the Digest of South

Figure 14.4b The Hector Pieterson Museum, Orlando, Soweto. History and memory emerged as common cause for remembering in the face of rapid change. The museum as a didactic site has seen the development of multiple learning landscapes across South Africa. Straddling the rural and the urban these programmes have provided fertile ground for spatial reimagining and the rewriting of museum as a transformed type. (A) Museum Plan. (B) Interior representations connect visitors with exterior sites of protest and conflict.

African Architecture (DoSA 2010–2017) as a reflection of its active participation in addressing local spatial transformation. Cato Manor township development, the Warrick Triangle precinct and the Mansell Road Arrival centre, and numerous Early Childhood Development centres, clinics on urban peripheries, libraries operating as learning centres and upgraded schools represent some of these projects. Each demonstrates an urban intervention that has significantly contributed to the manner within which previously disadvantaged communities have been incorporated into the city.

Harber/Masson's Mansel Road Settlement

This project predates yet parallels, albeit on a smaller scale, Johannesburg's Metro Mall, and exemplifies this phenomenon of incorporating locally specific activities as new spatial responses to problems of the post-apartheid city. Building from a social condition that constructed a contentious physical dislocation, a potentially highly problematic inner city invasion by rural women responding to their needs for overnight accommodation, the project was conceptualised through critical reintegration into the city, contributing a vital organ to a body under duress (KZNIA 1997). Whereas most other Metro Councils would have resorted to the corrective surgery of what would amount to post-apartheid forced removals, Durban's Metro has successfully incorporated the so-called "informal" into the so-called "formal".

A resolution of conflicting rationalities (Watson 2002) through the meeting of grassroots activists with bureaucratic management has realised the merging of top-down/bottom-up processes, affording added dimensions of sustainability and community building to the provision of shelter. In essence, a land occupation, that has not been challenged but has instead been successfully accommodated and incorporated within the inner city, affording mutual advantage to all stakeholders, particularly to the city, working as an inclusive and diverse social entity. The principled urban design approach, that values the pre-existent, as an extant community, diversity, with respect to complimentary functional and cultural uses, and integration, by connection with the larger order of the city, will reinforce the ultimate incorporation of Mansel Road land invasion into the City of Durban.

By virtue of its attempt to correspond socioeconomic issues within formal design, this attitude to urban intervention contributes significantly to the debates around cities in transition and, notwithstanding normal problems, represents a pilot that should be assessed and interpreted by all metros, notably the City of Cape Town, working under similar conditions. Durban-Ethikweni Metro, not unlike some other cities, such as across Asia and Latin America, has a record of such interventions and appears to deal with the local interpretation of the difficulties and potentials of rapid urbanisation that is characterised by uncertainty, scarce resources, disparity and social diversity, so as to genuinely engage and contribute toward the necessary discourse around urban spatial transformation – or a writing of the city otherwise.

Durban and Johannesburg, through their respective Metro Councils, have been intent on a process of achieving reconciled urban realms in their Central Business Districts (CBDs), establishing new possibilities for potentially conflictual differences to co-exist. The result has been evidenced in the growing disintegration of the historic spatial divide that characterised the apartheid city.

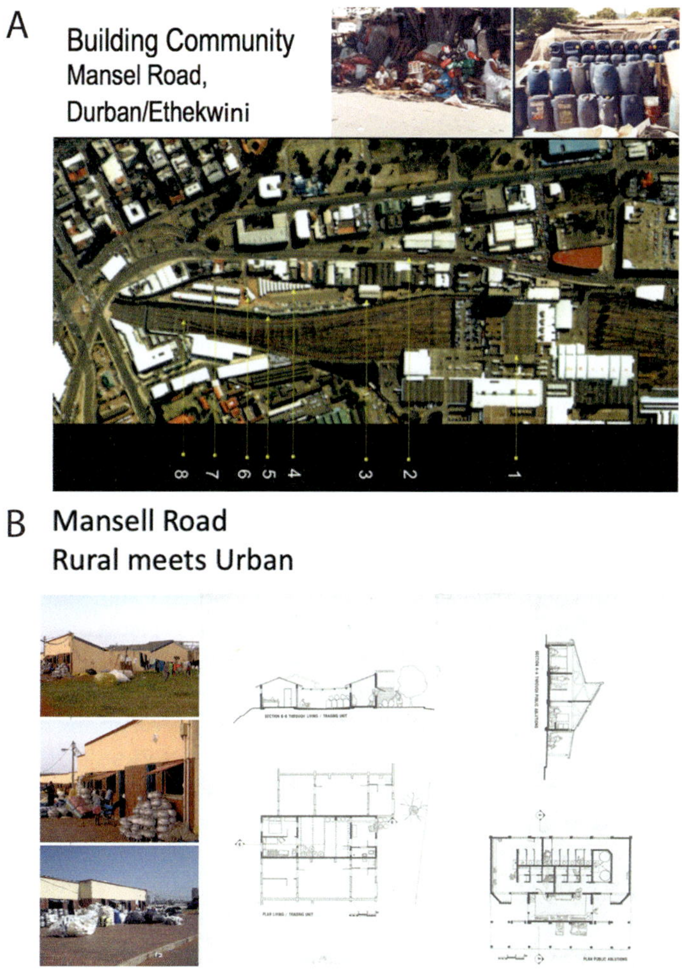

Figure 14.5 Harber/Masson's Mansel Road Settlement, Durban. The shift of the housing policy to one of breaking new ground (BNG) through the provision of human settlements was preceded by numerous design initiatives that sought to produce locality in response to highly specific needs of particular communities. This project represents the formalisation of an informal invasion of parastatal railway reserve land. (A) Mansell Rd Settlement formalised on Durban rail reserve. (B) Typical Live/Work unit Plan Central Shop/Ablution

Ultimately all citizens should genuinely and constructively begin to participate, not only in urban economics, but more so, in a socialised daily life that incorporates all possible aspects of urban dwelling. This is a temporal process, but its realisation is critically necessary for the constructive building of public culture and civil society. In this sense, strategic urban design principles have participated in laying ground for a longer-term realisation of urban vitality, wherein black and white communities might find productive engagement together.

Eastern Cape

The Nelson Mandela Museums in the Eastern Cape

The Nelson Mandela Museums in the Eastern Cape present a compelling case for spatial transformation at the urban/rural interface. The project held significant consequence for the potential of rural regeneration in an area of South Africa previously declared as a "homeland" – a pseudo-independent state within apartheid South Africa, that presented possibly the most alienating category of apartheid's legacy of systemic spatial dispossession and marginalisation.[2]

The Nelson Mandela Museum project was conceptualised so as to present Mandela again to the people in the province and domain of his birth. The Eastern Cape is constituted by land which the amaXhosa have occupied since their arrival and settlement in southern Africa around 500AD (SAHO). The contemporary provincial capital, Mthata, is approximately 50 km from the traditional village of Mvezo, Mandela's birthplace, and from the nearby Qunu, where Mandela spent his youth following the death of his father. Connected by virtue of the history of Mandela's early and later life, these three places co-constitute heritage sites for commemorating the life of Madiba in the Eastern Cape.

Designed and implemented by CohenJudin Architects, together with the Department of Public Works, in the late 90s, the museum interventions have been conceived of as locally produced in contesting the autonomy of the museum as a modern western colonial building type. Conceptualised as hybrid structures, they straddle the provision of infrastructure and culture through critical cross-programming. Represented as stilted pavilions installed within the rural landscape, they touch the earth lightly and, through their networked association, bring a new order or relations between villages and the urban to poverty stricken and semi-abandoned areas.

Constructed from a steel frame, they are infilled by wattle and adobe enclosures, erected by local artisans who are not only empowered through employment, but through the dignity of participation and their longer-term benefit of the plural utility afforded by the open building type. Whilst the pavilions each accommodate various elements and images of Mandela, they also operate as places of significance and historical connection across the rural terrain. They afford shelter to workers from surrounding fields, whilst also functioning as taxi pick up points or as watering places, and even as places of temporary storage, whilst functioning as heritage sites for outsiders to engage the local.

As "open", yet distinctly networked representations, their (re-)appropriative presence establishes a unique spatial orientation within the existing rural terrain. Interfacing between villages and the larger town, this cultural intervention has enabled the provision of infrastructure as a critical by-product. The cross-programmed project has enabled seemingly unforeseen interrelations between seemingly disconnected phenomena.

In providing a model for rural regeneration within a significantly threatened context, this project presents a highly imaginative response to spatial transformation. These pavilions then embody a unique interconnection between memory and justice – an interconnection that has been characterised as critical in terms of overcoming the *nomos* of apartheid (Barnard-Naudé 2017, 10–11). Their potential to intensify and support rural agriculture demonstrates the power of heritage when critically conceived of in order to engage local economic activity. This locates the agency of architectural design as an ethically politicised action, promoting counter memorialisation (2017, 13)

This introduction of a new order affords the possibility of restructuring rural life and rebuilding an alternative set of human relations. Centred in the socio-economic, new cultural dimensions for rural life may potentially transcend the tribal and provide for the basis of collective action. The production of the commons, or indeed of shared public spaces, then, represents an identifying condition of the writing of a decolonised *nomos*.[3] Its design and implementation was underpinned by a unique set of relations between a private architectural practice, the local public works department and a non-place-bound community of users.

Port Elizabeth's Red Location Museum

Noero Wolff's award-winning competition entry for the Apartheid Museum in Port Elizabeth's Red Location has been subjected to a fertile process of reflection. Brought on by the delays of implementation, it was reconceptualised as a Museum of Struggle. In its final form, it has come to incorporate the temporal dimensions of the living community – this within the familiarity of its factory-like iconography. In Red Location, the task is as much to rebuild the township as it is to provide a new institution. The urban principle of "city/street-making" abides in this project, as in most Noero projects (Noero 2009), and foresees the provision of housing as integral to the idea of the city.

Notwithstanding their predilection for form-making and the materialist bias of this architecture, an active interpretation of narrative process has been sought. The narrative process of inhabitation as ongoing story-telling is intended to provide for an inclusive continuum, most particularly, subsequent to the building's completion and its handing over to the community. Similar to the previously mentioned Nelson Mandela Museum(s), spectacle will be

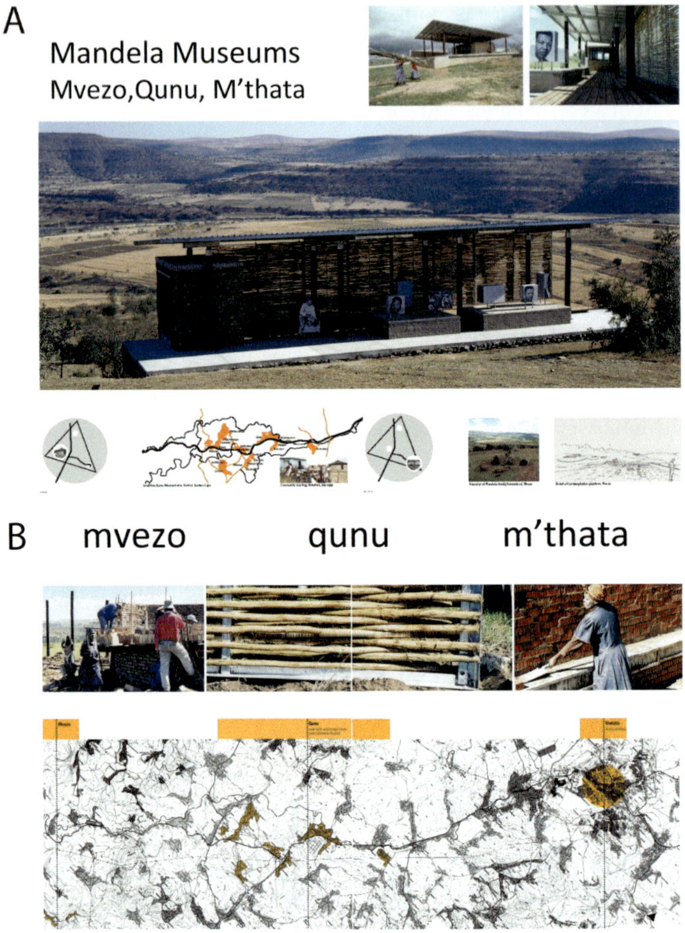

Figure 14.6 The Nelson Mandela Museums in the Eastern Cape. South Africa's apartheid "homelands" bequeathed an invidious socio-spatial landscape of radical marginalisation exemplified in a pervasive poverty and the concomitant genocidal destruction of local cultural practice. The potential of design to engage this legacy is demonstrated across many scales, from the tectonic material, through the built form of the individual building pavilions as simultaneously utilitarian and poetic, and to the networked reconfiguration of regional space between the urban centre and its rural periphery. (A) Typical Mandela Museum Pavilions. (B) Rural terrain network / Local labour-material tectonic.

maintained – not for its own sake – but through direct urban contribution to infrastructure as much as by the scale and intrigue imbued by such an intervention in an apartheid "black native township".

Commencing in its factory-like iconography, this is taken into the museum with the installation of the series of motorcrate-like memory boxes, which will afford a unique level of didactic empowerment, intended to cross all divides. Conceived of as open representations, these memory boxes may be reinstalled and reassessed through individual and collective interpretation, spanning both immediate and continuous time. In this way design process and experiential process may become interlinked in an open dialogue of sustained "rewriting".

Cape Town

Cape Town is South Africa's oldest city and despite a political transition now 25 years in the making, the Mother City's development framework seem to still be in the hands of the Dutch East India Company or the Vereenigde Oostindische Compagnie (United East Indies Company or VoC (Very Old Club!)) representatives of which still appear very much in command. Economic utilitarianism opportunistically rules and the previously marginalised continue to suffer

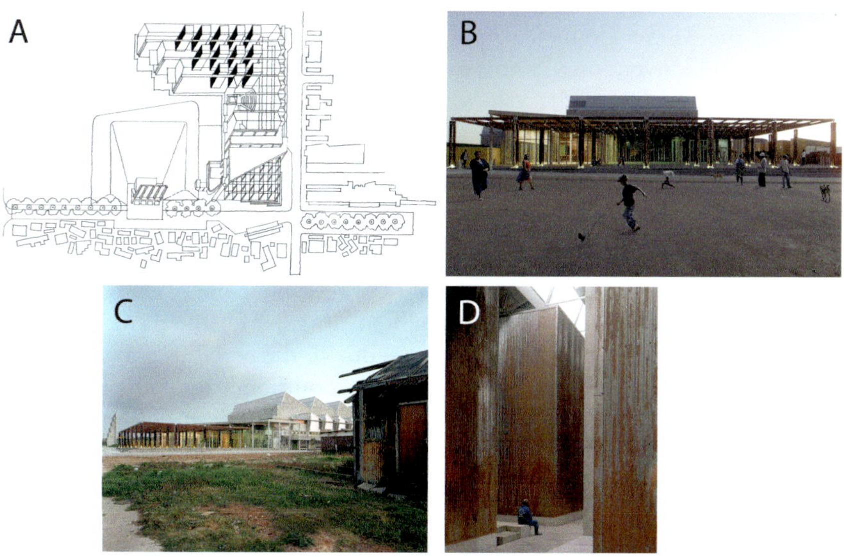

Figure 14.7 Red Location Struggle Museum, New Brighton, Port Elizabeth. Predicated on a political ambition to shift the colonial/apartheid centre from Port Elizabeth to New Brighton (Red Location), the project assembles new cultural facilities along an urban armature by linking Red Location to the railway station. (A) Museum Plan. (B) Museum entrance. (C) Townscape. (D) 'Crate' interior.

exclusion by virtue of their sustained dispossession at the periphery. Rampant urban migration is transforming the cities' demographic profile with radical implications for urbanity. Crime, gangsterism, HIV-AIDS, gender violence toward women and children, and corruption are pervasive. Needless to say, Cape Town is a time bomb waiting to explode. The disparities between rich and poor are among the worst in the country, with little prospect of real change. Urban spatial projects in the townships have, by and large, been located within the confines of extant neighbourhoods as black apartheid areas. While they have managed to address some of the omissions of the past, the approach can be characterised as (minimally) redressive, as opposed to progressively transformative. As such, these projects have predominantly failed in addressing the order of the apartheid city, and failed to address the racial divide, instead, perhaps, reinforcing it.

The geography of the Cape's landscape constitutes its main asset. Yet it is this very topography that manages to assist in maintaining privilege of position and comfort. A persistent "laissez-faire" attitude to development has prevailed, one that can be traced back to the city origins as a settlement run by a private company, the (VoC) and the 19th century British city (Dewar and Uytenbogaardt 1977). During the 20th century *Grands Projets* such as the Golden Acre development, that supplanted the old railway station, appropriated public streets and a portion of the historic Parade Ground – thereby effectively removing pedestrian privilege in the Heerengracht of the city's main commercial area. The subsequent and more contemporary the Uni-City renovation of the Metro Council complex, and the introduction of Cape Town International Convention Centre, each impose a compromised urbanism that is largely accountable to the values inculcated by the city lead [commercial] development alliances that construct them. Effectively one might discern a pattern of a "privatisation of the public realm", that is accountable to the effective abrogation of a primary local authority responsibility to ensure the public interest. Not dissimilar to public–private partnerships in other parts of the world, the private sector inevitably gains considerably more with drastic compromising consequences for the long-term quality of the public life of a city. In more recent times, this has played out especially in struggles for the introduction of affordable social housing in the inner city – due to the previous mayor's predilection for radically overwriting existing neighbourhoods by endorsing many compromised exemptions to development regulations (Ndifuna Ukwazi 2019).

Philippi Junction and Ngulube Drive Market

The production of the city's formidable spatial construct, lays in the collusion between topography and the imposition of colonial settlement. Its failure to transform emerges in the weakness of city officials and the consequent inadequacy of any urban policy to be implemented. Yet there have existed a number of attempts to spatially transform the greater metropolitan area. Within the Integrated Service Land Project (ISLP), and Municipal Spatial Development

Framework (Muni-SDF), a number of distinctive urban improvements have seen implementation in the outlaying townships. The work of Du Toit and Perrin stands out from amongst early urban design interventions in Cape Town's apartheid townshipscapes. Two of their projects are located on the North-South corridor along Emms Road/Ngulube Drive, intersecting with a major link of the townships to the inner city, Lansdowne Road, and which interconnects Nyanga with Philippi. The one project, at the extreme southern end of Ngulube Drive, attempts to address the "formalisation of the so-called informal" at Philippi Station. Not dissimilar to the Jeppe/Bree Taxi rank in Johannesburg, and many other South African urban conditions, the design harnesses the energy produced at an intermodal node, exploiting the move from one form of transport to another – by accommodating multiple forms of trade across the so-called formal/informal divide. An over-formalised control by means of "zoning" different trading activities has resulted in interesting local contestations of design decisions, and presents a compelling basis for a case study in the limits and possibilities of design in contributing toward spatial transformation. A deep understanding of local socioeconomic practices is absent – and indeed, the absence of both pre- and post-occupancy evaluation (POE) is a glaring one, an absence that sadly is predominantly neglected in local architectural practice and discourse (Appadurai 1996).

Given the enforced migrancy that apartheid imposed on all people of colour, it is not surprising that, as with design projects promoting culturally informed spatial transformation, the transit-based projects necessarily demand, promote and define a dimension of innovative spatial innovation predicated on the cross-programming of complementary functions necessary to ameliorate apartheid's wilful disjunctured spatialities. Consequently, in Philippi the design synthesis is intended on a unique confluence of interests to afford opportunity for a range of interactions between different levels of trading with commuters as residents, migrants or simply citizens. Despite some early teething problems, this early infrastructural offering represents the drawing together of numerous competing strands that characterise the contemporary township or global village – providing a basis for the beginnings of a newly formed and contemporary public realm, one where other difference is productively engaged (Low 2003).

The second project is complementary to the first, both by virtue of its programming, as well as by its location at the intersection of Emms Road and Lansdowne Road. Its design presents an attempt to set down a simple enabling framework whereby the previously divided phenomenon of formal and informal, building and city, past and future, living and working have become cojoined to provoke a new typology reflecting contemporary temporal relations. These confrontations have been woven together through design intelligence that has reimagined both what an urban intersection is and which different physical arrangements for living/working might support everyday life in the "new" South Africa. Reminiscent of HarberMasson's Mansel Road development in the inner city of Durban, the project set a critical precedent in Cape Town, constituting an early attempt to challenge the generally inadequate attempts of the city at urban regeneration in the black townships.

Predicated on the provision of infrastructure as opposed to the built form, these two projects provoke us to think in new ways about how design might surface and support the economic opportunity that is latent within a reconceptualised relation between becoming and being in the township. Genuine potential for an interactive public realm has been designed for, essentially in seeking reciprocal relations between seemingly dissimilar functions – with the intention to provoke a productive confrontation between the specificity of local community need, and the everyday necessities of transport infrastructure.

Weltevrede Valley and Philippi East Affordable Housing

Two further Cape Flats township residential schemes in the neighbourhoods of Weltevrede Valley and Philippi East have offered alternative urban arrangements for human settlements at the city periphery. As Provincial Government Western Cape (PGWC) projects, these are remarkable in that they significantly depart from accepted planning norms. In this instance, interior residential urban space has been reordered against the both prevalent transport and shelter standards, which have come to dominate township development in South Africa. A network of pedestrian friendly spaces has been established by the narrowing of streets to a width of 5 m. The resultant propinquity between dwellings fosters urban vigilance and privileges the elderly and children and pedestrian movement while "taming" vehicular activity. The introduction of "people places" for meeting and playing suggests a social fabric through which neighbours might begin to engage in community building, whilst the provision of an elongated site, bounded by two street edges enables expansion for either or both of second dwelling unit and an onsite economic work opportunity. A "new urbanism" that formalises, yet interprets, the social organisation of the spontaneous squatter settlements, has been suggested, albeit liminally.

Empower Shack – Site C, Khayelitsha, Cape Town

The reconfiguration of the new Empower Shack settlement at Site C in Khayelitsha represents perhaps one of the most advanced spatial transformations to have been successfully implemented in South Africa since 1994 (Low 2018). Despite having been reblocked from an informal organic to a cartesian planned settlement, the process of change reveals a set of complex interrelations whose qualitative resolution enables a set of previously unavailable dwelling arrangements.

The principle of coproduction across multiple dimensions of settlement making underpins the success of the project and its uniquely reconfigured socio-spatial arrangement. Predicated on horizontal relations between different stakeholders, the project endeavoured to first build community between participants and then embarked on design.

Figure 14.8 The Philippi Junction and Ngulube Drive EcoHub. The Dignified Public Project (DPP) originated in the City of Cape Town and intended to provide a series of public spaces within the city's apartheid townships that were of equivalence with those in the "white" colonial city. Conceived of as enabling structures, many of them have failed in that on the one hand they speak to white cultural practices, and on the other the programme failed to integrate any management or local facilitation process whereby they might have become integrated and functionally embedded. Many are "dysfunctional", or have simply been appropriated and become privatised. (A–G) Railstation and Crossroads - enabling installations that support economic opportunity and public space making.

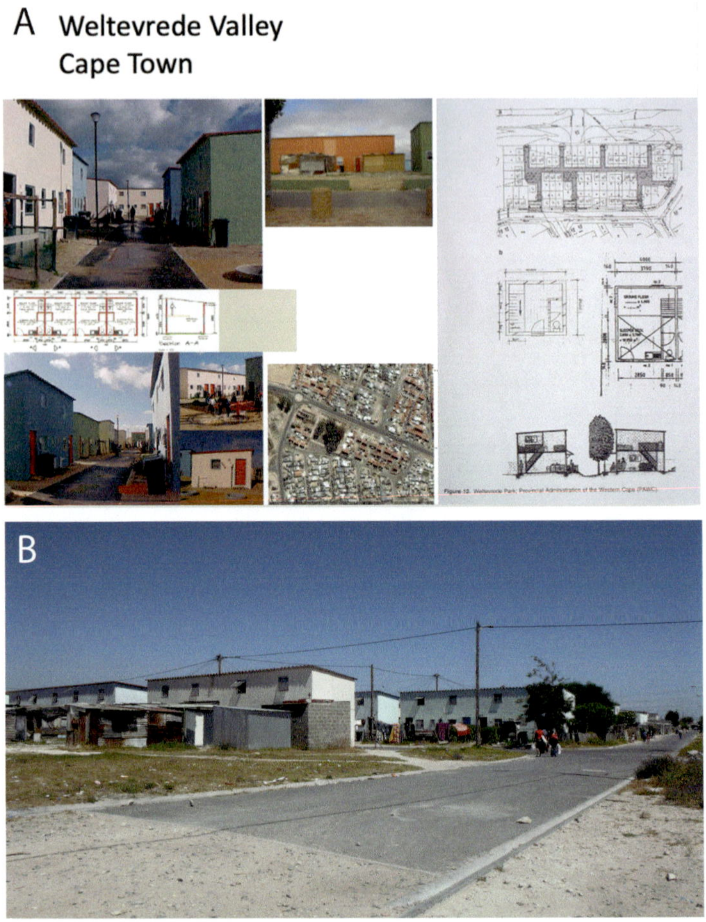

Figure 14.9 Weltevrede Valley and Philippi East Affordable Housing Model. This project represents a rare example of a provincial government housing department demonstrating initiative in interpreting the housing subsidy to offer an enabling starter home. Sited at the interior of a "superblock" – with a child and pedestrian friendly interior, it is capable of expanding to the rear toward a busy street offering significant commercial opportunity. Live/work and the potential for horizontal and vertical expansion afford both investment and alternative dwelling arrangement for accommodating extended family types. (A) Double Storey Starter Units. (B) Settlement layout Early evidence of inhabitiants rear selfbuild additions.

This process has delivered a project of potent valency that has raised the possibility of multiple and changing forms of occupancy. Despite being comprised of a series of individual attached units, the "connectedness" in this particular configuration allows for multiple permutations through unconventional divisions between fronts and rear on the one hand, and by contesting vertical and adjacent divisions on the other, thereby permitting for a variety of occupations; live-work, extended families, single resident occupation and work-only opportunities. Backyarding and homeworking may now become considered as new norms.

Soliciting local user needs and desire, through direct user participation, and conflating that information with a digitally based geospatial exercise – this process has enabled the allocation of sites according to highly particular individual preferences – effectively concluding in a 3-D volume of property which, whilst co-owned, maximises individual family choice through enabling continuing occupancy negotiation across the boundaries of conventional cartesian geometries that usually govern western planning practices.

As with most of the projects which have successfully concluded new spatial configurations, there is evidence of sustained commitment to research, testing and refinement in order to build the type of difference that is not only acceptable to local communities, but also possessing sufficient resilience to be sustained after its completion. The hybrid instrumentation that exists arises through an entrustment established by means of coproduction between the existing community, the foreign academic institution, the local NGO and the local authority. The presence of this resilient "institution" together with the agency leadership within each constituency has assured productive yet horizontal relations between parties who might conventionally have been hostile and conflicted (Watson 2002). The project represents an interesting contestation of the western norm, perhaps moving beyond transformation and suggesting a new or hybridised *nomos* for the post-apartheid postcolony predicated in Appadurai's notion of local relationality (1996).

Conclusion

The intentionality behind design decisions is what informs and shapes the final project. In the design professions, where image and form are frequently elevated above that of social purpose, common ground frequently becomes displaced and ultimately forfeited. From this perspective urban design may be characterised as "making space", instead of "taking space" or, as I have suggested throughout this contribution, as a kind of productive writing.

The past 25 years of continuous post-democracy rule constitutes a substantive period of time in which to have confronted the spatial legacies of apartheid. Nevertheless, we have yet to witness a genuine rupture with, or radical transformation from, the past and its concomitant pervasive spatial legacy. The unfortunate reality appears to reflect on the triumph of democracy having

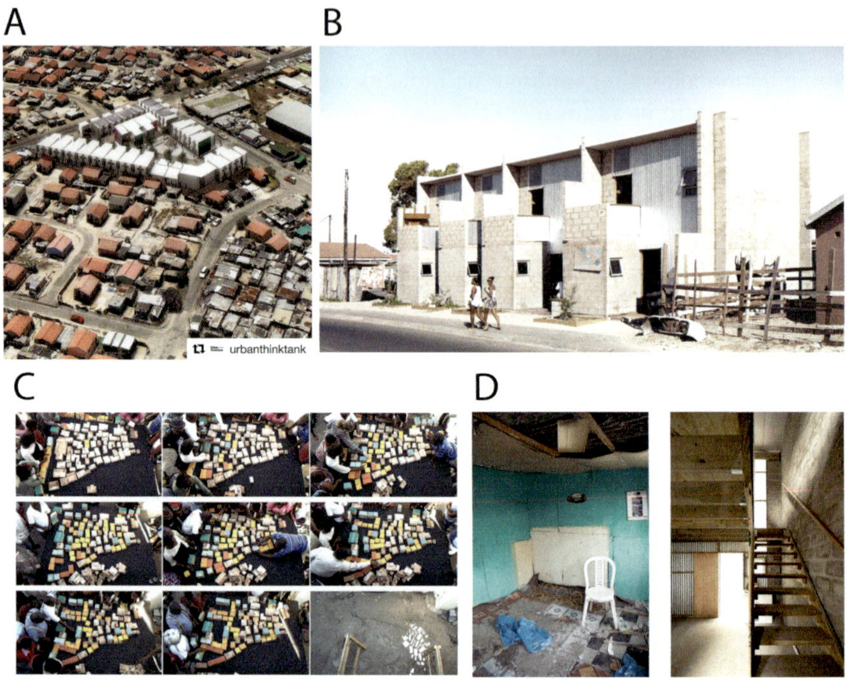

Figure 14.10 Empower Shack – Site C, Khayelitsha, Cape Town. U-TT/ETH Zurich with Ikhayalami. This urban upgrade represents an advanced experimentation in what Shack Dwellers International [SDI] terms reblocking – the reconfiguration of an informal shack type settlement to provide opportunity for service infrastructure, densification and safer, healthier environments. As an academic exercise it has benefitted from significant subsidisation and professional support. In the near future a post occupancy evaluation (POE) promises to surface an interesting set of critical information for advancing this approach. (A) Development. (B) Ph 3 – a 4 unit block. (C) Alternative layouts. (D) Interiors.

possibly been realised with the consolidation of a neoliberal agenda – one which serves to further entrench poverty and alienate the dispossessed. The coincidence of the "fall" of apartheid with the emergence of globalisation and its impact on a world economic order is significantly reflected in South Africa's exchange of one hegemony for another, a racialised past with the class structure of the present.

Having already delivered about four million housing opportunities since 1994, South Africa has realised a phenomenal transformational achievement when quantitatively measured. But despite the benefit of a radical legal and policy power set, including the most recently concluded National Development Plan (NDP 2013), which for the first time specifically addresses spatial transformation, the reality of apartheid spatial segregation remains the lived experience of the majority of South Africans. The lack of political will, the absence of intellectual capability and the concomitant failure of an ethical orientation across our society, has reduced delivery to a numerical task, burying spatial transformation within its path. Consequently, we have failed to overtly engage the project of social justice and its corollary of spatial equity in establishing a new *nomos* for the postcolony – one characterised in this contribution as the interplay of writing the city otherwise into being and writing the city into being otherwise.

Most of the projects discussed above represent contemporary responses to the provocation of the emergent inner city and the problematic of the apartheid condition, and have produced "new spaces" and building types. Building upon the idea of the city as a reality that is constructed by people, in respect of their unique "needs, wants and desires", it seems to me that the few architects involved have located their personal subjectivity within the collective of the larger South African project of transformation. In direct confrontation with the legacy of apartheid spatial practice, these designers have consciously engaged in rewriting architectural type – negotiating the complexity of our radicalised differences by projecting an alternative or new imaginary. In this manner, our unique South African issues are also finding connection with contemporary discourse, while directly attending to the needs of those originally disenfranchised – mediating the global through the specificity of our unique local.

In her reflection on the work of Schmitt through the lens of Hannah Arendt, Chryssostalis (2013, 162–3) has surfaced a challenge in Arendt's identification of the commons as a necessary humanistic mediator between the law and the land, and therefore demanding of the re-examination of the dialectic within architectural practice. Significantly positive evidence of transformed spatial practice appears to emerge most potently in the instances where the hegemony of the architectural and related professions have been challenged by co-productive modes of engagement through design and implementation. Where apartheid space has been contested constructively, it has been almost always through close attention to the production of localities, and where one can discern the presence of a third force of negotiation. Enabling change seems better realised with the precondition of outsider mediation between the State, or authority and all the various forms of community. Consequently, where these alternative projects have been more successful in producing new spatialities, there exists evidence of the valuing of human engagement as a form of necessary social infrastructure. The building of community appears as an essential pre-investment to the building of place – and consequently a precondition for spatial transformation. In each of these instances, the existence of a mediating instrument capable of negotiating the extremes of conflicting interests that characterise both the postcolonial and post-apartheid contexts, has been evident – and success through this form of mediation appears predominantly to reflect in the participation of non-government organisations (NGOs), community-based organisations (CBOs) and other non-aligned instruments.

A constructive interrelationship between organisational instrumentality and human agency seems to emerge as a necessary precondition for change. The prospect for both accelerated delivery and the successful expedition of spatially transformative environments seems aligned with adopting such an approach – however, additionally, through intervention at an increased scale that comprehensively addresses the need for spatial transformation at the scale of the Nation – thereby recognising the need for not only the rewriting of architectural type, but perhaps radical imaginative speculation regarding urban and rural reconfiguration.

In a sense, the failure of (spatial) transformation in South Africa may necessarily be laid at the feet of those who disabled the ruling ANC's original manifesto for change – the 1994 Reconstruction and Development Program (RDP). Perhaps then the current crisis in South Africa presents the opportunity to relaunch a new RDP, one reconstituted as a decentralised Reconstruction and Decolonisation Project or an RDP, with authority for speculative action and the mandate to structurally re-spatialise in the interest of social justice and spatial equity. Lest we forget the apartheid regime deployed the National Building Research Institute in order to spatially implement its grand plan of racial segregation.

The task of writing *nomos* otherwise in the South African postcolony is an onerous one. It is a work of space and transformation that must seek to rewrite the legacy of apartheid. Its boundaries are ill-defined, fluid and in a constant state of renegotiation. Spatial transformation, however, is fundamental to the post-apartheid, postcolonial project. Transformed space commences with altered forms of design inquiry that can only be sustained through imaginative explorations that genuinely dialogue with the contemporary needs of a heterogeneous society. Democracy is all about how difference co-exists, and only by acting differently can we begin to produce the critical difference on which writing *nomos* otherwise depends.

Acknowledgement

Jaco Barnard-Naudé and Julia Chryssostalis from the Spatial Justice and *Nomos* initiative, for including the architectural discipline, and in particular, for their critical insight and constructive commentary on my contribution.

Notes

1 Already in 2011, the National Planning Commission's [NPC] Diagnostic Report, recognised the inhibiting effects of the legacy of spatial division with respect to inclusive development.
2 An obsession with urbanisation has resulted in the neglect of reconfiguring the homelands "otherwise" - by both government and academia.
3 Cf. here also Palmer et al 2017.

References

Appadurai, A. 1996. *Modernity at large: Cultural dimensions of globalization.* Minneapolis, MN: University of Minnesota Press.

Awan N., T. Schneider, and J. Till. 2011. *Spatial agency: Other ways of doing architecture.* London: Routledge.

Barnard-Naudé, J. 2017. "Law, memory and post-apartheid spatiality: 'Reading Nomos otherwise,' 'mapping the heterotopic'." In *Spatial justice and the diaspora*, edited by E. Patchett and S. Keenan, 10-50. London: Counterpress.

Bremner, L. 2010. *Writing the city into being: Essays on Johannesburg 1998–2008.* Johannesburg: Fourthwall Books.

Constitution of the Republic of South Africa. 1996. https://www.gov.za/documents/constitution-republic-south-africa-1996

Chryssostalis, J. 2013. "Reading Arendt, 'reading' Schmitt: Reading Nomos otherwise?" In *Feminist encounters with legal philosophy*, edited by M. Drakopoulou, 158-184. New York and London: Routledge.

Dewar, D., and R. Uytenbogaardt. 1977. *Housing: A comparative evaluation of urbanism in Cape Town.* Cape Town: UPRU/UCT.

DoSA. 2010–2017. *Digest of South African architecture*, edited by I. Low. Cape Town: Picasso Headline/Tiso Blackstar.

Douzinas C., and J. Geary. 2005. *Critical jurisprudence: The political philosophy of justice.* Portland, OR: Hart.

Judin, H. and I. Vladislavic. Eds. 1998. blank______ Architecture, apartheid and after. Rotterdam: NAI Publishers.

KZNIA Journal. 1997. *KwaZulu-Natal institute of architects journal*, edited by W. Peters. Durban: KZNIA.

Lokko, L. 2002. *Arguments from Silence* Vivienne Japha and Len and Gunnel Hicks Memorial Lecture at the University of Cape Town's School of Architecture Planning and Geomatics. Unpublished manuscript, on file with author.

Low, I. 2003. "Space and reconciliation: Cape Town and the South African city under transformation." *Urban Design International* 8: 233–246. Basingstoke: Palgrave.

Low, I. 2004. "Space and transformation: Architecture and identity." In *Digest of South African Architecture vol 7*: 34–38 Cape Town: Picasso Headline.

Low, I. 2014. "Architecture in Africa: Situated modern and the production of locality." In *A critical history of contemporary architecture 1960–2010*, edited by E. Haddad and D. Rifkind, 291–310. London: Ashgate.

Low, I. 2018. "Family matters: Khayelitsha housing, Cape Town." *Intensity, Architectural Review*, 1451, May 2018, 91–96. London: Emap.

Matthews, D. 2018. *Obligations in the new climatic regime.* http://criticallegalthinking.com/2018/07/16/obligations-in-the-new-climate-regime/

Mbeki, T. 1998. *Statement by deputy president Mbeki at the African renaissance conference Johannesburg, 28 September 1998.* https://www.sahistory.org.za/archive/statement-deputy-president-mbeki-african-renaissance-conference-johannesburg-28-september-19

Memmi, A. 1965. *The colonizer and the colonized.* New York City: Orion.

National Development Plan 2030. 2013. NDP. https://www.gov.za/issues/national-development-plan-2030

National Planning Commission Diagnostic Report. 2011. https://www.nationalplanningcommission.org.za/Downloads/diagnostic-overview.pdf

Ndifuna Ukwazi. 2019. City leases: Cape Town's failure to redistribute land. Cape Town: Ndifuna Ukwazi. https://nu.org.za/publications-resources/#publications

Noero, J. 2009. *Everyday and the extraordinary: Three decades of architecture*. Cape Town: ADA Publishers.

Palmer H., S. da Silva, and I. Low. 2017. "Urban commons in the neoliberal global order: Commoning as counteraction." In N-AERUS XVII Conference Proceedings, Göteborg.

Reconstruction and Development Programme (RDP). 1994. https://www.gov.za/faq/finance-business/where-do-i-get-copy-reconstruction-and-development-programme-rdp

Schmitt, C. 2006. *The Nomos of the earth in the International Law of the Jus Publicum Europaeum*. New York City: Telos Press.

Simone, A-M. 2004. "People as infrastructure: Intersecting fragments in Johannesburg." *Public Culture* 16 (3): 407–429.

Watson, V. 2002. *Change and continuity in spatial planning: Metropolitan planning in Cape Town under political transition*. London: Routledge.

Index

Note: Page numbers in *italics* indicate figures, and references following "n" refer notes.

For Product Safety Concerns and Information please contact our EU representative GPSR@taylorandfrancis.com Taylor & Francis Verlag GmbH, Kaufingerstraße 24, 80331 München, Germany